"A fantastic journey through New York's 1970s underground music scene . . . Hermes moves effortlessly back and forth between the various musical genres while interspersing stories of New York at a time when the city was on the verge of financial ruin and moral collapse."
— June Sawyers, *Booklist* (starred review)

"[Hermes's] attitude, sharp ear and smart big-picture view turn what could have been a small book into something special. A hip, clever, informative look at an unjustifiably dismissed musical era that will have readers scouring iTunes for the perfect accompanying soundtrack."
— *Kirkus Reviews*

"I have to tell you [*Love Goes to Buildings on Fire*] is sort of mind-boggling—an incredibly scenic and detailed history of the music made in New York over a few years in the 70s. (It's one of the first things I've read that gives you an acute sense of all these musicians really walking the same streets on the same days—the sense that Willie Colón might have been packing up after a downtown gig while Patti Smith, just two blocks away, was coming home from the studio, the night before a legendary block party up in the Bronx . . .) It's a tremendous thing to have put together."
— Nitsuh Abebe on his Tumblr site, *a grammar*

"A panoramic nonfiction account of the bursting 1970s music scene in New York City."
— *Entertainment Weekly*

"Imaginative, poetic, and frequently humorous . . . As important a volume for music lovers as Michael Azerrad's *Our Band Could Be Your Life*."
— Jedd Beaudoin, *PopMatters* (Best Non-Fiction of 2011)

"What Hermes, a senior writer for *Rolling Stone* and an NPR contributor, captures so well is the burbling creative energy that gripped the city . . . [*Love Goes to Buildings on Fire* is a] big-hearted and inclusive embrace."
— Steve Futterman, *The Barnes & Noble Review*

"[A] breathtaking, panoramic portrait of five years . . . of that decade that music in New York City was alive, flourishing, and kicking out the jams."   —*Publishers Weekly* (starred review)

"A must-read for any music lover, *Love Goes to Buildings on Fire* will no doubt inspire nostalgia in readers who lived through the era, and make those who didn't wish they had."   —Liz Raftery, *The Boston Globe*

"Practically every paragraph about music here is also about something else just as fascinating—race, city planning, ambition, drugs, hair-dos. Braiding intricate research with his own teenage memories, Will Hermes has a bird's-eye view of a great city, and has his ear to the ground."   —Sarah Vowell, author of *Unfamiliar Fishes* and *The Wordy Shipmates*

"Will Hermes grew up in Queens, but *Love Goes to Buildings on Fire*, his new book on New York's 1970s music scene, is no nostalgia jag. It's a time machine that zooms in on everyone from the New York Dolls to Steve Reich and everything in between."   —*Rolling Stone*

"*Love Goes to Buildings on Fire* is an almost perfect portrait of New York music culture: specific yet comprehensive, enthusiastic yet objective, and as informed as it is personal. The five-page section of what (seemingly) every interesting person in New York City was doing on the night of the '77 blackout could have been a book unto itself."
—Chuck Klosterman, author of *Sex, Drugs, and Cocoa Puffs* and *Eating the Dinosaur*

"There's no mistaking that this book will have a special appeal for people who were exposed to this music when it was developing—mostly those living in New York in the mid-70s—but Hermes does what a good writer does. He makes the rest of us (this writer included) wish we'd been there."   —Georgia Young, *Paste*

"By simply putting things in chronological order, Will Hermes shows just how astonishing New York City's music was in the 1970s. But he does more than that: he brings depth and discernment and an eye for odd detail, making his book an essential work of cultural history."
—Luc Sante, author of *Low Life* and *Kill All Your Darlings*

LOVE GOES
TO BUILDINGS
ON FIRE

LOVE GOES
TO BUILDINGS
ON FIRE

FIVE YEARS IN NEW YORK
THAT CHANGED MUSIC FOREVER

WILL HERMES

FARRAR, STRAUS AND GIROUX

NEW YORK

Farrar, Straus and Giroux
18 West 18th Street, New York 10011

Printed in the United States of America
Published in 2011 by Faber and Faber, Inc.
First paperback edition, 2012

The Library of Congress has cataloged the hardcover edition as follows:
Hermes, Will.
Love goes to buildings on fire : five years in New York that changed music
forever / Will Hermes. — 1st ed.
    p.   cm.
Includes bibliographical references and index.
ISBN 978-0-86547-980-7 (cloth : alk. paper)
    1. Popular music—New York (State)—New York—1971–1980—History and
criticism.   I. Title.

ML3477.8.N48 H47 2011
781.6409747'109047—dc22

2011008445

Paperback ISBN: 978-0-374-53354-0

Designed by Jonathan D. Lippincott

Our books may be purchased in bulk for promotional, educational, or business use.
Please contact your local bookseller or the Macmillan Corporate and Premium
Sales Department at 1-800-221-7945, extension 5442, or by e-mail at
MacmillanSpecialMarkets@macmillan.com.

www.fsgbooks.com

18

FOR ANNE AND GIA

CONTENTS

CONTENTS

PREFACE

Beneath the postwar apartments and garden duplexes of Fresh Meadows—a neighborhood in Queens marked by a conspicuous shortage of meadows—there is a network of bomb shelters. They were constructed as part of the namesake housing development built by the New York Life Insurance Company back in the late '40s, and were accessible via doors in the apartment tower basements. If you had the key.

My friend Chris's dad worked in the complex, so Chris had the key. In the mid-'70s, when I was a teenager, the bomb shelters were our clubhouse. The bunch of us, all guys, hung out, smoked Marlboros and joints, drank Dr Pepper and Bud tall boys. We flipped through comic books, *MAD*, *National Lampoon*, porn; talked about girls (none would ever set foot down there); and marveled at the exploits of older kids—like Dave's brother, a premed Ivy Leaguer who had fallen into the barbecue at a family gathering while bombed on quaaludes. We talked about the movies we loved. And we talked about music. We were obsessed with music.

Sometimes, if the weather was nice—in summer, when dusk came late—we'd slip out of our houses after dinner and head for the roof of what we called the Thirteen-Story Building. Due to superstition, many tall buildings do not have thirteenth floors; their elevators have buttons for 12, then 14. This apartment tower accepted reality. I admired that.

We'd pile in, press 13, then scramble out, up the final flight of stairs, and through the fire door. And there it was: the city. We'd watch the sun sink behind the Manhattan skyline in a riot of pollution-enhanced reds and oranges, while countless unimaginable scenes played out behind countless glowing windows—a hundred thousand points of amazing and who-knew-how-depraved light. We were ready to fly to them.

•

Much has been written about New York City in the '70s, how bleak and desperate things were. The city had careened into bankruptcy, crime was out of control, the visionary idealism of the '60s was mostly kaput. For a kid growing up then, it was pretty dispiriting. The '60s was an awesome party that we had missed, and we were left to drink its backwash. The pot wasn't as cheap. The LSD wasn't as pure. The free love—as we saw in our parents' messy divorces and those health-class horror stories—was no longer so free.

Even the music was failing, it seemed. Jimi, Janis, and Jim were dead; the Beatles and the Velvet Underground had split. Sly and the Family Stone were unraveling amid mounds of cocaine. The Grateful Dead buried Pigpen. Dylan grew a beard and moved to Los Angeles. R&B was losing power as slick soul and featherweight funk took over. Jazz and "classical" music seemed irrelevant—the former groping fusions or post-Coltrane caterwauls, the latter dead-ended in sexless serialist cul-de-sacs.

There remains a myth that the early- to mid-'70s—post–Aquarian revolution, before punk and hip-hop begot the new age—was a cultural dead zone.

And yet, amid the skyscrapers we marveled at from the Thirteen-Story Building, down on the streets, artists were breaking music apart and rebuilding it for a new era. Kool Herc, Afrika Bambaataa, and Grandmaster Flash hot-wired street parties with collaged shards of vinyl LPs. The New York Dolls stripped rock 'n' roll to its frame and wrapped it in gender-fuck drag, taking a cue from Warhol's transvestite glamour queens. Bruce Springsteen and Patti Smith, both bussed in from Jersey, took a cue from the elusive Dylan, combining rock and poetry into new shapes.

Downtown, David Mancuso and Nicky Siano were inventing the modern disco and the art of club mixing. Uptown, Eddie Palmieri, Willie Colón, and the Fania All-Stars were hot-rodding Cuban music into multiculti salsa, making East Harlem and the South Bronx the global center of forward-looking Spanish-language music. In the wake of Miles Davis's funk fusions, jazz players were setting up shop in lofts and other repurposed spaces, exploding the music in all directions, synthesizing free-jazz passion with all that came before and after. Just blocks away,

Philip Glass and Steve Reich were imagining a new sort of classical music, pulling an end run on European tradition using jazz, rock, African and Indian sources, and some New York hustle.

All this activity—largely DIY moves by young iconoclasts on the edge of the mainstream—would grow into movements that continue to shape music around the world.

Which brings me back to the roof of the Thirteen-Story Building, from which we looked west toward Manhattan and Jersey, south to Brooklyn, and north to the bridges—Triborough, Whitestone, Throgs Neck— that led to the Bronx. Revolutions were unfolding, unseen, as we peered into the night.

This book attempts to see, with telescopic, panoramic, superhero vision, some of what happened during those years, and to zoom in on events—sometimes occurring simultaneously a subway ride away from one another—that made history. In most cases, they reveal people taking the lousy hands they'd been dealt and dreaming them into music of great consequence.

In this sense, it's an inspirational book. Sometimes the worst situations produce the deepest beauty, and the most profound change.

LOVE GOES
TO BUILDINGS
ON FIRE

1973

WILD SIDE WALKING

This is the era where everybody creates.
—Patti Smith[1]

An hour after midnight on January 1, 1973, Ernie Brooks was barreling down I-95 toward the city in his mother's Volvo. His band, the Modern Lovers, had been booked for a New Year's Eve show at the Mercer Arts Center. The New York Dolls were headlining. But his van died outside New Haven. So he hitched to his parents' house in New Canaan, got the family car, drove back to the van, jammed guitars and microphones into the Volvo, and drove like hell.

The Mercer was packed. There were teenage girls in miniskirts and garish makeup. There were guys in miniskirts and garish makeup. A woman wore a dress that had been cut into pieces and reassembled with safety pins.

The Modern Lovers went on at around 3:30 a.m., plugging into the Dolls' amplifiers. As a rule, they wore T-shirts and jeans, but for this gig their leader, Jonathan Richman, had bought a white dress shirt. During "Hospital," a love song as raw as a skinned knee, he ripped the shirt off. A girl standing beside the stage bent to pick up a stray button as a souvenir.

The Dolls went on just before dawn. The lead singer, David Johansen, wore a white blouse, tight white pants, and white platform heels. He swigged from a bottle of Miller, flipped back his hair, and introduced a song called "Trash." The band was sloppy—the bassist, who was wearing a yellow plastic tutu, could barely play—but thrilling. And the song sounded amazing, like some '50s rock 'n' roll gem retooled for a more jaded age.

There were lots of artists in the crowd that night; actors, dancers, musicians. Truman Capote was there. So was Richard Meyers, a poet who was beginning to play bass and write songs. He was impressed.

The Village Voice announced an "Invent the '70s" contest in its January 4 issue.

"If you know what the '70s are, or have any inkling where they're going," read the item, "write to [us] and any feasible answers will be printed."

The '70s had an identity crisis from the get-go. Richard Milhous Nixon was inaugurated to a second presidential term on January 20, 1973; thousands of troops remained in Vietnam. If a change was gonna come, as Sam Cooke had predicted, it was running way late.

You can hear this stasis in the music. Listen to the Grateful Dead's *Europe '72*, released just before the New Year. It's the '60s caught in amber, the Dead's prickly psychedelia smoothed out in a mix that reduces the audience's tripping howl to a distant murmur.

But the Dead were living the '70s. Their hard-partying singer/ harpman/organist Pigpen was so sick from years of alcohol abuse that he could barely sing. He played some keyboards on *Europe '72*, that's all, and on March 8 he joined his pal Janis Joplin in rock-star heaven. The Dead's first show after his death was a week later at the Nassau Coliseum on Long Island. They played mostly with their backs to the crowd, facing one another in a mourners' circle.[2]

As for the *Voice*'s "Invent the '70s" contest, there were no winners.

Meredith Monk wrapped a wineglass in foam rubber and newspaper and tucked it into an old 45 carrying case marked FRAGILE. She had a concert that night, January 11—her biggest to date, a coming-out party of sorts—and besides her remarkable voice, the glass would be her only instrument.

Monk, a thirty-year-old composer, singer, dancer, and multimedia artist, had rented Town Hall, a 1,500-seat theater on West Forty-third Street built by the League for Political Education, a bunch of monied idealists who'd fought hard for women's suffrage. In 1921, the year it opened, Margaret Sanger was hauled offstage and arrested for daring to speak to an audience of men and women about birth control. In '35, the great American contralto Marian Anderson gave her first New York recital there; in June '45, Dizzy Gillespie and Charlie Parker pretty much debuted bebop to the world there. Through the '70s, it remained accessible to artists who most promoters wouldn't touch.

Dressed entirely in white, her hair pulled back into tight braids, Monk walked downstairs from her new loft space on West Broadway ($400 a month, a stretch for her) and caught the uptown IRT at Franklin Street.

Monk performed *Our Lady of Late* that night, her wordless vocals dancing over a drone created by rubbing her finger around the rim of the wineglass. Sometimes she mirrored the drone perfectly, making microtonal shifts in her voice so it rippled like a banner in the wind. She purled out gorgeous, haunted, lowing melodies; sighed breathlessly in rhythm; applied severe vibrato to frightened babbling; bleated vowels and phonemes into unintelligible, sometimes hilarious chants. Her friend Collin Walcott, a multi-instrumentalist with an interest in world music, occasionally tapped out rhythms on another wineglass. Periodically, Monk sipped water from her own glass to alter its pitch.

A couple of days later she got a review in *The New York Times*, her first. John Rockwell called her "an incontestable virtuoso" and the concert "an extraordinarily consoling, meditative experience" that he heard as "a compendium of womanly experience, from birth to girlhood to motherhood to shamanistic ecstasy to grief to old age to death."[3]

It amazed her that the aesthetically conservative *Times* reviewed it. Even more amazingly, the writer seemed to get it.

That Sunday afternoon, twenty-five-year-old Laurie Anderson lay on Coney Island beach with the chill of the New Year swirling in the salt air. Her turtleneck was pulled up to her nose, her watchman's cap pulled down over her eyes. She was trying to sleep—perchance, to dream. It was a performance art piece sans audience, to be documented by snapshots and diary entries, part of what she called her "Institutional Dream Series."

The work was not entirely successful. Sleeping outside the women's bathroom in the Schermerhorn Library at Columbia University (where she'd recently earned an MFA in sculpture), she managed to dream that

the library was "an open-air market" and that all the shelves were stocked
with produce. She dreamed of "a bright white desert" in a boat berth at
the South Street Seaport, and had her camera confiscated while trying
to sleep on a bench in night court at 100 Centre Street, where, for some
reason, she couldn't dream.[4]

Dreaming would play a major role in Anderson's creative life. But at
the moment, she was just an ambitious midwestern art-school kid with
a viola, wanting New York City to shape her subconscious. As with many,
it did.

About twenty-five miles down the coast from where Anderson slept in
the sand was Asbury Park, a kindred seaside town in New Jersey where
Bruce Springsteen, age twenty-three, a small, skinny dude with a
scrubby beard, had been living in an apartment over a drugstore.
But he'd been evicted, and his buddy Big Danny Gallagher was letting
him crash on his living room floor. Springsteen wasn't around that Sunday; he was wrapping up a seven-day, fourteen-set run opening for David
Bromberg at Paul's Mall, a jazz and blues club in Boston. Some of the
ads misbilled him as "Rick Springsteen." But that was nothing new, and
Bromberg, being a gentleman, let him play nearly eighty minutes per
set, way more than most headliners would allow. Things were going
great; unbelievable, really. He'd done his first-ever live radio performance that week at the local WBCN-FM. And his debut album, *Greetings from Asbury Park, N.J.*, had been released by Columbia just over a
week ago.

Last spring, he'd ridden the bus into the Port Authority Bus Terminal with his acoustic guitar to audition for John Hammond, the producer
who had gotten Billie Holiday, Bob Dylan, and Aretha Franklin their record deals. Springsteen's manager, Mike Appel, an Irish-Catholic–Jewish
hustler from Flushing, had wrangled it. And the singer-songwriter did
well, impressing Hammond so much, the label don helped arrange a
last-minute showcase for him that night at the Gaslight Café on Bleecker
Street. Hammond wanted to see him in situ. He also wanted him back
the next day to record demos at the CBS studios on West Fifty-second
Street.

There were maybe eight people in the Gaslight audience that
Wednesday night, but like most any room in the city, it was full of

ghosts. Originally located in the basement of 116 MacDougal, where it helped spawn the Greenwich Village folk explosion (it was the site of a widely bootlegged 1962 Dylan performance), the club had recently moved into the basement of 152 Bleecker, formerly the Café au Go Go, where Lenny Bruce was arrested in 1964, and where the Dead had their first New York gig. Springsteen played originals: "Growin' Up," "It's Hard to Be a Saint in the City," "Arabian Nights." Hammond was wowed yet again.

In the studio the next day, the desire in Springsteen's voice was so aching, coiled, breathless, it was like he was about to explode, or pass out. In the first line of "Mary, Queen of Arkansas," he sang tenderly, "It's not too early for dreamin'."

Hammond thought that one was a bit melodramatic. But he was sold.

Springsteen signed a contract in the summer; deducting the money they needed for recording costs, he and Appel got to celebrate with an advance of $25,000.[5]

Hammond was convinced that the singer-songwriter's future was as a solo acoustic act. Springsteen liked playing the lone troubadour, and he could be riveting in that role. After all, he had caught the music bug as a kid in part from watching the guys in the folk-song circles on the Asbury Park beach, wooing girls with their acoustic guitars. "I'd be standing there like 'Someday I just wanna get good enough so that I can bring my guitar to the beach, sidle into that circle, and play along,'" he said years later after a rehearsal in the old Paramount Theater on the Asbury Park boardwalk. "That was the height of my ambition."

But ever since he began fronting the rock outfit Child in '69, playing beach parties and college peace rallies with his pal Danny Federici, he'd been, at heart, a band guy.[6] So, against the wishes of both Hammond and Appel, but with the support of Hammond's boss at the time, Clive Davis, *Greetings from Asbury Park* was recorded with Springsteen's bandmates. It riffed off rock history, and indulged in Dylan-style lyrical splatter-painting. The title, meanwhile, chosen by Springsteen, proudly proclaimed him a Jersey kid when Columbia was hoping to sell him as a New York poet.

The record tanked; it sold fewer than twelve thousand copies that year, despite full-page magazine ads showing the bearded singer in a tattered denim shirt beneath a headline declaring, "This man puts more thoughts, more ideas and images into one song than most people put into an album." The hype probably hurt more than it helped. Radio pretty much ignored the record; Dave Herman, DJ at the powerhouse New York rock station WNEW-FM, was so put off by the hard sell, he wouldn't even listen to it.[7] When *Rolling Stone* got around to running a review six months after its release, Lester Bangs described an artist singing verses that reveled in "the joy of utter crass showoff talent run amuck and totally out of control." For Bangs, the magazine's enfant terrible, this was a fairly positive review, but still.[8]

As a teenager, I found the record and its characters hypnotizing; I spent hours with it. This was not the noodling blues-rock or fantastical prog rock I heard on the radio. This music was virtuosic and expansive, but a sweatier, more hardscrabble thing, telling stories about neighborhood characters with a soulful, speed-freak poetry. Queens, like Jersey, was bridge-and-tunnel territory; we were all exiles from Manhattan's main stage, acting out small-potatoes, inconsequentially life-and-death dramas. I knew these people.

Springsteen began a six-night opening-act residency with his band at Max's Kansas City on January 31. The bar-restaurant, at 213 Park Avenue between Seventeenth and Eighteenth Streets, was the temple of New York's rock scene, home to the Velvet Underground until their split in '70, and now a proving ground for up-and-comers. Springsteen was out of his element there, the South Jersey rocker among the terminally cool downtown crowd. But Sam Hood was booking lots of folk music in the upstairs space, and Springsteen had been working in his solo singer-songwriter guise there. In '72 he opened there for Odetta, Dave Van Ronk, and the New York Dolls.[9] He'd usually play his last note, pack up his guitar, and grab a cab up to Port Authority to catch the last bus to Asbury Park. (He first saw the Dolls on a night he missed his bus, watching the show from beside the soundboard. "The scene was unusual for a provincial guy out of New Jersey," he recalled. "But they were incredible.")

Tonight, with his band, he impressed the crowd that had come for the hippie-folk wise guy Biff Rose, splitting his hour-long set between acoustic spiels and rockers. Along with songs from his debut was a Van

Morrison exercise, "Thundercrack," and "Bishop Danced," a boozy rocker about Catholicism that ends with drunken choirboys chasing a girl named Dinah—a play on "Dinah blow your horn," a cheap pun by a Catholic school kid who liked tweaking the Church.[10] The *Voice* critic Dan Nooger caught one of the Max's shows and predicted, "If he doesn't get lost under the attendant hype, Springsteen might even do something really amazing one of these days."

Bruce Springsteen was the least of the Church's worries in New York in 1973. The year began with the decision in *Roe v. Wade* on January 22, which legalized abortion in the first trimester. It was, as Andreas Killen suggests in *1973 Nervous Breakdown*, Year One of the Culture Wars.[11]

One of the year's biggest films—among the first true "blockbusters"—was William Friedkin's *The Exorcist*, which depicted a heroic Catholic priest saving a twelve-year-old girl (Linda Blair) from Satanic possession. Upon its release, the critic Andrew Sarris wrote that the film "may represent the most spectacular public relations coup for the Jesuits since the conquest of forensic television by William Buckley."[12]

The Exorcist hit home with everyone who felt America was a moral cesspool in need of soul-saving. And looking back, you could hardly be called a prude if you felt that way a little bit, especially in New York City, where the very stink of the place made simply wandering around Manhattan feel obscene.

Porn's great push into the mainstream began in June 1972 with the opening of *Deep Throat* at the New World Theater in Times Square. The film had legs, among other parts; its tale of a woman with a clitoris in her throat was one of '73's highest-grossing films, and it was quickly followed (with a nod to *The Exorcist*) by *The Devil in Miss Jones* and a flood of other titles.[13] Porn was not confined to the Times Square tittie-show ghetto; you could see *Behind the Green Door* at downtown art houses like the Cinema Village, over at the comfy Lido East on Fifty-ninth Street, or at the Capitol Cinema in Passaic, New Jersey, which hosted a personal appearance by the film's star, Marilyn Chambers—a onetime commercial model whose face was a cultural icon of purity thanks to a particular brand of clothing detergent ("Prints of the famous Ivory Snow package will be given away to each patron, plus personally autographed photos"). An ad for *Resurrection of Eve* quoted Kevin Saunders of ABC-TV exclaiming, "Marilyn Chambers is the first hard-core film star who has radiated the old-fashioned Hollywood-style glamour."

Even Fresh Meadows had its own porn palace: the Mayfair Theater, just off Utopia Parkway and Sixty-ninth Avenue. It had once been an arthouse cinema, but the local crowd (which included budding film enthusiasts Harvey and Bob Weinstein, who in those days pretty much lived there) couldn't sustain it. If I decided to walk to school—as I often did, since riding the young-thug-packed Q17 bus was the most dangerous part of the day—I'd pass the Mayfair en route to and from Ryan Junior High. I think it was open only at night; I can't recall ever seeing anyone go into it. The posters for *Behind the Green Door*, or whatever, hung in the marquee window, curling up at the edges.

Lou Reed's *Transformer*, produced by David Bowie and Mick Ronson, was released in November '72. It earned its name: it transformed Reed from rock musician into rock star. In early '73 the single "Walk on the Wild Side" was a radio staple, reaching number 16 on the *Billboard* charts despite, and because of, lyrics that peeped through a dirty window at New York City's gender-melting underground. Reed biographer Victor Bockris called it "the no. 1 jukebox hit in America in 1973," which may well be true; it was definitely worth a quarter to play it in a diner or pizzeria and watch heads turn. Most listeners had no clue that the song's characters—Holly the transvestite, Candy the blow-job queen, Little Joe the gay hustler, Sugar Plum Fairy the Harlem cruiser, Jackie the speed freak—were actual people: Holly Woodlawn, Candy Darling, Little Joe Dallesandro, Joe "Sugar Plum Fairy" Campbell, and Jackie Curtis were all members of Reed's extended artistic family at the Factory, Andy Warhol's salon/clubhouse/culture incubator, which at the time was located on the sixth floor of 33 Union Square West, just across the park from Max's.

Reed was born in Brooklyn and raised on Long Island. He was moody, pegged as a problem child, and the summer after he turned seventeen, a psychiatrist convinced his parents to send him to Creedmoor State Hospital in Queens for eight weeks of electroshock therapy, intended to cure him of his homosexual and antisocial sentiments. He attended Syracuse University, played in a rock band, took drugs, and studied with the poet Delmore Schwartz, whom he called "my teacher, my friend, and the man who changed my life." He moved back home to Long Island and got a job as a staff songwriter and session musician with Pickwick Records, where he met John Cale, an expat viola player from Wales.[14] The two became musical pals and drug buddies, and Reed moved into an apartment with Cale at 56 Ludlow Street, south of Delancey, in the old Jewish ghetto of the Lower East Side.

The two formed the Velvet Underground in 1965 with two other Long Island kids, the guitarist Sterling Morrison and the drummer Maureen Tucker. They were all fans of raw R&B: Ike and Tina Turner's "It's Gonna Work Out Fine," Eddie & Ernie's "Outcast." Reed also loved Ornette Coleman; Cale had worked with John Cage and, when the Velvets came together, was performing screechy, hypnotic drones with the composer La Monte Young in the latter's Theatre of Eternal Music ensemble.[15] The Velvets swiped their name from the title of a paperback about suburban sex kinks that Cale's friend Tony Conrad plucked from a Manhattan gutter, and they made music where scuzzy primitivism camouflaged brainy underpinnings, playing Reed's vérité rock songs about S&M and heroin at the height of international flower-power culture. As the critic John Rockwell noted, "Psychedelic weirdness never caught on very firmly in speedy, street-oriented New York."[16]

The Velvet Underground never made it big, but their aesthetic had a lasting effect. In a sense, the '70s began with them. And with *Transformer*, Reed became an idol. He still held court in the back room of Max's Kansas City, but his solo debut in January took place uptown, at two shows in Lincoln Center's Alice Tully Hall.

Tom Miller was tripping his balls off on LSD in his hometown of Wilmington, Delaware. The next thing he knew, a week later, he was in New York City, crashing in a crappy East Village apartment with his old friend Richard Meyers. They were both nineteen years old.

They'd met at Sanford, a boarding school for ne'er-do-wells and other types near Wilmington. Meyers was raised in Lexington, Kentucky, a town shadowed by the Lexington Narcotics Farm rehab facility, where William Burroughs and Sonny Rollins, among many others, had taken the cure. At fifteen, Meyers stole and wrecked a car; he was suspended from school and wound up at Sanford, but didn't last long there.

By late '66, he headed to New York City. He was besotted with Dylan Thomas, and intent on being a poet.

Miller stayed in touch and eventually followed. "Will be coming up Friday for good," Miller wrote to him in the summer of '68, scrawling on loose-leaf paper in ballpoint ink. "Had first acid trip on last Friday. Fucked me up and I know I found out some shit about everything." In the center of the page is a smiling cartoon figure caught in a whirlpool. Miller added that he'd probably be broke, and hoped Meyers and his girl-friend wouldn't mind him being around. He signed the missive, "Love, Tommy Poop."

Soon enough, Miller had a room at the seedy Village Hotel on Bleecker Street. He also saw himself as a poet. He and Meyers were now in thrall to the French Decadents, Baudelaire and Lautréamont, Rimbaud and Verlaine, Bréton and the Surrealists. Meyers was already self-publishing a tiny poetry magazine, *Genesis : Grasp*. The final issue, completed in 1971, featured a mysterious woman named Theresa Stern. Her poetry was actually the collaborative work of Meyers and Miller, her photo a composite of the two young men in drag. They liked the female alter ego, who Meyers imagined as a Hoboken hooker; a Stern chapbook called *Wanna Go Out?* followed.

They also adopted individual aliases—Tom Miller became Tom Verlaine, in honor of the poet; Richard Meyers became Richard Hell, in honor of the locale and Rimbaud's *Une Saison en Enfer.* Having enjoyed collaborative poetry, they turned their attention to music. Verlaine, who studied classical music and played sax in high school, worshipped Albert Ayler and John Coltrane. He'd begun playing guitar, further inspired by Hendrix, the Mahavishnu Orchestra's John McLaughlin, and the Grate-ful Dead's improv epic "Dark Star."[17] Shortly after he'd arrived in New York, he picked up a Fender Jazzmaster for ninety-five dollars up on Forty-eighth Street, and eventually persuaded Hell to buy a Danelectro bass at a pawnshop on Third Avenue.

Hell, who'd never studied music, was a fan of the Stooges. The two shared a love of the Velvet Underground; for the tight, mid-'60s British Invasion rock of the Stones, the Beatles, the Yardbirds, and the Who; and for the gnarly mid- to late-'60s American garage rock of bands like the Seeds and the Standells. Their taste for the latter had been stoked recently. Verlaine bought a box of old singles from a Hare Krishna kid in Washington Square, and also picked up the double-LP anthology titled

Nuggets, released in the fall of '72. A hard-boiled mix of the familiar and the forgotten, it was compiled by a rock critic, musician, and record-store clerk named Lenny Kaye, who called the music "punk-rock" in the liner notes.[18] Like Harry Smith's 1952 *Anthology of American Folk Music*— also curated by an erudite, record-collecting New Yorker—it caught the ears of many musicians. It was a between-acts staple on the sound system at Max's, where Hell and Verlaine would sometimes hang out, nursing drinks and rubbernecking, trying to make the scene.

Eventually they formed a trio called the Neon Boys with their old pal Billy Ficca, who came up from Delaware to join them in the fall of '72. They tried to recruit a second guitarist the way all local bands did, through an ad in the *Voice*. Theirs read: "Narcissistic rhythm guitarist wanted—minimal talent okay." A Brooklyn player, Chris Stein, tried out, but didn't like the material; according to Verlaine, he thought it too fast and uncommercial. A Queens kid named Douglas Colvin auditioned, but was too inept.[19]

The Neon Boys never found a second guitarist, but in April they decided to record some demos anyway, Hell playing bass and Verlaine playing both lead and rhythm. The six songs, including Hell's "Love Comes in Spurts" and Verlaine's "Hot Dog," were harsh and high-strung, in the spirit of *Nuggets*. Demos cut, they disbanded. Verlaine knocked around as a solo act with his Jazzmaster. Hell went back to the life of a writer, as he imagined it, living in a girlfriend's apartment overlooking the St. Mark's Church cemetery, working in a $16-a-week furnished room on East Tenth Street, where he would set up every day with a bottle of cheap wine and unspool words until he'd filled one single-spaced page. Before the end of the year he'd finished a short novel of surreal, horny, grim metafiction involving two young men, Caspar Skull and Arthur Black, that bore some resemblance to Hell and Verlaine. He titled it *The Voidoid*.[20]

Since last summer, the Mercer Arts Center, a theater complex at 240 Mercer Street, between Third and Bleecker, had become the New York Dolls' live-performance home. It was started in 1970 by the theatrical producer and off-Broadway pioneer Gene Frankel, who set up shop on two floors of the crumbling Broadway Central Hotel building with his partner Seymour C. Kaback—an engineering consultant who was the silent partner in another multiroom venue around the corner on Bleecker Street, Art D'Lugoff's Village Gate (where Bob Dylan wrote "A Hard Rain's Gonna Fall," in an apartment in the club's basement). The Mercer was primarily a theater space. It made its mark in '71 with a revival of the '65 Broadway production of *One Flew over the Cuckoo's Nest*, a play whose theme of inmates taking over the asylum seemed fitting for the place. Another early hit was *Tubstrip*, which was advertised as a "new play with all male cast . . . better than a trip to the baths."

The site itself had a storied past in the city's arts world. In the fall of 1850, the opera singer Jenny Lind—"the Swedish Nightingale"—had a historic fifteen-show run, arranged by her manager, P. T. Barnum, at Tripler Hall in the Lafarge House Hotel, which occupied the same footprint as the Mercer. In the 1860s it was the Winter Garden theater, hosting a legendary hundred-performance run of *Hamlet* with the renowned thespian Edwin Booth, brother of John Wilkes Booth (whose assassination of President Abraham Lincoln in 1865 made Edwin's life very difficult; he subsequently required a police escort to get through the hotel lobby to his dressing room so that he wouldn't be assaulted).

The Winter Garden burned down in 1869, and the hotel expanded, eventually renaming itself the Broadway Central. It saw lots of action. The Wall Street shyster and playboy James Fisk was shot dead on the grand stairway in 1872 by a jealous suitor over the affections of a showgirl. In the Gay '90s, Diamond Jim Brady partied hard in the hotel's restaurants. A bit later, one of the hotel's eateries—Trotsky's Kosher Restaurant—was allegedly a fave of a Russian visitor of the same name, the gentleman known, pre-Revolution, as Lev Bronstein.[21]

For their venue, Frankel and Kaback divided two floors in the Broadway Central (then functioning more or less as a welfare residence called the University Hotel) into seven small theaters. The Dolls usually played on the second floor in either the Oscar Wilde cabaret or—as they had for the New Year's Eve gig—the slightly larger O'Casey, which had tiered seating for three hundred or so people. They'd grown a good-sized following, and word was out; at one show, as legend has it, the seventy-one-year-old actress Marlene Dietrich—a fan of drag balls back in Weimar-era Berlin—turned up with some friends one night to check them out.

But it had been a nightmarish few months for the Dolls. In November, their drummer, Billy Murcia, died during their debut British tour after mixing champagne and Mandrax (the British brand name for methaqualone, the popular sedative/aphrodisiac/date-rape drug sold in the United States as Quaalude). The "friends" who attempted to revive the unconscious Murcia—killing time between gigs without his band-mates—heaved him into a filled bathtub and poured black coffee down his throat, quite possibly drowning him, and proving once again that serious drug users should study basic EMS.

Murcia's replacement, Jerry Nolan, joined the band just weeks be-fore the New Year's gig. He was a fairly seasoned musician—he played with Queen Elizabeth, among other local acts. But his debut with the Dolls, the early show at the Mercer on December 19, was a debacle of missed cues. Doubly unfortunate, it was in front of a room full of bizz-ers looking to sign the band. "That night we blew it fucking big," said Syl Sylvain. "Every major record company passed on us."[22]

At the late show, however, after Ahmet Ertegun and the other in-dustry folks left, the band played an awesome set. "Dolls are the new Rolling Stones," Patrick Carr typed breathlessly for his column in the Voice. "Dolls are the best New York City band in a decade."

In the April 19 issue of The Village Voice, an item in the "Scenes" col-umn noted that heroin, sniffed ("no needles, please"), was staging a comeback at parties in the Hollywood Hills, where people would "go downtown" with a snort, then "go uptown" with a wake-up toot of coke.

"You can bet that if it catches on out there," it read, "it will sweep its way through New York press parties by mid-summer."

The rioters at the Stonewall Inn in Greenwich Village in '69 were, by and large, not closet cases; they were warriors, and drag queens like Sylvia Rivera and Marsha P. (for "Pay It No Mind") Johnson were on the front line.[24] Richard Hell remembered James "Sweet Evening Breeze" Herndon, the real-life cross-dresser immortalized in Cormac McCarthy's Suttree, who cut a striking figure on the streets of Lexington.[25] In Hell's new home, Candy Darling, Jackie Curtis, and Holly Woodlawn—variously cast by Warhol in films such as Women in Revolt and Flesh—were celeb-rities. Queen Elizabeth's front man-woman Wayne County was mixing drag with crude garage rock, and the Lou Reed doppelgänger Ernie Thormahlen appeared in full drag on the back cover of *Transformer*. Now the Dolls, who played their first proper show in a Times Square welfare hotel with Curtis as a support act, were ramping up their own cross-dressing. Boys with long hair were no longer shocking, at least in New York. But add lipstick, panty hose, and high heels . . . people noticed. What, after all, was more badass and transgressive than a New York tranny?

The Dolls were émigrés in Manhattan. Sylvain Mizrahi began his musical career playing a toy oud in Cairo. His father was a banker there until 1956, when the Suez Crisis made Egypt an impossible place to be Jewish. The family moved to France, then to Buffalo, New York, and wound up in Queens, where Mizrahi got kicked out of Newtown High School for, as he put it, "lookin' like a fruitcake—because I was wearing bell-bottoms and had long hair."

He and his Queens pal Billy Murcia soon formed the Pox (with the inevitable "Catch the Pox!" gig flyers), playing their first gig at Craw-daddy's, a club in the West Fifties owned by the R&B legend Lloyd Price. The Pox played tough, hard rock à la the early Who. It wasn't hip-pie music, but something newer and older, with a sensibility the Dolls would inherit.

But not for a few years. When the Pox failed to take off, Mizrahi and Murcia turned their attention to the schmata trade. With help from Billy's Colombian mom, they set up a business—Truth and Soul Fashions—manufacturing trippy South American–style sweaters and tie-dyed biki-nis upstate in Woodstock. They sold wholesale to various shops; one customer was a young designer named Betsey Johnson. In '69, the men drove over to Bethel on the other side of the Catskill Mountains to sell their goods at the Woodstock Music and Arts Festival, which had been relocated out of town at the last minute. Restless hustlers, they soon pawned their designs to a large-scale manufacturer in Brooklyn, took the money to Europe, and blew it on hash, clothes, and musical gear.

Back home, they hooked up with the art school dropout Arthur Kane, a quiet, blond, extremely tall Irish kid from the Bronx, and Johnny Genzale, an Italian baseball obsessive and sartorial cockatoo from Queens who, like Mizrahi, had been kicked out of Newtown High School. The lead singer, David Johansen, was a troublemaker from Staten Island who had gotten expelled from Catholic school. "They just realized I was not the right person for them," he told me decades later in a café on Twentieth Street, exploding in a phlegmy laugh. "Because they couldn't break my spirit. They don't try to break everyone's spirit—only the people with spirit."

Johansen had been in San Francisco, mostly hanging around the Fillmore West; he worshipped Janis Joplin and pictured himself as her onstage, wailing hot-wired blues. When he wound up back home, he shifted his studies to the Fillmore East on Second Avenue, played with a few half-assed bands, got involved with the fringe theater scene. He hooked up with the Warhol actress Diane Poluski, a few years his senior, who introduced him to the inner circle at Max's. After a visit to the band's Upper West Side rehearsal space, located in the back of a bike shop, the twenty-one-year-old singer signed on.

The Dolls took their name from the New York Doll Hospital, a toy repair shop across the street from a midtown boutique Mizrahi had worked in. Ditching his last name, he became simply Sylvain Sylvain; Genzale became Johnny Thunders. The Dolls played dives, gobbled up drugs, and loved playing dress-up, their fashion sense inspired in equal parts by the Max's drag queens and Detroit glam rockers like Alice Cooper and the Stooges, in stacked heels, blouses, and makeup. They played simultaneously brute and campy rock 'n' roll that owed plenty to those bands—Thunders spewing metallic riffs, alternately squealing and spitting power chords, over Johansen's sashaying street-punk hollers.

"Personality Crisis" was their defining song, summing up a zeitgeist where who you were on the street, in the club, and in the bedroom was infinitely, confusingly mutable. "You're a prima ballerina on a spring afternoon," sang Johansen. "Change into the wolfman, you're howlin' at the moon—OWOOOOOOOOOO!"

One of their earliest gigs was at the cowboy-themed bathhouse Man's Country, located in the basement of 55 Pierrepont Street in Brooklyn Heights. During one set, Johansen pulled a prop saddle off the wall and put it on Arthur Kane's back and rode him around a bit. The first night, the band were all dosed on MDA. "I think I was selling it at the time," recalled Sylvain. "There was no audience, because all the guys stayed in their cubicles having sex. We weren't sure how to dress for the bathhouse, so the first night we went feminine; I wore hot pants. They didn't seem to appreciate the femme look, although we had a lot of fun on the MDA. The next night we came back in leather and chains and got more interest—everyone came out of their little cubicles to watch us."[26]

Few venues supported live music by rock acts playing original material; you pretty much had to be a cover band recycling the '60s. So the Dolls threw rent parties at their loft at 119 Chrystie Street, two dollars a head. When they heard the Mercer was booking bands, they went on a reconnaissance mission.

"They walked us all through the rooms and everything," Sylvain said. "You had to go through this one place, sort of like a cabaret, and the group Suicide were playing there. I don't know if they were doing their soundcheck or their first performance of the evening—there were like two people in the audience, black tablecloths on the table. And they scared the *shit* out of me. Marty Rev would glue together all this stuff to make these synthesizers, and Alan Vega was onstage in this wig looking like this kind of—I don't know how to describe him. He was wearing these glasses, like radiation glasses. I was like 'Oh my God, do we have to play *here*?'"[27]

But it was definitely a step up from the baths, so they did, with a residency that gave them the Oscar Wilde Room every Tuesday. They played there for seventeen weeks straight. Lou Reed turned up. Alice Cooper. And one night, David Bowie, the twenty-five-year-old British superstar, producer of Reed's *Transformer*. Bowie grilled the band about their clothing sources.

On March 20, the New York Dolls signed a two-album deal with Mercury and got a $25,000 advance. Their debut, *The New York Dolls*, was released on July 27.

And on August 3 at around 5:00 p.m., the Broadway Central Hotel building, with the Mercer Arts Center in it, collapsed. Rescue workers dug through the rubble with shovels and picks; twenty pine coffins were sent down to the site. Many people were carried out. Four people died.[28]

Eric Emerson and the Magic Tramps, a glam-rock band who also called the Mercer home, were rehearsing in the building when it came down. At first they thought it was an earthquake; they grabbed whatever instruments they could, and made it out. A Long Island band, Mushroom, had been rehearsing in another room; they made it out as well. Alan Vega was walking down the street and could see the Blue

Room, where Suicide had just played. "There was just a stage sitting there, with no building around it," he said.[29]

Until the following spring, New York's rock scene was essentially homeless. In the interim, the semifamous Dolls would travel to L.A., where Thunders would taste the heroin those *Voice* columnists had written about back in April while hanging around Hollywood with Iggy Pop, one of his heroes.

Thunders was nineteen. It was his first time. He liked it a lot.[30]

On certain days, if the sun was out and you cocked your head just so, you could still hear Sonny Rollins searching for a sound on the Williamsburg Bridge. Or at least you could imagine it. Rollins became a fixture up there in the early '60s, when he'd grown sick of the liquor-and-dope-fueled jazz club scene. He took a hiatus from gigging, and as he didn't want to disturb the neighbors in his Grand Street apartment on the Lower East Side, he hit on the idea to practice on the bridge. Out over the water, he'd parry with the sound of tugboat foghorns, weave around the steel-on-steel clatter of the BMT subway trains when they surfaced between boroughs, echo the hum and grind of the automobiles. He'd play for eight, twelve, fifteen hours at a stretch, the crisscrossing lines of girders and cables suggesting a physical geometry for his fast-changing melodic lines.

He bothered no one. After all, only fools even walked under the Williamsburg Bridge. The damn thing was so decrepit, it rained a steady shower of rust on the sidewalk below.

On April 5, the beleaguered mayor of New York, John V. Lindsay, presided over a ceremony and jam session at City Hall, declaring April to be "Jazz Month." Elected in 1966 with a campaign slogan of "He is fresh and everyone else is tired," Lindsay was now exhausted, in his final year of an eight-year run trying to hard-sell progressive politics to a city in fiscal meltdown. Hosting a jazz gig probably seemed a safe-enough move. Tellingly, the event was mostly old-schoolers: Billy Taylor, Roy Eldridge, Jo Jones, Willie "the Lion" Smith, Teddy Wilson.

It was a tough period for most New York jazz vets. Bebop and postbop seemed like ancient history. Coltrane had been dead for five years, Albert Ayler two. Sonny Rollins was back from yet another self-imposed retirement—spent partly in India—and playing brilliantly. But his comeback LP, *Sonny Rollins' Next Album*, was disappointing, and no one was setting the scene on fire.[31]

Not even Miles Davis, who, ever ahead of the curve, began inventing '70s jazz in 1969, first with the sublime electrified sounds of *In a Silent Way* and again, later that year, in New York City at Columbia Records Studio B (the same room where Springsteen would record his demos). At 10:00 a.m. on Tuesday, August 19—the morning after Jimi Hendrix closed the Woodstock festival a hundred miles upstate with his wildly improvisational take on "The Star-Spangled Banner"— Davis began recording *Bitches Brew*, the opening salvo of the jazz-fusion movement.[32]

That record sold well, but the jazz establishment hated it, and hated Davis's subsequent fusion records even more. After a stretch of declining sales and critical drubbing (the genre bible *Downbeat* dismissed the complex funk of 1972's *On the Corner* as "repetitious boredom"), the trumpeter was in a bad way, hoovering up cocaine, gulping down Tuinals and vodka.[33] He fired his manager of seventeen years, and one morning that fall, he fell asleep behind the wheel of his Ferrari on the West Side Highway—en route to an after-hours party in Harlem, as far as he could recall. He plowed into the divider, breaking both his ankles.

Davis began 1973 with crutches, hobbling onstage at the Village East (formerly the Fillmore East, on Second Avenue off Sixth Street) with another version of his endlessly mutating band. On February 23, he was busted with a girlfriend in front of his apartment building on West Seventy-seventh Street with a .25 automatic and three packets of coke. He'd been banging on the lobby door—he'd lost his keys—and a neighbor had called the cops.[34]

Miles's band boasted two Hendrix-influenced electric guitarists, Pete Cosey and Reggie Lucas. They came on like a lava flow, often working a single chord while the drummers would pile on churning crossrhythms. The records, produced by Teo Macero, continued to pioneer the use of tape collage and other postproduction trickery in a jazz context. But there was already a young generation of fusion musicians outshining Miles—many, like Herbie Hancock, Wayne Shorter, John McLaughlin, and Tony Williams, former sidemen/protégés of his. And like Lou Reed in the city's rock demimonde, Miles was at once of the scene and above it.

What generally gets called "free jazz"—improvised music that considers set chord changes, keys, time signatures, and bar lines optional—began in the explorations of Cecil Taylor and Ornette Coleman the late '50s, abetted by Coltrane, Ayler, and others in the '60s. In 1970, Coleman launched Artists House at 131 Prince Street, a combination performance space, recording studio, clubhouse, and apartment. Coleman was following Yoko Ono, one of his many musical collaborators, who hosted what was arguably the first New York loft concert in her sixth-floor walk-up at 112 Chambers Street one snowy night in December 1960. Soon a new generation of players took their cue from Coleman, building a scene in downtown industrial lofts repurposed as both homes and venues.

During July Fourth weekend in '72, the jazz promoter George Wein staged Newport—the World Cup of jazz festivals—in New York City for the first time. The festival had been kicked out of Newport, Rhode Island, the previous year after a mob of stoned kids, feeling music should be free and taking a cue from Woodstock, crashed the gates and freaked out the town elders. But New York presented its own problems. The city had emptied for the holiday, crowds were lean, and Miles was a no-show for a Carnegie Hall booking, allegedly due to a money dispute. There was a triumphant performance by Cecil Taylor (a single shape-shifting forty-minute piece that earned him a standing ovation), and the American premiere of Coleman's symphonic piece *Skies of America*, a composition funded by a recent contract with Columbia. But the bookings were otherwise typically conservative, largely ignoring the young loft scene.

Which, in fact, wasn't entirely young. The saxophonist Sam Rivers, who also played flute, piano, harmonica, and most anything else, was no newbie; the son of a Fisk Jubilee–schooled gospel singer and a student of the Armenian composer Alan Hovhaness, he was a transitional member of Miles's group in 1964, had albums on Blue Note as a leader, and at this point was pushing fifty. He'd moved into a loft at 24 Bond Street, between Bowery and Lafayette, back in '69, so he could give lessons and make music with his colleagues after hours.[35] Before long, it became a performance space, too: Studio Rivbea, named in part for his wife and comanager, Bea.

The drummer Rashied Ali, ten years Rivers's junior, also had a résumé, including his tenure as Coltrane's drummer during the saxophonist's final, farthest-out years. He'd been living in Williamsburg, in
a loft building on Bedford Avenue whose tenants included other jazz
players: Don Cherry, Archie Shepp, Roswell Rudd, Karl Berger, Marion
Brown. Ali was paying double rent—$100 a month—because he'd con-
nected two lofts. He had a good head for business, and was making
good money with Coltrane. In 1971, Ali moved into a second-floor space
in Manhattan, at 77 Greene Street, just off Spring. When the rag mer-
chant on the ground floor finally called it quits, the drummer nabbed
that space as well, and he, too, opened a performance venue: Ali's Alley.
His total rent there for both floors: around $200 a month.

Together, Rivers and Ali organized a Newport counterevent in '72
called the New York Musicians' Jazz Festival, staged simultaneously in
venues across the city. Rivbea presented Anthony Braxton, Dewey Redman, Andrew Hill, and Rivers. Studio We, run by the trumpeter James
Dubois and the drummer Juma Sultan at 193 Eldridge Street, hosted
Leon Thomas, Clifford Jordan, Cedar Walton, and Paul Bley. Pharoah
Sanders played up at Mount Morris Park in Harlem with a fledgling
bassist, Stanley Clarke, who had just turned twenty-one. There was
music at the University of the Streets on Seventh and A, Slug's on East
Third, Free Life Communication (run by the musicians Dave Liebman,
Bob Moses, and Richie Beirach) on West Thirty-sixth, the Third World
Cultural Center in the Bronx, and the Far East in St. Albans, Queens.[36]

Audiences were modest at best. "Despite its attempt to be rebel-
lious," pooh-poohed *The New Yorker*'s estimable jazz critic Whitney Balliett, the event "appears to be merely an inevitable overflow from the
Newport affair." But for the loft scene, it was galvanizing—a validation
and a baptism. Jazz players around the country heard about it, and New
York's gravitational pull grew that much stronger.[37]

For the '73 Newport Festival, the pragmatic Rivers worked in con-
junction with Wein, and the bookings reflected it. In addition to a
concert by Sun Ra and his Arkestra on July 6 (the synthesizer-playing
big-band leader released his trippy, landmark *Space Is the Place* in April),
Rivers led his own trio at the Wollman amphitheater in Central Park
on a July 5 afternoon bill that included the New York premiere of the Art
Ensemble of Chicago. Responses were mixed. Robert Palmer, a young
clarinetist and saxophonist from Little Rock, Arkansas, who also wrote

for *Rolling Stone* and had spent January in the Rif Mountains of Morocco with Ornette Coleman playing ritual music with the master musicians of the Jajouka village, penned an enthusiastic preview piece for *The New York Times*. In his *New Yorker* review, Balliett described the Art Ensemble's one-song set—staged with the tribal face paint and trailerload of percussion instruments that became their trademark—as "entertaining for a third of the forty-five minutes it lasted." He pronounced his feeling at the end of Rivers's "cantankerous" set as akin to "having just eased out of a pair of tight shoes."

But the Newport gig was a sign of things to come. Studio Rivbea was now at the center of the new jazz scene. The building at 24 Bond Street was lively. The landlady was the painter/art-world activist Virginia Admiral, whose son, Robert De Niro, a young actor, had just hit the Hollywood big time that summer with the baseball drama *Bang the Drum Slowly* (he had also finished a film called *Mean Streets*, which would open in October). The building had recently become home to a young photographer as well, Robert Mapplethorpe, who bought a loft on the fourth floor in late '72 for $15,000. Mapplethorpe had shot some portraits of Rivers, and would occasionally take the elevator down to Rivbea to check out the music. Ali's Alley, meanwhile, became home to regular gigs by the drummer's own group; he'd get a liquor license by the end of the year.

And soon players were coming in from around the country: from L.A., St. Louis, and especially Chicago. Many would stay. Jemeel Moondoc was a Chicago sax player who studied with Cecil Taylor when the pianist was briefly on the faculty at Antioch (Moondoc never enrolled; he just showed up to the class). The saxophonist soon moved to New York and assembled the band Muntu. Their playing was very free; gigs were hard to come by. Moondoc was ready to throw in the towel when Rivers offered his band a standing Thursday gig at the club in '73. And thus the scene grew.[38]

Of course, the loft scene was based on affordable lofts. And just as it gained momentum, the beginning of the end arrived on April 4, 1973: the official grand opening day of the twin 110-story towers of the World Trade Center.

Designed by Minoru Yamasaki, the towers were meant to reclaim and revive the area written off by Robert Moses in the early '60s, when the city's emperor-bureaucrat planned to level much of the areas now known as SoHo and TriBeCa for his unrealized Lower Manhattan Expressway project. Reclaim the area they did, when the financiers who moved into the WTC realized the potential of the surrounding loft district.[39]

It makes an odd kind of sense that the event to announce New York salsa's coming-of-age, and to reboot the career of Latin music's greatest living singer, would be a salsa remake of the Who's *Tommy* staged at Carnegie Hall.

The "rock opera" Pete Townshend had written a few years earlier represented more than his need to be perceived as an Artist in the wake of *Sgt. Pepper's Lonely Hearts Club Band*; it was a landmark of prog rock's hypervirtuosic, movin'-on-up sensibility of the early- to mid-'70s. Similarly, salsa wanted to travel beyond the barrio—to be seen, and to see itself, as more than just a ghetto dance-hall soundtrack. It was virtuoso music with deep history and an international pedigree; it wanted respect.

Appropriate to salsa's melting-pot culture, *Hommy, a Latin Opera* was cooked up by the flamboyant composer-bandleader Lawrence Ira Kahn, a.k.a. Larry Harlow. Kahn grew up in Brooklyn, the Jewish son of the opera singer Rose Sherman and Buddy Kahn, who worked for a while as bandleader at the Latin Quarter in Times Square under the stage name Buddy Harlowe. By the time he was a student at the High School of Music and Art up on West 135th Street in the '50s, Larry was obsessed with Latin music. He would head back to Manhattan on Sunday afternoons to see incredible bands at the Palladium Ballroom, the second-floor dance club on Fifty-third and Broadway—Arsenio Rodriguez, Machito, Tito Puente. Harlow was underage, but the owner, Max Hyman, a kindred Jewish mambo fan, would let him in anyway. In his late teens, Harlow went to Havana to study Cuban music. But the revolution soon forced him back to New York, where he followed in his father's footsteps—first playing Latin music, and, for a while, leading a Blood, Sweat & Tears–style rock band, Ambergris.[40]

The storyline of *Hommy* was written by Genaro "Heny" Alvarez, a Puerto Rican singer, drummer, and songwriter who worked days as a jewelry polisher in the Diamond District on West Forty-seventh Street.

It involved a blind and deaf boy with a talent not for pinball but for—what else?—Latin percussion. The music bore no resemblance to the Who's original; this was Cuban *son* and *guaguánco* spiced with jazz charts and other flavors. And who better to sing the production's signature number, thought Harlow, than Celia Cruz?

Cruz had been living in the New York area since declaring herself a political exile from her native Cuba in '62. But the music she'd been making in Havana as a singer with the great Sonora Matancera, and in New York with Tito Puente and others, had fallen out of fashion, overshadowed by Latin soul and boogaloo, as well as rock and the nascent pan-Latin salsa sound. At this point, she spent seven months of every year living and performing in Mexico.

Harlow met Cruz in Mexico and told her about his project. When Cruz returned to New York, she scheduled her first meeting with Jerry Masucci, cofounder (with the bandleader Johnny Pacheco) and business end of New York's preeminent Latin label, Fania. Cruz had come merely to talk. But it was a setup: when she arrived, she found a studio full of musicians ready to record. The song was *Hommy*'s equivalent of *Tommy*'s "Acid Queen," the kinetic "Gracia Divina." Cruz had never heard it before.

"I got so angry," she recounted in her memoir, "and I'm not an angry person." But the gracious and professional Cruz learned it and sang it.[41] Over a swirling, elegant *charanga*-style groove with full strings and gleaming brass, her bittersweet chocolate alto sound is unassailably regal. It's hard to know whether to dance or simply bow down.

Knocked off in a day, "Gracia Divina" became a massive hit on New York Latin radio: on Polito Vega's Spanish-language afternoon show on WBNX 1380, Joe Gaines's late-night English-language show on WEVD 1330, Felipe Luciano's Sunday specialty show on the jazz-minded WRVR 106.7. On March 29, Cruz sang "Gracia Divina" for a packed house in Carnegie Hall at *Hommy*'s world premiere, backed by the Orquesta Harlow and alongside the deep-voiced Cheo Feliciano, who had recently returned to claim his throne as the king of New York salsa singers after kicking a heroin addiction. The record flew out of the racks; the opera was produced in Puerto Rico and elsewhere.

But *Hommy*'s greatest effect was validating a group of young musicians, proving their music was worthy of Latin music's queen, and of one of the world's great concert halls. And performancewise, Harlow and the Fania crew would pull off something even more amazing by the end of the summer.

Latin music had been an integral part of New York's musical fabric for decades. Always part of the jazz scene, there were periods when the music's cultural presence ballooned. There was the mambo craze, which took off in the mid-'40s at the Palladium Ballroom. In the late '60s, there was the boogaloo era, in which Latin acts responded to R&B's golden era with their own hybrid soul music. Boogaloo was hated by Latin music purists, but it was perfect New York street pop, all simple, irresistible rhythmic and lyrical come-ons. (One critic dubbed it "cha cha with a backbeat.") Joe Cuba's "Bang Bang," Johnny Colon's "Boogaloo Blues," Ray Barretto's "El Watusi," and Pete Rodriguez's "I Like It Like That" are songs smart DJs still drop into dance mixes, and they always rock a party.

The "salsa" of the early '70s was not only more traditional than boogaloo, it was hotter, faster, brighter. It was not mellow, and it was not as refined as its Cuban models. Heard as a compressed radio signal blasting from shops, apartment windows, and passing cars, it sounded brassy and shrill—fun, hustling, terminally high-strung.

New York salsa was fusion music; you could hear urbane Havana *son* and country Puerto Rican *jibaro* styles, jazzy horn and flute solos, Santana-style rock guitar, wah-wah keyboards, long percussion jams that drew on funk and African music while mixing in various Caribbean and South American rhythms. It was integrated, like the city it came from.

To wit: on May 3 at the Lowe's Paradise—the spectacular old Bronx theater at 2413 Grand Concourse—a triple bill featured the formal debut of Tipica '73, the salsa group that had just splintered from the conguero Ray Barretto's band. With them was the Jersey City R&B crew Kool and the Gang, who were working on an album that would include a song called "Jungle Boogie." Rounding it out were the '60s pop-rockers Tommy James and the Shondells, whose '69 hit "Crystal Blue Persuasion" was a hit among Bronx soul fans, Latinos included; Joe Bataan and Tito Puente both covered it.[42]

It was an unusually mixed bill, given the tendency of music marketers to divide audiences along cultural lines. But salsa, R&B, and rock have a central thing in common: they worship rhythm. If it makes people move, it's all good. Not far from the Grand Concourse, a group of smart young DJs were learning this.

Hip-hop's ur-jam, described in Jeff Chang's sweeping hip-hop history *Can't Stop Won't Stop*, was a party held on the last week of August 11, 1973, in the west Bronx rec room of 1520 Sedgwick Avenue. There, Clive Campbell came of age as a DJ. He was a fairly recent immigrant, coming with his parents and siblings to the Bronx from Kingston, Jamaica, in 1967. It was a modest affair, coordinated by his younger sister Cindy, a budding businesswoman driven by a desire to buy herself a sweet back-to-school wardrobe.

Cindy's brother was known in the neighborhood as Kool Herc: the latter part of the nickname, short for "Hercules," was given to him by kids on the basketball court impressed with his size and power, the former inspired by a TV ad for the menthol cigarettes everyone smoked. Herc set up the gargantuan sound system he'd rigged with the Shure P.A. equipment that their dad, Keith—himself a hard-core music fan— used for gigs with a local R&B group. The siblings bought soda and malt liquor (Olde English 800 and Colt 45, the strongest brews of the era) and charged at the door. The space wasn't much for vibe—linoleum floors, steel-encased radiators, and a low, white-tiled drop ceiling with fluorescent lighting fixtures that a friend of the Campbells turned on and off to heighten the mood. Herc played some reggae sides—the kind that would fire up the yard parties he'd witnessed as a wide-eyed kid in Jamaica. Here, though, they didn't go over. Then he played some harder, funkier tracks: "It's Just Begun" by the Jimmy Castor Bunch, "Bongo Rock" and "Apache" by the Incredible Bongo Band, "The Mexican" by Babe Ruth, "Get Ready" by Rare Earth, Baby Huey's "Listen to Me," the Isley Brothers' "Get into Something," "Yellow Sunshine" by the Philly funk band of the same name, James Brown's "Give It Up or Turn It Loose."[43]

The crowd, mostly high schoolers, went bonkers. Being August, the side door of the building was opened to let the heat out. Kids hung by the Dumpsters smoking weed and drinking, and Herc's dad's sound system pumped beats out into the summer night, over the Major Deegan Expressway, up toward River Park Towers. It was Herc's first party under his own direction, on his own turf. The next day, it was the talk of the neighborhood.

In truth, the hard funk that the kids were sweating to that night was out of style in 1973. R&B was toning down and dressing up: Barry White's "I'm Gonna Love You Just a Little Bit More, Baby," Marvin Gaye's "Let's Get It On," and Harold Melvin and the Blue Notes' "The Love I Lost." Some grittier, funkier tracks still made the charts: War's "Cisco Kid" in May, Stevie Wonder's "Higher Ground" that fall. But by the year's end, the satin-sheeted "Love's Theme" by Philadelphia's Love Unlimited Orchestra would become a radio staple, followed the next spring by "TSOP (The Sound of Philadelphia)" by MFSB featuring the Three Degrees: the string-sweetened opening salvos of disco.

These were the records played by Herc's competition—guys like Anthony Holloway, who went by the moniker DJ Hollywood and played at grown-up clubs like Charles Gallery and A Bunch of Grapes, both on 125th Street in Harlem, places you generally had to look sharp to get into. Holloway became a DJ by accident, seeing a route out of the numbers running that helped land him in the Spofford Detention Center in the South Bronx during his high school years. His hero was Frankie Crocker, the king of New York soul radio, who made his own name at Harlem's WWRL-AM until he was hired away by the newly launched, black-owned WBLS-FM in '71. Crocker—who, coincidentally or not, also used the nickname "Hollywood," among others—often rhymed on-air between tracks, and his acolyte started doing the same in the clubs. Hollywood chanted things like "Throw your hands in the air, and wave 'em like ya just don't care. And if you got on clean underwear, somebody say 'Oh yeah!'" And then the crowd would shout back: "Oh yeah!"[44]

There were others in the game—the veteran R&B party-starter Pete DJ Jones; Edward Sturgis, a kid from Harlem's Douglas projects whose sobriquet was Eddie Cheeba; Brooklyn's Grandmaster Cameron Flowers, who played records in Yankee Stadium before James Brown's 1969 concert there. But at this point, Hollywood was the prince of the uptown discos.

Downtown, meanwhile, was a different story.

•

There is a pretty young woman standing on West Twenty-second Street, and she is screaming hysterically. Her pupils are pools of motor oil. Between shrieks, she tries to form words. One utterance sounds like "animal"; another like "gorilla." A young man with longish hair is trying to assist her, but he's laughing so hard he's nearly choking.

The scene takes place outside the Gallery, located on the second floor of an industrial loft building at 132 West Twenty-second Street. The nightspot began its life as a straight club in February 1973, but floundered. When it was reopened as an invitation-only, mainly gay dance club on June 28, 1973, the world's first modern disco was born.

Sure, there were "dance clubs" before the Gallery, and there were creative dance music DJs before its host, Nicky Siano. There was Francis Grasso, who mixed Chicago with Led Zeppelin at Sanctuary, the gay bacchanal palace located in a former German Baptist church at 407 West Forty-third Street that closed in 1972—partly on account of unruly patrons, who could often be found fucking in the hallways of nearby apartment buildings, but mostly because of its reputation as a mob-controlled drug supermarket (one of its owners, Shelly Bloom, was found murdered in his East Side apartment on the eve of testifying in a drug trial).[45] And there was the Timothy Leary acolyte David Mancuso, who began holding invitation-only parties at his home-based club, the Loft, at 647 Broadway just north of Houston, in early 1970. The Loft reimagined the French *discothèque* in terms of high-fidelity sound, thematic playlists, and the elusive element known as "vibe." It posited dancing not simply as a preface or overture to sex but as its equal.

The Gallery figured all these elements into the equation: a commercial club where admission was nevertheless on a members/friends-only basis, a crucible where room environment, social vibe, narrative-style song sequencing, sound effects, elaborate lighting, awesome sonics with extreme bass frequencies, and drugs combined to take people to places they'd never been before.

These were places not everyone wanted to go to. Thus, the pretty woman freaking out on Twenty-second Street.

"We had this big frog," recalled Nicky Siano. "It was a wading pool for kids, and the top of the frog had two big eyes; we hung it in the middle of the room, and when the room was crowded, all you saw over people's heads were these two weird eyes. One night we filled it with bananas, and we had this guy dressed up in a gorilla suit."

Siano laughed. "My friend Laurie is tripping hard, and she walks into the club and sees these two weird eyes over everyone's heads. So she says, 'Let me get out of here and go out onto the dance floor,' which was in a separate room. Then she turns the corner toward the dance floor and coming her way is this big gorilla! She ran out of the place screaming!"

Like his hero Mancuso, Siano knew how to throw a party. Raised in Sheepshead Bay in an extended family (he estimates more than a hundred cousins), he understood he was bisexual at an early age, and began running away from home at age fourteen. He started the Gallery as a partnership with his brother Joe, who was twenty-six and worked as an engineer. Joe was mainly an investor, and after a slow start, their $15,000 in loans began paying off. Siano was seventeen years old.

"There was no alcohol, but we'd have free food, punch, sometimes acid, lots of stuff," he recalled. "Things were not that expensive back then. The rent was like four-sixty a month, something like that, incredibly cheap. So, seven dollars times eight hundred, that would be fifty-six hundred a weekend, and your expenses would be . . . maybe you had like ten people working for you for fifty dollars each, which was five hundred. So you definitely turned a profit."

Back then, blotter acid was five, maybe six dollars a hit, and was strong enough that you could get four or five people very high off a single dose. Two of Siano's early employees, Frankie Knuckles and Larry Levan, were often in charge of distributing the LSD, either by dosing the punch or administering the drug to patrons individually, laying the sacramental blotters on tongues like communion wafers.

Like the San Francisco acid tests choreographed by Ken Kesey and his Merry Pranksters, Siano made sure the set and setting were conducive to revelers in altered states of mind. He and a friend painted one wall with puffy clouds; as a DJ, he was probably the first in New York to master the art of dropping out certain frequencies in a cut (usually the bass) at dramatic moments, then crashing them back in on the beat, à la dub reggae, detonating dance-floor pleasure bombs. He'd time these sonic sleights of hand with lighting effects, often cutting the lights altogether when a song reached a break and was building up to another crescendo. The result was breathtaking: you would suddenly be dancing in utter darkness, packed into a sweaty room full of screaming hedonists already out of their minds on drugs and adrenaline, their retinas still flickering with images, lights, and colors from a few seconds earlier. Then: WHAM! The lights were on and you were yanked back into reality, or some semblance of it.

Frankie Crocker had been playing the Wailers' *Catch a Fire* on WBLS.[46] Released in April, it came in a cool sleeve that looked and opened like a Zippo lighter. The reggae-driven film *The Harder They Come* had opened in February, and notwithstanding "Mother and Child Reunion," Paul Simon's Jamaican-flavored hit from the previous year, *Catch a Fire* was the first reggae music most non–West Indian New Yorkers had ever heard, and when the band came to Max's for a six-night run on their debut U.S. tour, it was the first time most of the crowd had ever seen a reggae band. The Wailers were a vocal trio—Peter Tosh, Bunny Livingstone, and the front man, Bob Marley—in the tradition of Curtis Mayfield's Impressions. Marley's presence was riveting, and the sound was hypnotizing. Many of the Max's regulars turned out. Lou Reed caught a show that week. So did the rock critic Lenny Kaye and his friend, a young poet and Max's regular, Patti Smith. They were both mesmerized.

The band played a new song called "Burnin' and Lootin'." Arson and robbery? Most locals could relate, no doubt—even the Jersey boosters who came to see the headliner, Bruce Springsteen.

Springsteen was in the throes of an endless promotional tour, and just coming off some of the worst shows of his life: opening a leg of an arena tour for the hit-making jazz-pop fluffballs Chicago. That group's Top 40–fed fans couldn't have cared less for him. At some dates, they threw things. He was booed offstage in Philadelphia. At Madison Square Garden in June, denied a soundcheck, he bombed so hard, even his supporters at Columbia Records were shaken. Afterward, he refused to play arenas—there was too great a rift, he thought, between the band and the audience—and refused to be an opening act unless he could play a full-length set.

Springsteen was exhausted, but happy to be back on familiar ground at Max's. That week he played two songs from his second album, which he was in the middle of recording upstate. "4th of July, Asbury Park (Sandy)" was a paradoxically romantic kiss-off to his hometown. "New York City Serenade" was a ten-minute elegy—lush, jazzy, deeply influenced by Van Morrison—for a town he also had mixed feelings for, full of hookers, small-time gangsters, and musicians who get the soul sucked out of them.

This life wasn't easy. Springsteen's band members were pulling around fifty dollars a week, when he could make payroll. By the end of the year, the bandleader had cleared about five grand for himself.

Released in September a mere eight months after his debut, *The Wild, the Innocent & the E Street Shuffle* was filled with New York imagery, from Bleecker to Fifty-seventh streets.

"It's midnight in Manhattan," Springsteen crooned to the crowd at Max's, strumming his acoustic against David Sancious's jazzy blue piano. "This is no time to get cute."

In early '73, Eddie Kendricks's "Girl You Need a Change of Mind" and the Temptations' "Law of the Land" represented a new kind of hit—the DJ club banger.[47] Both of the records were on the Motown label, but they weren't retreads of the label's signature sound: instead of compact pop songs, they were extended soul workouts with heavy percussion. Both prominently feature congas in their mix, and it's worth noting that the conga player on "Law of the Land" was King Errisson, the conguero who played with Kool Herc's beloved Incredible Bongo Band and also drove Kendricks's "Keep On Truckin'," the number 1 song in the country for two weeks in November. That Errisson's Caribbean hand drumming became a Rosetta stone of DJ beats is not surprising; hip-hop and disco were born of the same rhythmic gene pool.

And the city teemed with all sorts of DNA. The year's most unlikely hit was "Soul Makossa" by Manu Dibango, a previously unknown singer and saxophonist from Cameroon. The song was "discovered" in late '72 by the DJ David Mancuso on a French import during one of his vinyl-hunting expeditions in a West Indian record shop on Utica Avenue in Brooklyn. A low-riding funk track with a fierce groove undertow, "Soul Makossa" was all hot brass vamping, with Dibango's bassy "mama ko, mama sa, mama ma-kos-sa" chants riding over the top. Mancuso made it a hit at the Loft, and it quickly became the hottest vinyl in town. Nicky Siano and other DJs scarfed up the few available copies. Then Frankie Crocker got ahold of it and put it on heavy rotation at WBLS. Soon bootleg and cover versions were popping up. Finally, Ahmet Ertegun and Jerry Wexler of Atlantic Records licensed it for U.S. release. In June '73, "Soul Makossa" was on the pop charts. Black, white, Latino: everyone seemed to find it irresistible.[48]

Dibango's biggest U.S. gig, at the height of the song's popularity, was at Yankee Stadium in the Bronx, co-headlining an event billed in handwritten ads as the "1st Latin Soulrock Fiesta!"—although it could have been called the "1st Latin Soulrock Jazz Fusion African Proto-Disco Fiesta!" in its spectacular attempt to fuse nearly all the blooming local music scenes of the moment.

Sharing the bill were the jazz percussionist Mongo Santamaría, the rock guitarist Jorge Santana (Carlos Santana's brother, of the L.A. group Malo), and the fusion powerhouse drummer Billy Cobham (of the Mahavishnu Orchestra). Headlining, and yoking all these players together, were the Fania All-Stars, the supergroup led by Fania's co-owner Johnny Pacheco. The lineup featured the cream of the label's talent, including Ray Barretto, Willie Colón, Larry Harlow, Bobby Valentín, Héctor Lavoe, and their new member, Celia Cruz.

It was insane, of course: renting a baseball stadium to put on a salsa show. It happened because of the mad ambition of Jerry Masucci, an Italian lawyer and ex-cop from Brooklyn, who started Fania in 1964 with his divorce client turned partner Pacheco. Masucci was determined to make New York City salsa a global phenomenon, his label Fania its greatest exponent, and himself very rich.

It cost $280,000 to rent Yankee Stadium for the Friday night of August 24, with $50,000 security up front—mainly to insure the preservation of the field turf. (The stadium itself was slated to be demolished for a major renovation beginning that fall.) About 45,000 fans showed up, paying between $3.50 and $10 a head for tickets.

Manu Dibango played hard. "Soul Makossa" was a heady signifier, flexing the African roots of Latin music, speaking to the brotherhood of New York's black and Latino communities—a brotherhood damaged over the years by gang warfare while manifesting itself in the parallel political struggles of the Black Panthers and the Young Lords. (The impact of Cuban, and later New York, salsa on the music of West and Central Africa is a story unto itself.)

The setting was resonant, too. The year had begun with the death of the Puerto Rican–American baseball star Roberto Clemente, whose plane crashed into the sea during a New Year's Eve flight from San Juan to Nicaragua on a relief mission. The Pittsburgh Pirates' star player was dark-skinned and, in addition to his feats on the field, spoke out loudly about discrimination against blacks and Latinos, making him a hero to both communities. To witness such a bicultural celebration in a baseball stadium just eight months later made the evening even more profound.

By the time the Fania All-Stars get into their own set, the crowd, which has been prohibited from going onto the field, is getting restless. The band launches into Harlow's fire-spitting "Congo Bongo," and by the end—with Ray Barretto and Mongo Santamaría dueling furiously on tandem congas, and Billy Cobham, wearing a football jersey, thundering beneath and between the beats, lifting everything skyward—the crowd erupts. They burst past the barricades and swarm out over the field, dancing, cheering, and waving Puerto Rican flags. Jerry Masucci's brother Alex, one of the co-producers, is freaking, because he knows he can kiss that $50,000 deposit on the field adios. He tries to get the orchestra to stop, but they keep on pounding it out, Johnny Pacheco conducting wildly in an unbuttoned white dress shirt and stacked heels, hair flying like a crazed Caribbean Beethoven.

Finally they finish the tune, and security breaks down completely. Masucci decides to cut his losses and announces that the rest of the concert is now canceled. Bodyguards rush him to his car, headed for the after-party, while Alex hurries suitcases stuffed with box-office cash to another car. By now, the crowd is furious. People begin climbing onto the stage; some decide to go shopping. By the time things settle down, there is little left onstage besides cables and mic stands; someone has even made off with Larry Harlow's piano.

The most thrilling moment on the Fania All-Stars record *Live at Yankee Stadium Vol. 1* is when Héctor Lavoe, a twenty-six-year-old New York Puerto Rican—a Nuyorican—steps to the microphone in front of a cheering crowd and sings "Mi Gente," addressing the crowd as "my people" and declaring his pride, rhyming *"este mundo"* with *"orgullo profundo."*

Actually, Lavoe never sang the song at Yankee Stadium; the show had been shut down before he had a chance. The recording was made in Puerto Rico months later, at a performance staged to provide filler for two live albums and a film that Jerry Masucci had planned around the historic Bronx gig—a gig that never actually happened, beyond a few songs.

Lavoe had arrived in New York City from Puerto Rico as a talented teenager in 1963 intent on becoming a big-time musician, and he made his name as the singer in Willie Colón's band, a deal bartered by Masucci. Colón, born in the South Bronx to Puerto Rican parents, became Lavoe's mentor and sidekick. But Lavoe liked to get high, developed a taste for heroin, and became a wildly unreliable performer. By the time of the Yankee Stadium gig, the two were about to part ways.

Colón's dad had been a heroin addict. The young bandleader had been down that road before.

The title of Willie Colón's fiery 1972 album, *Cosa Nuestra*, declared its new-jack aesthetic ("Our Thing") while punning on "Cosa Nostra"— lingua franca for streetwise kids of all ethnicities with the release of Francis Ford Coppola's *The Godfather*. The LP sleeve had the skinny Bronx Nuyorican kid playing gangster dress-up, standing over a body bag, holding his trombone like a tommy gun. Colón's sharp wardrobe came partly from the film world. Colón's mother was dating Harry Belafonte's doorman, who had little use for the handsome silk ties the actor gave him. So he passed them on to her kid, the twenty-two-year-old salsa musician.

The thug persona wasn't empty role-playing: Colón moved amid street gangs, and had a reputation that earned him the nickname "El Malo," the title of his '67 Fania debut with Lavoe. (The nickname was also used by Latin music purists who thought his raw, rudimentary music was just plain bad.) It's odd that the cover depicts him ready to dump a body in the East River down by the Brooklyn Bridge, rather than up in his neck of the woods by the Triborough. Guess you don't shit where you eat.

The lead track of *Cosa Nuestra* was "Che Che Cole," which became one of Colón's biggest hits. He adapted it from a Ghanaian children's song learned from an African musician he knew, and built in a traditional Puerto Rican *bomba* rhythm, which in turn was probably rooted to some extent in the Ghanaian drum music that came over with the slave trade.[49]

"We're dancing African-style" is Héctor Lavoe's invitation at the song's head; the singer flashing homeboy *jibaro* phrasing while shouting out Panama and Venezuela, Puerto Rican music reconnecting with Motherland roots in the stew of New York City salsa.[50]

It's interesting to note that Willie Colón shares his last name with the Genoese seaman Cristobal Colón, a.k.a. Christopher Columbus, who, back in the fifteenth century, spent time in what is now Ghana, on the so-called Gold Coast of Africa, where the Portuguese operated a slave-trading castle and where the explorer no doubt learned some unpleasant things about human nature.[51] That his namesake was a New World explorer who celebrated America as a polyglot culture is a small, sweet irony of history.

In 2006, Willie Colón sat in Victor's Café, the posh Cuban restaurant in Times Square, where he is still received as royalty. "To be out in the field in Yankee Stadium?" he said, his heavy-lidded brown eyes widening. "It felt like we were up there with the Beatles and the Rolling Stones. And I just don't know how it happened, man. This music was marginalized. We were used to playing the wedding room up at 149th Street behind the Lowe's theater."

Looking wistfully across the dining room and back in time, all Colón could do was shake his head and say: "Oh, my God."

Two days after the Yankee Stadium concert, on August 26, about a hundred miles north of the city, a different sort of salsa was being made by Eddie Palmieri. In front of a small audience at the Woodstock Playhouse, a modest hike down the road from where John Cage premiered "4'33"," the Harlem-born pianist led his band through "Adoración." It begins with an extended, free-form, neoclassical piano section with some electric guitar and upright bass colorings, before launching into a *son* with a fire-spitting *montuno* section where Palmieri hurls his body at the keyboard, crashing out massive note clusters with his forearms, like a beefy Cecil Taylor. The song, from Palmieri's LP *Sentido*, pushed salsa further out musically than it had ever gone before.

But it was just a warm-up for his next project, which he describes in the voiceover to the short film made around the gig, *Salsa in Woodstock*. Palmieri mentions a new composition, "Un Día Bonito," talks about feeling Dylan's vibes, and confesses a wish that he could have played on

Yasgur's farm in 1969, to represent Latin music to the people. (He doesn't mention Santana's appearance.)[52]

Although the Lindsay administration was spending $10 million a year trying to erase it, graffiti culture was in full bloom in 1973—the year scrawled spray paint script began morphing into huge 3-D bubble letters and cartoon characters, a new kind of art.

The first spotlight was a front-page *New York Times* article in 1971 on the tagger Taki 183, who simply wrote his nickname and street number on trains and brick walls with a fat-tipped Magic Marker. A '73 feature in *New York* magazine titled "This Thing Has Completely Gotten Out of Hand"—by Richard Goldstein, who began his career as a pioneer rock critic at *The Village Voice*—called graffiti "the first genuine teenage street culture since the fifties." By this time, writers such as Phase 2, Blade, and Super Kool 223 were innovating; the latter is credited with the first "end-to-end"—spray-painting the entire length of a subway car. A ghetto salon known as the Writer's Corner grew up on the benches at one end of the 149th Street elevated IRT station. In late '72, a sociology major named Hugo Martinez organized the first graffiti art exhibit at City College and launched a writers' group called the United Graffiti Artists (UGA). By April, the downtown choreographer Twyla Tharpe had enlisted a rotating cast of eighteen writers to spray-paint live during her piece *Deuce Coupe*.[53]

In Queens in the mid-'70s, you would occasionally see artful tags on the E and F trains. But the IRT lines had the best graffiti: wild, multicolored murals. The Flushing 7 train that ran on the elevated line into Manhattan had some; the lines that ran up to the Bronx, especially the 2 and the 5, had the cream.

As a pop-culture junkie, I moved from Marvel and DC comics to underground ones like the R. Crumb vehicle *Zap* and Vaughn Bode's *Junkwaffel*, books that had a strong influence on the early graffiti artists. Wacky Packages, the *MAD* magazine–influenced bubble-gum sticker cards, were introduced in 1973. The cartoon parodies of consumer products—Jail-O, Quacker Oats, Minute Lice, Crust toothpaste, Skimpy peanut butter, Blisterine mouthwash, Chock Full O' Nuts and Bolts coffee—subverted commercial design with a graffiti-like spirit. Many of the concepts came from Art Spiegelman, a cartoon fanatic who worked for the Topps bubble-gum company in Brooklyn.[54] Taking received culture and violating it, breaking it up, transforming it into something funnier, weirder, fresher, more exciting—and one's own: this was the aesthetic engine of '70s art.

Music added its own imagery to the mix. Roger Dean did the lush fantasy art for LPs by Yes and other prog-rock acts; along with Rick Griffin and some of the San Francisco poster artists of the late '60s, he was another influence on the graffiti scene. I drew the fluid-lettered Yes logo on every available surface: school desks, notebooks, Levi's denim jackets. (Wrangler and Lee were, of course, out of the question.)

But I didn't do buses, which were ruled by the black and Hispanic kids who were redistricted from southern Queens to George J. Ryan Junior High School in Fresh Meadows. Most of them would take the Q17, which originated at the Jamaica Bus Terminal and ran north along 188th Street to Horace Harding Expressway, the service road for the Long Island Expressway. As soon as the bus was full enough that the driver's rearview mirror sight line was blocked, kids would light up cigarettes and pop the caps off their fat-tips, making the rear of the bus a sauna of marker fumes and Kool smoke.

These were tense times in northeastern Queens. Across the LIE from Ryan was Francis Lewis High, where white thugs with leather jackets and greased-up ducktails smoked cigarettes against vintage cars like it was still the '50s. They unapologetically used the word *nigger*, and there were regular "race riots" between them and the bussed in kids. At points the atmosphere was so violent that students were sent home early, or the entire day's classes canceled outright.

I was no thug, but in a gesture of both terror and boldness, I often came to school with a gravity knife tucked into my desert boot. Thankfully, I was never called on to use it for anything more aggressive than carving Granny Smith apples into hash pipes.

On October 31, the New York Dolls played the Waldorf-Astoria Grand Ballroom. Their debut LP had been out for three months—Ellen Willis, *The New Yorker*'s pop music critic, wrote that it had "virtually no competition as the most exciting hard-rock album of the year"—and although they did a week of shows at Max's in late August, this was their

New York City coming-out party. They'd just returned from their first proper tour; they'd been on TV in Los Angeles, and Johansen had been jailed in Memphis for "lewd public behavior" and "inciting a riot" after a boy kissed him on the lips during a show.

The Halloween homecoming gig was conceived as a spectacle. The promoter, Howard Stein, took out a full-page ad in *The Village Voice*. Tickets were steep at $7.50, though they automatically entered the holder in the Best Costume competition (one prize: a weekend for three at a hotel in Newark).[55] The Waldorf-Astoria was the epitome of uptown, uptight, upper-crust New York; whoever agreed to give the ballroom over to the Dolls and their wasted fans was either clueless or wickedly subversive.

By midnight, a thousand-some freaks of various stripes were packed into the ballroom entryway, pressing against doors that were supposed to have opened at 11:00. Tempers flared, doors were smashed, and someone lit a stink bomb in the hotel lobby in protest. Security guards admitted a portion of the mob, but hundreds were turned away. Arthur Bell described the scene as "Malcolm McDowell in *A Clockwork Orange* and Joel Grey in *Cabaret* by the dozens, chains and hoods, silver buttocks, scarlet breasts, dildoed noses," with old-school trannies washing down Demerol capsules with swigs of whiskey.[56] It even occasioned a lock-up-your-daughters (and sons) TV news report by Tony Hernandez of WNBC. Walking through the crowd, he described the Dolls as "a rock group with an aura of bisexuality" and as "a group of five tough Brooklyn street kids."

"The Dolls usually play at a sound level of 130 decibels!" Hernandez bellowed at the camera. "A jet plane at take-off has a decibel level of 115!"

The band finally came onstage at about two a.m., with Johansen in a white tux and a black top hat: for a dude who generally walked around in semidrag, men's clothing constituted a Halloween costume. They proceeded to play what may have been their greatest gig. By the finale of "Frankenstein," Johansen was shirtless, yelling into the mic with his top hat teetering on his head and his lush brown curls sticking to both sides of his face.

"New Yawk City!" he shouted near the song's end, in his camp Howlin' Wolf–meets–storefront–preacher delivery. "It's Halloween, and it's the night you're all gonna get down and do it really *evil* if you're ever gonna do it at all . . . And before you go home tonight to do it, I'm gonna ask you one question about yourself: Do you think that . . ."

Johnny Thunders hit a monstrous power chord.

". . . you can make it . . ."

Another Thunders explosion, this one lower, gurgling, the sound a man makes after being poisoned and before he falls to the ground.

". . . with Frank-en-steeeeeeeiiiiiiiiiiiiiiiiiin?!"

Thunders's and Sylvain's guitars hurled feedback; Johansen yelled "Happy Halloween, everybody!" over the squall, grinned broadly, pivoted in his top hat, and strutted offstage, turning to throw a kiss perfectly synched with one last Thunders power chord.[57]

A few days later the Dolls were back in England for the first time since Billy Murcia's death. Their most important gig was on the BBC music show *The Old Grey Whistle Test*, hosted by the absurdly tweedy Bob Harris, who introduced them with withering condescension as practitioners of "mock rock." Their performance of "Jet Boy" and "Looking for a Kiss" made an incalculable impression on countless impressionable youths. "I couldn't believe it," recalled the future Sex Pistols guitarist Steve Jones. "They was just all falling about all over the place, all their hair down, all knocking into each other. Had these great big platform boots on. They just didn't give a shit, y'know? I thought it was great."

The future president of the New York Dolls fan club and future lead singer of the Smiths, Steven Morrissey, was also watching. "I was thirteen," he recalled, "and it was my first real emotional experience."[58]

"It's ten o'clock: Do you know where your children are?"

To answer the question posed nightly by an ominous broadcaster's voice on the bump before the 10:00 p.m. Channel 5 news: my parents' children—me and my sister, Liz—were usually in our rooms, either asleep or pretending to be. I'd stay up reading comics like *Unexpected* or *Ghost Rider*, mags like *MAD* and *National Lampoon*, or books by Ray Bradbury and H. P. Lovecraft while listening to Led Zeppelin, King Crimson, Deep Purple, Black Sabbath, Yes, or ELP. My allowance was five dollars a week. The Korvettes department store sold new records at three for ten dollars. But the Music Box on Union Turnpike sold used titles for one or two bucks. It was run by Keith, a glam rocker with long straight hair and bangs. He had a band called the Brats, who I'd never actually heard; they had a following and eventually became regulars at Max's. He'd point things out for me. By the end of '73, I'd begun a decent record collection.

Other than as a sensationalist news item, the New York Dolls didn't make it onto television in their hometown. The only real outlet for rock on TV at the time was ABC's *In Concert*, channel 7, Fridays at 11:30 p.m., simulcast on WPLJ 95.5 FM. Whenever my father went to bed early, I'd sneak down to the basement and watch the procession of British acts. The show gave me my first black-and-white glimpse of a rock concert that August: the Electric Light Orchestra (not bad, I thought) with Black Oak Arkansas (lame). I sat there, riveted, until the station signed off the air, footage of an American flag flapping in the wind while "The Star-Spangled Banner"—not Hendrix's—wheezed away in the background. What was happening in Manhattan, I had no idea.

In 1963, as music director for the San Francisco Mime Troupe, Steve Reich pulled together a group with his Mills College cohorts Phil Lesh and Tom Constanten. The idea was to create an improvisatory music-theater piece with dancers, brightly colored lights, and chaotic/hypnotic music. Soon afterward, Lesh (and later Constanten) joined the Grateful Dead. In his memoir, Lesh describes the Mime Troupe production—titled *Event III/Coffee Break*—as the prototype for Ken Kesey's Acid Tests, the "happenings" that help launch the Dead's musical journey.[59]

Reich, meanwhile, followed a different path. Raised on the Upper West Side, he'd studied music and philosophy upstate at Cornell, continued his music studies at Juilliard on West Sixty-sixth Street, then headed west to Mills in Oakland, where he worked with the composer Luciano Berio. Like his pal Lesh, Reich fell hard for the music of John Coltrane, whose gigs he caught whenever possible, often at the Jazz Workshop in North Beach. Around the time of his Mime Troupe stint, Reich began experimenting with magnetic tape, making loops and collages. He also began a working relationship with Terry Riley, a composer who lived down the street from him.

In the fall of '64, Riley—well known in Reich's circles—attended a concert by Reich's group at the Mime Troupe theater in San Francisco's

Mission District. Bored, he left midway through it. The next day, Reich walked down the block to Riley's garage, where Riley kept his piano, and confronted him about the previous evening. They smoothed things over, and Riley showed Reich a new composition written on a single sheet of paper.

In C was a series of fifty-three melodic modules, each to be repeated by each group member as often as he or she liked, until moving on to the next, each at his or her own pace. It was simplistic, anarchic, and, in practice, ecstatic. Reich loved it and offered to help arrange it. That November, the piece premiered at the San Francisco Tape Music Center, with Reich playing percussion and his girlfriend playing piano. It received a rapturous review in the *San Francisco Chronicle*.

Reich was completely taken with the piece. He began experimenting with repetitive structures. The first fruit was *It's Gonna Rain*, composed for multiple tape loops of a preacher's voice that begin in unison and gradually slip out of phase. Reich was still interested in performing with live musicians, though. So in the fall of '65, with hippie culture heating up and Lesh having run off to join the circus, Reich headed back to New York, where he figured he'd have better luck finding kindred spirits.

Riley wound up back in New York that fall, too. He wasn't pleased when he discovered Reich pursuing ideas Riley felt were his, and they never worked together again. Reich did strike up a friendship with another like-minded composer, Philip Glass, a Juilliard classmate who reintroduced himself at a concert Reich gave at Paula Cooper's Park Place Gallery—the foremost exhibition space for minimalist artists such as Sol LeWitt—in early '67. Reich and Glass soon formed a collective ensemble to perform each other's work. They also formed a furniture-moving company, Chelsea Light Moving, as neither of them made enough money from their music to pay their bills.

Meanwhile, Reich's longtime interest in drumming was rising up. He was inspired to visit Ghana in 1970 by Alfred Ladzekpo, a Ghanaian drummer teaching at Columbia University. (Ladzekpo's *African Dances and Games* LP, which may have seeded Willie Colón's "Che Che Cole," had just been released.) The trip was something of a nightmare—Reich contracted malaria and left a month earlier than planned—but his studies there blew his mind, confirming many of his ideas on rhythm.[60] At the end of '71 he premiered his extended *Drumming*—for bongo drums, marimbas, glockenspiels, female voices, piccolo, and a whistler (for now, himself)—over two weeks at three concerts: at the Museum of Modern Art, the Brooklyn Academy of Music, and Town Hall. As a new-music composer, he had arrived.

Still, a gig at Carnegie Hall, the bastion of old-school classical music, was not on his to-do list when the phone rang in late '72. Yet the guy on the line—Michael Tilson Thomas, twenty-seven-year-old conductor of the Boston Symphony—was knowledgeable and enthusiastic about Reich's music. He was curating a new-music program for Carnegie Hall called the Spectrum series, which hoped to lure a younger audience. Thomas wanted Reich in it.

Reich agreed. His *Four Organs*, an extended piece employing extreme repetition and performed with four Farfisa electric organs and some Latin Percussion rawhide-and-buckshot maracas, was presented in Boston without incident. The performance in his hometown on January 18, 1973, was another story.[61]

Four Organs was not new to New York, having premiered at the Guggenheim Museum back in 1970, with Glass at one of the keyboards. Performed this evening by the musicians in shirtsleeves—a statement in itself on the formal Carnegie Hall stage—the performance lasted about sixteen minutes.[62] The music was amplified, but it wasn't rock-concert loud. After a few minutes, the performers could hear the noise of the audience—more old guard than the young vanguard they'd hoped for—fidgeting in their seats, coughing, murmuring, and rustling their programs. Soon, this was joined by groans and, eventually, straight-out shouting and heckling.

The musicians traded glances. There was nothing to do but to keep playing the repeated, stabbing phrases, over and over and over. The audience noise grew so loud, they couldn't hear one another play; they had to mouth their cues, and eventually yell them, to keep the piece from falling apart. The audience was literally trying to stop the performance by shouting it down. At one point, a woman got out of her seat and walked down the aisle toward the musicians. All eyes were on her, and when she reached the lip of the stage, she began mock-banging her head against it repeatedly, wailing: "Stop, stop—I confess!"[63]

When the piece ended, there was a moment of silence, then a tidal wave of boos and catcalls. The musicians bowed, and walked offstage with as much composure as they could muster.

In his review, Harold C. Schonberg of *The New York Times* described the audience reaction "as though red-hot needles were being inserted under fingernails," adding that he himself had heard "nothing much to like, nothing much to dislike." Alan Rich of *New York* magazine praised it as a "marvelous, original invention about musical time and rate of change."[64]

Afterward, Steve Reich returned to his element, giving free performances of works-in-progress alongside exhibitions by his new friend Sol LeWitt at the John Weber Gallery.[65] When Reich's old colleague Phil Lesh came east to play Nassau Coliseum with the Dead that March, they did not see each other.

The Carnegie Hall *Four Organs* was the most striking aboveground display for the New York school of music branded "minimalism," after the art movement. Some critics called it "static music" (for its apparent lack of motion, not its resemblance to white noise—although using the latter was not out of the question). The composer Tom Johnson, who was also the *Voice*'s classical music critic, wrote of the "New York Hypnotic School"—Reich, Glass, Riley, and the school's provost, La Monte Young—composers who made music "that lulls, hypnotizes, and draws you into its world." It was music that functioned as a more or less flat field, not unlike the visual work of LeWitt, Frank Stella, Donald Judd, and the Nashville jazz saxophonist turned painter Robert Ryman. Static, however, did not necessarily equal boring. "A pitch changes slightly, a rhythm is altered, something fades in or out. They are not big changes, but they are changes," Johnson wrote, "and there are more than enough of them to sustain one's interest, provided he can tune in on this minimal level."[66]

La Monte Young was raised as a Mormon in Idaho and studied music in Los Angeles, where he focused on the saxophone. He was an L.A. City College classmate of Eric Dolphy, who he beat out for a spot in the college dance band in 1956; he also led a group with the drummer Billy Higgins, and occasionally played with another Ornette Coleman associate, the trumpeter Don Cherry.[67] Around the same time, Young became obsessed with a record of ragas by Ustad Ali Akbar Khan, and especially by the drone sound of the tamboura; he listened to it so incessantly while living in his grandmother's house that she worriedly wrote the words "Opium Music" on the LP jacket. His interest in sustained tones grew, and during the summer of 1958 he wrote the roughly hour-long *Trio for Strings* at the great organ in Royce Hall at UCLA, where he'd just completed his BA. He presented the piece during his first semester of graduate studies at Berkeley, to a composition class held in the home of Professor Seymour Schiffrin; his classmates included Terry Riley, Pauline Oliveros, and David Del Tredici. The work's vast fields of drones and silences were alien territory. It was the birth of minimalist composition.[68]

Arriving in New York City in the fall of 1960 on a Berkeley scholarship, at age twenty-five, Young became a proto–rock star, moving through galleries and performance halls in a black cape in the shadow of his hero turned rival John Cage. Within two months he was involved with the Fluxus art movement, curating the first loft concert series with Yoko Ono at her place on Chambers Street.[69] Young was composing busily, swinging between Cagean conceptualism and tonal minimalism. *Piano Piece for David Tudor #1* (Tudor was a close associate of Cage) instructs the performer to "bring a bale of hay and a bucket of water onto the stage for the piano to eat and drink. The performer may then feed the piano, or leave it to eat by itself." The droning *Composition 1960 #7* consists of a B and an F-sharp, notated on a staff with the direction "to be held for a long time."[70] *Arabic Numeral (Any Integer) for Henry Flynt* (1960) called for a loud percussive sound to be repeated at will; in one performance, Young played a piano chord 1,698 times.[71] Unlike music made in uptown performance halls, which generally divided concerts into five- to thirty-minute slots for individual works, loft settings gave composers the option of presenting extended pieces. In this way, Young and Ono's brief series changed the sound of modern composition.

By the time John Cale began working with Young in his Theatre of Eternal Music ensemble in the mid-'60s, radically sustained notes and chords were at the core of the work. With his new wife, the light artist turned singer Marian Zazeela, Young moved into a loft space at 275 Church Street, where the group would perform for hours, through the night; a waking day for the couple would last anywhere from eighteen to twenty-seven hours or longer.[72] A recording from April 1965 features the table-saw drones of Tony Conrad's violin and John Cale's viola, their modulations stretching clock time like putty.[73]

The group continued in various forms throughout the '60s, occasionally touring and performing in galleries and museums. But as Young became more obsessed with the idea of the eternal in music—of a work that might literally last forever—he began setting up what he called "Dream House" installations: rooms in which music was produced continuously by precisely tuned sine-wave generators, sometimes with human accompaniment. The initial and primary one was in his loft; it ran pretty much uninterrupted from September '66 through January '70, when Young and Zazeela began their long relationship with the North Indian master singer Pandit Pran Nath, and continued intermittently after that.

Recordings of this music were somewhat beside the point. But Young often rolled tape, and in '73 he captured what became a French LP called *Dream House 78' 17"*. The number denotes the duration of the LP, and the "song titles" note simply the date, time, and locale of the recording. "13 I 73 5:35–6:14:03 PM NYC" demonstrated vocal techniques inspired by Pran Nath. "Drift Study 14 VII 73 9:27:27–10:06:41 PM NYC" was the sound of three sine-wave generators, which presumably burbled out strange harmonics before the recorder was turned on, and continued after it was shut off.

Performances of extreme duration—lasting as long as, say, a psychedelic drug experience—were being explored by many artists of the era. The *New York Times* critic John Rockwell identified a "newly meditational mode of perception" in audiences, partly code for saying everyone would be stoned. According to the trumpeter Jon Hassell, a devotee of Miles Davis's electric experiments who studied and played with Young, "the history of drugs in America is inextricably interlaced with early minimalism." To him, there was a need in the '70s for a new sort of classical music that "one could actually enjoy listening to, that you could float away to."[74] Young's music catered to this need and reveled in it. He had been a weed smoker since his jazz days, and by his own account, the Theatre of Eternal Music got high for every concert.[75] And according to the photographer Billy Name of Andy Warhol's Factory posse, who played with an early version of the ensemble, the scene at the Church Street loft was a heady one:

La Monte Young was the best drug connection in New York. He had the best drugs—the best! Great big acid pills, and opium, and grass, too. When you went over to La Monte and Marian's place, you were there for a minimum of seven hours—probably end up to be two or three days. It was a pad with everything on the floor and beads and great hashish and street people coming and scoring, and this droning music going on.[76]

In his autobiography, John Cale writes about being busted for selling opium when he was working for Young. Of course, by 1973 drugs were a part of every music scene, for players and listeners both. When I started sixth grade that fall, my friend Ron's older brother, a music fanatic, offered to smoke some of his "Acapulco Gold" with us if we'd alphabetize his vast LP collection. We did, and he did. I didn't get high, but filing all those records had a lasting effect.

The New York artist who played most spectacularly to Rockwell's "newly meditational mode of perception" was in fact not a musician. It was the playwright Robert Wilson, who in December presented *The Life and Times of Joseph Stalin* at the Brooklyn Academy of Music in Fort Greene. The work ran from 7:00 p.m. to 7:00 a.m. A casting call in the theater column of the November 15 *Soho Weekly News* read:

> Robert Wilson is looking for 32 dancing ostriches, over 100 sleep-walkers (experienced and non-experienced), bears, mammies, fishing ladies, apes, a pregnant woman, a Wilhelm Reich- and an Alexander Graham Bell look-alike for his latest epic . . . Anyone interested (no professional experience of any kind necessary) may call Mel at 966-1365 or stop by Wilson's Soho studio, 147 Spring St., this Thursday night from 8–12.

Philip Glass, a composer also interested in extended forms, was in the audience for one of the performances with a friend and a bag of sandwiches. At the cast party/breakfast afterward, Glass and Wilson met for the first time and hit on the idea of working together.[77]

Glass was born in Baltimore in 1937; his dad had a radio repair shop that also sold records, both classical and popular. He began studying violin at age six, and followed a conventional prodigy path through to Juilliard. He detoured in 1964 to study with Nadia Boulanger in Paris, and also worked with the sitarist Ravi Shankar, transcribing his music. By the time he returned to New York City in '67 and reconnected with his old classmate Steve Reich, he was ready to make a new sort of music.[78]

Throughout '73 Glass worked on *Music in Twelve Parts*; by the time he completed it in '74, it was around four hours long. He frequently presented his music in Sunday concerts in his loft on Elizabeth Street, just off Bleecker. Glass and his players would sit in a circle around a ring of electric organs, surrounded by audience members, most either seated cross-legged or lying on their backs on the hardwood floor, eyes closed.[79]

John Rockwell describes a ninety-minute performance of an earlier work, *Music in Changing Parts*, that spring at the loft of Glass's pal Donald Judd, the sculptor:

> Glass's ensemble that night played with the spirit and precision that only years together can bring. The music danced and pulsed with a special life, its motoric rhythms, burbling, highly amplified figurations and mournful sustained notes booming out through the huge black windows and filling up the bleak industrial neighborhood. It was so loud that the dancers Douglas Dunn and Sara Rudner, who were strolling down Wooster Street, sat on a stoop and enjoyed the concert together from afar. A pack of teenagers kept up an ecstatic dance of their own. And across the street, silhouetted high up in a window, a lone saxophone player improvised in silent accompaniment like some faded postcard of fifties Greenwich Village Bohemia. It was a good night to be in New York City.[80]

The chugging rhythms of *Music in Changing Parts* were a sharp contrast to La Monte Young's sprawling drones, the same way the New York Dolls stood in opposition to noodling psychedelic guitar jams. It's as if the pulses and beats of '70s sounds were necessary to march music out of the miasma of the late '60s. *Music in Changing Parts* unrolls sustained pitches roughly the length of a loooong breath—by trumpet, violin, voices, flutes, and saxophones—over a rigorous electric-organ pulse. There's some improvisation in the drone placement, and some psychoacoustical magic going on too, the way chords rise up like ghosts from the typing-pool swirl of keyboard patterns.

Glass's attitude toward recording, and commerce in general, was also different from Young's. And it was informed by rock 'n' roll. In 1970, a friend of Glass's was dating Jerry Leiber of Leiber and Stoller, who wrote songs for Elvis Presley, among many others. It turned out Leiber and Glass had gone to the same Baltimore high school; and though Leiber was four years older, he knew and adored Glass's mom, who was the school librarian. Leiber invited the composer to come by his office in the Brill Building. When he did, after passing down a hallway lined with gold records, Glass saw a room full of people sitting at desks in front of typewriters and telephones.

"What are they doing?" he asked.

"Finding money under stones," Leiber replied. "This is publishing. This is how you make a living at music."

Always a quick study, Glass went down to the county clerk's office shortly thereafter, plunked down two hundred dollars, and registered Dunvagen Music as his publishing company. He also started his own record label, Chatham Square, and released his first record in late '73: *Music in Changing Parts*. It didn't go gold. But he owned it.

On December 10, CBGB and OMFUG—the acronym standing for Country, Bluegrass, Blues, and Other Music for Uplifting Gourmandisers ("voracious eaters of music," as the proprietor explained)—opened its doors in an appalling space under the Palace Hotel, a flophouse at 315 Bowery, where Bleecker ends. The proprietor was a hirsute Russian Jew named Hillel Kristal, a singer, violinist, and ex-marine who was part of Radio City Music Hall's house chorus in the '50s until the chorus was canned. In 1959 Max Gordon hired him to manage the Village Vanguard, a long-running club that had recently switched to an all-jazz format.[81] Kristal had found his calling.

He soon opened Hilly's on East Thirteenth Street, which showcased folk and blues acts through the '60s until the bottom fell out of the folk scene and locals began filing noise complaints. In the fall of 1973, he finally closed up shop, throwing a party for the neighborhood Hell's Angels chapter as a farewell fuck-you to the neighbors.

But Kristal had another venue, a wino bar on the Bowery he'd acquired in '69 for around twenty grand. Named Hilly's on the Bowery, he operated it primarily for a clientele of derelicts. "Bums would be lining up at eight in the morning when I opened the doors," he told Roman Kozak, author of *This Ain't No Disco: The Story of CBGB.* "They would come in and fall on their faces even before they had their first drink."[82]

Now the place had his full attention. Before renaming it CBGB, Kristal had bands perform on the small side stage near the entrance. One was Suicide, the duo that had terrified Sylvain Sylvain at the Mercer Arts Center. Alan Vega, who was also a visual artist, loved the aesthetic violence of the Stooges, the roaring drones of La Monte Young, and the heavy minimalism of the Velvet Undeground. Martin Rev, meanwhile, had studied with the postbop pianist Lennie Tristano and was a Cecil Taylor fanatic. Together they made chaos using microphone feedback and a fifty-dollar electronic keyboard. Vega, dressed in studded leather, stalked the stage like a combination of animal trainer and animal, swinging a motorcycle chain like a whip, cutting his face with a switchblade just to freak people out.[83]

Another Hilly's band was Queen Elizabeth, fronted by Wayne County. A drag queen from Marietta, Georgia (born Wayne Rogers), who got off the Greyhound bus just in time to join in the Stonewall riots, County fell in with the Warhol crowd and Charles Ludlam's Ridiculous Theatrical Company, and after being laughed offstage at an audition for the part of King Herod in the Broadway premiere of *Jesus Christ Superstar,* he started a rock band. At that time, Wayne's act with Queen Elizabeth involved a strap-on vagina, a dildo, and a can of shaving cream. In a low-budget black-and-white promotional reel made in a friend's apartment with acoustic guitars and bongos, the singer cleans up the act a bit, refining David Johansen's gutter-punk snap-queen routine on the song "Wonder Woman" in stockings and a swastikaed policeman's cap. "Max's Kansas City," meanwhile, was a catchy girl-group number shouting out the Dolls and Bowie along with the club.[84]

Hilly's booked jazz, too. Rashied Ali played there frequently; for years, a black-and-white photo of Ali and his wife, Patricia, standing in front of the club hung on his living room wall.

How well the music went over with the Bowery locals is hard to say. The traditional dumping ground for the city's down-and-out, the Bowery has a long history as a boozer's ghetto. As Luc Sante recounts in *Low Life,* the area's first bar was probably Cornelis Aertszen's inn, established in 1665, but the neighborhood didn't really become notorious until the nineteenth century, when grocery stores fronting grog shops began popping up—joints like Rosetta Peer's, opened in 1825, home base to the Forty Thieves, one of the city's first armed gangs. The Atlantic Garden, a massive German-style beer garden on two floors that could accommodate a thousand patrons, operated for nearly fifty years next door to the Old Bowery Theatre, just up and across the street from the site of CBGB. Beer there was five cents, although other Bowery dives began selling it for three: the catch was no glasses—you sucked your drink through a thin rubber tube, taking as much as you could until you had to stop for a breath.[85]

By 1891, more than half the saloons below Fourteenth Street were on the Bowery—sixty-five on the street's west side, seventeen on the east. Among the latter was the Bowery's worst dive, McGurk's Suicide Hall, just above Houston. Opened in 1895, with a four-story interior, it attracted whores and roughnecks who were generally at the end of their rope. It earned its name; in 1899 alone there were reportedly more than thirteen suicide attempts there, six of them successful. Its reputation made it something of a tourist attraction; when it was shut down in 1902, its owner reportedly retired to California with around half a million dollars to show for his efforts.[86]

That a band named Suicide would play this strip for a bunch of winos almost eighty years later was grimly appropriate. Hilly's certainly conjured the Bowery spirit. The space was a dump; it reeked of beer, sweat, pee, and decay. A photo of Suicide from around this time shows Vega embracing a parking meter, Rev standing behind him, and—a few feet up the street—a bum collapsed in the gutter in a pile of garbage, with the Empire State Building looming in the distance.

On December 16, 1973, due west of Hilly's, a cement truck was heading up the West Side Elevated Highway near Gansevoort Street when a sixty-foot section of the roadway collapsed.

The truck, as it happened, was bringing cement to repair the road. But like many things in town, the West Side Highway was beyond repair.[87]

On Christmas Day up in the Bronx, Puerto Rican families were carving up *lechon asado*, cooking rice and pigeon peas, and drinking *coquitos*.

Countless stereos played Fania's two *Asalto Navideño* LPs—classics of salsafied Puerto Rican *jíbaro* holiday songs. The joke is that while *asalto navideño* is the boricua equivalent of door-to-door caroling, *asalto* also means "assault." The cover of Volume One showed Willie Colón, in a variation on his usual gangsta pose, as a cigar-chomping Santa, stealing the presents and the TV set. The newly released Volume Two showed Colón, Héctor Lavoe, and the cuatro virtuoso Yomo Toro in a timely variation, given the current fuel shortage: holding up a gas station.

The big New Year's Eve rock event was at the Academy of Music, a crumbling old theater on Fourteenth Street, just east of Union Square. Headlining the early and the late show was the Blue Öyster Cult, a heavy outfit cooked up by a bunch of kids on Long Island with input from the rock journalist Sandy Pearlman. Also on the bill were Kiss, a newly signed bunch of hard-rockers from Queens, and Teenage Lust, a glammy repurposing of the Lower East Side, the backing band of the pothead activist and John Lennon buddy David Peel. In from Detroit were Iggy and the Stooges. (In a coincidental culture swap, the New York Dolls were playing that night in Detroit, at the Michigan Palace.)

The Stooges released two records of dark, heavy rock in '69 and '70 that spiritually had little to do with flower power and San Francisco hippie culture: the music was about being young, bored, horny, disgusted with almost everything, and hell-bent for kicks. Younger brothers to Detroit's MC5, the Stooges similarly dug raw electric blues and Coltrane's modal freakouts, and their front man was inspired by the audience-confrontation tactics of the Doors' Jim Morrison. They also loved the nasty drone of the Velvet Underground, so much so that they had John Cale produce and play on their debut. But both records tanked commercially, and except for the guitarist Ron Asheton, everyone in the band had acquired nasty drug habits, and by '71 they'd been dumped by their label, Elektra Records.

Their second act began later that year, when David Bowie, in New York to sign his U.S. deal with RCA, began asking about the band, whose records fascinated him. After a dinner at Ginger Man on West Sixty-fourth Street, where Bowie met his labelmate Lou Reed, another hero of his—the beginning of the relationship that produced *Transformer*—the entourage headed down to the back room of Max's. Danny

Fields was with them, a music journalist turned scene *macher* from Queens who got both the Stooges and the MC5 signed, and he happened to have James Newell Osterberg, Jr. (who got the nickname Iggy from his high school band, the Iguanas, and later added Pop as a surname) crashing on his couch. So Fields went home, splashed water on his ward's face, and dragged him to Max's. In a matter of days, Iggy Pop was booked on a flight to London to record a new record with Bowie's management company, MainMan. Pop took his childhood pal James Williamson, who had recently joined the Stooges as a second guitarist. Bowie's people wanted a solo act, but eventually Iggy managed to convene the Stooges in London to make their third LP.

Raw Power, released on Columbia in February '73, condensed, amplified, and accelerated the negative energy of their first two records. Sonically, it was an assault, all screeching high end, Iggy's death-tripping lyrics ("I'm a street-walkin' cheetah with a heart full of napalm / I'm a runaway son of the nuclear A-bomb"), Williamson's stabbing guitar shifting between loudest and louder still, Ron Asheton—now on bass—and his brother Scott pounding out brute rhythms. It was raw, muddy, thrillingly nihilistic, and there was no market for it. By the end of summer, both CBS and MainMan had cut them loose.

But *Raw Power* had lots of fans in New York. Back in May, *Rolling Stone* published a review by Lenny Kaye, the *Nuggets* curator who also worked at the Village Oldies record shop at 118 West Third Street, just off Sixth Avenue. "The Ig," he wrote. "Nobody does it better, nobody does it worse, nobody does it, period. Others tiptoe around the edges, make little running starts and half-hearted passes; but when you're talking about the O mind, the very central eye of the universe that opens up like a huge, gaping, sucking maw, step aside for The Stooges."

Kiss, meanwhile, had played some loft gigs around town, including one back in April opening for Queen Elizabeth in a rivet-making factory at 54 Bleecker, just off Lafayette. They were another bunch of New York Dolls–style tranny rockers, minus the wit. But tonight they'd become something else. They'd just finished recording their Casablanca debut, yet to come out, and they took the stage in full Kabuki-alien face paint (Stein brand, Clown White and Clown Black), with a four-foot illuminated sign that spelled out their name as backdrop. The playing was ham-handed and deafeningly loud, and when the bass player did a fire-breathing trick, the right side of his hair momentarily went up in flames.

He also flung a piece of flash paper into the crowd, accidentally singeing the eyebrows of a kid up front. But the crowd loved it.

Iggy Pop, meanwhile, was high as hell. The Stooges blasted through the early show, but by the late show Iggy was so fucked-up he could barely perform. In *Please Kill Me*, the artist-writer Duncan Hannah, a recent Parsons School of Design grad who was celebrating the New Year, recalled:

> I don't know what he did, it was like he shot two quarts of vodka or something. He comes out and he barfs all over everything, he falls off the stage, he can't remember any of the lyrics, the band starts a song, they stop, they start, they stop. They're mad as hell, but Iggy just can't stand up. He just doesn't know what's going on.[88]

By spring, after another few flame-out gigs, the Stooges were done. But the kids they inspired were just getting started.

Back in April, Phil Ochs was down at Folk City on Bleecker Street talking to the owner, Mike Porco, trying to get a "good ol' days" hootenanny together at the venerable club—Dylan's launch pad—with some of the surviving old gang: Dave Van Ronk, Carolyn Hester, John Paul Hammond. It was an uphill battle, and all in all, a rough year. The Vietnam War continued. During a trip through Africa, Ochs was attacked in Tanzania by thieves and strangled, which left his vocal cords damaged. On September 11, the inspirational government of Salvador Allende in Chile was overthrown in what everybody knew was a U.S.-backed military coup. Soon after, Ochs's friend Victor Jara, the radical Chilean folksinger, was publicly tortured—his hands crushed by rifle butts—then murdered.

Ochs ended the year with a six-night stand—not at Folk City, but at Max's Kansas City, from December 26 through 31. The shows were good, despite Ochs's drinking and the loss of his upper-register singing voice. The highlight was a relatively new song, "Here's to the State of Richard Nixon," which updated Ochs's '60s civil rights anthem "Here's to the State of Mississippi," rhyming "the land you've torn out the heart of" with "find yourself another country to be part of." Impeachment hearings would begin in the spring.

As for Bob Dylan, the giant of the New York folk scene—a scene unto himself at this point—had stepped off his pedestal. He released two middling albums in '73, *Pat Garrett & Billy the Kid* and *Dylan*. By the end of the year, insiders had heard the forthcoming *Planet Waves*. It was an improvement, yet its muted, domestic tone suggested that rock's greatest poet was still in something of a creative retirement.

Opening for Ochs at Max's that week was Patti Smith. There is a black-and-white photo of her taken by her friend Judy Linn in 1971: Smith sits in a wicker chair, wearing what looks like a boy's school uniform jacket over bell-bottom jeans and snakeskin boots. Covering her face is a magazine picture of Dylan circa '66, his tousled hair fusing with hers.[89] In a review of *Planet Waves* for the Detroit-based *Creem* magazine, Smith described an epiphany she had while listening to it:

> Playing "Dirge" over and over. Drawing a picture. I thought it was Rimbaud but it was Dylan. I thought it was Dylan but it was me I was making.[90]

Another photograph of Smith, taken by the poet Gerard Malanga, shows her standing on the edge of a subway platform in knee-high boots, an Indian print shawl around her shoulders and a crucifix on a leather lanyard around her neck that hangs down to her exposed navel. In her hands is a manila portfolio, perhaps filled with verses; she fixes the camera with a burning stare and a Mona Lisa smile.

Lenny Kaye, the rock critic and record store clerk, backed Smith at Max's on electric guitar. They'd been performing as a duo, Kaye transforming Smith's incantatory poetic rants into something like rock 'n' roll. But this was their first extended gig, and the first time Kaye stayed onstage for her entire set.[91]

Standing in a torn T-shirt, spitting between hollered verses, Smith came on like a homeless delinquent who'd just bum-rushed the stage. The older folkies in the crowd were between baffled and repulsed. "She looked like a scarecrow in a garden of chickpeas," wrote Frank Rose in the *Voice* about one of her sets. "It was all very hard and furious."

"Don't be afraid of me," Smith reassured the audience that night. "I'm just a nice little girl."

1974

INVENT YOURSELF

I'm in love with this modern feeling . . .
I've got the magic power of bleakness.
—Jonathan Richman, "Roadrunner" (early version)

The city's first Jewish mayor, Abraham Beame, was sworn in on a rainy New Year's Eve at his rented apartment in Queens. The next morning, he addressed a small gathering from the steps of City Hall. "I hope to be a matchmaker in the years of my administration," he said, "wedding our people to their city, encouraging them to identify with this great metropolis that is their home."[1]

Mazel tov, sorta. It was a strange note to strike on taking office, since everybody knew the city was near bankruptcy; by fall, its short-term debt would hit $5.3 billion.[2] Unemployment was rising, and along with crime and filth there was a new physical manifestation of the fiscal crisis: lines at fuel pumps. They stretched for blocks, if you were lucky; in some areas, virtually all the stations were closed because there was no gas to sell. "With 1973, an era died," a *Times* op-ed piece declared, "an era of profligacy unprecedented in human experience when most Americans embarked on an orgy of consumption, following the lean years of the depression and World War II. This New Year's Day, symbolized by dimmed lights, chilly rooms, and empty gas tanks, ushers in a new era . . ."[3]

Patti Smith swaggered up to the lectern of St. Mark's Church at the Poetry Project's annual New Year's Day reading. She noticed Victor Bockris, a young writer working for Warhol's magazine *Interview*, and spat on the floor as she passed him.

"You owe me money, motherfucker!" she snarled.

This was her home turf: she'd first played here with Lenny Kaye in '71, and now lived down the block on Tenth Street with her new boyfriend, Allen Lanier, who played keyboards and guitar with Blue Öyster Cult. Though she'd done some singing with them, and even co-wrote a song on their new record, *Tyranny and Mutation*, hers would be a different kind of rock 'n' roll.

There was an amp on the altar; Kaye plugged in. Just off their week at Max's, he and Smith reprised their St. Mark's debut with the accrued power of three years spent experimenting and woodshedding. As Kaye slashed out his final chords, Smith bolted off the altar, down the aisle, and out the church doors. The crowd roared. William S. Burroughs—who had just returned to New York from London, and would soon move into a repurposed YMCA gymnasium at 222 Bowery—leaned over to his twenty-one-year-old companion, James Grauerholz, and croaked, "She's really got it."[4]

Smith's first full poetry collection was published by Gotham Book Mart in September. It was titled *Witt*, and the cover was a bare-shouldered portrait of her photographed by her pal Robert Mapplethorpe. Like her fellow poets Richard Hell and Tom Verlaine, she wanted to tap the rock 'n' roll power grid. "Nine years ago," the critic Tom McCarthy wrote of the book, "Bob Dylan was given credit for introducing poetry to rock 'n' roll. Now Patti Smith has simply reversed the process."[5]

Of course, the impulse to fuse poetry and music had been in the New York air for some time—understandable in a city informed by the rhythms of jackhammers, subways, car horns, and people who won't shut up. Amiri Baraka and the Beats drew on bebop and free jazz in the early '60s. In the early '70s, the Last Poets unspooled polemics over Afro-Caribbean drumming, while others (including the Chicago-born NYC transplant Gil Scott-Heron) explored similar ideas. On Harlem's WWRL, Super 1600 AM, DJs like Hank "the Soul Server" Spann, Jocko Henderson, Jerry Bledsoe, Gary Byrd, and, especially, Frankie Crocker rock 'n' rolled rhymes over and between the songs:

This is an album that's bound to put more dips in your hips, more cut in your strut, and more glide in your stride. If you don't dig it you got a hole in your soul. Other cats be laughin' and jokin', Frankie Crocker steady takin' care of business, cookin' and smokin'. For there is no other like this soul brother, tall, tan, young and fly. Any time you want me I'm your guy. Young and single and I love to mingle, can I mingle with you baby? Closer than white's on rice, closer than cool's on ice, closer than the collar's on a dog, closer than a ham that's on a country hog: Gonna get next to you, mama.[6]

And nightclub DJs were beginning to do the same thing, shouting out friends and alliterative catchphrases while the records spun, separate data streams rubbing together like riders on a rush-hour A train.

Smith had arrived in New York via bus in the spring of 1967. She'd gotten pregnant by a friend back home in Woodbury Gardens, New Jersey, delivered the child, then arranged for an adoption. At first she slept on the subway, in parks, or on the street; eventually she landed a job at Brentano's bookstore on Fifth Avenue. She hung around Pratt Institute in Clinton Hill, Brooklyn, hoping to absorb some direction—she'd decided during her pregnancy that she would be an artist—and met Robert Mapplethorpe, a nineteen-year-old art student who became a friend and lover. In '69, they moved into the smallest room in the Chelsea Hotel, number 1017. They began haunting Max's, so Robert could break into the Warhol circle. Eventually Mapplethorpe realized he was gay, but he and Smith remained soul mates.

Smith's creative fire began to flare; she was writing poetry, and her interest in music grew. She was befriended by Bob Neuwirth and Todd Rundgren; met Jimi Hendrix and Janis Joplin. Through Rundgren she met Sam Shepard, a playwright and moonlighting drummer with the Holy Modal Rounders.[7] The two began an affair (Shepard was married) and produced a baby of sorts: the play *Cowboy Mouth*, written by the couple "together on the same typewriter, like a battle," as Smith described the process, and performed by the two of them exactly once.[8] She bought herself an old beat-up black Martin acoustic guitar, learned a few chords, and, in addition to her poems, began writing songs.

She also began writing about rock music for the magazines *Crawdaddy*, *Circus*, and *Rolling Stone*. Smith met Lenny Kaye after reading a piece he wrote on New Jersey doo-wop groups of the early '60s and tracking him down at Village Oldies to tell him how much she liked it.

She would come down during his shifts to hang out; they'd listen to old records like the Dovells' "Bristol Stomp" and dance in the store.

When Mapplethorpe helped wrangle Smith a slot at a St. Mark's Poetry Project reading—opening for Gerard Malanga, part of the Warhol clan—she had to decide what to read. Shepard suggested she add music, and Smith remembered Lenny saying he was a guitarist. So she asked him if he wanted to rehearse something with her. That night in '71, in front of a crowd including Warhol, Rundgren, Lou Reed, and others, Smith read "Oath," which began, "Christ died for somebody's sins / But not mine." She spoke-sang "Fire of Unknown Origin," and ended with a piece about Shepard, "Ballad of a Bad Boy." For that one, Kaye played behind her, simulating the sound of a road race and a car wreck with his Gibson Melody Maker, the first time anyone could recall hearing an electric guitar in the church.

"It seemed to have a negative effect" on the audience, Smith later observed. "I took that as a positive sign."[9]

The performance put her on the map. She was contacted with proposals for publishing her poems, for readings in Europe, even a recording deal, from the small Blue Sky Records, which had just been launched by the guitarist Rick Derringer. But Smith turned the latter down: she thought it was premature.

Wayne Rogers, meanwhile, was more than ready for his deal. He took his stage name, Wayne County, from the Michigan birthplace of his beloved Stooges, and at this point he'd made a name in fringe theater; he even performed opposite Patti Smith in a short-running play called *Island*, as a transvestite revolutionary (she played a Rolling Stones–obsessed speed freak). But what really got Wayne noticed was his role in Andy Warhol's *Pork*, a pornographic, semifictional farce based on Warhol's Factory family. After a successful run at the experimental theater space La Mama, one of Warhol's art dealers mounted a production in London, which scandalized the theater scene there.

David Bowie and his wife, Angie, saw it and loved it. So when Bowie and his MainMan operation heard that County had a rock band, Queen Elizabeth, they invited him to join the team, as they'd done with Iggy. Surrounding Bowie—who was now Ziggy Stardust, in partial tribute to Iggy—with a roster of even freakier acts, they reasoned, would only burnish his star brighter. MainMan hired County's roommate, Leee Black Childers, as a vice president (whatever that meant) and set the pair up in a swanky uptown apartment. County did some shows in London that were so wild, he made the cover of *Melody Maker* in October '73. The next move was to mount a full-scale theatrical rock show in New York, the most outrageous, *Pork*-like thing ever, and then head into the studio to cut an album.[10]

On January 17, *Wayne at the Trucks* was staged at the Westbeth Theater, near the West Side docks and the deserted truck-trailers where dudes and transgenders liked to bare their souls. Where Ziggy Stardust flirted with androgyny and homosexuality, Wayne County rubbed people's faces in it. Opening on a Latin rock groove (the guitarist quoted a lick from Santana's "Black Magic Woman"), County, dressed in a green lamé miniskirt festooned with semi-inflated condoms, slid onstage through the mouth of a cartoon backdrop of his own made-up face—puking himself into the spotlight, as it were. Then, like Dorothy in *The Wizard of Oz*, he found a pair of magic shoes (though his were shaped like huge, curved penises), slipped them on, and started to rock, with his band set up offstage. "Stick It in Me," with a Velvet Underground snarl wound up into a whiplash rhythm, was as raw an expression of punk—in both the original and revised sense of the word—as anyone had ever attempted. "Queen of the truck / If you wanna fuck!" he barked.

The next day, Wayne was set to fly to London to begin recording. Backstage after the show, he got word that the plans had been canceled. It was never clear exactly why, but the assumption was that Bowie's team was hit with a combination of cold feet and, with Bowie's fame shooting into the mainstream, prudent business sense.

Soon, MainMan pulled the plug on his apartment, and County moved up to a cheaper place on Seventy-seventh and Broadway. And he moved a vastly downscaled version of his show to Club 82, the little tranny joint at Fourth Street and Second Avenue.

Another odd rock band that had yet to release a record resurfaced in January, when the Modern Lovers played the Townhouse Theatre, a tiny, eighty-eight-seat venue at 120 West Forty-fourth Street near Times Square.[11] Jonathan Richman, age twenty-two, now had a ghost of a mustache, the sort that would inspire a fifteen-year-old to rooster-strut around the schoolyard. He sang a churning, thrilling, electric-guitar-driven number that resembled the Velvet Underground's "Sister Ray," with a heady, nasal voice, all adolescent passion and clogged nostrils.

The song, "Roadrunner," was about embracing reality, about not living in the past, about hurtling oneself into the future on an engine of drums and guitars, about being in love with the modern world and all its meshugas. Can someone be in love with an industrial park? It's a question that "minimalist" fiction writers such as Frederick Barthelme would begin asking in the '70s, answering sure, why not? "Are the Modern Lovers serious? Are they for real?" asked Frank Rose, reviewing the Townhouse show in the *Voice*. "Jonathan insists they are, but his eyes contradict him."[12]

The band came together in early 1971 after a party in the Cambridge, Massachusetts, apartment of Jerry Harrison and Ernie Brooks, when Richman showed up with a brand-new copy of the Velvet Underground's *Loaded* and drafted both men into his new musical project. The Modern Lovers were definitely not a hippie band. This was clear to those who had heard the unknown Richman playing his guitar in the parks of Cambridge, yelling things like "I'm not a hippie!" and "I'm not stoned!" to anyone within earshot, and playing songs like "I'm Straight," in which the singer tries to woo a girl away from a character named "Hippie Johnny."

"Jonathan had a message that went against the grain of the times," Harrison told a writer. "To me he captured a certain kind of teen frustration practically better than anything that's ever been written."[13] The Modern Lovers' opening gig for the New York Dolls' New Year's Eve show at the Mercer last year had been one of their first New York shows; now they were headliners.

But they still couldn't get a record out. They'd earned enough label interest to bankroll demos produced by John Cale in '72, which eventually became the posthumous debut *The Modern Lovers*. "Roadrunner," "Pablo Picasso," and "She Cracked" are noisy, propulsive, proto-punk rock 'n' roll rooted in the Velvets. But Richman was mercurial, and his interests were now shifting toward quieter, faux-naïf songs with titles like "Hey Mr. Insect." He'd recorded another, somewhat gentler set of demos in late '73 with the California producer Kim Fowley, but labels remained baffled, and by the time of the Townhouse gig, the band was falling apart.

After the show, a slight, acne-scarred musician named Arthur Russell struck up a conversation with the bassist, Ernie Brooks. They hit it off, and a week later, Russell showed up at Brooks's place in Cambridge with his guitar. Brooks liked his lyrics, which shared a kinship with Richman's, and his voice, which Brooks thought "still held a lot of small-town Iowa."

Russell was born in 1952 in Oskaloosa, Iowa, where he began playing cello, moved to San Francisco to study European and North Indian classical music, then moved to New York in the fall of '73 after being accepted to the Manhattan School of Music. He made connections quickly. He looked up Allen Ginsberg, who he'd met in San Francisco, and soon Russell was living with the poet, more or less platonically, in the latter's apartment on Tenth Street. They became collaborators: Russell taught Ginsberg about music, he taught Russell about poetry, and eventually they would perform together, mixing poetry and music.

Russell also worked with Philip Glass, who thought he "could sit down with a cello and sing with it in a way that no one on this earth has ever done before."[14] And with Brooks, he tried to blend his composer's sense with what Brooks describes as "the transcendent and egalitarian possibilities of pop."[15] On a '74 demo with Brooks called "Time Away," Russell declares "I'm taking time away to dream" in a voice that gently mirrors Lou Reed. On another, "This Time Dad You're Wrong," over gentle electric-guitar chords that shift like beach sand in strong winds, he sweetly insists to his father that his dreaming is worthwhile. "I'm not just a fool, no," he croons, "I'll prove it to you."

That fall, Russell landed a gig as the musical director of the Kitchen, a video/art space born in one room—a former banquet hall kitchen, in fact, from the Broadway Central Hotel days—of the late Mercer Arts Center. With the Mercer gone, the Kitchen's new home was a loft at the corner of Wooster and Broome.[16] Russell booked the Modern Lovers in early 1975 (after which Brooks often slept in the venue, on the foam pillows that otherwise functioned as seating). It was a perfect job: from John Cage to rock and free jazz, Russell indulged the full breadth of his musical appetites there, as both presenter and performer.

•

A few days before the end of '73, Nicky Siano headed uptown to Columbia Records to scam some vinyl with David Rodriguez, his Puerto Rican mentor-cum-sidekick. The former rail-thin with long hair and full lips, the latter a cherub with curly locks and a thick mustache, they came on like a snap-queen Abbott and Costello.[17]

Columbia's Laverne Perry played them a single by a group called MFSB—an acronym for Mother Father Sister Brother—on the Philadelphia International label, which had a distribution deal with Columbia's parent company, CBS. The title was an acronym as well: "TSOP (The Sound of Philadelphia)." Originally commissioned for the national TV show *Soul Train*, which used it to replace King Curtis's funky but old-school "Hot Potatoes" as its signature theme, "TSOP" was essentially an instrumental, although a girl vocal group called the Three Degrees chirp the lines "People all over the world!" and "It's getting hard, it's time to get down!" The bass line struts alongside hot brass stabs, churning gospel organ, and an athletic string section, with a conga-spiced drum groove.

The two DJs loved it—so much that, after convincing Perry to give them one of the only two copies, they swiped the other on their way out, ensuring no other DJs in town would have it. Over Christmas and New Year's the men played the song repeatedly for rapturous dancers at the Gallery and the Continental Baths (where Rodriguez spun), confirming it as a hit even before it was released.[18]

"TSOP (The Sound of Philadelphia)" was the second major example of a new dance-club-friendly sound coming out of Philly. The first, "The Love I Lost" by Harold Melvin and the Blue Notes, was still on the charts in January 1974, an impressive feat, since it first hit in September. Part of the record's appeal, clearly, was the beat. It begins with a churchy organ and a sprinkle of shimmering electric-guitar notes. Then the string section and drums engage, the latter with a playful little three-beat pattern that shifts into a metronomic 4/4 bounce for kick drum and high-hat—the ur-beat of what became known as disco.

Its inventor was Earl Young, house drummer for Philadelphia International Records, who was looking to distinguish himself and his crew from their legendary R&B competitors in Detroit. As he explains in Tim Lawrence's definitive history of early dance music, *Love Saves the Day*:

Motown used four-four on the snare—khh, khh, khh, khh—and the heartbeat on the bass—dmm-dmm, dmm-dmm, dmm-dmm, dmm-dmm. And they also used four-four on the tambourines. I would use cymbals more than the average drummer, and I realized if I played the four-four on the bass, I could work different patterns on the cymbals.[19]

The third song in the label's trifecta was "Love Is the Message," the title track of the MFSB album that also contained "TSOP." Another instrumental track, this one with no vocals whatsoever, "Love" had voicelike saxophone breaks that glided over the song's silvery surface, an uplifting mix of swirling strings and brass charts over Young's steady drum pulse and cymbal spangles. The groove shifts gave hypnotized dancers a chance to switch up their moves, the smooth sax defined the upscale tone of soul jazz. For sound as well as titular sentiment, Nicky Siano immediately made it his theme song.[20]

Siano continued to sculpt records during his DJ sets, manipulating the bass and treble controls on the mixer, or cutting out the tweeters or bass horns altogether, punching them back in at key points. He also added a third turntable to his rig, which he sometimes used to deploy sound effects over his mixes. One favorite, the sound of an airplane taking off, drove dancers to screaming and jumping so intensely the floor would shake.[21]

If the musical birthplace of disco, in its strictest aesthetic definition, is Philly, its cultural birthplace is unquestionably New York, where records like Eddie Kendricks's "Girl You Need a Change of Mind," the Temptations' "Law of the Land," and "TSOP" achieved their full expressive potential in clubs where DJs "performed" the music in a context where it could move people in a profoundly new way.

Unfortunately, disco culture suffered a setback that spring akin to the one that hit the rock scene when the Mercer collapsed. In fact, it was partly an aftershock of that event. Most assumed the Mercer Arts Center building had collapsed because it was decrepit, but an investigation revealed that it probably fell because a support column was removed during a renovation. Looking for similar violations, the New York City Department of Buildings fixed its sights on the Loft, Mancuso's club at 645–647 Broadway, just a few blocks from the Mercer site, which had recently expanded into the adjacent building.

At 10:00 p.m. on Friday, May 31, a group of cops and building inspectors gathered outside the Loft in a show for journalists and posted an eviction order for Mancuso. Although the DJ didn't allow the group into the building that night and didn't vacate for a while, the original Loft was *finis*.

Later that summer, the Fire Department turned up at the Gallery one busy night and ordered it shut down immediately, ostensibly due to inadequate fire exits. Per legend, Nicky Siano brought out a box of enhanced strawberries and placed them on the hood of an NYPD cruiser as a farewell offering to his guests and his nemeses. He then went back into his club, opened the windows, and cranked "Love Is the Message" at full volume.

Around this time, you could see a double feature at the St. Mark's Cinema for a dollar. In late February there was a good one. *Westworld* was about a futuristic theme park where, among other things, one could have a shootout with a cowboy robot played by Yul Brynner, who since *The King and I* had slipped a few notches. *Soylent Green*, in a metaphor that might have impressed the food activist Michael Pollan, was about state-sponsored cannibalism by unsuspecting diners—one of whom famously declared "Soylent Green is . . . *people!*" in a moment of realization foreshadowing the horror of moms discovering high-fructose corn syrup on the ingredients lists of their kids' lunch items.

In '74 I subscribed to *Famous Monsters of Filmland* and saw every horror and sci-fi movie I could. Along with like-minded comics and books, these films melded with the reality of the city to colonize my imagination. I had dreams in which my friends and I wandered deserted streets in the wake of some biological holocaust, like Charlton Heston in the '71 B-movie classic *The Omega Man*. Outside my house in Queens, utility workers had dug up the street to replace ancient water and drainage pipes. The excavations were nearly eight feet deep, and the repairs took months. After school and on weekends, these ruts—scented with machine oil and sewage—were our unauthorized playground, and a backdrop for postapocalyptic imaginings.

Like disco, dystopian sci-fi seemed part of an escapist, fiddling-while-Rome-burned spectacle—it just got off on darker aspects of the hard times. At Hilly's and later CBGB, the aesthetic similarly seemed less about escaping the nastiness of the city than reveling in it, amping it up to a cinematic scale, drawing a narrative in which artists could wage heroic battle.

Stevie Wonder was back. Last summer he'd nearly died in a car crash. In March, he played a triumphant comeback gig at Madison Square Garden. Around twenty thousand people sang every word of "Living for the City" and danced on chairs for a version of "Superstition" featuring Roberta Flack, Eddie Kendricks, and Sly Stone, each taking a verse, with the band seguing briefly into Sly's "Higher."

"In all its integrated optimism, [it] was like a one-night Summer of Love," wrote Robert Christgau in the *Voice*. "The next day, everything looked like 1974 again, but for a brief time we could feel our power to defeat our own death wish."

Television played their debut gig on March 2 at the Townhouse, the tiny Times Square art-house movie theater that the Modern Lovers had played. Admission was two dollars. The band rented the venue themselves, and stuck up flyers around the Village and the Lower East Side.[22] Television was the former Neon Boys, revised with a new member: Richard Lloyd, a twenty-two-year-old bleached-blond Pittsburgh guitarist who was living with William a.k.a. Terry Ork, a Warhol associate and bookstore manager looking to mentor a band like Warhol had the Velvets. Ork became Television's manager. Lloyd and Tom Verlaine played guitar, Richard Hell played bass, Billy Ficca played drums. Hell and Verlaine settled on the name because they both hated the medium and figured they could be a living, bleeding alternative to it. They thought they could "tell a vision." And though he didn't crow about it, Verlaine thought it fit nicely with his initials. They spent all winter rehearsing.

One chilly afternoon, Hilly Kristal was putting up a new canopy at 315 Bowery when Lloyd and Verlaine walked by. The two musicians were scraggly and thin. Verlaine had short brown hair and fine, aquiline features, elongated like those in a Modigliani figure; he moved with a sort of lanky, aristocratic grace. Lloyd was more street urchin, hair scruffy and mid-length, in torn jeans and a cheap black leather jacket.

The pair got Hilly off his ladder and went inside. He offered them drinks; Verlaine had a White Russian. They asked if they could play at his club. Hilly asked them what sort of music they made, and when they said rock, he said he didn't want rock bands. He explained the acronym CBGB.

"If you listen to it, you'd hear country, you'd hear blues—elements of it, but it's original!" said Lloyd, a devoted Hendrix fan. "It's like nothing you've heard before!"[23]

Kristal wasn't sold, but Lloyd returned later with Ork, who convinced Hilly to let Television play a Sunday, the club's slowest night. Ork promised to fill the place with hard-drinking friends, and if the bar tab didn't equal that of Hilly's best night, Ork would buy drinks for the room.

Kristal agreed, and Television played there on Sunday, March 31. The tiny, hand-drawn CBGB ad in that week's *Voice* announced the gig along with a three-night stand of Elly Greenberg's "country blues" and Erik Frandsen's "fancy guitar pickin's [sic]." The band lured as many friends as they could, and Ork bought a shitload of beers. The set was sloppy but intense and, at moments, stunning. Hell's "Love Comes in Spurts" dated back to the Neon Boys; "Venus," "I Don't Care," and "Eat the Light" were new. So was "Blank Generation," a song that, on a bootleg recording from that night, can't seem to decide what it wants to be. Hell's vocals are pinched, inflamed, not fucking around: "I belong to the blank generation," he sneers, "I can take it or leave it each time." Ficca's drums lumber behind, while the guitars careen: chattering, squealing, sputtering, following a shifty melody that at one point resembles "Big Spender," the campy come-on from *Sweet Charity* best known at the time as the soundtrack to a Muriel cigar commercial. The guitarists sound like they're goofing, except when the lines occasionally synch and bloom like fireworks.

Hell wasn't wild about Verlaine and Lloyd's approach. He thought "Blank Generation" should be played hard and serious.[24] But the show was encouraging. Hilly made a little money, and though he thought the band was terrible, he let them play the next Sunday, and the next. The arrangement went on for most of the year.[25] A tiny review in the *Soho Weekly News* on April 25, mistakenly identifying them as "Television Set," declared: "The great thing about this band is they have absolutely no musically or socially redeeming characteristics and they know it."

•

On Easter Sunday, Patti Smith and Lenny Kaye were returning down-town from the New York premiere of *Ladies and Gentlemen, the Rolling Stones* at the posh Ziegfeld up on Fifty-fourth Street. The event was a fiasco: originally conceived as a screening plus hippie street fair, the promoters sobered up and canceled the festival portion at the eleventh hour. Kaye covered it all for *Hit Parader*, a fan magazine that had hired his friend Lisa Robinson as editor in chief.

Smith suggested they go see her pal Richard's new band on the Bowery. He was a fellow rock 'n' roll poet. Smith and Kaye were both impressed by Television's ragged, lyrical ambition, which seemed pierc-ingly real after the spectacle they'd just left at the Ziegfeld. Smith was especially wowed by Verlaine: his delicate fingers squeezing out crystal-line guitar notes; his beautiful long neck.

Smith and Kaye became Sunday-night regulars at CBGB.[26] Over the summer, Smith hyped Television in the *Soho News*, and wrote a two-page feature on them for *Rock Scene*.[27] Verlaine's guitar playing, Smith wrote, was the sound of "a thousand bluebirds screaming." And he himself was "a languid boy with the confused grace of a child in paradise. A guy worth losing your virginity to."[28]

That spring, Smith gave Hell a blank hardcover diary as a gift. On one of the first pages, he wrote: "Take each idea, thought, conjecture that makes the heart sick and elaborate on and reveal it in every detail as exhaustively as possible."

He also wrote: "Heroin possesses no negative qualities. You Asshole."

The night before Television's CBGB debut, March 30, the Ramones played their own debut at the Performance Studio, Tommy Erdelyi's rehearsal and recording space at 23 East Twentieth Street, between Broadway and Park Avenue South. The band had been practicing there since January. Erdelyi himself was not yet a member; for their first show, the band was a trio: Douglas "Dee Dee" Colvin on bass and vocals, John Cummings on guitar, and Jeffrey a.k.a. Joey Hyman on drums and oc-casional vocals. They'd handed out flyers, mostly to friends, charged two dollars, and probably had too much to drink before they started playing. Colvin was so jittery, he stepped on his bass and broke its neck. They played brute-simple bar-chord rock at a medium-fast tempo. It would get faster.[29]

The four men spent their teenage years in Forest Hills, a middle-class Queens neighborhood of solid apartment buildings and handsome single-family homes surrounded by the Grand Central Parkway, the Interboro (now the Jackie Robinson) Parkway, and the huge, heavily wooded Forest Park. Cutting through the neighborhood's heart is Queens Boulevard, a multilane thoroughfare connecting Queens to Manhattan that's so wide and hectic at parts, crossing the street can feel like an expedition. Among Outer Borough bedroom communities, Forest Hills proper always felt especially claustrophobic. The manicured lawns and faux-English village vibe of its core, Forest Hills Gardens (the first planned community in the United States, designed by Frederick Law Olmstead, Jr.), were hemmed between tightly packed apartment blocks, like the basket of a catapult pointed toward Manhattan.

Erdelyi and Cummings were the oldest; both graduated Forest Hills High in '67. Born to a Jewish family in Hungary who emigrated when he was a little kid, Erdelyi was driven. He dug experimental art and had a career epiphany after seeing Phil Spector on a talk show. He landed a gig as an intern at the Record Plant, where he helped out during the production of Jimi Hendrix's *Band of Gypsies*, and after seeing the New York Dolls at the Mercer, started his own leather-glam band called Butch. Cummings was mostly a layabout. "He was the first person to introduce me to really good pot," recalled Colvin, who met him hanging out on the street near his house. "John said, 'Dee Dee, I promise you, three tokes of this and you'll be out of it.' And I would be!"[30]

Talking about bands they dug, like the Stooges, Colvin and Cummings became friends, and eventually went up to Manny's Music on West Forty-eighth Street together to buy themselves instruments—Cummings a fifty-dollar Mosrite guitar with a single pickup, Colvin a similarly cheap, lightweight Danelectro Longhorn bass. Colvin learned to play, barely (though not well enough for the Neon Boys). Meanwhile, the impossibly gangly Jeff Hyman—a sickly kid who'd done time in a psychiatric hospital—was fronting a glitter band called Sniper in makeup, a black jumpsuit, women's scarves, lavender platform boots, and silver gloves. A devout David Bowie fan, he called himself "Jeff Starship."[31] Hyman and Colvin met at a Sniper show at the Coventry, a rock club on Queens Boulevard near Forty-seventh Street. They met again at a New York Dolls show and became fast friends. They both dug the Dolls. Hyman was also impressed by the Dictators, a band of leather-jacketed outer-boroughs wiseguys who played funny, ass-kicking, British Invasion–style rock at the Coventry, where they were pretty much the house band.

For a while, after Hyman was kicked out of his house for being a freak, he and Colvin lived clandestinely in the back of the Art Garden, a gallery on Queens Boulevard owned by Hyman's mother. And when Sniper imploded after a loft gig with Suicide, the trio of Dee Dee, Joey, and Johnny came together. Hoping to get some input, Cummings called Erdelyi, and the trio shlepped into his Manhattan studio, Cummings carrying his guitar on the subway in a shopping bag because he didn't have a case for it. "It was the worst thing I'd ever heard," Erdelyi recalled of the rehearsal. "But I thought it was *great*."

Erdelyi unofficially signed on as manager-mentor, and soon realized that Hyman, with his compellingly weird Queens street punk/faux-Brit accent, was better utilized as a singer. The band began auditioning drummers, looking for a straightforward timekeeper. But after an endless parade of dudes playing wild-armed imitations of John Bonham and Carmen Appice, Erdelyi decided it was easier to just become the drummer himself, though he'd never played drums before.

After some more rehearsing, the Ramones—named for Paul McCartney's touring alias during his Beatles days, Paul Ramone—got themselves a two-night weekend gig at CBGB, August 16 and 17.

"We were glamorous when we started—almost like a glitter group," recalled Dee Dee. "Joey would wear rubber clothes and John would wear vinyl clothes or silver pants."[32] Johnny had a leather jacket at the time, but not biker style: it had fake leopard-skin fur on the collar.[33]

They still needed work. But Alan Vega saw them that first weekend and thought they were fantastic.[34] Hilly Kristal also liked them straight off, but he doubted anyone else would.

The best rock radio station in New York was WNEW-FM 102.7; its DJs were Dave Herman, Jonathan Schwartz, Pete Fornatale, Dick Neer, Dennis Elsas, Scott Muni, and Alison Steele. Ads in newspapers and on subway billboards showed the seven of them seated like deities atop a cloud (weed smoke?), the buildings and chimneys of New York peeking up behind them. Steele—"The Night Bird"—would read poems in a sexy, husky voice and play album sides by prog rockers like Yes, Genesis, and ELP.

As for rock in print, there was the San Francisco–based *Rolling Stone*, which stood above teenybopper rags like *Tiger Beat*, as did *Crawdaddy*, the East Coast intellectual version of *Rolling Stone*, which it predated. *Circus* tried to split the difference between the fan mags and the counterculture digests.

But "rock journalism" was still being invented in 1974. There was *Creem*, based in Detroit, and *Who Put the Bomp!*, a fanzine published in L.A. by the record fiend Greg Shaw, both parsing rock in post-hippie voices that were contentious and funny. *Trans-Oceanic Trouser Press*, a British-rock fanzine started by Ira Robbins, Dave Schulps, and Karen Rose in New York, made its mimeographed debut in March.

And then there was *Rock Scene*, a photo-heavy fan magazine written and edited by Richard Robinson, his wife, Lisa Robinson, and Lenny Kaye. Its parent company also published the long-running *Hit Parader*, a vehicle for reprinted pop-song lyrics with tacked-on interviews and slight features. When the owners handed the editorial reins of *Hit Parader* to Lisa Robinson, beginning with the May '74 issue, she remade it in the vein of *Rock Scene*, with a redesigned art-deco masthead. Where the April issue had trumpeted the soft-rock AM radio hitmakers Jim Croce and Gilbert O'Sullivan, its follow-up had cover lines announcing "Stones Do Europe" and "The Dead's First Seven Years." She also managed to write a syndicated newspaper column, Rock Talk, and freelance for *Creem* (where she did a fashion-cum-gossip column, Eleganza) and the *Soho Weekly News*.

Robinson was pretty, brassy, and not easily offended. Her features on acts like Zeppelin and the Stones—personal friends whose entourage she'd travel with—didn't bother much with pop-crit sociology, but they had a chatty intimacy few others could touch. She defined the hanging-out-with-the-megastars school of insider, bon vivant rock journalism. In the March issue of *Rock Scene*, Robinson mugged in a photo with David Johansen for her cover story on the Dolls; a feature on Led Zeppelin's private jet included a shot of her deplaning with John Paul Jones and label boss Ahmet Ertegun, looking as elegant as her subjects.

As a local scene booster, Robinson showcased her friends as rockers of consequence in much the same way. Gerard Malanga's portrait of Patti Smith as a fiery-eyed poetess clutching a book on the edge of a subway platform ran in *Hit Parader* between shots of Foghat and Ringo

Starr—never mind that the poet had yet to make a record. Robinson ran early features on the Dolls, Television, and the Ramones; she even had Wayne County do an advice column for *Rock Scene*. (Once a kid wrote to ask him how to start a band even though he couldn't afford equipment, and County responded "Lie! Cheat! Steal! Rob people! . . . Rock & roll comes first!" He got another letter from the kid a few months later saying he'd taken County's advice, held up a liquor store, and was now writing him from prison.[35])

The April *Hit Parader* featured two pieces by Lenny Kaye: a long, heartfelt appreciation of the Grateful Dead, and a review of Bruce Springsteen's *The Wild, the Innocent & the E Street Shuffle*, which had come out in September. Kaye described catching Springsteen's early band, Child, at Monmouth College in New Jersey years earlier. "Led by a Neanderthal guitar player who sunk back on his heels, closed his eyes, and hunched into his music in a way that magnetically riveted all available attention," Kaye wrote, "the group was astonishingly mobile and self-possessed."

Kaye saw Springsteen solo at Max's and, unlike John Hammond, was not so impressed: he thought the singer came off as too much of a Bob Dylan/Van Morrison manqué. But Kaye thought his new record was back on track, with songs that were "not so much verbal paroxysm as definitive image," walking "a thin line between melodrama and tense emotionalism."

By June, Kaye would be in the studio with Patti Smith, recording a song that might be described the same way.

Ellen Willis was the city's most compelling music writer—and since the death of Australian émigré Lillian Roxon of the *New York Post* last summer from an asthma attack in her apartment, the only prominent woman music journalist besides Lisa Robinson. Born in Manhattan and raised in the boroughs, with a degree from Barnard, she was hired as *The New Yorker's* pop critic in 1968. She wrote not like an insider or a frustrated Ph.D. candidate but as a thoughtful, super-smart fan. Her pieces were feminist, feminine, and personal; she wrote about nineteen-year-old David Johansen's "sulky, leashed sexuality," and offered a sharp sociological analysis of the Dolls' stylish Mercer Arts Center crowd while worrying about her own wardrobe. Jonathan Richman, she declared, was

"an oddball's oddball—the archetypal Queens high-school creep," while
Lou Reed "is such a genius that once when I was face to face with him
in a hotel room I couldn't say a word (what I wanted to say was 'Your
music changed my life,' which would have been most uncool)." This was
before tearing into *Transformer*, in the same elegantly breathless sentence,
as "terrible—lame, pseudo-decadent lyrics, lame, pseudo-something-or-
other singing, and a just plain lame band." Even if you knew nothing
about the music she was discussing, her prose made you feel it.

The biggest shift on the local music journalism scene began in August, when the rock critic Robert Christgau (Willis's ex-boyfriend) returned to *The Village Voice* as a senior editor after a two-year stint at
Long Island Newsday. The *Voice*'s music coverage was already notable:
in the mid-'60s it published Richard Goldstein, by most measures the
first professional rock critic. There were Christgau's columns, which ran
from '69 until '72; jazz coverage by Gary Giddins; and Tom Johnson's
writing on New York minimalism. But by early '74 the holes in its coverage—rock, salsa, new jazz, disco, R&B—were obvious.

"It was absurd," Christgau said over gin-and-tonics at his cluttered
East Village apartment in 2008. "There were all these really great writers out there. And you didn't even have to use N.Y. writers. Call Lester
Bangs at *Creem* in Detroit and ask him to review the new Rolling Stones
record. Which I did. It was that simple."

Christgau was born and raised in Queens. He went to Flushing
High School, majored in English at Dartmouth, and did some newspaper reporting after graduating. Meanwhile, he was a huge music fan,
and began writing about it. For a minute he was a rock columnist at
Esquire for the astronomical sum of four hundred dollars a column.
The gig fell through, but he'd found his calling. He jumped to the *Voice*
in 1969, where he began a regular column for forty dollars a throw. In
the July 10 issue, he began writing his Consumer Guide, a series of
pithy, poetic, paragraph-long record reviews capped by a letter grade.[36]

When he took the job, Christgau was still living at 308 East Eighth
Street, between Avenues B and C, in an apartment that ran him $77 a
month and may have formerly accommodated Richie Havens. When he
wasn't at home playing records, Christgau would hike over to the offices
at 80 University Place, at the northwest corner of Eleventh Street, and
set to work. Beginning with a piece on Waylon Jennings by Richard
Meltzer—author of *The Aesthetics of Rock*—and a Jackson 5 review by

Vince Aletti, already the foremost writer on disco, Christgau set out to make the *Voice* music section a must-read nationally as well as locally.

Meanwhile, musicians were writing about their own scenes. Richard Hell joined Kaye, Patti Smith, and Wayne County in covering local bands. The composer-performer Joan La Barbara, who sang with Philip Glass and Steve Reich as well as assorted jazz artists, followed her colleague Tom Johnson into journalism, writing on new music for the *Voice* challenger *The Soho Weekly News*, launched in late 1973. Its jazz critic, Peter Ochiogrosso, who would cover the loft scene more thoroughly than anyone, was joined by the drummer Stanley Crouch, who also wrote for the *Voice*. The DJ Tom Moulton would write about dance music for *Billboard*. Alongside John Rockwell, who covered rock, classical music, and just about everything else, the saxophonist and clarinetist Robert Palmer also became a pop critic at *The New York Times*. His band, the Insect Trust, was finished by '71, but its weird mix of rock, folk, and out jazz had been groping for a new form of expression, like many of its New York peers.

Gary Giddins launched a regular jazz column for the *Voice* in late summer. He named it "Weather Bird," after the Louis Armstrong/Earl Hines recording—which the writer considered the greatest jazz duet extant, and thus a good metaphor for an idealized pas de deux between reader and critic—and also for the allusions to Charlie Parker and to Dylan's "Subterranean Homesick Blues." The column would run for just shy of thirty years.

"I would like to try and explain," Giddins wrote in his debut column, "why so much jazz criticism, particularly that of younger critics, is paranoid, bitter, and esoteric."

His own work, however, demonstrated the opposite: enthusiasm, plainspoken erudition, and love of music outshone his complaints, even during trying times. And indeed, the times were strange for jazz. Duke Ellington died on May 24. The most discussed and applauded LPs of the year were *Interstellar Space* and *The Africa Brass Sessions, Vol. 2*, both posthumous releases by John Coltrane, who had died in 1967. "Until about 1975, his sound was like a dust cloud," wrote Ben Ratliff years later in *Coltrane: The Story of a Sound*, "it spread out through jazz and finely infiltrated it."

You could hear it in Dave Holland's *Conference of the Birds*, maybe the year's best document of new jazz. It brought together Sam Rivers and the Chicago émigré Anthony Braxton, two sax-playing composers who learned from twentieth-century "classical" music as well as from Coltrane. Recorded downtown at Allegro Studio in late '72 and issued on the young Munich-based ECM label, it featured the drummer Barry Altschul, who made his name with Paul Bley in the '60s and had more recently played with Braxton, Holland, and the ex-Miles sideman Chick Corea in the group Circle. The music could swing hard ("See Saw"), and while the sax duels are often blistering, the flute-sax exchanges on the title composition—inspired by Holland's attention to birdsong—are tender and pretty. The playing is out, but Holland's yoking bass and focused arrangements hold it together. It's a model of balance between the old school and the new.

Cecil Taylor's *Spring of Two Blue-J's* was the year's other great jazz epiphany. After his triumphant gig at Newport in '72, Taylor returned to NYC from his teaching exile at Antioch; he began to play shows and launched his own label, Unit Core. *Two Blue-J's* was its second release, a live recording made at a Town Hall concert on November 4, 1973. Side one was a blinding-bright solo performance; side two a firebrand band session with Jimmy Lyons, Sirone, and Andrew Cyrille. Then there was Keith Jarrett's *Solo Concerts: Bremen Lausanne*, a remarkable pair of hour-plus piano improvs by another former Miles sideman, which conjured pop, folk, and European classical music along with Bud Powell and early John Cage. And there were two releases by Miles Davis himself: *Big Fun* and *Get Up with It*. Few bought these records, and in jazz's capital, the most innovative music went largely unheard. In May, John Swenson wrote of a transcendent performance by the honey-toned, occasionally yodeling vocalist Leon Thomas, performing at the Bitter End on Bleecker Street for an audience of seven, himself included. Despite growing interest and some small-potatoes support from the National Endowment for the Arts and other arts organizations, the jazz lofts struggled.

Yet jazz-rock fusion acts like the Mahavishnu Orchestra, Return to Forever, and Weather Report were packing halls with young audiences.[37] The biggest-selling "jazz" record of the period, released in late 1973, was *Head Hunters* by Herbie Hancock—another former Miles sideman, like the leaders of all the aforementioned groups. Recorded in San Francisco in the figurative shadow of Hancock's new musical hero,

Sly Stone (an influence for Miles as well), *Head Hunters'* catchy instrumental funk-pop was in the Top 40 for twenty-one weeks in 1974.

For his part, Giddins had little patience for crossover jazz. A piece on the popular Argentine fusionist Gato Barbieri laments how the rich ideas of Coltrane and Dolphy could have led to such shallow playing ("It's all spinach to me . . . I call it pop music"). A review of Jarrett's *Solo Concerts* finds it admirable but often dull. A report on a Miles Davis concert at Avery Fisher Hall in September praised its innovative spirit, but concluded that Davis ultimately seemed "locked in a cul-de-sac," adding with a note of sadness: "He has become predictable."

In March, the Brazilian keyboardist Eumir Deodato won a Grammy for an unlikely remake of Richard Strauss's "Also Sprach Zarathustra," a spangled jazz-pop fusion instrumental featuring Ray Barretto's congas that hit number 2 on the *Billboard* Hot 100 chart. It was produced by Creed Taylor—the man who signed Coltrane to Impulse! Records and won a Record of the Year Grammy in 1964 for producing the Stan Getz/ Astrud Gilberto single "The Girl from Ipanema." Taylor believed in the idea of jazz as pop music when he launched the CTI label in 1968 in partnership with A&M; the company guaranteed him a minimum of $1 million over the next five years.

They got their money's worth. The label became known for velvety instrumental records with radio-friendly sparkle. Straightforward jazz sets with light funk underpinnings, such as Freddie Hubbard's 1970 soul-bop session *Red Clay*, defined the sound. With Deodato's *Prelude* and the "Also Sprach Zarathustra" single, CTI found a bona fide pop audience. But it soon found something else, too. *Deodato 2* featured "Super Strut," a Latin-funk number with John Tropea's jazz-rock guitar squealing like a stuck pig. While it didn't cross over to pop radio, it did catch the ear of dance club DJs, who loved it. Suddenly, after an exile that began with the beginning of the bebop era, it seemed jazz could be dance music again.

By late '74, disco DJs were coming by the CTI offices and lining up for vinyl. Taylor had developed a subsidiary label, Kudu, to market more R&B-flavored jazz to a primarily black audience: Afrocentric incense largely sans politics. In November, Kudu's flagship act, the saxophonist Grover Washington, Jr., set up in Rudy Van Gelder's studios in Englewood Hills, New Jersey, up on the Palisades across the Hudson River from Inwood Park on Manhattan's northern tip. The state-of-the-art

room, based on the architecture of Frank Lloyd Wright and run by
Gelder—a retired optometrist who became one of modern jazz's great
engineers and background figures—was where John Coltrane recorded
A Love Supreme ten years earlier, almost to the day.

Washington saw himself as a creative jazzman after Coltrane's example. A sideman who lucked his way into a hit solo debut with *Inner
City Blues* when the saxophonist Hank Crawford was a no-show for his
own LP session (the bandleader had been busted for weed possession in
Memphis), Washington suddenly found himself a pop star, with serious
cash coming in. For his fourth set, he didn't rock the boat, recording his
smoothest music yet: boogie-down soul jazz with beefcake brass arrangements, pillowy strings, and the undeniable drumming of Harvey
Mason, who also played with Hancock's Head Hunters.

Yet Washington chafed. Taylor was making many of the creative
decisions. The saxophonist didn't like the proposed album title, *Mister
Magic*, and he didn't like the cover concept: a photo of him emerging
from a swimming pool, bare chest glistening, a plume of water streaming playfully from his lips. This was not how a serious jazz player represented. But Washington acquiesced, and not long after its release the
following spring, *Mister Magic* was number 10 on the pop charts.

Latin musicians, who suffered the attrition of their own dancing fan
base when rock took over in the mid-'60s, were paying attention to CTI's
success, too. Joe Bataan was an ex-con with a sweet tenor voice who had
some early Latin soul hits with Fania before splitting with the label over
money issues (at one point, he tried to stage a sit-in at the Fania offices
with other label acts to get a better pay rate). Jumping to the small Mericana label, he recorded a cover of Deodato's "Super Strut" called "Latin
Strut," for an LP titled *Salsoul*, toning down the original's guitar, pumping up the percussion, and throwing in a *charanga*-flavored flute solo. It
didn't impress salsa fans much, but at discos and South Bronx park parties, the dancers went wild.

CTI didn't impress serious jazz fans much, either—in fact, it was
reviled, and Creed Taylor was considered an aesthetic Antichrist. But
that didn't stop the records from selling.

The New York salsa scene was at its apex in 1974, but if you were an
outsider to the culture, you'd hardly know it. The *Times* gave it only

passing mention, ditto the *Voice*, although coverage improved markedly when Christgau, on the recommendation of Fania Records' chief, Jerry Masucci, brought in John Storm Roberts, a Kenya-raised Englishman steeped in the scene, with a deep knowledge of African and Afro-Caribbean music.

Spanish-language publications couldn't help the music cross over to most non-Latin audiences. But they also missed the many second- and third-generation Latinos in New York whose English was better than their Spanish. Launched in 1967, the English-language *Latin NY* attempted to solve this problem, but went bust after eight issues.[38] In 1973, Izzy Sanabria, a Puerto Rican writer and graphic artist who had worked on the original edition, teamed up with another Puerto Rican artist, Walter Velez, and relaunched it as a free tabloid/newsprint flyer. By May '74, *Latin NY* appeared on newsstands as a full-fledged magazine.

Latin NY covered Fania acts heavily—the label had most of the genre's major acts and also bought large ads in the magazine. It was a conflict of interest that made for critical blind spots and no doubt much backroom drama, but the mag's relationship with Fania also gave it access no one else had.

It's hard to overstate how central the magazine was to the salsa scene. It arguably gave the scene its name, although that's still a topic of debate, fueled in part by cultural competition between Cubans who feel "salsa" is Cuban music hijacked—roughed up, and renamed by a bunch of Puerto Ricans without giving proper credit or compensation—and the Nuyoricans, who contend that their streetwise fusions gave old Cuban styles a new life. Both factions are correct.

In his book *Mambo Kingdom*, the *Latin NY* contributor Max Salazar traces use of the term *salsa* to describe upbeat Latin dance music back to "Échale Salsita," written in 1933 by the Cuban composer Ignacio Pineiro. The term may have been planted in the modern New York scene via "Salsa y Bembé," written by Jimmy Sabater and sung by Cheo Feliciano on Joe Cuba's 1962 *Steppin Out* LP. In 1963 Charlie Palmieri released *Salsa Na' Ma'*. In 1964, Cal Tjader's Latin jazz hit *Soul Sauce* triggered the colloquial use of *salsa* among West Coast Mexican-Americans in reference to hot Latin jams, and the usage spread back east. In November of 1973, Sanabria began a short-lived TV program called *Salsa*, a multimedia corollary to *Latin NY*, on UHF channel 41. Sanabria became "Mr. Salsa," as much a cultural mascot as a journalist.

At this point, *salsa* was the catchall brand name for new Latin music, in large part due to its use in the pages of *Latin NY.*

Larry Harlow's follow-up to *Hommy*, released in early '74, was also called *Salsa*. It was an even better record. Looking to tap the music's roots, he spent hours with Rene Lopez, who pretty much had the city's best collection of Cuban recordings—as hard to find as Cuban cigars since the post–Missile Crisis trade embargo. It featured two songs by Harlow's hero Arsenio Rodriguez, the great Cuban bandleader who had died in 1970. "La Cartera" was the hit, a mash-up of New World salsa brass and jazz improv with old-school *charanga* violins. Johnny Pacheco, a master of the latter style, played flute.

Rodriguez, sightless from birth, was known as "El Ciego Maravilloso"—"The Blind Marvel." At the break before Harlow takes a piano solo on "La Cartera," the *corista* Adalberto Santiago shouts out *"ahora viene el maravilloso"* by way of introducing his boss. The singer Junior González responds *"el judío maravilloso"*—"the Jewish Marvel." The nickname stuck, and Harlow, the former outsider, wore it like a crown.[39]

> The one mile of the Cross-Bronx Expressway through East Tremont was completed in 1960. By 1965, the community's "very good, solid housing stock," the apartment buildings that had been so precious to the people who had lived in them, were ravaged hulks. Windows, glassless except for the jagged edges around their frames, stared out on the street like sightless eyes.[40]   —Robert Caro, *The Power Broker*

Most descriptions of the South Bronx between 1973 and 1977 conjured an urban version of Brueghel's *Triumph of Death*, flames lapping from ruined buildings amid scenes of spectacular human suffering. There was some truth to this. The construction of the Cross-Bronx Expressway in the 1950s, spearheaded by Robert Moses, displaced tens of thousands of people and triggered a downward spiral of abandonment that, abetted by the recession, left the area gutted. In the families who stayed, largely black and Latino, poverty was entrenched. Meanwhile, landlords sold out to slumlords, who often found it more profitable to burn down buildings for the insurance money rather than maintain and rent them. The area during this period averaged twelve thousand fires a year—more than thirty a day. It lost about 40 percent of its usable housing stock, along with hundreds of thousands of residents. Those who stayed faced staggering unemployment rates and rampant crime.[41]

And yet there was still music, still dancing. After Kool Herc's South Bronx rec room party in the summer of '73, word was out about his bad-ass sound system and vinyl collection. Rec rooms were now too small. So he began throwing parties up the road in Cedar Park on 179th Street between Sedgwick and Cedar avenues, a park pitch-black at night except for the spot near the single functional streetlight, which Herc tapped into for electricity to power his system. Herc also began spinning records around this time at the Hevalo Club on Jerome Avenue between Burnside and Tremont. He recalls working there in late '73, though other accounts place his residency there later.[42] What is clear is that the segment of Herc's set called "The Merry Go Round"—which involved isolating the most rhythmic passages of songs (what would later be called breakbeats) and playing them back-to-back—was developed at both the Hevalo and the park parties. "The Merry Go Round" was hip-hop music's moment of conception.

As Herc perfected it, "The Merry Go Round" often began with a segment of "Apache," a song by the Incredible Bongo Band—not a band at all, really, but a bunch of L.A. studio session dudes convened as a lark by the young MGM film music executive Michael Viner. "Apache" was a much-covered instrumental with a varied life, including iterations as surf jams by the Ventures and the Shadows. In the early '70s, Bruce Springsteen occasionally included it in his live set.[43]

The Bongo Band version was a percussive firestorm with R&B horns, rock guitar, and heavy drumming. Produced by black and white players with Latin-inflected percussion, it was a melting-pot record that resonated mightily with Herc's audience. "I started playing it at [the Hevalo] week after week," he said, "and I'm studying people waiting for particular parts of records to break into their dance moves. And this record was perfect for that."

At first, Herc played the best break songs straight through, one at a time: "Apache," "Bongo Rock" (also by the Bongo Band), James Brown's "Give It Up or Turn It Loose," Babe Ruth's "The Mexican." But he soon realized that he could isolate the percussion breaks and play them on their own, sandwiched between other breaks. And by purchasing a second copy of a record, he could extend individual percussion breaks indefinitely, using his mixer to cut from the end of the break on one turntable to the beginning of the same break on another.

But Herc's DJ gigs were less about turntable trickery than about his love of obscure funk tracks with wild percussion, and the overwhelming power of his sound system, which emulated the roof-rattling bass of the systems he knew growing up in Jamaica. The extended percussion break, in fact, was at the heart of the dub reggae music being created in Jamaica around this time by pioneers such as King Tubby, where extended, echo-laden drum segments gave stoned dance-hall revelers space to get lost in. As Herc found out at his earliest DJ gigs, however, most of the Bronx kids had no taste for reggae—it was immigrant, old-world music. So he applied the same logic to hyperactive, Latin-flavored American funk.

The kid who really made his name with the double-record breakbeat routine, meanwhile, who first truly mastered it, was Joseph Saddler, a.k.a. Grandmaster Flash, one of five kids born to parents from Barbados and living on 163rd and Fox Street, in the South Bronx neighborhood that the local cops at the 41st Precinct nicknamed—in an amusing coincidence—"Fort Apache."

In May, Saddler was walking around the neighborhood and he saw a flyer:

> DJ KOOL HERC and the Herculoids return with . . . THE
> BAD MACHINE !!!SURE SHOCKER!!! With COKE LA
> ROCK & DJ CLARK KENT . . . a birthday celebration for . . .
> *Wendy & Alvira!!* Saturday, May 25, 1974 CEDAR PARK REC
> CENTER 9:00 p.m.–??? 16–18 ONLY!!! I.D. REQ. Free Admission . . . no guns—no alcoholic beverages—no drugs.[44]

He had heard about Herc's parties on Sedgwick Avenue. Saddler was thirteen, a geeky kid with a scientist's instincts and a passion for electronics. Saddler and his pals had a jerry-rigged clubhouse in the basement of a Faile Street brownstone in the Bronx, which doubled as his sound laboratory. He'd worked at home until he made the mistake of bringing home a couple of meatpacking drums that he'd salvaged from a Dumpster—pork barrels, literally, used to ship bacon—with plans to use them as loudspeaker cabinets. He never washed them out, and soon the stench of rotten meat led his mother to evict his lab.[45]

In the basement clubhouse, Saddler blacked out the windows, hung Christmas lights, got some old couches and a mattress, and wired up a sound system. He and his friends listened to Stevie Wonder's *Innervisions*, the Ohio Players' *Fire* (the trademark nude on the cover holding a firehose this time), and records by Eddie Kendricks and the Temptations that were also electrifying revelers at gay discos 150 blocks south. Saddler counted MFSB's "Love Is the Message," just like Nicky Siano, as one of his most beloved records.

Two blocks from Cedar Park that Saturday, Saddler could hear Herc's sound system pounding out Babe Ruth's "The Mexican"—a genuinely strange Afro-flamenco prog-rock funk jam with a face-slapping snare-drum beat stoked by tambourine, congas, and the occasional castanet flourish. "I had never heard sound, let alone music, that loud in my whole life," Saddler wrote in his autobiography, *The Adventures of Grandmaster Flash*. "I could feel the boom of the bass coming up through my Super Pro Keds."

By the time he got closer, Herc faded in "I Wouldn't Change a Thing" by Coke Escovedo—but the middle of the song, near the rhythmic break. He did this again and again, with song after song: pieces of "Give It Up or Turn It Loose" and "Hot Pants," Aretha Franklin's "Rock Steady," the conga-funk title track of Johnny Pate's *Shaft in Africa* soundtrack, and of course "Apache," all booming through huge cabinets via a monster McIntosh power amp.[46] Dancers were going bananas, pulling wild moves. Herc or his sidekick Coke La Rock or another of his crew would chant "Yes yes y'all" and "Herc Herc" into a mic, triggering the echo chamber on the mixer so the phrases reverberated out into the evening and up into the sky.

Saddler spent the next few weeks fooling around with his turntable, and by high summer, he took his sound system out to the streets, eventually settling on the park at Mott Haven Houses on 142nd and Willis, near the enormous Patterson Houses projects. He was intent on making Herc's style into something of his own.

•

A week after the Cedar Park party, there was another historic New York jam, down at Town Hall on Forty-third Street: stripped-down, heavily rhythmic, hypnotic music that was presented through a serious sound system and that ran well into the night.

Music in Twelve Parts took Philip Glass three years to finish. It was four hours long, and while he'd played pieces of it in his loft gigs and in various recital halls, the June 1 concert was the world premiere of the complete work—his first uptown concert hall performance. Tom Johnson called it a major accomplishment that "never became dull or repetitious, despite all the repetition."[47]

Johnson also praised the sound system, which was built by Kurt Munkacsi, Glass's devoted audio engineer. Munkacsi began his career at nineteen building crazy audio systems for La Monte Young at the latter's Church Street performance loft. Munkacsi also worked with Young's old pal Yoko Ono and her fairly new husband, the New York transplant John Lennon. Glass was a rock fan himself: he had his epiphany at the Fillmore East during a Jefferson Airplane concert. "I want to be like *that*," he thought. "I want to be *loud*."[48]

When Munkacsi first heard Glass's music at the Whitney in the summer of '69, it was already amplified, mixing the electric keyboards, sax, and wordless vocals that would inform *Music in Twelve Parts*. But both men figured it would be interesting to apply serious rock technologies to the music: superhigh amplification, ultradeep bass. And so they did. When Glass would present his work at his loft apartment on Elizabeth Street with his band—Munkacsi included—surrounded by the audience and a huge, pummeling quad sound system, listeners sometimes fled; others, tripping hard, saw God. The players themselves demurred. "Drop acid and try to do a Philip Glass performance? You couldn't possibly," says Munkacsi. "The music was too complicated. The most anybody did was maybe have a glass of wine or smoke a joint."

In any case, the music itself was mind-altering. Brian Eno called the London performance he attended in '71 with his friend David Bowie "one of the most extraordinary musical experiences of my life—sound made completely physical and as dense as concrete by sheer volume and repetition. For me it was like a viscous bath of pure, thick energy."

Glass booked Town Hall himself for the big debut, and Munkacsi set up their sound system, which they'd recently upgraded from Altec 604 speakers to huge bi-amplified JBLs.[49] The sound was glorious. Down the block in Times Square, hookers fought with their pimps, sad men jerked off in porn houses, junkies hustled theatergoers for change, and Jersey kids copped dubious drugs from street dealers. But just as Herc's gigantic beats erased the pain beyond Cedar Park, Glass's sublime, cheerily chug-chugging rhythm cycles made one section of Forty-third Street, for roughly four hours, an awesomely beautiful place.

If Glass's and Reich's use of electric keyboards was an affront to the classical music status quo, as was Joe Zawinul's to jazz purists, Larry Harlow's use of them, starting with the 1971 LP *Electric Harlow*, was no less radical. Salsa groups like Tipica '73 used electronics and rock textures, too. Out West, Santana's Latin guitar rock loomed as the primary route to a crossover audience. But New York salsa players kept their fusions rooted in Cuban *son* and *charanga*, Puerto Rican *bomba* and *plena*. Jazz was an important element in salsa since Mario Bauza took the "cubop" fusion he cooked up in the '30s with Dizzy Gillespie and applied it to Machito and his Afro-Cubans, a Latin dance band led by Bauza's brother-in-law Frank "Machito" Grillo in the '40s. During the '60s and '70s, the Monday-night Salsa Meets Jazz sessions at the Village Gate, at Bleecker and Thompson, stoked the fusion fire. But for most New York players, especially the Fania acts, improvisation was held in check by the dictates of rhythm. Salsa was for dancing—or it was arguably not salsa at all.

The artist who flaunted this rule most spectacularly was Eddie Palmieri. And in 1974, he released *The Sun of Latin Music*, the most far-reaching recording salsa had ever produced.

Palmieri was a musical powerhouse and, like Miles Davis, a restless innovator. Born to Puerto Rican parents in Spanish Harlem, he was a prodigy who was playing talent shows with his brother Charlie at age eight. He revered Thelonious Monk and McCoy Tyner. He formed the band La Perfecta in 1961 at age twenty-five, which introduced the notion of performing Cuban charangas with a pair of braying trombones instead of the usual old-world trumpets and violins. Willie Colón would take that idea and run with it a few years later, though by then, Palmieri was moving in other directions. In 1970 he made *Harlem River Drive*, a

Latin soul record steeped in jazz that was visionary but didn't sell. Palmieri was as mercurial as he was creative, and had trouble making a
living. By 1973, in a turn that promised to get him back on track, he
teamed up with the producer/manager Harvey Averne.

Born to Eastern European Jews in Brooklyn, Averne discovered
Cuban music as a teenager playing accordion with dance bands in the
Catskills. (His band, Arvito and the Latin Rhythms, featured Averne's
pal Larry Harlow for a while, until Averne fired him for not taking direction, telling him to start his own band.) Averne was a hustler: he took
a job with Fania early on, producing Ray Barretto's boogaloo-flavored
Acid for them in '67. Working as a bandleader around the same time, he
was similarly fusion-minded: he had a supple Latin soul hit for Atlantic
in '68, "My Dream," by the Harvey Averne Dozen, and one of the earliest disco hits in '72 as leader of the Cakatchas, a Belgian studio group
whose porn-funk "Jungle Fever" slowed and flipped the "Soul Makossa"
groove, while stealing its heavy-breathing routine from Serge Gainsbourg and Jane Birkin's French hit "Je t'aime . . . moi non plus." Around
this time, Averne had signed on with United Artists as an executive to
head up its Latin music division. But he didn't see a future in it, and
with Fania's business booming, he decided to start his own label, Mango,
a takeoff on the Beatles' Apple. When he received a cease-and-desist
order from Chris Blackwell's Island Records, which had already registered the name for a subsidiary, Averne changed his label's name to
Coco. And one of the first things he did was plop down $35,000 in
cash to buy Palmieri's recording contract from the very shady owner of
Roulette Records, Morris Levy, along with another $10,000 for his
management/booking contract.

To Averne, the segregation of the Latin audience that occurred a
decade earlier when rock exploded was tragic; suddenly, the twist (pio-
neered in part, ironically, by Roulette releases like Joey Dee's "Peppermint Twist") replaced the cha-cha. Touch-dancing was *finito*, and soon
listeners who once might have chilled out to Latin jazz were more interested in arty, psychedelic rock. Averne and Palmieri figured they could
make a new fusion, something that could cross over to sophisticated
rock and jazz listeners without betraying the Latin dancers. This thinking informed his production on Palmieri's *Sentido*—with "Adoración,"
the song that capped Palmieri's show at the Woodstock Playhouse
in '73—and even more so on *The Sun of Latin Music*.

It was recorded, tellingly, at Jimi Hendrix's Electric Lady Studios on Eighth Street. The horn charts, by the venerable Cuban arranger Rene Hernandez, are supple and bright, the percussion sharp and swinging. "Nada de Ti" is merely a well-produced salsa record until the two-minute mark, when the twenty-year-old Cuban Alfredo de la Fé saws into the mix with an electric violin, building a rough-edged solo that's more hallucinatory country music than proper Cuban charanga, ending with a pizzicato flourish and disappearing into a tunnel of reverb. The singer Lalo Rodriguez, all of sixteen years old, is already a tough-sounding salsero and songwriter; on "Deseo Salvaje," a smoky ballad, his croon dips low, veering between the left and right channels as if he's an animal pacing around his cage, horns rising like steam from a manhole cover at the end of a dark street.

But the centerpiece is "Un Dia Bonito," a fourteen-minute epic that begins with a piano solo haunted by electronic ghosts and dissonant violin scribbles, careening between delicate melodic exploration and pianistic cluster bombs à la Cecil Taylor or Henry Cowell (Palmieri admired both musicians; his bassist Andy Gonzales introduced him to the latter). Eventually, the free-form piano resolves into an elegant, hot-shit Afro-Cuban jam with Rodriguez shouting out San Francisco, a firestorm of trombones and forearm-powered keyboard-bashing finally immolated into a tape-feedback whiteout. It's an avant-garde South Bronx salsa answer to Santana's Mesoamerican acid rock.[50]

The Sun of Latin Music's rival for the year's greatest salsa LP was *Celia and Johnny*, Celia Cruz's formal declaration of allegiance to the new school in her adopted homeland. Johnny Pacheco, age forty-four, was a good partner: in addition to being Fania's co-owner, able to marshal all its resources, the bandleader and flutist was also, at heart, a traditionalist weaned on Cruz's early Cuban recordings with Sonora Matancera. Cruz was open to experimentation, but fiercely proud of her tradition. Mainly a set of straightforward Cuban *sones*, *Celia and Johnny* was played with killing New York swagger.

The album's high point is "Quimbará," a brassy rumba *guaguancó* written by Junior Cepeda, a Nuyorican who included the song on a demo he'd sent to Fania. The label thought it too old-fashioned, but Cruz liked it straightaway. With its rootsy Afro-Cuban call-and-response opening between Celia and the conguero Johnny Rodriguez, it captured the Afrophilia of the cultural moment, while its liquid midsection—

churning under Celia's growls of "Azúcar!"—was old-school dance-floor sugar.[51]

It was a hit, and remains one of Celia Cruz's greatest numbers. Sadly, the songwriter never savored it: Cepeda, then twenty-two, was killed during a lovers' quarrel in their Bronx apartment just two days before the album's release.[52]

Like Cruz, Patti Smith had one hand in the old, one reaching for the new. She revered Jimi Hendrix, Jim Morrison, Brian Jones, even palled around a bit with Janis Joplin when the latter was in New York. But when Smith and Lenny Kaye followed Eddie Palmieri into Electric Lady Studios with the pianist Richard Sohl and their new pal, Television guitarist Tom Verlaine, to record Smith's first single on June 5, they sprang off history like cliff divers.

They had two songs. "Hey Joe (Version)" remakes the much-covered folk standard whose most well-known iteration was by Hendrix. Smith's version bore little resemblance; it begins with her voice, unaccompanied, breathy, challenging, coming on to Hendrix's ghost: "Honey, the way you play guitar makes me feel so . . . masochistic." Then she invokes Patty Hearst, a timely reference: the granddaughter heiress of the news baron William Randolph Hearst was kidnapped in February by the dubious revolutionaries of the Symbionese Liberation Army, and in April was videotaped robbing a bank in San Francisco with her captors. Eventually, Kaye's tick-tock rhythm guitar comes in, then Sohl's piano, and the song emerges, about a man killing his unfaithful girlfriend. The tempo builds, Verlaine's twitchy lead guitar rises, then explodes into spasms, and soon Smith breaks the lyric pattern completely; she becomes Patty Hearst, spitting the line "I'm nobody's million-dollar baby" like an heiress spitting on her trust-fund statement. It's a bit too impressed with its own transgression, but flecked with incandescent magic.

The B side, "Piss Factory," is for the ages. Beginning quietly with Sohl's simple chords and Kaye's alternately slithering and strutting lead (Verlaine sits this one out), the men build a five-minute jam-vamp under Smith's prose-poetry, which dances to the music without clinging to it. She begins her story about working for thirty-six dollars a week in a sweatshop with women who threaten to beat her up for doing her piece-work too fast. She's wishing for a radio, to hear James Brown singin' "I Lost Someone." Then she's peeping through a porthole at a convent, imagining the freedom of the nuns, imagining their smell, and then the forbidden smell of boys, and the way "their dicks droop like lilacs."

Then she's yanked back to the foul workaday scent of Dot Hook, the archetypal battle-ax who works beside her on the line. Smith is about to faint from the heat, but she fights it, Kaye's circling electric-guitar notes and Sohl's piano runs, part Debussy and part Jerry Lee Lewis, pulsing like the blood in her temples, lifting the song higher. Finally Smith decides to flee. She's naked now, confessing desire that's absurd, desperate, deeply true, exploded in flames. "I'm gonna get on that train and go to New York City," she sings as the song hits its peak, declaring her intent to be famous, to be a star, to never return.

And the music keeps circling like wind in the aftermath of a storm, scattering ashes and debris. Smith takes a breath and tosses a final fuck-you to Dot Hook as the 8-track tape in Studio B unwinds and the clock strikes midnight at the recording session they booked with money hustled by their pal Robert Mapplethorpe, at the studio Hendrix built to revolutionize music. In fact, she'd met Hendrix briefly at the opening party there in 1970. But he died before he got a chance to use it, age twenty-seven—the same age as Smith when she finished the take and headed out toward Sixth Avenue in the early hours of a summer morning.[53]

And if "Piss Factory" remains the most powerful song Smith ever sang, it's because its words seem to contain the voices of multitudes, of every musician and artist and hard-luck dreamer working their ass off in the urine stench of New York City in the summer of 1974.

In Boston, touring in support of *The Wild, the Innocent & the E Street Shuffle*, Bruce Springsteen played two shows at the Harvard Square Theater. The late show on May 9 was so fiery that Jon Landau—in a column that ran in May in *The Real Paper*, Boston's *Village Voice*—knocked out a personal, inspirationally hyperventilating review that declared: "I saw rock and roll future and its name is Bruce Springsteen," playing with hyperbole like Springsteen played with rock's carnival-barker bluster.

This was not some proto-blogger blowing wind. Landau's day job was reviews editor for *Rolling Stone*, a gig he'd held since 1970, and he was as much a parent to rock 'n' roll criticism as anyone. Prior to that, he was the main critic for *Crawdaddy*; his definitive review of the Stones' *Between the Buttons* ran in '67, before *Rolling Stone* even existed. Jann Wenner hired him as part of the latter's start-up team, and at this point his was the most powerful voice on the scene. He was writing in a regional weekly (he'd been living in Boston), but there was no doubt the piece would have legs.

Landau was raised in New York; his parents moved the family to Massachusetts when he was a teenager. He went to Brandeis, dropped out due to health problems, got a job at a record store, and started to write about rock and R&B with seriousness and a sense of political mission. He also made music and was fascinated by the production process, which he often addressed in reviews. In '69, thanks in part to his *Rolling Stone* juice, he got to try his hand at it. There was a failed attempt with the J. Geils Band, which Landau championed to Atlantic and whose lead singer, Peter Wolf, he'd met back at Brandeis. Then there was *Back in the USA*, the second album by the Detroit wildmen MC5. From the psychedelic-punk feedback sprawl of the band's live debut, Landau stripped things down '50s-style, to a tight, tinny, bare-knuckled primitivism, all in-your-face vocals, guitar blasts, and snare hits, nearly every song between two and three minutes long. The set was bookended with two covers, frantic takes on Little Richard's "Tutti Frutti" and the Chuck Berry title track that were object lessons in Landau's no-bullshit, less-is-more rock aesthetic. The record didn't sell, but it was admired by musicians and critics—among them Patti Smith and Lenny Kaye, who in '74 were both writing for Landau.

By July, his Springsteen review had been repurposed as ad copy for *The Wild, the Innocent & the E Street Shuffle*, the "rock and roll's future" bit its banner headline.[54] Landau was a reluctant New Yorker—he'd left the city in '72 after a brief stint helming *Rolling Stone*'s satellite office on East Fifty-sixth Street. But now twenty-seven, he moved back to town, getting himself an apartment just around the way, at 400 East Fifty-seventh Street.

That summer, Springsteen was booked as an ill-advised replacement for Boz Scaggs, slotted between the folk-rockers Brewer & Shipley and the fluffy country-pop headliner Anne Murray at the popular Schaefer concert series in Central Park's Wollman skating rink. He blew the place up, ending with "Rosalita" and a standing ovation from a crowd of around five thousand, many of whom heartily booed Murray before heading for the gates. "Like all demon rock and rollers," wrote Robert Christgau, "Springsteen sells youth at its best, in all its zany, irresponsible compassion and doomed arrogance. That commodity is scarce in this cowardly time, and a lot of us—kids looking for an exemplar and aging holdouts who refuse to give up on the promise of an exemplary spirit—are hooked on it."

Printed below those words in the *Voice* was a tiny, column-wide ad that read "AT LAST Patti Smith single 'Hey, Joe' b/w 'Piss Factory' NOW AVAILABLE," followed by a list of the tiny bookstores and record shops that carried it.[55] It was a nice juxtaposition: after all, the New Jersey working-class escape fantasy of "Piss Factory" wasn't far away from the piano-colored storytelling on *The Wild, the Innocent & the E Street Shuffle*.

Smith and Springsteen were both imagining the future of rock 'n' roll as rock's biggest heroes seemed ready to bail. Dylan and the Band did two intense comeback shows at Madison Square Garden, but the musicians were ambivalent about the ballyhoo and their fame; they made their point at the January 31 show, which began with a trio of kiss-off songs, "Most Likely You'll Go Your Way," "It Ain't Me, Babe," and the venomous "Ballad of a Thin Man," after which the Band amusingly segued into "Stage Fright." The double-LP document of the tour, *Before the Flood*, toned down that sentiment and was full of powerful music, but it felt like a replay of the glory years.[56]

Ditto the Stones' *It's Only Rock 'n' Roll*, which threw Detroit's Lester Bangs—himself trying to imagine rock's future through his writing—into a tizzy. ("This album is false," he wrote in the *Voice*. "Numb. But it cuts like a dull blade."[57]) Even David Bowie, the young glam savior, had fallen from grace like Major Tom; the young critic James Wolcott described the new *Diamond Dogs* as "so desiccated and sluggish, so bereft of wit and energy, that not even the most feebleminded of Camp-followers will be able to coast with it."[58] Lou Reed, Bowie's New York pal, reanimated Velvet Underground classics on the live *Rock n Roll Animal* with mascara, flash pots, and glammy guitar wank.

On top of everything, the New York Dolls were stumbling in their high heels. *Too Much Too Soon* had been released in May. Lisa Robinson praised it in *Hit Parader*, which ran a two-part feature by Kaye around its recording sessions with the veteran producer Shadow Morton.

But the British writer Nick Kent, a fan who had seen the band in their glory (burning and wisecracking through a set at the tiny Bleecker Street haunt Kenny's Castaways) and at their lowest (Thunders repeatedly vomiting during a show in Paris), wrote in London's *New Musical Express* that the record was "messy and shot through with unfulfilled potential." *Circus* called it "cut after cut of annoying screeching." Some months later, *Creem* awarded the band Worst Group of the Year in their Readers' Poll.[59]

Given the Dolls' reverence for old-school rock 'n' roll, *Too Much Too Soon* was a great concept on paper. Morton was best known for his '60s work with the Shangri-Las. The *Nuggets*-style garage-band crunch of "It's Too Late," the Stonesy stomp of "Puss 'N' Boots," and the sax-studded roar of "Human Being" were, in fact, fairly awesome. But the campy backup vocals on "Who Are the Mystery Girls?" and the girl-group drag of "(There's Gonna Be a) Showdown" didn't help translate the Dolls aesthetic beyond Lower Manhattan.

And the band was not in a good way. Thunders still possessed the best hair and one of the greatest right hands in rock, the latter so impressive that even Jimmy Page courted him as a peer when Led Zeppelin came to New York. But Thunders was a mess, using methedrine as well as heroin at this point, according to biographer Nina Antonia. Most of the rest of the band was using one thing or another. Members of their crew were dealing; there were trashed hotel rooms and girlfriend dramas; and their label and management were rapidly losing faith.

By the end of a train-wreck summer tour, Arthur Kane was drinking so heavily he left the band to recuperate, and the Dolls were back to playing tiny joints like Club 82, where the drag queens and glam scenesters showed them hometown love. The cops didn't, however, shutting down their August 19 show there for overcrowding.[60]

The first issue of *High Times* magazine appeared on newsstands in early June. On glossy paper, fifty-two pages long, it included a feature on the origin of the hemp trade, along with info on new psychoactives (Special K), domestic price quotes, and photos of robust cannabis buds.

Despite the harsh Rockefeller Drug Laws, enacted on September 1, 1973, the drug culture in New York City appeared essentially unchanged. As Lester Bangs wrote that summer for a *Creem* cover story, illustrated with a photo of a gumball machine full of pills and pot pipes and coke vials: "The drug culture is still around; in fact, it's so far permeated this society as to not be an 'other' culture at all any more."[61]

It's hard to convey the extent to which drugs were a part of life in New York during the mid-'70s. Kids would generally encounter marijuana in sixth or seventh grade. With public school extracurricular activities mostly axed due to the city's budget woes, many partied with the sort of drive, diligence, and devotion others might bring to Little League, tennis, or debate club. Young burnouts saved for the best equipment, like the water pipes made by U.S. Bongs, ultrathick colored Lucite tubes with wooden-sleeved one-hit bowls. There were modular brass pipes with built-in chambers where you could resinate your stash to make it more potent. Power hitters were essentially plastic bicycle-style water bottles tricked out so a joint could be inserted into the cap, lit end in; when you squeezed the bottle, smoke shot out the mouthpiece. And who could forget the strap-on, resuscitator-style "grass mask" pipes?

Older brothers and friends of friends would come back from vacations with blond hash, black hash, hash oil, Thai stick, Hawaiian green buds, red buds, gold buds. There was LSD in blue pills, on green blotter, and occasionally, if you were lucky, as drops on sugar cubes—just like in the movies. There were psilocybin mushrooms, and the dreaded purple PCP tabs. The drug-education programs in the schools doubled as primers about the marvelous diversity of the pharmacopoeia. Kids hit the library to study the *Physicians' Desk Reference*, which detailed every prescription drug and its potential effects. Seconals, Tuinals, and of course quaaludes were popular, and would occasionally turn up in the medicine cabinets of parents and grandparents.

Valium, the subject of the Stones' "Mother's Little Helper," was Father's Little Helper in my house: Mom used a paring knife to split the 10-milligram blue tablets, leaving half on the counter as a cocktail for my dad when he returned from work. A World War II vet who went to vocational school for commercial art after returning from the service, he became an art director at an ad agency, and his accounts were primarily pharmaceutical; at one photo shoot, he'd scored a thousand-tab bottle of Valium, which he kept in the kitchen cabinet next to the vitamins, but hid years later when his kids suddenly began acting suspiciously tranquil.

Maybe exercising control over one's consciousness was compensation for being unable to exert control over anything else.

The August 1 issue of the *Voice* trumpeted "Countdown to Impeachment," accompanied by a Jules Feiffer cartoon of Nixon shackled to a dungeon wall while one military general announces to another, "Wonderful news! He beat the rap on Cambodia." By September, Nixon had been pardoned by Gerald Ford.

Robert Caro published *The Power Broker* that fall, his doorstop biography of the New York überplanner/overlord Robert Moses. In some 1,200 pages, it detailed how the most powerful figure in twentieth-century New York politics—the creator of Long Island's beachfront state park system, the region's parkway and expressway system, plus an astounding number of urban playgrounds, pools, housing projects, and public buildings—was ultimately a corrupt and out-of-touch megalomaniac whose initiatives crippled working-class neighborhoods and helped trigger the city's current decline.

Even the guy who created Jones Beach was a crook.

The entertainment industry, of course, tried to fill the Great Man void with hero tales. *Death Wish* was especially resonant. It featured Charles Bronson—a "Cro-Magnon Man and America's latest gift to cultural anthropology," per the critic Molly Haskell—as an Upper West Side architectural engineer turned vigilante who stalks Riverside Park in search of muggers, then guns them down.

New York's crime rate had already become a punch line, although the jokes usually involved Central Park. And not without cause: by early October, the year's tally there was 486 muggings and/or robberies, 19 rapes, and 2 murders. The *Voice*'s October 24 cover story was billed as "A True Tale of New York: Our Man Walks Through Central Park at Night (Now Read What Happened . . .)" What happened was nothing—although the author did pretend to have a gun under his jacket, Bronson-style, at one point when he passed some suspicious-looking men.

To keep me out of trouble, my parents sent me off to sleepaway camp that summer, where I stole a canoe and learned how to fire a gun. On August 7, I was awarded a certification of Marksman First Class through the authority of the National Rifle Association. It seemed a useful skill.

Aside from firearms, a hobby I couldn't pursue at home due to the lack of official firing ranges, my greatest obsession remained music. I couldn't wait for new records to turn up at my local music store. I would check the ads in the *Long Island Press*, strap on my army-navy store backpack, jump on my ten-speed racer, and ride the four miles to Korvettes in Douglaston to survey the latest titles and the cutouts, pop history shrink-wrapped at 99 cents a throw.

The last stretch of the trip was a breathtaking hill, a dip in the road alongside Alley Pond Park where Horace Harding Expressway drops sharply into a valley as the Long Island Expressway intersects with the Cross Island Parkway in a tangle of entry and exit ramps. There was no shoulder, no place to stop once you joined the flow of cars, which were usually doing 55 mph or more. So you'd look out from the hilltop at the white obelisk of the department store in the distance, cross yourself, and take the plunge, pedaling your ass off until you shot up Douglaston Parkway and onto the parking lot ramp on the other side of the ravine and arrived, hopefully intact.

Philippe Petit stepped off the South Tower of the World Trade Center at approximately 7:15 on the morning of August 7. He and a crew of friends illegally smuggled a steel cable up to the building's roof and spent the night there, stringing it across to the North Tower. Petit was a week shy of his twenty-fifth birthday.

There was poetry to his walk; the aerialist danced, bounced, lay on his back. It was conducted without hordes of digital media-gatherers; there are just a handful of photographs.

There was a metaphor here: art-making could be like a criminal act, wild-eyed aesthetic lawbreaking in front of a few wowed onlookers that could subsequently go viral. Petit was arrested after his forty-five-minute performance. But he'd earned his immortality.

The summer was exceptionally hot. It gave Laurie Anderson the idea to hitchhike to the North Pole. She spent a couple of weeks amassing supplies in her new apartment, located in a building occupied mostly by junkies at 223 East Second Street between Avenues B and C. Then she heaved a seventy-pound backpack onto her shoulders, walked down to Houston Street, and stuck out her thumb. She never got to the true north, the magnetic pole. But she got close. She camped out, cooked, smoked, and watched the northern lights dance across the sky.

While she was away, someone cut a hole big enough to crawl through into the wall between her apartment and the hallway. When Anderson came back in September, pretty much everything she owned, including her artwork, had been either stolen or destroyed.⁶²

Richard Nixon resigned the presidency of the United States live on national television.

Politics went out of fashion in music in the seventies: so says conventional wisdom. It's true, but not entirely. In 1970, twenty-year-old Gil Scott-Heron released his debut LP, *Small Talk at 125th and Lenox*, a live recording made in Harlem. It included "The Revolution Will Not Be Televised," a grimly funny spoken-word piece recited over a hand-drum groove. By the time he issued *Winter in America* in May '74 on the independent jazz label Strata-East, he was fronting a full band led by the keyboardist/flutist Brian Jackson, and had figured out how to build his internally rhyming raps into soul-jazz song structures, singing with a handsome, crying baritone.

In September, Scott-Heron joined Eddie Palmieri and Celia Cruz to perform at the Nation of Islam's Black Family Day at Downing Stadium on Randall's Island, at the top of the East River below the Triborough Bridge. A stone's throw from where Robert Moses and the Triborough Commission ran their empire, Brother Reverend Louis Farrakhan spoke for two hours to around twenty thousand people, denouncing the United States as "the wickedest nation on the face of the earth" under sunny fall skies. Jimmy Cliff sang, "I'd rather be a free man in my grave, than living as a puppet or a slave."

Elsewhere in the city's music, political impulses hid out: in Bronx DJ parties powered by hijacked electricity, in Wayne County's post-Stonewall drag punk, in the DIY jazz lofts.

Unemployment was at 5.8 percent; 5 million Americans were out of work, not counting housewives and kids. The city was hard-hit. Almost a third of its 87,000 construction workers, for instance, were jobless. "Let's face it," Tommy Cush, a Vietnam vet and unemployed New York ironworker told the journalist Pete Hamill, "the Depression is in the air."[63] By the time Treasury Secretary William Simon conceded, "The United States is in a recession," on November 7, it was old news.[64]

Dance club culture was not just popularizing records but was also beginning to influence the way a certain kind of dance music—now known specifically as "disco"—was made. The success of Hues Corporation's "Rock the Boat," which reached number 1 on the pop charts on July 6, and George McCrae's astonishingly similar "Rock Your Baby," which took its place a week later, was credited in part to club DJs, who'd been playing "Rock the Boat" since the beginning of the year.[65] Labels were beginning to understand how particular beats and song structures appealed to dancers and DJs. If they wanted to tap their power to propel hits, they needed to shape their music accordingly.

Thus was born the "disco mix" and the 12-inch single. Both can be credited to the DJ Tom Moulton.

Moulton was a fiercely handsome white dude with caterpillar eyebrows, a porn-star mustache, and a Cheshire cat grin who had done some modeling (he was a Marlboro Man, among other roles) and had worked on the business side for King Records—home of James Brown—in the '60s. In the summer of '72, Moulton made a series of sophisticated R&B mix tapes for a gay disco called the Sandpiper on Fire Island, the ribbon of beachfront off Long Island that was the summer haven of choice for the city's gay community.[66] Through careful overlaying and beat-matching, Moulton created seamless song transitions that kept dancers stuck blissfully on the floor like flies in honey. He updated his tapes weekly with the latest records—which he hustled, like Nicky Siano, from record companies.

One day Moulton was on a vinyl run and swung by Scepter Records at 254 West Fifty-fourth Street. The label was run by Florence Greenberg, one of the first female record company chiefs; it had helped launch the girl-group craze with the Shirelles in '59, had a string of hits with Burt Bacharach and Dionne Warwick, and was just breaking into disco, thanks to the ear and instincts of Mel Cheren, a dedicated dance music fan who adored the Loft and the Gallery. Familiar with Moulton's work, he gave the DJ a multitrack master copy of "Dream World" by Don Downing—a tough, string-draped Motown-style jam—and told him to have fun with it.

Because the song modulated to a lower key near the end, Moulton couldn't simply extend the song by looping it back to an earlier segment. So at around the 2:15 mark, he spliced in an instrumental section, built up by layering strings over the track's martial trap drums, and stretched the song out to a dance-floor-friendly four and a half minutes. Fashioning with tape manipulation what acts like the Incredible Bongo Band did in session and guys like Kool Herc and Flash did on turntables, Moulton—a DJ, not a "producer"—created the first disco edit.[67] According to Cheren, the remix moved ten thousand copies without radio airplay.[68]

Instantly, Moulton became the disco doctor. "They would bring me their sick record, and I would fix it," he told the writer Tim Lawrence. Labels clamored for his services.[69] He accepted an invitation to write the Disco Action column in *Billboard*. As with the city's other scenes, disco generated its own writers. The *Voice* contributor Vince Aletti began his column for the trade magazine *Record World* around the same time as Moulton's.[70] Disco was now officially a genre.

Like the edited break, the 12-inch single was also born somewhat accidentally—and, coincidentally enough, with a record by Don Downing's brother. In late '74, Moulton was remixing Al Downing's "I'll Be Holding On" for Chicago's Chess Records, and he wanted test pressings for DJing that weekend. Usually these were done on 7-inch acetates, but the engineer was out of them. So he used regular 12-inch hard vinyl discs, spreading the grooves out to fill the disc surface. When Moulton played it back, he freaked: the sound was *massive*, much fuller and clearer than a 7-inch single, since the grooves were not squeezed together. He played it that Friday at his preweekend listening session with the DJs Walter Gibbons, David Rodriguez, and others. They freaked, too.

The label ultimately released the remix as a 7-inch. But the genie of the 12-inch disco single was out of the bottle. And the song topped the dance charts anyway. As for "Big" Al Downing, the Oklahoma singer-songwriter moved on; his next hit was "Mr. Jones," a decidedly non-disco country-music weeper about a kindly black sharecropper and his troubled white son.[71] His brother, who became known as "Doctor Boogie," pledged allegiance to the dance floor.

•

By November, Nicky Siano had the Gallery up and running again in a new space on Mercer and Houston, bigger and better. In December came the Flamingo, a gymnasium-sized gay disco and cruising ground in Chelsea. It was an excellent time to be a gay dance music fan in New York City.

Disco was a sociocultural movement as well as a rhythmic one. As its sound and aesthetic were being shaped, disco was in turn shaping gay men, flush with post-Stonewall pride. Being gay no longer meant being sad, lonely, and isolated. In New York, it could just as well mean dancing shamelessly and ecstatically with all the coolest people.[72] People who weren't gay, strictly speaking, seemed to wish they were. Rock presented sexuality as an androgynous, polymorphously perverse playground. The New York Dolls may have been largely straight, but David Johansen kept people guessing, flinging quips like "I'm trisexual: I'll try anything." Patti Smith, whose first boyish haircut was a hit with the Max's crowd, was no less ambiguous. Lou Reed had an anatomically male girlfriend named Rachel.

For the purpose of pleasure, there was a self-righteous sense of anything goes. And between the gay rights and women's movements, bisexuality could seem like a political imperative as well as a hedonistic one. "To be sexual is to be bisexual," wrote David Starkweather in the *Voice*. Movies heralded a brave new era. "You've been reading about the bi-sexual chic phenomenon. Now—for the first time see it at work and play!" read an ad for *Score* by the New York director Radley Metzger, an adaptation of an off-Broadway play that had featured a fledgling actor named Sylvester Stallone. Long-haired boys like me often got cruised by older dudes, which was sometimes flattering, sometimes creepy. Polyglot sex was a rock 'n' roll right of passage.

As a wise friend once said: "It's hard enough finding someone you can really *be* with. Worrying about gender seems beside the point."

In September, along with James Brown and other American acts, the Fania All-Stars traveled to Zaire to play the festivities around the Muhammad Ali–George Foreman fight, ballyhooed around the world as the "Rumble in the Jungle." Unfortunately, as the band found out mid-flight, Foreman was injured during training, and the fight was post-poned—for over a month, as it turned out. But the "Zaire '74" concerts took place as planned, and the All-Stars were greeted as conquering heroes by roughly eighty thousand Africans as keen on Cuban music as they were. Héctor Lavoe, onstage in high-waisted red satin slacks and a wide-collared green dress shirt embroidered with dragons, led a stadium-wide sing-along on "Mi Gente." And at one point in his set, he jumped down into the crowd to dance while Larry Harlow vamped out piano chords and drove the *descarga* home. Celia Cruz, in a backless, brightly colored sequined gown, hair swept up into a towering African 'do, did "Quimbara" and a magnificent version of "Guantanamera," turning the old Cuban folk song about the peasant girl from Guantánamo into a turbocharged international anthem. The All-Stars also played a private show for President Mobutu at his palace. Jerry Masucci had convinced the Fania musicians to perform the entire festival for free, according to Harlow. But they did get stories to tell their grandkids.

Willie Colón, meanwhile, never got on the plane. He was strung out from cocaine and terrified of the inoculations required before arriving in Africa, which made many ill. At Kennedy with his bandmates, he was sweating bullets, and thought he heard God speaking to him, telling him not to go. "After an hour, I told Jerry I was going to the bathroom," he recalled, "went outside, and hailed a taxi home." He didn't even bother retrieving his baggage.

With virtually the entire Fania roster out of the country, Colón took over Good Vibrations Sound Studios at Fortieth and Broadway to begin work on his first post-Lavoe record, and to reinvent his career. (As it turned out, *The Good, the Bad, the Ugly* would include two tracks with Lavoe, recorded on his return from Kinshasa.) Colón worked up backing tracks with all the musicians left in town, experimenting with Brazilian rhythms, Yomo Toro's *jíbaro cuatro*, and some hot blues-rock guitar. Colón even recorded his first-ever vocal lead, on a brassy cover of the Baden Powell bossa nova "Cua Cua Ra, Cua Cua."

He also recorded a song by a guy who worked in Fania's mail room. Rubén Blades had moved to New York earlier in the year, arriving from Miami by Greyhound. He'd graduated law school in Panama in June, but had no interest in working as a lawyer under a military dictatorship. He was already a moonlighting singer and songwriter; he had visited New York as a student back in 1969 and even got to record an album with the Pete Rodriguez Orquestra (*De Panamá a New York*), which tanked. He figured the mail-room gig would give him access to ears. But his colleagues thought his songs, as rooted in socially conscious *nueva canción* as in New York party music, were too depressing to be commercial.

Still, he kept writing. Ray Barretto soon hired him as a singer for his new band, a gig that netted him $35 a gig on top of his $125-a-week mail-room job. When Colón heard a demo tape of "El Cazangero," about life in a Panama prison, he wanted Lavoe to record it for *The Good, the Bad, the Ugly*. But Lavoe had no feel for the mix of poetics and jailhouse slang, which Blades based on his student-thesis experience working at a penal colony. So Colón invited the writer to sing it.

It was a great performance, full of empathy; its mix of Caribbean and Brazilian percussion—the *cuíca* friction drum conjuring the sound of crows in the prison farm plot—was especially striking. Barretto, having lost a lot of musicians recently (his entire band deserted him the previous year to form Tipica '73), wasn't happy. But his new singer wasn't jumping ship just yet.

After the Fania crew returned from Zaire, Celia Cruz performed a string of New York shows, and she was on fire. Crowds danced, laughed, wept at the intensity of the music. "Oh God!" yelled a young Latina during one performance. "It's *so* deep! It's so damn *deep*!"[73]

Allen Ginsberg was attacked while walking near his apartment on East Tenth Street at seven o'clock on Halloween night. He wrote a poem about it, "Mugging":

> dragged slowly onto the fire-soiled floor of an abandoned
> store, laundry candy counter 1929—
> now a mess of papers & pillows & plastic covers cracked
> cockroach corpsed ground—

The muggers got a plastic wallet and seventy dollars.

Stevie Wonder played Madison Square Garden again on December 6, the last of three comeback shows in the area. A party before his Nassau

Coliseum gig in September had drawn Mick Jagger and other celebrities to pay their respect. Also on the guest list were Patti Smith and David Johansen, their downtown stardom reduced to fandom as they watched from the sidelines.

The Ramones, preparing to record their debut in January, didn't have the best holiday. Tommy was hit by a cab, which laid him out for a while. Johnny wound up in the hospital with appendicitis.[74]

Chris Frantz, a young drummer, and his girlfriend Tina Weymouth, a painter, moved into a loft at 195 Chrystie Street with a friend from the Rhode Island School of Design, David Byrne. Their plans: uncertain.

Philip Glass was working on a collaborative project with Robert Wilson. The two men had been having lunch at a Sullivan Street restaurant nearly every Thursday since Glass premiered *Music in Twelve Parts* in the spring. They were searching for a historical figure to center the work on. Charlie Chaplin? Adolf Hitler? Mahatma Gandhi? All were considered, rejected. Finally something clicked. The provisional title of their new work: *Einstein on the Beach on Wall Street.*[75]

Glass's onetime comrade Steve Reich was working on his own large-scale work, which, once he settled on the number of players, would be called *Music for 18 Musicians.* His friends rehearsed at his loft space downtown every two to four weeks into the next year, essentially for free. Russ Hartenberger and Bob Becker came in from Connecticut, where they were both studying non-Western music at Wesleyan. Reich, doing what he could, covered their bus fare.[76]

Elsewhere, Bob Blank, a session guitarist, realizing his chops were not enough to earn him a living, decided to set up a recording studio in his loft on Twentieth Street between Sixth and Seventh. He bought a 16-track recorder and built the mixer himself. He called the studio Blank Tapes. It was rudimentary, but it worked. So did he, fast and cheap. He recorded disco. He recorded salsa. He recorded rock— anything, really, weird or straight, that needed to be done inexpensively with a minimum of fuss. There was no running water in the building between the hours of 6:00 p.m. and 8:00 a.m. But things like that, you work around.

Television played CBGB every Sunday. Up at the Academy of Music on Fourteenth Street, a group of commuter kids who came in to see the prog rockers Renaissance, a favorite of Alison Steele on WNEW-FM, bought a nice-looking chunk of blond hash in the bathroom.

The drummer Billy Cobham, a free agent since the split of the Mahavishnu Orchestra who had played with Cruz and Colón at Yankee Stadium, was leading his new band through a holiday run at the Bottom Line, a small club with great sight lines and an ambitious booking policy that had opened in February on West Fourth Street at Mercer.

For New Year's Eve, the most successful New York rockers, Long Island's Blue Öyster Cult, were back at the Academy of Music, although with no Iggy this time. Nearby, at Second Avenue and Seventh Street, Ike and Tina Turner played a show at the New Fillmore East, a short-lived attempt to rekindle the hall's '60s glory days. Operating the psychedelic light show was John Holmstrom, a School of Visual Arts student originally from Connecticut. He wasn't into hippie shit. But this was the first night of his first rock 'n' roll–related job, and he was psyched.

After their second day of deliberation, the jury was still out on the Watergate trial. In Hawaii, the Mauna Loa volcano erupted. In Albany, at the Executive Mansion, Hugh L. Carey—a fifty-five-year-old former Brooklyn congressman—was sworn in as the fifty-first governor of New York State, the first Democratic governor in sixteen years. In the small upstate New York town of Olean, Anthony Barbaro, seventeen, was apprehended after a shooting spree at his high school that left three dead and nine wounded.

In Times Square, a cold rain fell on revelers. On screens across the city, bodies plummeted from skyscraper windows in *Earthquake*. To show the film, which boasted a soundtrack filmed in Sensurround, theaters had to rent a special seat-rumbling speaker system. Its designer, Richard Long, had also helped create the state-of-the-art sound system with David Mancuso at the Loft.

With buildings crumbling around him on-screen, Charlton Heston, the dean of mid-'70s disaster flicks, tried to manage the chaos. Across town, he was doing the same in *Airport '75* as yet another plane plunged into the abyss.

1975

JUNGLELAND

Jack: We gotta let the cops handle this, Dad!
Paul: Yeah?

—*Death Wish*

For most of January, if you walked down Sixth Avenue in the Village between Third and Eighth, you would come across a red-and-white panel truck—its side cut away as if with a can opener—and a small group of people huddled around it, listening. The truck's owner was a bearded busker named Silverbell, and inside was his life: books, dolls, a bed, a kerosene lantern, two long-haired Afghan hounds, and an ancient upright piano, on which he played pop and classical tunes. A piano tuner and repairman by trade, he tinkered endlessly with his instrument; its insides were completely exposed, a number of its keys broken. Yet the instrument had a soul.

"It's got magic," he declared. "I used to own plenty of pianos. But now this one owns me."[1]

Around lunchtime on January 24, a bomb exploded at 101 Broad Street in the annex of Fraunces Tavern, the oldest building in New York City. Credit was taken by the FALN—Fuerzas Armadas de Liberación Nacional—a Puerto Rican nationalist group that had been active since the late '60s. They'd set off other bombs in the city, most notably the previous October, when five exploded within minutes of one another at a variety of banks and corporate buildings. But those bombs went off in the wee hours of the morning, destroying only property. This time, four people died; sixty-three were injured.

The bombers remained a mystery. In a typewritten letter, the group labeled the act retaliation for a "CIA ordered" bombing in Puerto Rico earlier in the month. It was signed "Comando Griselio Torresola"—the name of the Puerto Rican nationalist killed in a failed assassination attempt on Harry Truman in 1950.[2]

According to Bambaataa Kahim Aasim, his cousin, the young guy everyone knew as Soulski, was gunned down by police in the Bronx on January 6. "They shot him all in the lungs and chest," said Aasim, "a whole bunch of spots. They tore him up."[3]

A dark-skinned young man with a linebacker build, Aasim was a warlord in the Black Spades street gang through the early '70s. But after the intergang truce of late 1971 and a trip to the Ivory Coast and Nigeria (won as a prize in an essay-writing contest), he began having different ideas. Along with some former gangbangers near the end of 1973, he conceived the Bronx River Organization, a sort of party-promoting community-group-cum-art-tribe that recruited black and Latino kids under a banner of "Peace, Love, Unity, and Having Fun."[4]

After his cousin's death, Aasim's mission was confirmed. He'd seen Kool Herc turn parties out. He honed his own DJ skills, and began hosting events around the Bronx River housing projects near the heart of the borough. The Bronx River Organization became the Universal Zulu Nation, and Aasim was renamed Afrika Bambaataa, the "master of records." A set might juxtapose James Brown's "Give It Up or Turnit a Loose" and Brother Bones's "Sweet Georgia Brown," Funkadelic and Grand Funk Railroad, the Monkees and the Fania All-Stars. Bambaataa's omnivorous mixes, which took Frankie Crocker's eclectic programming on WBLS-FM to the next level, were born of both taste and necessity: peacekeeping at parties attracting rival gangs required a soundtrack everyone could get with: African-American, West Indian, Puerto Rican. But in practice it was musical revelation, demonstrating that genres, like racial divisions, were largely false constructs. If the rhythm was right, that was all that mattered.

Things were going well for DJ Hollywood. He was making money, more than five hundred dollars a week—enough to pay an apprentice, a Puerto Rican DJ nicknamed Junebug, along with a few girls who danced onstage to heat things up. In addition to Manhattan gigs, he began playing up in the Bronx at a place called Club 371. There, with Junebug playing records, Hollywood could get on the mic and concentrate on being an emcee.[5]

The DJ was at home previewing records one day, and he put on Isaac Hayes's *Black Moses*—hardly a go-to record in the discos he worked at. But he liked the lyrics to "Good Love," a funk-rock jam with cackling laughter, a TV ad-man schtick, and soft-porn couplets over the top. Hollywood used his own nursery-rhyme exhortations to hype crowds over the years, talking between songs and over the instrumental bits; hell, at this point he was selling his mixes on 8-track tapes for fifteen dollars a shot—what he used to make for a whole night DJing at Lovey's on 148th Street and Seventh Avenue. But he was looking to do something more mature, sexier, more like telling a story. So Hollywood took Hayes's lover man boasts and flipped them a bit, changing the line about having "thirty years' experience with sweet young girls" to "twenty-one years," as Hollywood was still a young man.[6]

He ran the rhymes over and over in his head. This is gonna be good, he thought.

"To bid farewell to 1974 is in many ways a relief," began the year's first op-ed piece in *The New York Times*—phoned in, perhaps, by a writer vacationing in Acapulco.[7] But '75 wasn't shaping up as much better. On New Year's Day, the Watergate crew—Mitchell, Haldeman, Erlichman—were convicted in the cover-up. Unemployment was at 7.1 percent, and budget cuts were squeezing city services. This included the Parks Department's Pest Control Division, which meant a shocking increase in the population of jumbo Norway rats in Central Park. Even a walk in the park was no walk in the park.

It was a golden era for American TV, though. Like millions of others in those pre-TiVo times, I spent Saturday nights watching CBS: *All in the Family* at 8:00 p.m., *The Jeffersons*—which debuted on January 18—at 8:30, Mary Tyler Moore at 9:00, Bob Newhart at 9:30, Carol Burnett at 10:00. The big rock records, on the other hand, were British: Led Zeppelin's *Houses of the Holy*, Emerson, Lake and Palmer's triple-LP *Welcome Back My Friends to the Show That Never Ends*. When tickets went on sale Monday morning, January 6, for the Zeppelin shows at Madison Square Garden and Nassau Coliseum in February, there were near-riots. At the Ticketron outlet in Macy's department store at the Roosevelt Field Mall on Long Island, more than a thousand kids were met by twenty-five Nassau County cops; six were arrested. I had planned to get tickets that afternoon after school. By then, they'd been sold out for hours.

And then I heard Bob Dylan's *Blood on the Tracks*, released on January 17. Dylan had begun writing songs for the record in Minnesota last summer. His nine-year marriage to Sara Lowndes, a.k.a. "Sad Eyed Lady of the Lowlands," a.k.a. Shirley Nozinsky, was crumbling, and he'd been spending time with a twenty-four-year-old A&R woman at his label. That spring, he'd returned from his self-imposed exile upstate in Woodstock to his old stomping ground, Greenwich Village. He'd begun taking art classes with a gurulike seventy-three-year-old teacher, Norman Raeben.[8] Scruffy and undercover, Dylan would hail a cab uptown to Carnegie Hall and take the elevator to the eleventh-floor studio spaces, where Raeben schooled him in new ways of seeing—eight hours a day, five days a week, for two months, chastising him like the other students. Dylan loved it, and applied the new ideas to his songwriting. Sure enough, *Blood* was a profoundly imagistic, almost cubist work of storytelling, unlike anything Dylan had done before.

It was the record that showed me how bone-deep music could make you feel. West Coast psychedelia and British prog-rock records were brainteasers—fun to ponder, like an M. C. Escher etching—but *Blood on the Tracks* pushed its calloused fingers into my chest like an Aztec priest trying to rip my heart loose. Hyperbole? I was fourteen. I'd had my heart broken: at sleepaway camp, in homeroom. When Dylan sang "he didn't see her anywhere / he told himself he didn't care," I knew *exactly* what he meant. I'd lie on the blue-green shag carpet of my Queens bedroom, and when side one ended—if I was feeling in a particular mood—I'd click the switch on the BSR turntable in my compact stereo and play it again. Other times, I'd flip the LP and listen to "Lily, Rosemary and the Jack of Hearts," which I could visualize like a film, each scene played out in Dylan's magically compressed verses. *Blood on the Tracks* was a Niagara Falls of words, its rush of language soothing, instantly familiar; its creation famously split between Minnesota and New York, its verbal momentum was all New York City—you can imagine Dylan as a cabbie, cruising down the Grand Central Parkway from

La Guardia toward the limitless skyline, telling his tales: half invented, all true.

It's fascinating to listen to the New York City *Blood* sessions, originally released as a bootleg on vinyl, now floating around the Internet. The most striking track is "Tangled Up in Blue," with key lyrics cast in the third person. The album's revised, superior version, largely rewritten in the first person, was recorded at eleventh-hour sessions on Dylan's old home ground in Minneapolis—a subtle shift in language, entirely different emotional results. It makes me think about New York as a culture of aliases and personal reinventions. Dylan was abandoning certain masks; maybe he needed to go home to remember how to be himself.

In March, Ellen Willis wrote a poignant essay on the LP for *The New Yorker* ("In a sense, 'Shelter from the Storm' is a 'My Back Pages' for the seventies"). *Rolling Stone* ran two separate reviews of the record in the same issue. Jon Landau compared Dylan with Charlie Chaplin, the populist cinematic revolutionary; Jonathan Cott invoked Rimbaud, Baudelaire, and Dante. Landau's piece ran over 2,000 words, Cott's over 3,000. I remember studying the reviews and researching their sources for some clue as to why the record made me feel the way it did. I never did get to the bottom of it. But the writers' seriousness of purpose, and their sense that the entire world of art and culture and human emotion could be compressed into a vinyl recording, left a deep impression on me.

Two bands humped their gear into CBGB for a Friday-night gig. One was Television. The other was called Blondie. It was obvious, there on the sidewalk, who their lead singer was.

Things were starting to happen for Television. The band was being courted by Island Records—the force behind Bob Marley, Jimmy Cliff, and other reggae acts, plus an eclectic rock roster including Traffic, Richard and Linda Thompson, and the Velvet Underground expats John Cale and Nico. Island's Chris Blackwell also signed the Roxy Music émigré Brian Eno, who had just released his solo debut, *Here Come the Warm Jets*—a wired set with a faintly obscene title and a thrillingly demented glam-rock song called "Baby's on Fire."

Now Television were set to make some demos for Island over at

Good Vibrations near Times Square, where Willie Colón had just finished *The Good, the Bad, the Ugly*, and Eno's pal Richard Williams—a rock journalist turned A&R guy who had written the first piece about Roxy Music on the basis of a demo tape—invited Eno to the sessions.[9] Over three nights, the band finished five songs, including a hypnotizing seven-minute guitar showcase, "Marquee Moon," that recalled the Velvet Underground at their most expansive. But Verlaine thought the demo's sound was thin, and didn't want to make the record with Eno, which was part of Island's signing offer. Also, there was friction between Verlaine, the virtuoso Coltrane freak, and Hell, the punk auteur and party animal whose bass-playing skills were at best rudimentary. None of Hell's songs were demoed, and Verlaine had begun cutting them from the band's set list, too.

Deborah Harry was raised, like Patti Smith, in the Jersey suburbs. An adopted child, she was smart, restless, alienated, with beautiful features and dark brown hair. She defected to New York the minute she finished high school. She worked as a bar dancer in Union City, N.J., as a bunny-eared hostess at the Playboy Club on East Fifty-ninth Street, and as a waitress in Max's. Meanwhile, she passed through a number of musical identities. In '69 she was a twenty-four-year-old hippie folk siren singing with the Wind in the Willows, who made a forgettable record for Capitol. A few years later, she joined the scene diva Elda Gentile in the Stilettos, a trash-camp, performance-art take on '60s girl groups like the Ronettes.

Chris Stein was an arty intellectual Jewish kid born to Eastern European parents and raised in Midwood, Brooklyn. Kicked out of high school for having long hair, he wound up at Quintano's School for Young Professionals, an art school for misfits at 154 West Fifty-sixth Street, behind Carnegie Hall, where he was a classmate of Johnny Thunders. He began his adult subcultural life as a hippie, lighting out to San Francisco in '67, trekking up to Woodstock in '69. Back in New York, he played in various bands, one of which opened for the Velvet Undergound, and he took classes at the School of Visual Arts, including one in electronic music taught by Steve Reich. ("All that talk about polyrhythms went over my head," he later confessed."[10])

Stein watched the Dolls come up, and occasionally played guitar with their glammy Mercer Arts cohorts Eric Emerson and the Magic Tramps. Through Emerson he met Gentile—who had a baby with Emerson and later dated Richard Hell—and one night in the fall of 1973, Stein was invited to see the Stilettos perform. It was their second-ever gig, at the Bourbon Tavern, a dive on Twenty-eighth Street in Chelsea. The place was nasty, but he found one of the singers to be sumptuous. Stein and Harry bonded, and the Stilettos suddenly had a new guitarist. They opened for Television at CBGB in May of '74.

By the summer, though, the group had fractured. Gentile was out; Harry and Stein remade the band with Harry as its focal point. At first they were called Angel and the Snakes; after a couple of gigs, they recruited as backup singers the Bronx-bred sister team Tish and Snooky (Patrice and Eileen Bellomo of the Palm Casino Revue, a cabaret show that had been running at the Bouwerie Lane Theatre across the street from CBGB). Stein and Harry changed their band's name to Blondie and the Banzai Babes. Their second guitarist was the Czech ex-pat Ivan Kral, the bassist was Fred Smith, and the drummer was Billy O'Connor.[11]

This lineup was also short-lived. The downtown rock scene was small and incestuous; allegiances were mercurial. Kral defected to join what seemed the more promising Patti Smith Group in December; then O'Connor left for law school.

In early '75, Blondie was auditioning drummers at Tommy Ramone's studio on Twenty-third Street. A twenty-one-year-old from New Jersey named Clem Burke was on the stool, and Patti Smith drifted into the room. This wasn't unusual; though Harry and Smith weren't exactly friends, they knew each other.

When Burke stopped playing, Smith, in her nasal come-hither sneer, said, "Heeeeey, you're pretty good. What's your name?"

Harry stared daggers at her. Ivan Kral had defected to her band only a few weeks earlier.

"Patti," she said. "I'm working with this guy."

"Oh," responded Patti casually.[12]

Smith soon left. Not long afterward, Burke auditioned for her, but didn't get the job. He played his first gig with Blondie—who were still being billed in CBGB ads as the Stilettos—in March. That night, Fred Smith told his bandmates he was leaving to join Television. He would be replacing Richard Hell, who was tired of deferring to Tom Verlaine. Verlaine was in CBGB that night, Patti Smith beside him. But they didn't linger.

Fred Smith's replacement would be Gary Valentine, a New Jersey fuckup who liked to occasionally go out in drag and had a talent for songwriting. For a while he lived with Harry and Stein in Harry's tiny one-bedroom at 105 Thompson Street; Stein was subletting his own place at 18 First Avenue off First Street to Tommy Ramone. Harry had a '67 Camaro that opposite-side-of-the-street parking rules required her or Stein to move back and forth in the early morning, but it was beloved; on summer days she'd drive the guys to Jones Beach or Coney Island, looking like a modern version of a Shangri-Las song where the girl had the wheels and called the shots.

While there was plenty of style-mixing, aesthetic lines were being drawn. There were the pop-rockers in one clique: the Ramones, the Dictators, the Miamis, and Blondie (and later the Heartbreakers). And there was the art-rock clique centered around Patti Smith and Television, now fronted solely by her now close friend Tom Verlaine.

The divide grew. "I may be paranoid," Harry reflected in the wake of all the musical chairs, "but I think that whole clique wanted to destroy us."[13]

Television's last shows with Richard Hell, in early March, were as the openers for a band that helped inspire them in the first place: the New York Dolls. Wayne County was the DJ. They were strange evenings, bringing together punk and glam in a sort of graduation ceremony. They would be the original Dolls' final New York shows.

After some debauched months of touring on *Too Much Too Soon*, which sold far more poorly than Mercury Records had hoped, the Dolls were booked to record demos for a third album. But the band was too wasted to pull a session together. By early '75, Mercury had given up on them. Their A&R guy, Paul Nelson, left the label and returned to music journalism, and their management team pretty much cut them off.

Enter Malcolm McLaren, a British clothing-designer-cum-culture-hustler who'd seen the Dolls in better days and fallen in love with them. He temporarily set up shop in New York with plans to resurrect the group, and on February 28, after some warm-up gigs at My Father's

Place, a hippie-rock bar in Roslyn, Long Island, they made their comeback—not at Max's Kansas City, shuttered since December, or CBGB,
which was not to McLaren's liking. ("I didn't look very commercial, and
I didn't fancy talking to the people who ran it. They looked a bit rough."[14])
Instead, now functioning as their unofficial manager, he booked them
into a drag club/disco at 227 East Fifty-sixth Street called the Little
Hippodrome. With their downtown fans packing the house, the Dolls
came out in more or less matching skintight red outfits designed by Mc-
Laren and his partner, Vivienne Westwood. If this wasn't odd enough,
they performed in front of a huge Communist Party flag, hand-sewn by
David Johansen's girlfriend, Cyrinda Foxe.

The "Better Red Than Dead" conceit, which McLaren saw as high-
concept pop art and the band saw as an attention-getting goof, confused
everyone (political theory and the Dolls made no sense at all) and
the shows, with Jerry Nolan and Arthur Kane partly sidelined due to
substance-abuse issues, were not the group's finest moments. A few
weeks later, on a final, cursed tour of Florida, the group finally exploded,
after a feud in a Tampa trailer park over Jerry Nolan's mom's dinner table. Thunders and Nolan, junk buddies who didn't like being away from
their New York City sources, headed straight to the airport.

After landing in New York, Thunders rang up Richard Hell. In a
few weeks, with Nolan, they had a new band called the Heartbreakers.
Looking for a second guitarist, the band got together with Blondie's
Chris Stein. They jammed, but nothing came of it.[15]

Saturday night, March 15, Felt Forum, early show. Al Green is falling
apart onstage. "You playin' too loud for me," he castigates his band. "I
want to be able to *relate* to the people." Later: "We'd like to stop for five
minutes and give honor to the most high." He mumbles a few more dis-
jointed phrases. "Pepsi Cola, man. Pepsi Cola." He leaves the stage after
half an hour and never returns. His face "was contorted," wrote the
critic Wayne Robins, "his mouth twitched, his eyes were glazed." As a
woman in the audience described him, shaking her head ruefully:
"Stoned as a sixteen-year-old."[16]

Two months earlier, a young Caribbean writer named Elaine Cynthia Potter Richardson reviewed Sly and the Family Stone at the first of
a six-night stand at Radio City Music Hall. "Uninspired is the word that

most readily comes to mind," the critic—who had begun calling herself Jamaica Kincaid—wrote in *The Village Voice*. "Sly is not in touch with any kind of new black music even when it's dominated by variations of his old sound." She noted that the crowd seemed much more excited during the opening set by the jazzy Jersey City funk clan Kool and the Gang.[17]

April 2, 3: Four more FALN bombs explode around midnight. One had been planted in the garbage bags outside a Blimpie at 5 West Forty-sixth Street, another by the entrance door of the Met Life building at 340 Park Avenue. Total damage was assessed at around $180,000. No one was injured. Again a typed communiqué was issued by the group, which took responsibility for targeting corporations "at the heart of Yanki imerialism [*sic*]."[18]

April 5: The German electronic group Kraftwerk plays the Beacon Theater, a once-lavish 1920s movie palace on Broadway and Seventy-fourth Street. Their new album, *Autobahn*, with its cool, enginelike rhythms inspired (like Jonathan Richman's "Roadrunner") by the idea of driving as transcendence, is a surprise hit—number 5 on the *Billboard* charts—and is getting local airplay on WNEW-FM. Ralf Hütter and Florian Schneider tell the Detroit journalist Lester Bangs that, of all American music, they are especially fond of the Stooges and the Velvet Underground. Bangs figures these machine-heads are, in some way, the future of rock 'n' roll.

The same month, Jon Gibson, age thirty-five, sat down at the pipe organ in Washington Square Church to perform and record *Cycles*, a waterfall of droning, sustained-tone harmonics. The composer had played at the premiere of Terry Riley's *In C* in '64, with La Monte Young in the Theatre of Eternal Music during the late '60s, and with Steve Reich at the premiere of *Drumming* in '73. Gibson was currently working with Philip Glass on *Einstein on the Beach*. His own music had received far less notice than that of his collaborators. But sitting before the organ, with the huge chords of *Cycles* filling the church, just as they had a year earlier for the work's debut, he felt beatific.[19]

The Patti Smith Group played a double bill with the new Television on Thursday, March 20, just a couple of weeks after the Hippodrome shows. It was the first date of a collaborative seven-week residency for the bands at CBGB—four nights a week, two double-header shows a night. Aside from a one-off in February, these were the first gigs Smith had played at the club, although she'd hung out there frequently since she and Lenny Kaye had first caught Television there nearly a year ago. Her star was ascendant: the *Voice* put an inset photo of her on the cover—a close-up of her declaiming at the annual St. Mark's Poetry Project benefit back in January—and record companies were courting.

Smith's trio—with Kaye on guitar and Richard Sohl on piano—had been performing only once or twice a month at cabarets like Reno Sweeney, and at Max's, where she'd done a weekend double bill with Television last summer. They played a few dates in California, including an audition night at San Francisco's Winterland, where, according to legend, Jonathan Richman sat in on drums. Smith and Kaye knew they needed to get a drummer and woodshed if they wanted to make a good record. Between gigs, they rehearsed in an office space rented by Smith's manager, Jane Friedman, behind a billboard on Forty-sixth Street off Times Square. Smith kept writing poems. She hung out at the local laundromat—a place she found comforting—doing her and Allen Lanier's clothes. And she attended Television gigs, handing Verlaine flowers onstage. Debbie Harry once caught them kissing out on Extra Place, the alley behind CBGB.[20]

The Patti Smith–Television shows put CBGB on the map. The lyrical attitude was new, snarling and diffident. And while the music was aggressive, it was also kind of psychedelic. With Hell out of the mix, Television's finest moments became songs like "Marquee Moon" and "Little Johnny Jewel," with lyrical guitar solos that could push them past the ten-minute mark. Smith's band, too, played songs that would stretch into vast improvisatory spaces that Kaye calls "fields."

"They were areas in which the song could find out what direction it wanted to move in," he said in 2005 in his Brooklyn apartment near the foot of the Manhattan Bridge. On the living room worktable is a Macintosh computer and a synthesizer keyboard. Kaye makes a pot of strong black tea in the kitchen, and, sitting at an old Formica table, talks about the past with astonishing recall.

"That seven-week stand was the first continuous gig we ever had.

We could play the songs four nights a week—Television and us alternated opening and closing the sets. It gave us a kind of continuum to have the songs grow, to add a little emphasis or syncopation or a chord, and then be able to remember them the next night without writing them down or even speaking about them."

As if making an extended piece of performance art, night after night that spring, the two groups hung out and played, '60s boundlessness and '70s nihilism ravishing each other in a dark and dingy room. On a bootleg dated April 17, the final weekend, Television's new bassist, Fred Smith, holds down a frantic version of "Foxhole" while the guitarists explode chords around him. Billy Ficca's drums charge across a cover of the 13th Floor Elevators' "Fire Engine," Verlaine whispering "Let me take you to the empty place" over hushed riffs that ratchet up along with his hysteria. On "Venus," he squeals about falling into, and walking out of, the Venus de Milo's arms like he is having a panic attack. Was Patti Venus? "I remember how the darkness doubled," he yelps on "Marquee Moon," stretching lines into unintelligibility, the double guitar lines sloppy, sweaty, as inevitable as a closing-time make-out session.

Smith now had Ivan Kral as bassist and second guitarist, and the CBGB soundman, Jay Dee Daugherty, drummer for the Mumps, began sitting in occasionally. Her set on that recording begins with the Velvet Underground's "We're Gonna Have a Real Good Time Together," a gimme-the-torch declaration of aesthetic solidarity. Sohl pounds the keys, Kaye and Kral grind out the rhythms, Patti sings about smack uptown, yelling "Shoot, shoot" like a gangster moll or a junkie cheerleader, an abstract correlative to Richard Hell's homemade "Please Kill Me" bull's-eye T-shirt. Then the sexy "Redondo Beach" with just Sohl's piano, the guys ooh-oohing like street-corner doo-woppers. Patti's goofy, free-associative banter—something about Martians and the Mets—and then she goes dead serious, with no segue between the absurd and the appalling. "The French let Jean Genet out of prison, but the Americans left Wilhelm Reich to die in his. So every day, his little son Peter would go looking for his dad at night to come back down to get him on a big black UFO . . . Oh . . . Oh . . . Oh . . . Oh . . ," she incants over blue piano chords, and glides into the lament "Birdland," Kaye's and Kral's guitars weeping gently, then then spiraling into fury.

And then "Distant Fingers," about long-distance love, perhaps Martian love. Daugherty is sitting in now, cymbals shimmering. "Me and

Allen Lanier wrote that one; me and a generation wrote this one," Smith
says to introduce her reconstruction of Van Morrison's "Gloria," framed by
the line "Jesus died for somebody's sins, but not mine," from a poem she
had been declaiming since her first performance with Kaye at St. Mark's
Church four years earlier. She unspools lust for a sweet young thing she
spies from the window of a dull party, a girl leaning on a parking meter.
She spits the phrase "Anything's allowed" as both challenge and statement of incontrovertible fact, the band building steam slowly until she
begins spelling the girl's name, shifting into the 1964 Them B-side, the
guitarists locking gears on the chorus, then shifting back to her own
poetic reverie, then back into "Gloria," claiming it like a lover, spelling
the name one last time: G-L-O-R-I-A. Then yelling out "Them!"—a
final gesture of respect—before the song slams the history book shut, a
new line scrawled into it like fat-tip marker graffiti.

Word got out, lines grew around the block. Journalists came and
crowed, bizzers sniffed. Lou Reed, ghostly pale and rail thin, came one
night with his friend Clive Davis—former president of Columbia Records, where he signed Springsteen and Iggy Pop, now head of the deep-
pocketed Arista. Davis would return again during the run, and by the
time it was over Patti Smith had a deal: seven albums, $750,000, full
creative control over releases and media campaigns.

For everyone on the CBGB scene, the stakes were now completely
different.

Miles Davis had toured the world through the end of '74 and into '75.
Drug problems notwithstanding, he was making powerful music. On
February 1, during a string of Japanese dates, he played two shows of
ferocious large-group improvs at Osaka Festival Hall, later released on
the LPs *Agharta* and *Pangaea*—writhing masses of organ, wah-wah guitar licks, funk bass, salsa-style congas, fat rock drum grooves, and voicelike, electrically mutated trumpet. Yet the jazz community had largely
thrown up their hands. You could read the prevailing attitude toward
Miles's new music on a poster advertising a Carnegie Hall program on
February 15: "The New York Jazz Repertory Company Plays the Music
of Miles Davis 1950–1965."

The trumpeter spent most of the spring in the hospital, then toured—
embarrassingly enough—as the opening act for his former sideman

Herbie Hancock. By June, Miles had decided to stop playing. He had "nothing else to say musically," he declared.[21]

> Cecil Taylor packing them into the Five Spot for three solid
> weeks! Cecil Taylor playing encores to get off the stand! Cecil
> Taylor—iconoclast, super-avant-gardist, mysterioso pianist—a
> matinee idol! Incredible but true.
>
> —Whitney Balliett, *The New Yorker*

The best jazz radio in town was still WRVR, an ex-public station supported primarily by the Riverside Church and other donors until '71, when it went commercial. Its MVP was Ed Beach, a self-confessed "third-rate" jazz pianist who had left Portland, Oregon, for New York to try to make it as an actor before finding his true calling. By 1975, he'd been at the station nearly fifteen years, and during his shows—the thematic "Just Jazz," or the 10:00 a.m. to 2:00 p.m. slot he held down that spring—he'd unspool backstory and value judgments about records like a firebrand soloist with a sixteen-bar window. No one in New York had ever presented jazz quite like this before. But things had begun to shift in February when the station, which had given programmers pretty free rein, instituted a play pattern policy, mandating some "commercial jazz" and soul every hour. Fiscal problems mounted, and there were rumors of the station's demise.[22]

However, WRVR played little of the music being forged in the city's loft scene. The big news in 1975 was that Steve Backer, A&R man and producer for Impulse! during Coltrane's years, had convinced Clive Davis to bankroll progressive jazz as part of his new label. While Arista's initial titles were mostly reclamations of older recordings (by Albert Ayler, Marion Brown, Julius Hemphill), Backer got funding for new projects, too. "We signed the Brecker Brothers to pay the bills, and people like Larry Coryell and Steve Khan," says the producer Michael Cuscuna, Backer's project partner. "Then we signed a lot of very avant-garde guys—Anthony Braxton, Oliver Lake, Air."

Cuscuna had a track record as an advocate of far-out jazz; he'd helped sign the Art Ensemble of Chicago to Atlantic Records during his tenure there, after being floored by the band's performance at a festival he'd been asked to record. "I brought the tape back to [the producer]

Joel Dorn at Atlantic and said, 'I wanna sign this band. In fact I want to put this out, this whole set,'" Cuscuna said. "So Dorn went to Nesuhi Ertegun's apartment, and was smart enough to give Nesuhi a joint before he listened to it. And Nesuhi just said, 'Absolutely! This is great! Reminds me of the first time I heard Ornette Coleman. Go ahead, do it!'"[23]

It's amusing that Braxton, generally regarded as the most forebodingly oblique of the era's jazz avant-gardists, was among the first to land a major-label contract—after all, this was the guy who released a double LP of unaccompanied solo sax improvs (the 1969 landmark For Alto) and whose graphic song titles often resembled molecular geometry. Where many of his peers dressed like African royalty, Anthony Braxton came on like a professor: a handsome, pipe-smoking, light-brown-skinned gentleman with an unkempt Afro, muttonchop sideburns, and round wire-rimmed glasses. He had grown up in '50s Chicago on Elvis, Chuck Berry, and the Platters, studied clarinet, and got turned on to Miles and Brubeck. Serving in Korea, he played in army bands; he heard Coltrane's Ascension, listened to the music of Ayler, Cage, and Schoenberg. Back in Chicago he got involved with the Association for the Advancement of Creative Musicians (AACM), a progressive black cultural group shepherded primarily by the pianist Muhal Richard Abrams and which included the future core of the Art Ensemble of Chicago.

Like many American art mavericks before him, Braxton decided to try Europe. As the composer and AACM historian George Lewis writes in A Power Stronger Than Itself, it's unclear which AACM faction had the idea first. The Art Ensemble crew—the trumpeter Lester Bowie, the singer (and Bowie's wife) Fontella Bass, the saxophonists Roscoe Mitchell and Joseph Jarman, and the bassist Malachi Favors—set off to Paris in May 1969, followed a number of weeks later by Braxton, the violinist Leroy Jenkins, and the trumpeter Leo Smith. There was definitely competition in the air. The latter trio, which became a quartet in France with the addition of the expat AACM drummer Steve McCall, were less theatrical and political in their presentation than the Art Ensemble, and liked to play with tropes of European classical music (they were so geeky they became known as "the slide-rule boys"). The Art Ensemble made flamboyantly jump-cut music whose logic was more

like a film soundtrack than serialist composition, with some Dada gestures thrown in for kicks; their groundbreaking 1970 *Les Stances à
Sophie* was in fact a film soundtrack. As Lewis described their approach:

> The music of "l'école de Chicago" had broken sharply with the
> sustained high-energy performances that characterized 1960s
> free jazz. Quick changes of mood were the rule, ranging from
> the reverent to the ludic. A quiet, sustained, "spiritual" texture
> offered by one musician might be rudely interrupted by an ah-
> ooh-gah horn or a field holler from another. A New Orleans–
> style brass fanfare would quickly be dunked in a roiling sea of
> tuned metal trash cans. An ironically demented fake-bebop
> theme could be cut up into a series of miniatures, punctuated
> by long silences and derisively terminated by a Marx Brothers
> raspberry . . . No sound was excluded and no tradition was sac-
> rosanct, and French audiences and the jazz press quickly fell in
> love with the ruptures and surprises.[24]

Struggling soul brothers in Chicago, the musicians were stars in
Paris. They shared festival stages with rock bands, including a Black
Panther benefit with the Anglo-French psychedelic tribe Gong. The
competition didn't splinter the musicians; Braxton sometimes sat in
with the Art Ensemble, and for a time they all lived together, hippie-
style, in a farmhouse on the outskirts of Paris—until locals, fearing the
foment of black revolution, told them it was time to move on.

When they were ready to take their music back to America, the
players decamped to New York. And just as Philly soul jump-started
disco culture and Detroit's Stooges inspired punk, Chicago's AACM
crew profoundly shaped the New York loft jazz sound.

Stateside, Braxton moved in with Ornette Coleman, and made money
as a chess hustler on the concrete boards in Washington Square Park.
He saw himself increasingly as a composer, and for a while he stopped
playing altogether. He began working with Chick Corea (yet another
ex-Miles sideman) in the quartet Circle. But soon Corea turned his attention to a new group, Return to Forever, a Brazilian-jazz experiment
that turned into a fusion juggernaut. By the time Braxton was signed in

1974, he was exploding with ideas; now he had the means to realize them. For his first Arista sessions that fall, he recorded with a quartet featuring the trumpeter Kenny Wheeler, the bassist Dave Holland, and the drummer Jerome Cooper, adding the violinist Leroy Jenkins (who led his own New York trio, the Revolutionary Ensemble, with Cooper and Sirone). Another session paired him with the Moog player Richard Teitelbaum. A third gathered Julius Hemphill on alto, Oliver Lake on tenor, and Hamiet Bluiett on baritone—a grouping that, swapping out Braxton for the young L.A. expat David Murray, went on to become the World Saxophone Quartet.

Braxton's Arista debut, *New York, Fall 1974*, was released in March 1975, hot on the heels of a standards set on the Steeplechase label, *In the Tradition* (which he dedicated to Roche Pharmaceuticals, makers of Valium, a drug he subsisted on to control his anxiety). Yet even the abstract originals on *Fall 1974* weren't entirely out of the tradition. *Opus 23B*, otherwise known as:

$$6 \text{———} 77AR\text{-}\text{-}36K$$
$$|$$
$$(NJD)$$
$$|$$
$$T$$

was impressionistic bop that the composer described as "an atonal version" of Charlie Parker's "Donna Lee." Braxton's subsequent Arista LP, *Five Pieces 1975*, would include a playful read on "You Stepped out of a Dream"; later releases deconstructed "Maple Leaf Rag" and "Giant Steps." Braxton was hardly ignorant of jazz tradition, but he had a restless imagination. He did what he liked—and, among other things, he liked to wind folks up.[25]

At this point, Braxton had relocated two hours upstate to the old artists' colony of Woodstock, a Catskills town where classical, jazz, and pop musicians had long retreated to settle minds, tend souls, and court muses. He became intimately involved with the Creative Music Studio, a musicians' retreat and think tank founded by the German expat vibraphonist Karl Berger; his partner, the singer Ingrid Sertso; and, nominally, Berger's friend and aesthetic comrade Ornette Coleman. (Berger recalls Coleman's quip on agreeing to sign on as cofounder: "You handle

the not-for-profit part. I'm more interested in the for-profit.") CMS became a woodsy outpost of the city's loft scene, a sort of new-jazz ashram,
developing a tradition of freely improvised music that aspired, among other
things, to draw every form of world music into its vocabulary.

In a house on Chestnut Hill Road, surrounded by old-growth forest,
in a light-filled rehearsal space, with a woodstove at one end and a chess
board (with clock) at the ready for downtimes, Braxton and his cohorts
worked on their modern music, the birds and bullfrogs sitting in. The
composer had a swivel chair surrounded by four music stands, each
holding a work in progress. When he was writing, he would spin from
one to another as the ideas came to him.

Arista wasn't the only major label trying to market the new jazz. Im-
pulse!, the ABC Records subsidiary, released Sam Rivers's remarkable
Crystals in February, with Rivers playing tenor, soprano, and flute, lead-
ing a group of eleven additional horn players plus bass and percussion.
But the greatest activity was among new indie labels, following in the
DIY footsteps of Sun Ra's El Saturn label, which he had incorporated in
Philly in 1956, and ESP-Disk', the New York label that released Albert
Ayler's pioneering records in the mid-'60s.[26] Strata-East was started
in '71 by the Florida-born trumpeter Charles Tolliver and the Ohio-born
pianist Stanley Cowell, charting a middle ground between free jazz and
tradition; they released Gil Scott-Heron's *Winter in America* in '74, along
with *Celebrations and Solitudes*, a kindred fusion of jazz and firebrand
poetry by Ornette Coleman's ex-wife, Jayne Cortez, and bassist Richard
Davis. The Bronx-born drummer Steve Reid started his own Mustevic
label in '72, releasing sets by his Legendary Master Brotherhood group
and others. Bob Cummins, a corporate lawyer and major jazz fan, began
the India Navigation label in '72 as well. It devoted itself almost entirely
to new jazz being made in New York; its riveting first release was by the
Revolutionary Ensemble.

Then there were European labels. Steeplechase was started by a
Danish student, Nils Winther, who used a study grant to press up some
Jackie McLean LPs in '72; the label put out records by Braxton and
helped relaunch the careers of Andrew Hill and Dexter Gordon, the
latter long expatriated in Paris. Black Saint, launched in Italy by the
well-heeled jazz fan Giacomo Pelliciotti in '75, became a hugely impor-

tant label for the loft scene. To a lesser extent, so did the short-lived Whynot, begun the same year by Masahiko Yuh, a Japanese business-man who fell hard for the Chicago school before setting his sights on New York. The indie labels owed a tremendous amount to Carla Bley and Michael Mantler, jazz musicians who founded the Jazz Composers' Orchestra Association and the New Music Distribution Service (NMDS), which helped small labels get their sounds into shops; Philip Glass's Chatham Square Records was also among their clients. The commer-cial prospects for this music were minimal, after all; the history of labels screwing musicians was long, and the '60s spirit of self-determination, black and otherwise, still held sway. It was a DIY world.

For his part, Rashied Ali was running Ali's Alley at 77 Greene Street, in the ground-floor space below his loft apartment, leading a group there nearly every weekend with the bassist Benny Wilson and a rotating cast of pianists: Hilton Ruiz, Andrew Hill, John Hicks, Charles Eubanks. In partnership with the saxophonist Frank Lowe, Ali ran his own label, too, Survival Records. The drummer had some basic re-cording equipment and rolled tape at the club whenever possible, stock-piling boxes of quarter-inch reels in his cabinets. He was a self-contained jazz culture factory.

On June 19, the club's first anniversary, Ali was recording. His group featured the alto saxophonist Jimmy Vass, Marvin Blackman on tenor, and the singer Royal Blue, a talented, eccentric young bluesman with drink and woman trouble. That night he unfurled his chocolaty, aching tenor over Eubanks's loose comps and Ali's skittery, swinging pulse—tradition locking horns with the moment.

"New York ain't so bad," Royal Blue sang. "Where you gonna go, anyway?"

That same weekend, Charles Mingus played at the Bottom Line. A new group, Talking Heads, played a double bill with the Ramones at CBGB. In its *Voice* ad that week, the club invited local bands to audi-tion for a "rock festival," which would begin on July 16.

Billy Cobham, a Panamanian who moved to New York as a kid, was a monster drummer, a speed demon and powerhouse who got his start with Miles and made his name with the Mahavishnu Orchestra. Cob-ham played open-handed: he didn't cross his arms when playing the snare/hi-hat combo—the common approach—but hurled himself into them arms open. He could swing; he could rock; he could play in clave, as he did with the Fania All-Stars at Yankee Stadium in '73; and he could play huge grooves, as he did on his '75 solo record *A Funky Thide of Sings.* He wasn't so good at laying back, which is one reason he wound up as a bandleader.

Joseph Saddler had grown up in the Bronx listening to all kinds of music. His sister loved salsa. His dad was a jazz fan. So it isn't that surprising that, after months of studying Kool Herc's technique, a drum break by Cobham would catch his ear.

By this time, Saddler's mom had kicked him out of the house. He was eighteen, his girlfriend was pregnant, he had a crappy job delivering fabric in Manhattan, and he took his paychecks to Uncle Nick at Downstairs Records—the disco and oldies shop in the subway arcade at Sixth Avenue at Forty-second Street where Herc got his music—and spent most of his earnings on obscure grooves. Then he'd hole up at home and practice his turntable technique.

It was with "A Funky Kind of Thing," the nine-minute drum solo on Cobham's album, that he perfected it. He bought two copies of the record, and tried to quick-cut between the end of a break on one copy and the beginning on the other by syncing them together. "Finally," he recalled in his autobiography, "I found a way to start the first record with my hand physically on the vinyl itself. The platter would turn but the music wouldn't play because the needle wouldn't be traveling through the groove. However, when I took my hand off the record . . . BAM!" He'd flick the fader switch, and after many tries, the beats matched up.

Soon he refined the process by tracing the length of the breakbeat on the surface of a record using a grease pencil while the record spun, so he could see exactly where it began and ended. Then he moved from extending a single break to jump-cutting between breaks. And sometimes, when spinning a record backward by hand to cue it up, he'd throw the fader and catch the *zhuk* of the backspin through the speaker, just before releasing the record to play the beat. Sometimes he'd move the record back and forth a few times, for dramatic effect, before letting the record go.

You couldn't really call it scratching. That creative leap was made later. Saddler had a protégé, Gene Livingston, who would help him warm up the crowd at gigs. But Gene couldn't get the hang of Saddler's new moves. "I really wanted him to learn this technique so that we could go out as a team and introduce this new style of DJing all throughout the city," Saddler wrote. "I tried showing him over and over and over again, countless times, and he just could not understand what it was that I was doing."[27]

Neither, it seems, could Saddler's audience. When he debuted his new beat-juggling style at a party at 23 Park on 166th Street and Tinton Avenue, a crowd of hundreds just stood there and looked at him. He went home and cried.

But Theodore Livingston, Gene's younger brother, understood. He hung with Saddler, studied his techniques, and wound up taking Gene's place. Theodore debuted alongside Saddler at the P.S. 63 school yard on Boston Road at 169th Street, by which time Saddler had learned to read an audience, and folks had warmed to his style. The crowd went wild for Saddler—now becoming known as Grandmaster Flash via his graffiti tag, Flash 163, which came from his street number plus his childhood nickname, acquired by being fast and being a Flash Gordon fan.

The crowd liked Theodore, too, who was like a mini-Flash. But like any real artist, he had to define his own style. One day Livingston was at home practicing when his mother banged on his door and asked him to turn the volume down. He stopped the record with his hand to speak to her, then began moving it back and forth. "Flash invented this way of rubbing a record," Livingston recalled, "but he usually just rubbed it once and let it go. What I did was give it a rhythm; I made a tune out of it, rubbing it for three, four minutes, making it a scratch."

The first time he tried it for a crowd was at the Sparkle on Mount Eden and Jerome avenues, where Herc played regularly. "I wanted to do something different with this record 'Johnny the Fox' by Thin Lizzy," Livingston said. "I'd play the drum part over and over. People were like, 'Whoa!'"[28]

And as Saddler became Grandmaster Flash, Livingston became Grand Wizard Theodore, sometimes adding an extra z to his honorific— Wizzard—for flavor.

It was hard to decide who was the cutest. Perhaps *cute* is the wrong word; *magnetic* is better. The boy singer was tall, wiry, and nervous, as if the electricity going through the pickup on his acoustic guitar was also short-circuiting through his body. He had thick eyebrows and remarkably hairy forearms. The girl was petite and blond with a page-boy haircut that made her faintly androgynous. Her bass, a short-scaled Fender Mustang that she'd bought on layaway at We Buy Guitars on Forty-eighth, dwarfed her even so, but she made it percolate. When she played, she stared at the boy with a combination of rapt attention and fascination, as if she were watching a strange, engaging TV show.

Some things written about David Byrne that may be true: Growing up in Baltimore, Byrne played ukulele. He knew all ten verses of Dylan's "Desolation Row" by heart, and bought the Beatles' *Let It Be* the week it was released in 1970. He got into both the Massachusetts Institute of Technology and the Rhode Island School of Design in Providence, and chose the latter, casting his vote for art. He stayed a year, dropped out, lived briefly with an old girlfriend on a commune in Kentucky called the Flying Frog Farm. He moved back to his hometown, hung in a crowd that shadowed the filmmaker John Waters, and became friendly with Edith the Egg Lady from Waters's *Pink Flamingos*. He went to California, then moved back to Providence. He became friendly with an RISD film student named Gus Van Sant. He smoked pot, played violin, and got into performance art with some friends. In one piece, he cut himself while shaving his face, dripping blood onstage like Iggy Pop. He joined a band called the Artistics, nicknamed the Autistics, writing songs and playing guitar. He performed the song "Psycho Killer" for the first time on Valentine's Day 1974, at an RISD masquerade ball.

Tina Weymouth was a Catholic girl, the daughter of a navy man who eventually became an admiral. She grew up all over: San Diego, Hawaii, Switzerland, Belgium, France, Washington, D.C. She spent time at Barnard, dropped out, and transferred to RISD. She graduated in August '74. She aspired to be a painter, but got discouraged and gave it up.

Weymouth's boyfriend, also an aspiring painter, was Chris Frantz, who had seen the Beatles on *Ed Sullivan* and been impressed by Ringo. He played drums with the Artistics, moved to New York with Tina in the fall of '74, saw the Ramones with her at CBGB, and convinced Byrne to start another band. They couldn't find a bassist who fit their aesthetic bill, so Tina put money down on the used Mustang, and Byrne, eventually, taught her to play. In December '74, Frantz rented a loft space at 195 Chrystie Street—south of Houston and east of the Bowery, a short walk from CBGB—and they all moved in. Rent was $250 a month. They had no refrigerator or stove. Tina bought a hot plate; they stacked perishables outside on the window ledge until the spring thaw, when they bought a mini-fridge. And for the next six months, they practiced. They also thought about their visual style. Dressing like prep school students among the black-leather downtown decadents fit nicely with what was shaping up to be as much of a conceptual art project as a band.

Talking Heads played their first show on June 5 at CBGB. Headlining were the Ramones. The middle act was the Mumps, a glammy rock band fronted by Lance Loud, a gay man who became famous in early '73 when the pioneering reality-television show *An American Family*, filmed in '71, began its twelve-episode run on public television. The series, centering on the collapse of his parents' marriage and on Loud's sexuality, was set in California. Shortly after it aired, Loud lit out to New York with some high school friends, including Jay Dee Daugherty, joined the outcast-celebrity demimonde at Max's, and started a band.

As far as anyone recalls, Talking Heads' first song of their first gig was "The Girls Want to Be with the Girls." The title seems a classic rock 'n' roll predicament—an exasperated guy venting his inability to get with the ladies. In part it's about sexual inarticulateness: "And the boys say, 'What do you meeeean?'" sings Byrne on a demo recorded that year, in a spasmodically high-strung, emotionally ambiguous sing-talk—it isn't quite clear whether the "boys" are requesting clarification, or are outraged at being rebuffed at first base. Yet the alienation in his tone is visceral, scarier in its way than "Psycho Killer."[29] As for the music, the band sounded like a cross between the Modern Lovers and Television minus the latter's guitar sparks: strangulated vocals, rudimentary bass lines, and martial little-drummer-boy beats that hinted at soul music. Byrne had just turned twenty-three; Tina and Chris were twenty-four.

Reaction was mixed. Suicide's Alan Vega disliked the new band. ("[Byrne] didn't make any twitchy gestures without something in his head saying, 'Make a twitchy gesture now,'" he said. "It always turned me off."[30]) Lenny Kaye appreciated their sneaky rhythmic ties to R&B. The Artistics had covered R&B classics—Al Green's "Love and Happiness," Smokey Robinson's "Tears of a Clown"—and Frantz and Weymouth were serious fans of funk and groove music. An early version of "The Book I Read" had a rhythm guitar bridge that echoed the '74 disco hits "Rock the Boat" and "Rock Your Baby." Frantz wrote an instrumental based on a salsa rhythm that he cheekily dubbed "Atom a Bomba." Byrne listened to everything. On Monday nights, he'd often check out Salsa Meets Jazz, the long-running cross-genre jam session up at the Village Gate.

In terms of sexual presentation, Weymouth was halfway between CBGB's other two great heroines, the scrappily boyish Patti Smith and the ur-feminine Debbie Harry. Byrne, Tom Verlaine's rival for New York rock's sexiest neck, would become the third of CBGB's lanky matinee idols, along with Joey Ramone.

Hilly Kristal liked Talking Heads, and invited the band to play all three nights the next weekend. Paired with the Ramones on double bills, they were the hyperanxious Manhattan yin to their roaring-id Queens yang.

In Times Square, Bruce Springsteen was recording his follow-up to *The Wild, the Innocent & the E Street Shuffle*—a great record that, by the go-for-the-gold standards of Columbia, was another flop. He'd been working on it for a year and a half. All he had to show for it was one finished track.

It was a good one: "Born to Run." The suits at Columbia weren't especially impressed with it—they needed an album, and in any case, their belief in Springsteen's ability to sell records had pretty much evaporated. But the song bought Springsteen some time. Hoping to generate hype, his manager-producer Mike Appel sent bootleg cassettes of "Born to Run" to thirty radio stations around the country that had been supportive in the past. Suddenly, the song was on heavy rotation in major markets—but no one could buy it. The label was livid. The enthusiasm, however, convinced them that maybe, if they gave Springsteen time and money enough to finish the album, there might be a decent payoff.

By now, the band that recorded "Born to Run" in '74 no longer existed. The keyboardist David Sancious was offered a contract to make jazz-fusion records with his own group, Tone, and Springsteen's drummer, Ernest "Boom" Carter, joined him. So like any bar-band musician looking for players, Springsteen placed an ad in the *Voice*. After sixty auditions he got a new keyboardist, Roy Bittan, a seasoned player from Far Rockaway; and a drummer, Max Weinberg, a Broadway pit professional weaned on rock and happy to jump ship. It is worth nothing that both new recruits had done time in religious-rock musicals: *Jesus Christ Superstar* and *Godspell*, respectively.

They were now mired in endless retakes, endless overdubs, and endless second-guessing by Springsteen of every song the band played. This was make-or-break time. Another record that sold like the first two, and he was certain he'd be dropped by Columbia. He sweated every detail. By May, his new bandmates were broken in.

There was a new coproducer, too. *Rolling Stone*'s Jon Landau had been coming to Springsteen's shows regularly ever since the Harvard Square Theater show he'd written about last year; in fact, Landau had seen the live premiere of "Born to Run" that night, which the singer included knowing that the *Rolling Stone* critic would be in the house. The two became fast friends; Springsteen would crash at Landau's apartment on East Fifty-seventh Street when he was in town late and didn't want to take the bus back to New Jersey. They would stay up all night talking music, listening to records. Landau was thrilled to be participating, however indirectly, in the music-making process, as opposed to simply judging it from afar; Springsteen, desperate to make a great album, was thrilled to have the input of the most powerful rock critic in America. Together, they decided that Springsteen and Appel needed another set of ears. Appel was not pleased, but he deferred, and by April, Landau was officially signed on.

Landau convinced Bruce to move the session from the dinky but inexpensive 914 Studios in Blauvelt to the Record Plant, the state-of-the-art facility at 321 West Forty-fourth Street, between Eighth and Ninth Avenues, where Todd Rudgren produced the first New York Dolls LP. The engineer was Jimmy Iovine, a coolheaded twenty-two-year-old from Red Hook, Brooklyn. With the only acceptable outcome a Record for the Ages, they all worked around the clock, often to the point of delirium, eventually stumbling into the morning light or passing out with their heads on the mixing console.

"The album became a monster," Springsteen later told Landau's *Rolling Stone* colleague Dave Marsh. "It wanted everything. It just ate up everyone's life."

The single "Born to Run," completed in Blauvelt, is an example of its early appetite, a song bulked up layer by layer like a Phil Spector production on steroids; the final version included piano, organ synthesizer, Fender Rhodes, multiple electric and acoustic guitars, bass, sax, a string ensemble, choral vocals, tambourines, drums, and an indelible glockenspiel. Clarence Clemons's epic sax solo at the end of "Jungleland," completed at the Record Plant, was the fruit of a sixteen-hour recording session during which Springsteen helped Clemons chisel each note, and the two men resisted the urge to strangle each other.

Another logjam was the brass arrangement, or lack thereof, for "Tenth Avenue Freeze-Out." Two of the highest-paid session horn players in New York, the brothers Randy and Michael Brecker, had been hired, and there they were, stuck, staring at sketchy charts that no one was happy with. As it happened, "Miami" Steve Van Zandt, Springsteen's former bandmate and Asbury Park crony, had come into the city to record backing vocals. As the story goes, he cocked his straw fedora, pimp-rolled into the studio, told the pair to ditch the charts, and sang a Stax/Volt-style horn part. They played it back at him. It was perfect. The band had a new member. The work ground on.

That June, Patti Smith took LSD for the very first time with her acid-loving compadre Robert Mapplethorpe. "It was at the time of a garbage strike, and I recall thinking there was a lot of corruption in the world. Robert said, 'Patti, it's supposed to make you feel *good*.' Instead, I felt like John Brown. I felt like all around was filth and corruption." They walked down Christopher Street and saw the leather men and drag queens cavorting. For all Smith's fascination with decadence, this was a disturbing scene for a first acid trip.[31]

The imagery stuck with her as she rehearsed her band that summer, in a practice space just two blocks from where Springsteen was recording. Smith would return to Electric Lady Studios in the fall to make her debut LP, and she wanted to be ready. She filed her farewell piece for *Creem*, and it ran in the June issue: a rambling prose poem that described her rain-soaked pilgrimage to Jim Morrison's grave in Paris, where she sat until she was ready to head home to make her own music, "to focus my floodlight on the rhythm within."

In Connecticut, Thurston Moore read the piece. He was sixteen, and he worried that an era was ending before he'd even gotten a proper taste.[32]

In Queens, Russell Simmons graduated August Martin High School in June. He wanted to be an entrepreneur. He'd stopped running with gangs, and was enrolled in City College for the fall as a sociology major. He didn't like being broke. So he spent the summer the way he'd spent most of the past year, selling weed on the corner of Hollis Avenue and 205th Street. He did very good business.[33]

In late June, the Stones played a weeklong run at Madison Square Garden. To judge from most accounts, or from the long-circulating *Discover New York* bootleg, they remained the Greatest Rock 'n' Roll Band in the World. But like Dylan's comeback shows last year, they showed gods somewhat diminished. The great slide guitarist Mick Taylor had left the band in December (replaced by Ron Wood of the Faces), and while the Richards/Wyman/Watts engine remained awesomely powerful, Jagger had become less a Satanic majesty than a superhero court jester. "Mick plays that masterpiece of lubricity 'Star Star' for yuks," wrote a disappointed Ellen Willis about the opening night show in *The New Yorker*, "sparring with an inflated phallic prop that looks like Casper the Friendly Ghost." The same night, they played "Sympathy for the Devil" for the first time in the United States since Altamont, a mythic moment undercut, in Willis's estimation, by the addition of a steel drum battery and a guest guitar solo by Eric Clapton. Yet on the following Friday, per another bootleg recording, the band achieved evil beatitude with the trifecta of "Midnight Rambler," "Rip This Joint," and "Street Fighting Man."

The previous night, Patti Smith achieved her own beatitude on Bleecker Street. The '60s folk-scene chapel the Bitter End had reopened as the Other End, and Patti was working the flip side of her Dylan fixation—the Stones. It was a last-minute booking, a fill-in for Ronee Blakley, who had made the cover of *Newsweek* for her role in Robert Altman's just-released masterpiece *Nashville*. During her second set, Smith unbuttoned her black silk blouse to display a white T-shirt bearing an image of Keith Richards's head. She sang "Time Is on My Side" with Lenny Kaye slashing the melody and their new drummer, Jay Dee Daugherty, doing a ramshackle Charlie Watts.

Halfway through the chorus, Bob Dylan slipped into the club and took a seat in the back. He wore a striped T-shirt and a thin black leather jacket; he had a scrubby beard and his curly hair hung shoulder length. Smith recognized him, but played it cool. Between songs, she flirted in code, free-associating off of Dylan verses. "You got a lotta nerve sayin' you won't be *my* parking meter," she declared, then tore into "Break It Up" and "Piss Factory," closing with a possessed version of "Gloria," her bum-rush up Mount Olympus, in which a girl leans come-hither on the parking meter Dylan once warned his generation to watch.

Dylan stuck his head in the dressing room afterwards, a madhouse of journalists and photographers.

"Any poets around here?"

"I don't like poetry anymore," Smith blurted. "Poetry sucks!"

They talked about her band, the way her musicians followed her freestyle word flights.

"I wish I would have stayed with just one group," Dylan said. "If I'd had the same group all this time, how well we would have known the ins and outs of each other." The experience of reworking *Blood on the Tracks* at the eleventh hour was still fresh.

The photographers snapped away, telling them to move closer to each other. Smith laughed, pushing Dylan away. "Fuck you . . . take my picture, boys!" Then she put her arm around him and posed. He put his arms around her; they beamed at each other. Smith felt she had passed an initiation.

Dylan was cruising old haunts, untethered. He'd just turned thirty-four. He went to see the Stones at the Garden the following night. Pictures of his summit with Smith made the covers of both the *Voice* and the *Soho News.*

Smith ran into him near her apartment on MacDougal Street a week later. She was feeling self-conscious about how she'd acted with him after her show; she felt she had come off as a jerk.

Dylan grinned and brandished a copy of the *Voice* cover. "Who are these two people? You know who these people are?"[34]

On Saturday of the July Fourth weekend, the Ramones and Blondie played CBGB, while Dylan, Smith, Tom Verlaine, and Bob Neuwirth (who'd befriended Smith some years back) headed over to the Other End for something called "The First Annual Village Folk Festival." Neuwirth played some songs, and he coaxed Dylan onstage. Soon Smith joined Dylan at the piano. Along with a crowd of veteran and latter-day folkies, they sang "Amazing Grace," "Banks of the Ohio," and that chipper suicide threat popularized by the Weavers, "Goodnight, Irene."

Overheard in the audience: "Isn't it amazing, man? It's all happening again. It's just like the sixties. It's all gonna happen again."[35]

No, it wasn't. Neil Young knew that much. The week of the Dylan-Smith summit, Reprise Records released *Tonight's the Night*—maybe Young's greatest record, definitely his rawest, darkest, most toxic. It's about drugs and death and violence and hippie illusions. It's mumbled, muted, caked with feedback, and after the sun-kissed gorgeousness of his mega-hit *Harvest*, it's startlingly, marvelously ugly. More than any other record by a Woodstock-era superstar, it's an unsparing eulogy for the sixties.

A punk record, in its way.

The summer of '75 was hot and wet (a record-breaking twenty-two inches of rain), and the stench in the subway was even fouler than usual. The economy was still stalled, and the city's deficit was estimated at around $3 billion. When Mayor Beame and Governor Carey rode into Washington to ask for $1.5 billion in aid to stave off default, President Ford turned them down.

The drug economy, though, was thriving. On the Lower East Side heroin was shockingly cheap; you could get a bag for two or three dollars. And, as *High Times* magazine confirmed, there was no shortage of high-grade weed around.

Plenty of it was being burned on June 18 as Mayor Beame, courting the city's West Indian community, introduced Bob Marley and the Wailers onstage in Central Park. It was the second show of the season at the Schaefer Music Festival, which was celebrating its tenth anniversary in the park's dilapidated Wollman Skating Rink. With tickets between $1.50 and $2.50, the festival—sponsored by the local beer—was one of the summer's best cheap escapes, with a schedule that generally included a salsa blowout (this year's featured Ray Barretto and Willie Colón), big-ticket jazz fusion (Return to Forever), and various shades of pop, rock, folk, and country. Yet the '75 season was otherwise pretty dull, padded with pop radio acts like Three Dog Night and America, flashbacks like Sha Na Na and Frankie Valli, and various Woodstock Nation B-listers.

Disco music, meanwhile, was everywhere. WPIX-FM had recently remade itself as a 24/7 boogie station ("Disco 102") and clubgoing was a less underground activity. On July 1, around five hundred revelers packed into Le Jardin, in the basement of the Diplomat Hotel on West Forty-third Street near Sixth Avenue, to see the disco don Barry White, who had a hit with "What Am I Gonna Do with You?" in the spring.

Opened two summers back, Le Jardin had become the first truly mixed disco. Gay and straight, black and white, everyone came—and unlike the Gallery and the Loft, it was never membership-only. It was an instant celebrity magnet, with an exclusive rooftop garden. Patti Smith hosted a tribute to her beloved Rimbaud there shortly after it opened in '73. David Johansen and his girlfriend, the Warhol actress Cyrinda Foxe, were fans; Truman Capote raved about the club's fabulousness to Johnny Carson and millions of American viewers on *The Tonight Show*.[36] In time, the cognoscenti moved on, leaving the club to the bridge-and-tunnel crowd, who were happy to have it. It had a booming sound system: 2,000 watts of amplifier power driving eight Bose 901s and two huge bass cabinets. It also had two of the city's great DJs: Bobby Guttadaro and Michael Cappello.

The crowd on July 1 is getting down; the room is steamy, the scent mostly sweat and weed smoke. Dancers wobble, shuffle, shimmy, swoon on blocky platform heels; Davy the quaalude dealer floats through the room. Guttadaro, better known as Bobby DJ, segues into the Ritchie Family's "Brazil"—the summer's samba-spiced, horn-pumped disco anthem—and the crowd hoots wildly. Hands fly up, shirts are yanked off, the beat goes on.

"It takes about an hour to get them up like this, where everyone feels like they're tripping!" Guttadaro yells into the ear of a reporter, trying to be heard over the pummeling beats. "They're so fabulously *hiiigh!*" He grins crazily.

Barry White never shows. Nobody seems to notice.

David Mancuso, still clubless, was fighting a battle with his new neighbors to reopen the Loft at 99 Prince Street. Michael Goldstein, publisher of the *Soho Weekly News* and with business interests in the area, was spearheading a campaign against him, convinced that discos would destroy the "quality of life" in the neighborhood. In his downtime, Mancuso decided to gather his fellow DJs into a defensive power bloc. He used his Prince Street space to launch Record Pool Inc. with writer Vince Aletti and the DJ Steve D'Acquisto—a not-for-profit operation that distributed thousands of records to a membership that, by July, was 162 DJs strong. Theoretically, the Pool DJs exposed new music to around a quarter million clubgoers a week. The labels would have no choice but to deal with them.

Also that summer, Tom Moulton's '74 reference-disc accident became a new standard when Bobby Moore's "Call Me Your Anything Man" was released as a 12-inch promo single, thanks to Moulton's pal Mel Cheren at Scepter Records. The format wouldn't fully take off until the following summer. But turntable DJing would never be the same.[37]

Meanwhile, disco culture had spread beyond New York. Jersey had the Follies in Passaic, the Last Resort in Long Branch, and Players Disco in Union City. There was the Dimples chain (twenty-one clubs around the country, all attached to Emerson Steak Houses). Boston, San Francisco, and L.A. all had growing scenes, and disco records were being made for love and/or money by all sorts of artists: fusion jazzers, salseros, MOR pop stars. In June, the Jackson 5, left for dead, released a disco cover of the Supremes' "Forever Came Today" (with Michael as Diana Ross) that only reached number 60 on the pop charts but topped the dance charts.[38] Fellow vets the Isley Brothers scored with the unusually political "Fight the Power." The collective urge to dance was so powerful, cultural divisions were steamrolled. White dancers flipped for Consumer Rapport's version of *The Wiz*'s "Ease On Down the Road" and Bohannon's "Foot Stompin' Music"; black dancers went crazy for Elton John's "Philadelphia Freedom" and David Bowie's "Fame."[39]

And everyone loved Van McCoy's "The Hustle," which landed in the spring and ruled all summer. The dance it canonized had been around for a few years, in the Latin ballrooms in the Bronx—a sped-up, more freestyle variant of salsa dancing. The song itself was a fluke. Early in the year, McCoy was finishing an instrumental LP at Mediasound studios, which occupied the former Manhattan Baptist Church on West Fifty-seventh Street, when his partner came back from the Adam's Apple disco, over on East Sixty-first, around midnight. He had two wide-eyed dancers with him, who demonstrated the Hustle for

McCoy right there in the church. McCoy worked up the song's groove and signature *doo doo doo / doo doo doo doo doo doo* melody on the spot, and recorded it the next day in his last hours of studio time, the beat driven by the session ace Steve Gadd. (The drummer also concocted the funky groove for Paul Simon's "50 Ways to Leave Your Lover," which followed "The Hustle" to number 1.)[40]

And though it was released last year, you could still hear the mesmerizing synth whine of "Summer Madness," by Jersey City's own Kool and the Gang, wafting out of windows, rising through the humid air like the buzz of cicadas, the ultimate urban chill-out song. It, too, was recorded in that old church on Fifty-seventh Street. Something about that room still brought out the holy.

By the end of the year, the city supported around five hundred discos—a count that probably included some pizzerias with backroom jukeboxes, but still: that's a lot of rooms with people shaking ass in them. Across the nation, the count was estimated at ten thousand and climbing.[41]

Salsoul, nominally the equation of *salsa* plus *soul*, was a small New York indie label run by the Cayre brothers, Joe, Ken, and Stan: a business-minded family of NY-Miami *machers* who were early players in 8-track tape distribution and dealt Mexican music on their Mericana label. When they issued Joe Bataan's *Salsoul* on Mericana in '73—paying him a flat five thousand dollars—it became a club hit, and they saw an opening. They renamed the label, teamed up with Bataan (who, still smarting from his experience with Fania, wisely asked for a 25 percent share), and released the singer's *Afrofilipino* LP the following year. It featured "La Botella," an instrumental cover of Gil Scott-Heron's "The Bottle" with a hot brass section arranged by Springsteen associates the Brecker Brothers and a steam-kettle sax solo by the David Bowie collaborator David Sanborn. If the city's musical revolutions were partly a result of cultural cross-pollination, the session players were often the honeybees.

By March '75, Salsoul had cut a deal with Epic Records for national distribution, with $100,000 up front. The Cayres knew the value of good session men. So they took their nest egg and quickly poached the key players (including the ur-drummer Earl Young) from disco's championship team, the Philadelphia International house band—the force behind MFSB's "Love Is the Message"—to create their own hit machine, the Salsoul Orchestra. Using the advance from Epic, a subsidiary of CBS Records, to hijack musicians from Philly International, also in bed with CBS, may have been impolite. But business is business.

The Latin scene Salsoul emerged from was still indie. Fania remained the talent monopoly; in 1975, every major salsa act recorded for Fania or one of its acquisitions (Vaya, Tico, Allegre), with the notable exception of Eddie Palmieri, still with Harvey Averne's Coco label.[42] In the wake of the Yankee Stadium spectacle, Masucci's label and the Brooklyn promoter Ralph Mercado—to salsa management and bookings what Fania was to recordings—rented Madison Square Garden for blowouts that generally made up in vibe what they lacked in sound design and crowd control. In February, seventeen thousand people turned out for a pan-Latin *habichuela* fest with Héctor Lavoe and Ismael Rivera, salsa's two best male singers. Machito and his band represented for the old school; the saxophonist Felix del Rosario came from the Dominican Republic with merengue, the frantic regional dance style whose presence in New York was growing. In July, an even bigger Garden show featured Rivera, Cheo Feliciano, Celia Cruz, Roberto Roena y Su Apollo Sound, and the entire Fania All-Star posse. For his finale, Héctor Lavoe was lowered on a cable strung from the Madison Square Garden support beams—as Mick Jagger had been just days earlier—to sing "Mi Gente."

The few non-Latinos paying attention to this cultural explosion came largely from the disco community, where its rhythm science was understood. Vince Aletti attended the Garden blowout in July and called it "the most impressive and exciting show I've seen in years." New York disco DJs were salting salsa records into their sets: Eddie Palmieri's "Puerto Rico," Ray Barretto's "El Negro y Ray," the Fania All-Stars' "Chanchullo" (from *Latin-Soul-Rock*, a makeup session of songs with Billy Cobham and Jorge Santana that never got played at Yankee Stadium because of the audience melee). They were also combing the shops for other international grooves. The Nigerian bandleader Fela Kuti was introduced to the United States via New York disco DJs playing "Shakara (Oloje)" and "Roforofo Fight" on import pressings that made it over in '75.

The biggest Latin crossover event of the year was the Latin Music Awards, cooked up by Izzy Sanabria under the *Latin N.Y.* banner. The first event of its kind in the United States, remarkably enough, it was held May 4 at the Beacon Theater, featuring everyone from Tito Puente and Eddie Palmieri on down. The evening's most telling moment was when Stevie Wonder was led onstage. "Black music is very much influenced by Latin music," he announced. "I've been very influenced by it myself." The crowd shouted back affectionately: "We know!"

The next day, with usual 20/20 hindsight, the Grammy Awards people announced that they would add the category of "Best Latin Recording" to their laurel list. And before the summer ended, there would be another breakthrough, modest though it might seem: Ray Barretto played a three-night stand at the Bottom Line, the Greenwich Village showcase boîte for white record company executives.

"Well," said the trumpeter Papi Roman backstage, "if they don't like us here, then fuck 'em; we'll take the place apart and carry it uptown with us!"

"Hey, you can't do that, man," chimed in the flutist Artie Webb. "How would it look?"

"Like the Puerto Ricans did it again!" yelled Barretto.

"See?" said Roman. "Can't take us anywhere!"

In addition to "Ban Ban Quere," a Rubén Blades vehicle from his new Fania LP, *Barretto,* and the solo-mad staple "Cocinando," Barretto played tracks from *The Other Road*, a fusion-minded jazz set from the previous year that bombed with his Latin fan base. With it he encountered the classic dilemma facing Eddie Palmieri and the other salsa pioneers: innovate too much and risk your livelihood. Barretto and Palmieri tried to have it both ways, because the idea that the American music they helped invent might remain either aesthetically stale or culturally marginalized was simply unacceptable to them.

"We're very proud and nervous to be the first Latin band to play here," Barretto told the largely Anglo Bottom Line audience. "Hopefully we won't be the last."

He added: "If you notice anger among Latin people, it's because we haven't been recognized, and we're tired of people taking our rhythms and using us. *We* are the source, and we want to be it."[43]

At the Metropolitan Opera on March 29, the soprano Birgit Nilsson sings *Götterdämmerung*, the final opera of Wagner's *Ring* cycle, as she has countless times before. As Brünnhilde, staring at death, apocalypse, the death of the old gods, and the possibility of a new world, she lights the bonfire. The ovation lasts twenty-one minutes. The *New York Times* critic Raymond Emerson winds up with tears streaming down his face. In the *Voice*, Leighton Kerner describes the performance as "something that grandchildren will be told about in the next century."[44]

The venerable German classical music label Deutsche Grammophon released a handsome triple-LP box set that month devoted to the music of Steve Reich, centered on his 1971 piece *Drumming*. The composer followed the LP's release with four concerts at the Kitchen billed as "Work in Progress for 21 Musicians and Singers." The *Voice* critic Tom Johnson devoted an entire column to it. To his mind, it confirmed the death of New York minimalism. He lamented that the music sounded closer to Ravel or Mahler than Reich's earlier music, and doubted it could offend even the most conservative listeners. "Over everything," he wrote, "is a pall of lushness."

Perhaps. Yet thrumming through that pall—a rising and falling lattice of marimba and xylophone and metallophone notes, cello, violin, clarinets, pianos, and women's voices—was music of the spheres, its shimmering harmonies and melodic patterns laser-focused yet diaphanous, enveloping. Of all the New York composers working with notions of repetition and modulation, none had come up with anything that sounded quite like this. It was the full flowering of the orchestral minimalism posited back in '65 by Terry Riley's *In C*, whose premiere Reich helped pull together.

Years later, the *New Yorker* critic Alex Ross would write about the final iteration of Reich's work-in-progress, *Music for 18 Musicians*: "The seeming stasis of the sound encourages the listener to zero in on seemingly inconsequential details, so that the smallest changes have the force of seismic shocks and something as simple as a bass line going down a half step sends chills up the spine."[45] Listening to it, one could indeed imagine a new world, with new gods.

Desperate to balance the books, Mayor Beame laid off 5,034 cops and more than 3,000 garbage men. In solidarity, the remaining 10,000-plus city sanitation workers went on strike. At the end of three pungent summer days (during which Patti Smith took her first hit of LSD), Beame caved, agreeing to reinstate a couple thousand police officers and most of the sanitation workers. In the meantime, the ones returning to work had about fifty thousand tons of rotting trash to collect from the city curbs. Despite the rains, the scent seemed to linger for the rest of the summer.

This was the backdrop for the CBGB Rock Festival (advertised subtitle: "Top 40 New York Unrecorded Rock TALENT"), which ran from July 16 through August 3. The festival was a smart bit of marketing by Hilly Kristal. Crowds and press came out in force, including writers from the English pop rags *New Musical Express* and *Melody Maker*. Television, the still-unsigned forefathers, performed. Richard Hell played with his new band, the Heartbreakers, with the ex-Dolls Johnny Thunders and Jerry Nolan as born-again punks. The Ramones, Blondie, and Talking Heads played; so did the hard-rock wise guys Tuff Darts and the heavy electric blues outfit White Lightning. The Shirts—an amiable bunch of rockers with catchy songs and a strong-voiced, *Little Rascals*–style frontwoman, Annie Golden—came over from Park Slope.

Talking Heads, who'd played their first show less than two months earlier, got their picture on the cover of the *Voice*, illustrating a festival recap by James Wolcott titled "The Conservative Impulse of the New Rock Underground." In trying to pin down what was happening, Wolcott—emerging as the scene's authoritative critical voice at age twenty-two—quoted Pete Townshend, who felt that "rock music as it was is not really contemporary to these times. It's really the music of yesteryear." Wolcott's reply both agreed and disagreed: "What's changed is the nature of the impulse to create rock. No longer is the impulse revolutionary—ie: the transformation of oneself and society—but conservative: to carry on the rock tradition."

As David Byrne remarked some years later: "The days of naïve, primitive rock bands are gone. The punk thing was a very self-aware reaction and in that sense it's very historically oriented. Part of its meaning and importance comes out of that historical perspective. Without that I don't think it would have seemed important at all."[46]

About the era's best jazz and salsa—even DJ music and modern composition—one might say exactly the same thing.

•

June 26: Columbia Records released *The Basement Tapes*, which documented home recordings made by Bob Dylan and the Band up in Woodstock in '67, buffed up a bit with overdubs. Although most of the songs
had circulated for years—notably on '69's *The Great White Wonder*, the
first high-profile bootleg rock LP—they sounded here like a matter-of-
fact manifesto on gimmick-free music making: an anti–*Sgt. Pepper*, a
folk-rock *Raw Power*. Out of the box, critics declared it the album of the
year. Christgau gave it a rare A+ rating, impressed with an artist "armed
in the mystery of his songs but divested of the mystique of celebrity,"
wondering how rock history might have played out if the recordings had
been released earlier. ("We don't have to bow our heads in shame because this is the best album of 1975," he wrote. "It would have been the
best album of 1967, too.") Together with *Blood on the Tracks*, Dylan had
managed not merely a comeback but the year-to-date's two best albums—one by his new self and one by his old self, a self-contained
continuum of American music that itself contained multitudes.

July 19: In the wee hours of the morning, Bruce Springsteen and his
bandmates left the Record Plant to get some sleep. The album was finally done. The band had crawled to the finish line; Springsteen was so
spent, he dozed off during the final mix of "Thunder Road" and wound
up leaving a sax track on the entire song, when he'd intended to use it
on just the final chorus.[47]

The musicians napped at the studio until around 3:00 p.m. They
rehearsed their live show with the new material straight through until
ten the next morning, when they all piled into a van headed to Providence, Rhode Island, the first stop on the *Born to Run* tour. Making his
debut that night with the E Street Band would be their new guitarist,
Steve Van Zandt. Named for a residential block in Asbury Park, the new
band, truth be told, had come together in New York City.

Each day, the line stretched from Fourth Street all the way up Mercer.

The first week in August, the Bottom Line had booked the multi-
horn magician Rahsaan Roland Kirk; the second, the free-jazz shaman
Sun Ra and his Arkestra. Beginning on the thirteenth, the Bottom Line
was proud to present the first of five evenings with Bruce Springsteen
and the E Street Band.

The first night, Wednesday, began with Springsteen at the piano, plinking the tender opening notes of "Thunder Road" under the blue beam of a single spotlight. He started singing. Mary lets the screen door slam and dances across the porch, perhaps to "Only the Lonely," while her dirty-hooded suitor woos her to join him in flight, cut her losses, stop praying in vain for a savior to rise from their streets.

Springsteen plays that first-person suitor to the hilt, the guy who "got that guitar" and "learned how to make it talk." He makes it explicit in the song that he's "no hero." But a hero was needed. Rock radio had been playing "Born to Run" since the spring, and while the LP wouldn't be released until the end of the month, advance copies had been circulating. The Bottom Line shows, for which writers flew in from everywhere, sealed the deification deal. Even jaded locals bowed. "Dear *Soho Weekly News* readers," wrote Ken Tucker after the opening-night show, "I have just come from the best rock & roll performance I've ever seen in my long, decadent life." (He was 21 at the time, but still.) In a cover-billed story titled "Is Springsteen Worth the Hype?" Paul Nelson—the man who signed the New York Dolls—reflected after Sunday's final-night performance in the *Voice*: "On my feet, clapping, never wanting it to end, I ask myself when I've ever been so moved by a concert."[48]

Patti Smith walked to Electric Lady Studios from her apartment at 107 MacDougal Street on September 2. When she arrived at 52 West Eighth Street—the former site of the Village Barn, a country-music nightclub that opened in 1930 and soldiered on until 1967—she headed down the stairs, just as she had the previous year when she cut her debut single. Now as then, she was conscious of working in the house Hendrix built to bum-rush the future of rock. He "never came back to create his new musical language," she later recalled, "but he left behind a studio that resonated all his hopes for the future of our cultural voice. These things were in my mind from the first moment I entered the vocal booth." She wrote the title track of *Horses*, and its final track, "Elegie," with Hendrix in mind. Producing the sessions, at Smith's request, was John Cale.

Earlier in the year, Springsteen turned up at an after-party following a Faces and Blue Öyster Cult concert at the Garden. Smith was there, and they spoke; Springsteen cheekily told her that he fell in love with her after seeing her picture in *Creem.*[49] As she prepared to make her record, the mania around the just-released *Born to Run* and the shows at the Bottom Line, located just a few blocks from Electric Lady, was palpable; it pulsed through the Village like pheromones radiating up from the pavement.

Smith and the band recorded through September, coming in at odd hours, when the studio rates were lowest. They woke at four o'clock one morning and recorded "Redondo Beach," which had developed a reggae groove during rehearsals. Smith, used to improvising with her boys around her, was put off at having to sing behind the glass walls of a vocal booth. But she warmed to it.

"I remember to this day improvising 'Birdland,'" Smith said in 2005 over tea in a MacDougal Street café, a brief stroll from both her old apartment at 107 and her current one down the block. She was preparing for a thirtieth-anniversary performance of *Horses* at the Brooklyn Academy of Music, and she was dressed in her signature uniform: a man's white dress shirt, a tattered black suit jacket.

"Richard Sohl was such a brilliant accompanist. Even though I was just hearing him through headphones, I could feel him following me no matter where I went. Lenny, Richard, and I could just move on a canvas together; we were so in sync."

She sipped her tea.

"And I remember the exact moment where I peaked: there's a line in it, 'Shoot 'em up like light / like Muhammad boxer'—my little tribute to Muhammad Ali. That moment something happened. It was a moment where you shiver, y'know?"

Smith adored three-chord rock—her band did a great version of "Louie Louie"—but, like Tom Verlaine, she was also drawn to the idea of free, unbridled improvisation. "Birdland" shares its name with one of the city's great jazz clubs, where John Coltrane recorded a stupendous live album in 1963. In fact, Smith credits two key influences in her music making: Johnny Carson and John Coltrane.

"My two Johnnys," she said, laughing. "Watching Johnny Carson taught me how to spar with people, to not be daunted by hecklers. 'Cause I got heckled *a lot* in the early years—really a lot. And I just learned to shoot back at them. And from Coltrane I learned about a more spiritual kind of improvisation. Coltrane talked to God, visited the universe, went really far out. But then he came back—because, as a performer, his responsibility was to return. I learned I could cast a line very far out, but you still have to reel yourself back in."

There was a third Johnny in Smith's trinity, the character she sings about in "Gloria," the Johnny apparently being stabbed—or raped—against a locker: a locker in a high school, a bus terminal, a bathhouse. Smith recalled her LSD trip with Mapplethorpe, her poet's tour of hell, the streets piled high with garbage, the leather men cruising each other at the piers, and her soul mate Robert, at home in it all. Perhaps the song's Johnny was a little bit him.

Smith finished recording "Elegie" on September 18, the fifth anniversary of Hendrix's death. The record was complete. The sessions drained her: rail thin from the beginning, she was down to ninety-three pounds. The two men in her life, Allen Lanier and Tom Verlaine, had both contributed as cowriters and guitarists. And while Smith and Cale clashed repeatedly over process and direction, they made a great album, triangulating Hendrix and the Velvet Underground and the garage rock that Kaye had canonized with his archival *Nuggets* LPs.

The cover photograph was shot by Robert Mapplethorpe in his boyfriend Sam Wagstaff's newly purchased and still-empty penthouse apartment at 1 Fifth Avenue, just off Washington Square Park. On the morning of the shoot, Smith was dawdling with Mapplethorpe over a late breakfast at the Pink Tea Cup on Grove Street in the West Village. When he realized they were going to lose the afternoon light, the pair dashed across town.

"It was just the two of us, no assistants," she said, smiling, eyes wet. "We shot like twelve pictures for the cover and a few extras, maybe twenty-four in all. After like eight he said, 'I got it.' And I remember saying, 'How do you know?' And he just said, 'I know.'"

He was right, although Clive Davis didn't think so: the label chief hated the androgynous black-and-white portrait. But Smith's contract gave her full creative control. She even refused to let the art department airbrush out the trace of hair on her upper lip; she felt "it would be like having plastic surgery."[50]

The photo is iconic: Smith in a white dress shirt, purchased a few days earlier from the Salvation Army, cuffs ripped off, unbuttoned at the neck, tucked into tight dark slacks in front, tails hanging in back. A thin necktie draped around her collar, untied, its ends also tucked in, resembling suspenders. She holds a black jacket—casually tossed, Sinatra-like, over her left shoulder—with a delicate hand, a simple ring on its middle finger juxtaposed with a lapel pin of a tiny horse (a gift from Allen Lanier) on the jacket collar. Her right hand reaches over her chest, barely touching the left, covering her breasts, though there is no trace of a bust, or shame. Her expression is unsmiling yet undisturbed, eyes puffy but resolute, lips full, a shadow falling over the right side of her face, her hair a perfectly uncombed bird's nest, lips full, kissable, gender not so much indeterminate as double-barreled, negatively capable, 360 degrees of possibility.

It's a picture I spent a lot of time studying, from the moment my thirteen-year-old sister brought the record home from the Music Box on Union Turnpike. It seemed to be a portal to myriad ways of conducting your life, of channeling sex and passion, of dressing your dreams. The record spun out its images of women seducing women, men fucking men; of sand and snow, funeral cars and stallions; of bodies dancing, naked, ripped open. Propped up on elbows, Koss headphones hugging my skull, the scratch of shag carpeting against skin, I listened.

Born to Run and *Horses* were released on August 25 and December 13, 1975, respectively. The similarity between the two records is striking. Both have black-and-white, three-quarter-framed portraits on the cover, the singer-songwriters standing against blank backdrops. Both have the artist's name and the album title in sans-serif type in the jacket's upper right-hand corner. And both albums show artists stepping onto mythic rock 'n' roll turf with an ear to history and their place in it. *Born to Run* begins by invoking Roy Orbison's romantic existentialism, *Horses* by invoking Van Morrison's ecstatic garage-band horniness—a clue to their aesthetic differences.

But both South Jersey kids were maximalists, given to extended and verbose songs. And both embraced rock 'n' roll as a kind of religion. Springsteen was more the fundamentalist, testifying to old-school verities; Smith more the Sufi-style mystic. But, at core, both were telling stories of escape, from narrow hometowns and narrow conceptions of life's possibilities. And for both, escape equaled New York City, because if you grow up in Jersey or the Outer Boroughs—or other states or even nations beyond—New York was where you ran away to, the place where real life was. Springsteen's characters drove back and forth over the Jersey state line; they had sketchy deals brewing across the river, where they could feel two grand practically sitting in their pockets. They might walk into some kind of trouble on Tenth Avenue on the desolate far West Side, close to the Lincoln Tunnel approach, preparing to "bust this city in half." On *Horses*, perhaps because she had already put her roots in the Village, Smith looked farther afield: to the Maine outpost of Wilhelm Reich, the imaginary Lesbos of L.A.'s Redondo Beach, to fantastical spaces where horses breathe fire and sand melts into glass rivers. Yet it all felt refracted through the lens of that first single, when Smith declared she was going to go to New York City "and be a big star."

I desperately wanted to see Springsteen at the Bottom Line, having spent much of the summer lost in his first two records. But the club's eighteen-and-over policy was notoriously strict; you needed two forms of ID, and studying the defects in my "Identification Card," which I had purchased at a novelty shop in Times Square, I knew it was hopeless.

It may have been nowhere in his mind—Springsteen has said as much—but when, near the end of the album, he sings about how rock 'n' roll bands "faced off against each other out in the street," he might have been imagining his own band, walking southeast from the Record Plant or the Bottom Line toward CBGB to take their stand, switchblade guitars in hand, there in the middle of Bowery, and see if anyone could step to them.

In truth, Springsteen and his band were on a mission of an entirely different scale. By the end of October, his face would appear simultaneously on the covers of *Time* and *Newsweek*.

Television, meanwhile, remained unsigned. They booked their first out-of-town gig in Cleveland, where a parallel punk scene had been brewing among bands like the Mirrors, the Electric Eels, and Rocket from the Tombs (who opened their shows at the Piccadilly Penthouse). Television played "Little Johnny Jewel," a song they'd record that fall for their debut release, a 7-inch single with the seven-minutes-plus track split into two parts over both sides. Punk's equivalent of the Grateful Dead's "Dark Star," "Little Johnny Jewel" was a curious combination of teenage-kicks attitude—Verlaine hiccup-yelping, "Little Johnny Jewel / He's so cool"—and beautiful guitar abstractions. It wasn't yet as incandescent as the song would become live. But it was a document. The band now existed on vinyl.

Around this time, at the urging of a friend, I took the E train into the city to see Television at CBGB. My fake ID couldn't get me into the Bottom Line, but the handsome dark-haired woman at the door of CBGB barely looked at it. I wore a loud polyester-print Huk-A-Poo dress shirt, thinking it would make me look older than fourteen. Too timid to attempt buying a beer, I found a place to stand near the side of the stage. The music was intense and dazzling. I recall Verlaine's hands, which seemed freakishly huge, like spiders. And I remember "Little Johnny Jewel," which seemed to go on forever.

Amid all the creative ferment, the city rattled toward bankruptcy like an old IRT train. "It may happen in the coming month of August," wrote Phil Tracy in the *Voice*. "It might occur after Labor Day. It is even possible that the city could stagger through until October, when the $3 billion that Big MAC is authorized to borrow (presuming it can find someone to lend it that much) runs out. But one way or another, the city is going under."[51]

What would this mean? A citywide teachers' strike looked inevitable—the last major one, in 1968, had closed my elementary school for a month. City College, swallowing hard at an $87 million budget cut, was likely to end free tuition. After the firefighter layoffs, there were 5,500 recorded cases of arson in the South Bronx alone in seventeen months.[52] In February, a blaze raged for fifteen hours in New York Telephone's central offices on Second Avenue, taking out service on more than 170,000 phones. Even after the sanitation men returned to work, there was an excess of trash in the streets, as recession-strapped businesses and restaurants dumped their waste illegally rather than paying private haulers. The city's shorthanded sanitation police helplessly looked the other way.

In the Village, two guys went into the Orange Julius on the corner of Sixth Avenue and Eighth Street, night after night, demanding protection money. Nearby, the charming, old-world Mamie's Ice Cream Parlor, at 35 West Eighth Street, got held up; the Flame Steakhouse was burgled after hours. At the Lord Byron Arms restaurant on Sixth Avenue near Thirteenth Street, three men with handguns cleaned out the register, making five customers empty their pockets and then strip naked.

On September 5, the Manson Family cult member Lynette "Squeaky" Fromme pointed a Colt .45 semiautomatic at President Ford in Sacramento and pulled the trigger. Though the clip was loaded, there was no bullet in the chamber. Sara Jane Moore, a quintuple divorcée and Patty Hearst fan, came closer to assassinating Ford two and a half weeks later in San Francisco, using a .38 revolver with a sight that was off-register by about six inches. The bullet whizzed by him.

At the Emotional Outlet, a clothing store on Sixteenth Street off Seventh Avenue, a customer inexplicably punched a salesgirl in the face. And in October, in a bizarre case of life imitating art imitating life, a burnout named Ray "Cat" Olsen held up the Bankers Trust on Sixth Avenue with a rifle, taking hostages à la Al Pacino in the current hit film *Dog Day Afternoon* (itself based on a crazy New York City bank robbery from the summer of '72). Declaring himself a member of the Symbionese Liberation Army, Olsen demanded the release of Patty Hearst, who'd just been arrested in San Francisco.

"On any night, the Grateful Dead are the best fuckin' rock 'n' roll band in the world," Olsen told a live radio audience via phone over his favorite radio station, WNEW-FM, which fed his voice over the airwaves while his gun was trained on ten hostages. "I want to thank Jerry Garcia. I want to thank Phil Lesh . . . They have made me high over the years. I'm psychedelic." He spoke with Scott Muni, who played Dylan's "Stuck Inside of Mobile" for him and then went down to the bank to try to talk him down. The gunman was finally arrested after trading two hostages for a six-pack, and then passing out.[53]

If people seemed higher as well as crazier, it was understandable: among other drugs, an estimated two hundred kilos of heroin was coming through Harlem every week. In the spring, Frank Lucas—a businessman whose story would be told in *American Gangster*—became the first high-profile black heroin importer, challenging the Gambinos and Luccheses. The upshot was lots of Southeast Asian brown on the streets and a bloody turf war that included one body dragged out of the Passaic River, and another found in a car under the West Side Highway with its stomach slit open.[54]

Musicians kept coming to town. Where else would they go? David Murray, a twenty-year-old saxophonist and student at Pomona College outside Los Angeles, arrived in March to do an independent study project on saxophone music from 1957 to the present. He interviewed Ornette Coleman, Cecil Taylor, John Cage, and Dewey Redman; the latter told him: "Put down that pencil and pick up your saxophone." Murray began turning heads at Studio Rivbea and elsewhere. His sound was huge, already distinctive—brutish yet melodic, focused, damp with emotion. He was capable of unbridled free blowing, sizzling with extended technique, phrases stretched via circular breathing, colored with unusual breath attacks and key rattling. But he could also puff out velvety Ben Webster–style phrases in between ferocious gospel-style shouts and honks. By the end of the year, he had written "Flowers for Albert," a lilting composition he had conceived while walking beside the East River near where the radical saxophonist Albert Ayler was found floating facedown in 1970.

By the end of summer, Murray had become roommates with Stanley Crouch, his teacher and colleague in L.A. They'd rented a loft space on the second floor of 2 East Second Street, across the Bowery from Studio Rivbea and just around the corner from CBGB, and began putting on shows. They called their space Studio Infinity. Crouch was a burly drummer whose interest in extended technique was steeped, like Murray's, in a love and knowledge of jazz history. He played an ancient kit with loosened heads, using sticks, mallets, hands, and elbows, creating a vocabulary that might be used for ping-ponging free play or a percussion-only solo version of "It Don't Mean a Thing." Murray and Crouch weren't unlike Tom Verlaine and Patti Smith: exploring their music's early roots via the form-smashing freedom of the sixties.

Both men were visionaries and badasses. Crouch was an outspoken jazz critic. He'd often hang out and debate aesthetics with the writers Ralph Ellison and Albert Murray—Crouch had studied jazz criticism with the latter, who was working on a book called *Stomping the Blues*. Unafraid to shit where he ate, Crouch began writing barbed criticism for both the *Soho News* and the *Voice*. Reviewing a Keith Jarrett concert in the latter, he declared Jarrett's music as "very slight, even pretentiously naïve" and lacking "balls."[55] Crouch developed a rep as a fighter, intellectually and (when necessary) physically, and was not one to back down.

Murray wasn't anyone to mess with, either. Gary Giddins, who wrote glowingly of the saxophonist during Murray's first summer in town, remembers standing around between sets outside the Tin Palace, the jazz club beneath Murray and Crouch's apartment. Murray was beginning to generate some record company interest, and he had a meeting scheduled with a major-label rep. The older musicians were giving him sage advice along the lines of "Those guys are sharks, man—you gotta watch yourself." As Giddins recalls, Murray replied, "I'll be OK; I have my piece"—a reference to the hunting shotgun he brought with him from California. He admits to having in his car on at least one occasion when picking up receipts from a club owner who was trying to stiff him.

Henry Threadgill also arrived in New York in '75. A Chicago AACM composer who played saxophones and other instruments, he was the fulcrum of a collective trio called Air, with the bassist Fred Hopkins and the drummer Steve McCall. In September they recorded their debut LP, *Air Song*, which contained some of the most thrilling jazz made in '75: formally free, swinging hard, and stuffed with musical ideas—as the twelve-minute opener, "Untitled Tango," made clear. It was released on the tiny Whynot label, and almost no one heard it.

Also in September, Threadgill's colleagues in the Art Ensemble of Chicago began a two-week residency at the Five Spot, at 2 St. Mark's Place in the East Village. On one night, they opened a set with the saxophonist Joseph Jarman and the drummer Don Moye, faces painted African-tribal-style, staggering onstage as if they were drunk. Lester Bowie, the trumpeter—dressed in cutoff denim shorts, a ripped denim vest, and a visor—called them over to a table onstage, yelling: "None of this music shit; we're gonna play some cards!" Bowie produced a deck and began dealing wildly while swigging from a pint bottle. Then he produced a pool cue, pointed it at the bassist, Malachi Favors, and yelled, "Here's your cue"—upon which the band, springing off the pun, began a single, uninterrupted piece of free-form music played on an array of instruments: saxes, from sopranino to bass; various flutes; vibes; gongs, log drums, and other percussion devices. At times the music was meditative; other times, it blew like a typhoon.

During the theatrical introduction, according to *Downbeat*'s critic Scott Albin, the audience "sat in silence, looking stunned and disoriented." This was jazz as performance art, medicine-show shtick, esoteric

ritual. Even seasoned fans of cutting-edge New York free-improv were
puzzled. Yet the music itself was often breathtaking, and the Five Spot
shows were talked about for months afterward.

October 27: The FALN pull off their most spectacular display to date.
Ten bombs explode nearly simultaneously in three cities: Chicago, New
York, and Washington, D.C. One was planted behind a shrub outside
the United Nations on First Avenue; another outside the Chase Manhattan Bank on West Fifty-seventh Street. No one is injured.

The weather forecast for October 30 was sunny and cool, highs in the
mid-fifties. The forecast for New York City's future: not so good. Speaking
to the National Press Club, President Ford declared flatly: "I can tell you
now that I am prepared to veto any bill that has as its purpose a federal
bailout of New York City to prevent default." He had decided along with
his advisors, including Chief of Staff Donald Rumsfeld, that the Big
Apple represented everything that was wrong with the welfare state and
the New Deal approach to government. Letting the liberal city collapse
would be an object lesson not just for the nation but for the world.

That night, the *Daily News* managing editor, William Brink, came
up with the next day's headline. It read: "FORD TO CITY: DROP
DEAD."

Rumor was that the original idea was "FORD TO CITY: F***
OFF." Still, the fifteen-cent tabloid cover shouted across the five boroughs. People snapped up copies and saved them in plastic dry-cleaning
bags, as they did with papers covering the *Apollo 11* moonwalk and the
JFK assassination. I still remember a strange mix of anger and pride at
the sight of it. One can imagine the millions of pairs of eyes narrowing
at breakfast tables, the curses muttered; commuters paused at news
racks, shoulders rolled back, eyebrows arched in New York "You must
be kidding me" code, middle fingers reflexively flipping up.

The rest of the country hated us, sure. But the world responded to
Ford's object lesson at the premiere G6 summit in France two weeks
later by scolding him that the city's default could create a global eco-
nomic disaster. And so he backpedaled, extending the city credit with
federal spending oversight.

The night of the headline, Labelle started a four-night run at the Beacon. The trio, a latter-day girl group formerly known as Patti La-Belle and the Bluebells, were reborn not long ago just across the street, at the Continental Baths, the gay bathhouse in the Ansonia, a posh Beaux Arts residential "hotel" where they, along with DJs Bobby Guttadaro, Frankie Knuckles, and Larry Levan, played for crowds of naked, ecstatic men. Ignoring the self-segregating conventional wisdom of black music marketing (like their Detroit brethren in the Parliament-Funkadelic clan), Labelle fused rock, funk, and R&B, dressed in platform boots, form-fitting spacesuits, and feathered headdresses, and had hit number 1 in the spring with "Lady Marmalade," a polyglot praise song to a Creole prostitute. They returned to their old neighborhood as conquering glamazons.

The kid was in the Esplanade Tunnel, the air thick with spray-paint fumes. His radio was tuned to WBLS-FM. The DJ's patter was like a back rub:

B.T. Express at 107.5 in New York. Giant love peace pipe that everybody can smoke and get high on. Talking 'bout being high on each other and high on love. Put that in your peace pipe and smoke it on out.

This was where the IRT number 5 cars sat overnight on layover. And Blade 1—the lanky kid with the giant Afro, propped up with his back against the tunnel wall and his sneakers against the side of the train—knew this was his finest hour.

Blade (Steve to his family) had been tagging subway cars seriously since '72. Now he was leader of the Crazy Five crew, and the acknowledged master of the 2 and 5 lines. Tonight he'd do something no one had pulled off anywhere in the city. A full end-to-end piece dominated by his name, the red-white-and-yellow 3-D block letters lying down and leaning left, stretching to a horizon of snowcapped mountains with a flaming sunrise behind them. Framing this on the right of the subway car's rightmost sliding doors was an angry Grim Reaper, yelling and pointing to the left—where, framing the other side of the mega-tag, was what resembled an ancient Easter Island head with a cartoon speech balloon declaring, "W.B.L.S. IN ESPLANADE!"[56]

Like Masaccio in fifteenth-century Florence, Blade 1 introduced linear perspective to the graffiti world. By daybreak of October 31, the image was bound for Manhattan to spread its maker's name. The president may have told the city to drop dead. But on Halloween morning, there was a different headline, and new work to make. The Reaper could wait.

The two men asked to see the vacant loft space. Then they beat the shit out of him.

George Maciunas, founder of the Fluxus collective, was also an unconventional real estate developer who helped invent SoHo as an artist community. In the mid-'60s he had organized artist co-ops at 16 Greene Street and 80 Wooster; in the latter building, you could buy a space for $2,000 down. Ornette Coleman bought a loft from him; so did Jonas Mekas and Nam June Paik. (His pal La Monte Young almost did but, sensing some fiscal funny business, pulled out of the deal.) In 1970, an artist could still purchase a finished loft space between 1,200 and 3,600 square feet for around $5,000. Now it was approaching $50,000.

A congenital prankster, Maciunas played fast and loose. He never bothered registering his co-ops with the attorney general's office, as the law required, and as the stakes rose, his clients suffered the fallout. At one point, the city shut off fuel to the co-op he started at 141 Wooster after finding a hundred violations. By the time of the attack, which left him with four broken ribs, thirty-six stitches in his head, and one blind eye, he'd made more than a few enemies.

Soon afterward, Maciunas decided to leave SoHo and the New York real estate business. As he told a reporter, "I don't want to lose my other eye."[57]

Christopher Street, the center of New York gay male culture, was now a tourist destination for hetero gawkers. Gay clubs were no longer subcultural secrets: even bathhouses (like the Continental, hero of the indie film *Saturday Night at the Baths*, released in June) were drawing straight hipsters to their DJ and performance nights. Gay patrons "began to feel like wallpaper, as if we had paid admission to be the backdrop for somebody else's evening out," complained one observer; "the people sitting next to us were laughing a little too hard."[58]

Yet if disco was gay culture's ambassador, it had brokered a remarkable alliance with the mainstream. That notion was inescapable at Madison Square Garden on November 28, the Friday after Thanksgiving, always a busy night at the dance clubs. Billed as "The World's Biggest Discotheque" and hosted by Richard Nader, a promoter and advocate of Werner Erhard's self-realization training program (est), the event featured a gigantic dance floor with balloons, lasers, dry ice, choreographed kung-fu fighters, acrobats, and a variety of stage dancers, plus live performances by the Trammps (a new band assembled by the busy drummer Earl Young), Brooklyn's Crown Heights Affair, and Gloria "Queen of the Discos" Gaynor. The anonymous DJs played the hits—"Rock the Boat," "Lady Marmalade," "Fly, Robin, Fly." Given the rare chance to get into a "real" disco, underage kids came out in force, dressed to impress. Over four hours, a crowd of 14,000—in three-piece suits, satin gowns, and far less—attempted the hustle with varying degrees of success.

It was fitting that, after seventeen months off-line, David Mancuso was finally able to reopen the Loft at 99 Prince Street. The new space was bigger and less intimate than his old space on Broadway, and there were problems with the new sound system, but Mancuso still made magic. So did Siano at the reopened Gallery, who remained, like Mancuso and their colleagues at 12 West, the Flamingo, and Reade Street, a primary tastemaker for the music. Siano even got a personal thank-you note from Barbra Streisand for championing her surprisingly soulful disco cover of the Four Tops' "Shake Me, Wake Me (When It's Over)" from her *Lazy Afternoon* album. But the culture they'd helped invent and shape was evolving fast, beyond their aesthetic control.

Some months after Springsteen's departure from 914 Sound Studios in Blauvelt, the Ramones trudged up there to record some new demos. They'd opened for Johnny Winter in Waterbury, Connecticut, and were nearly killed by an outraged blues-rock crowd. In October, they played some dates at Mother's, a gay bar for aging queens on Eighth Avenue at Twenty-third Street with wood paneling and red tablecloths. Linda Stein, the wife of Sire Records' Seymour Stein, saw them and flipped out. A few days later, the Ramones auditioned for the Steins at Tommy's loft studio and signed a deal. They got $20,000 up front. They hired Joey's brother, Mickey Leigh, as their roadie for $50 a week. In November,

Stein saw Talking Heads by accident at CBGB and offered them a deal, too. They passed on it. They didn't want to be a short-lived curiosity; they wanted to be great. And they knew they weren't yet.

CBGB reprised its summer Unsigned Bands fest with a Christmas Rock Festival. But now that Hilly Kristal had revived the scene, he had competition. Max's Kansas City had reopened in the summer and began booking bands again in the fall. Mother's booked Blondie and the Heartbreakers, along with the Ramones. Even Club 82, the tranny dive on East Fourth Street that hosted the Dolls and Wayne County, was regularly booking bands.

Talking Heads played two nights at CBGB in late December. In a blurry black-and-white clip that later surfaced on YouTube, David Byrne appears to be doing a mic check, but instead of the usual "one-two" he sputters "Uh, uh, uh" over and over, like an autistic kid in a lock groove. Tina Weymouth stands stock-still, her bass nearly the size of her torso, her hands draped over the top, waiting. She wears a dress shirt under a pullover, her hair in a blond bob. She resembles Olga Korbut, the era's famous teenage Olympic gymnast. Byrne looks equally neat and preppy, dress shirt open at the neck, sleeves rolled up. Chris Frantz, behind his drum kit in the rear, wears a similar light-colored shirt; his head is cut off in the framing.

"The name of this band is Talking Heads," Byrne says in a faint, tremulous voice, "and the name of this song is 'Psycho Killer.'"

Tina Weymouth begins the taut nine-note bassline, Frantz coming in with a chugging, disco-like beat. Then Byrne begins strumming his acoustic guitar, off-rhythm at first, then locking in. He begins singing softly, expressionless, with little inflection, the delivery on verse and chorus identical, almost murmured, his eyes fixed absently on the microphone, or shifting down to his hands on the guitar.

Before long, Byrne would be hamming it up, playing the psycho. But here, the "fa fa fa's" are more like tics, or placeholders for forgotten lyrics, than melodic devices, the "ai-yi-yi-yi-ooos" less outbursts than quiet convulsions. Only at the bridge, after the French bit about hurling himself toward glory, does he raise his voice a bit beyond the murmuring drone, making guttural noises and declaring: "I hate people when they're / not polite."

It was clearly performance art as much as pop music. Of course, the Ramones were performance art as well, in their way. Suicide, too.

The band had finished writing a new song around this time, called "Love Goes to Building on Fire." It was an anthem set to a loose march rhythm, its chorus revolving around Byrne's insistent, catchy declaration of "it's *not* love," and the comparison of his feelings to a building on fire. Between neighborhood tales of Gasoline Gomez, the mythic arsonist, and endless TV news footage of flames licking out of local apartment windows against the night sky, Byrne's metaphor was a resonant one. And the part where he yelps "They go tweet tweet tweet tweet tweet tweet tweet" like he's having a seizure was unforgettable.

That summer, as part of their fight against the City Hall cuts, the fire and police unions enlisted a PR firm and produced a leaflet for distribution at New York airports and bus terminals. On the cover was a shrouded skull beneath the words "Welcome to Fear City." It counseled visitors to stay off the streets after 6:00 p.m., to avoid public transportation ("You should never ride the subway for any reason whatsoever"), and to be aware of fire hazards ("You may have to evacuate quarters without assistance if a fire should occur"). It was like life during wartime. But as in wars, life went on: love was kindled; music was made.

Bob Dylan asked Patti Smith to join him on the Rolling Thunder Revue, his name for a large-scale tour he was developing in the spirit of their ad-hoc hootenanny at the Other End in July. She dropped by a rehearsal, but passed. *Horses* was about to be released, and whatever the truth about her rumored fling with Dylan, she had her own music to make.

"I thought it was real sweet of him, but he's so restless," she said. "At this point we're not chemically suited to be around each other . . . It's like if you have an electric chair, you need somebody to electrocute; you don't bring in another electric chair."[59]

Dylan previewed the tour on Thursday, October 30 (the evening of the "Drop Dead" headline), at Folk City—the site of his artistic birthplace back in '61, now relocated from 11 West Fourth Street to West Third, a few doors down from Village Oldies. Joan Baez, Bob Neuwirth, Allen Ginsberg, Ramblin' Jack Elliott, Ronee Blakley, and some others joined Dylan. Though she didn't perform, Smith was there, too. As was Phil Ochs, who still harbored a deep love-hate for his old friend onstage.

After the show, Dylan rode off in a red Cadillac El Dorado, Kerouac-style, to play small-scale shows in unconventional venues—an auditorium in Plymouth, Massachusetts; a women's prison in New Jersey. Along with the entourage of musicians, Dylan also enlisted a film crew, which included Smith's old flame Sam Shepherd, whose job it would be to script the thing. In part, Dylan was trying to create a microcosmic movable feast of the '60s-style folk community. It worked, sort of. He played the dates around the northeast, then finished the tour with a December 8 show at Madison Square Garden, a fund-and-consciousness-raising benefit for Rubin "Hurricane" Carter, a black prizefighter in jail for a 1967 triple murder that many believed he didn't commit. Dylan wrote a topical song, just like in the old days, asserting his innocence, and released it as a single. He played two other new songs, "Isis" and "Sara," which were clearly about the end of his marriage.

He also played a repurposed version of his race-minded 1963 protest song "The Lonesome Death of Hattie Carroll," its campfire–sing-along flow supplanted by a staccato, spitting, nearly shouted delivery that was entirely new for Dylan. He sounded, in fact, like Patti Smith, and the strangled glam-rock guitar solo (by the tour's wild card, Mick Ronson, David Bowie's former guitarist) wouldn't have sounded out of place at CBGB.

Later in November, Patti Smith played a three-night stand at the Bottom Line. It was her coming-out party, like Springsteen's in August. Dylan didn't make it this time, but Springsteen did; so did Lou Reed, David Johansen, and Tommy Ramone. Even Hilly Kristal, like an uncle attending his niece's bat mitzvah, came by. John Rockwell of the *Times* reviewed the first night's late show. He found Smith's opening poetry reading incoherent, and guessed she was "scared or stoned." But then the band came out, and they killed.

"It was as if a different person had inhabited her body," he wrote. "It was a 'performance' terrifying in its intensity, like some cosmic, moral struggle between demons and angels."[60] At one point, she fell to the floor and began slamming her head against Richard Sohl's keyboards, Iggy Pop–style.

Lou Reed's *Metal Machine Music* had been released over the summer. A double LP of electric guitar feedback drones, it was a minimalist statement, like the music John Cale made with La Monte Young's Theatre of Eternal Music (as the back cover credits note, "Drone cognizance and harmonic possibilities vis a vis Lamont [sic] Young's Dream Music"). Reed suggested to his label, RCA, that it be released as a classical LP. But if the album was serious, it was also a prank—an amplified sneer suggesting the very idea of the rock record was hopelessly outdated—and a trump card: an act of transgression that no leather-jacketed twenty-something punk could top. That it seemed unlistenable by normal "rock" standards seemed beside the point. Perhaps it was the point. He'd described it to Talking Heads' Tina Weymouth, at his apartment with her bandmates seeking career advice, as "shit on a platter."

Everyone assumed he was out of his mind on speed, anyway.

Reed had certainly been producing LPs at a furious rate: his self-titled debut and *Transformer* were issued in '72, *Berlin* in '73, the live *Rock n Roll Animal* and *Sally Can't Dance* in '74. Early in '75, RCA released yet another concert recording, *Lou Reed Live,* and wanted more product from him. But after three weeks in the stores, his label essentially deleted *Metal Machine Music,* after numerous returns by angry/confused customers who bought the record thinking it was a set of more or less conventional songs.

Reed's third record of '75, *Coney Island Baby,* came out the week of Smith's Bottom Line stand. Careerwise, it was a Hail Mary pass of haunting pop songs that echoed both *Transformer* and the great doo-wop-scented ballads of *The Velvet Underground and Nico.* Reed had demoed what became its title track at Electric Lady back in January: a nostalgic reverie about identity and belonging sung-spoke over gently strummed guitar that gradually builds steam as much through language as rhythm; formally, it was not unlike Patti Smith's "Piss Factory." He wound up recording the LP uptown at Mediasound, the little church, in October. During the sessions, RCA put him up in a suite at the Gramercy Park Hotel, where Dylan and the Rolling Thunder entourage were camped out in preparation for their tour. Reed received an invitation to join their ranks. But, like Smith, he declined.

The final weekend in November, Reed went down to CBGB to catch the Ramones. He returned to see them again a day later, taping them from his seat with his Sony portable cassette recorder.[61] He'd recorded Television there, too, earlier in the year—although Tom Verlaine caught him and took him to task for it.

•

The Ramones played a New Year's Eve double bill with the Heartbreakers at a loft space called the Sea of Clouds, on the fifth floor of 5 East
Sixteenth Street. Wayne County was the DJ, and the $7.50 cover in-
cluded champagne. The Heartbreakers had been playing a great cover
of "(I'm Not Your) Stepping Stone," first recorded by the Idaho garage
rockers Paul Revere and the Raiders, later redone by the made-for-TV
rock stars the Monkees. The Heartbreakers turned it into an anthem of
marginalization just as pointed as "Blank Generation."

Richard Hell wrote in his diary with pride about a show the previous week: "Johnny furiously started ripping chords from his guitar like
they were love letters he stopped himself just in time from sending."
Earlier, he'd written: "Using a lot of junk, but not as much as Jerry."

While the Heartbreakers rang in 1976 near Union Square, David
Johansen and Syl Sylvain played with pickup musicians as the New York
Dolls at the Beacon uptown. The ad for the gig showed the two men
dressed down, with startled, vaguely surly expressions, standing under an
umbrella. Tickets were $7.50 at the door, no champagne included.

Television played CBGB that night. Ivan Kral, Patti Smith's new
guitarist, was shooting black-and-white stock with a 16mm Bolex for a
short art film about the scene. Kral moves down the length of the narrow bar with the camera in his hand, squeezing through the crowd,
getting jostled, then resteadying himself. His bandmates Jay Dee Daugherty and Lenny Kaye mug with blowout noisemakers in their mouths.
Tina Weymouth smiles and shimmies in what looks like a bathrobe.
The lanky Tom Verlaine, head tilted down in conversation, peeks skep-
tically from under his brow. Hilly Kristal (who sprang for tablecloths to
make things festive) chats with Richard Robinson. Lisa Robinson works
the crowd. A long-haired Chris Stein talks to Blondie's new bassist,
Gary Valentine, both hypothesizing new wave fashion in skinny ties and
Salvation Army sports coats. Debbie Harry stands nearby with a tiara
on her head, grinning and waving a cigarette. Chris Frantz stands alone
with a lei around his neck, nursing a drink and observing the scene.
David Byrne, in a wide-lapeled sports jacket over a sweatshirt and a polo
shirt, sits in a group but stares off into the distance. And John Cale, a
paper hat on his head, scans the room, wild-eyed, looking for something
or someone.[62]

The Sex Pistols had played their first gig in London on November 6.
The Dolls' former benefactor, Malcolm McLaren, was now their man-

ager. He imagined them as made-for-TV rock stars, of a sort, inspired by both the Dolls and Television, who he met at their Hippodrome shows in March. As it happened, the Pistols also played a wicked version of "Stepping Stone."

Meanwhile, on lampposts around the East Village, handmade posters started appearing: "Watch out! PUNK is coming!"

1976

THESE ARE THE DAYS, MY FRIENDS

> I don't know why I love you. Could be you remind me of my-
> self. —Gil Scott-Heron, "New York City"

A cartoon of Lou Reed as Frankenstein graced the premiere cover of *Punk*, a magazine cooked up by three Connecticut kids—now living in a Chelsea storefront—obsessed with comics, films, and the seamy side of rock 'n' roll. The cover Q&A grilled Reed on the Ramones, Television, and Patti Smith, all of whom he liked.

PUNK: How 'bout Springsteen?
REED: *Oh*, I *love* him.
PUNK: You do . . . (?)
REED: He's one of *us*.
PUNK: Thank you.
REED: He's a *shit*—what are you talking about, what kind of stupid question is that?!

The first issue was produced out of 356 Tenth Avenue, in the former office space of a trucking company that the trio had been renting since November for $195 a month. They nicknamed their new home "The Punk Dump." The magazine was hand-drawn and lettered by John Holmstrom, a comic book fan who had done time with Chris Stein at the School of Visual Arts. Ged Dunn handled the business end. By default, Eddie McNeil became a writer, and something of a cartoon character/mascot as well, whom Holstrom renamed "Legs." Holstrom and McNeil lucked into their cover story at one of CBGB's Ramones shows in November, when they saw Reed at a table with his girl-styled friend Rachel and coaxed him into an interview on the spot.

The trio didn't coin the term *punk*, an archaic slang for "prostitute" used by Shakespeare before them, and which had evolved over time to connote a male hustler, sexual and/or otherwise. It was first used to describe rock 'n' roll by the Detroit writer Dave Marsh in 1971 in *Creem*, in reference to the Michigan garage-rockers ? and the Mysterians; Lenny Kaye used it in the liner notes to the '72 *Nuggets* album, and by '75 it was being thrown around to describe Patti Smith, Bruce Springsteen, and the CBGB scene. But by grabbing it for their name, *Punk* accelerated its transformation into a cultural brand.

Their debut also included an introductory editorial signed by Holmstrom that declared, "DEATH TO DISCO SHIT!" noting that it was "the epitome of all that's wrong with western civilization."

It was meant as a joke by a guy weaned on *MAD* magazine. But as Holmstrom later recognized, "everyone took it very seriously."[1]

There were plenty of other aesthetic arguments made against disco. Reviewing the Thanksgiving Madison Square Garden blowout, co-critics Cynthia Heimel and Stephen Saban decided the music is "like a Chinese meal—satisfying for the moment, but two hours later, there you are with your stomach empty."[2] The reviewer Vernon Gibbs was more alarmist: "If anyone doubts that we have entered a dangerous new era of conformity and mindless partying, they should have been at the Garden Friday night . . ."

Others put the music in cultural context. Robert Palmer of the *Times* IDed it as a Western form of "trance music." Vince Aletti took aim at rock-crit prejudice, targeting a Dave Marsh pan in *Rolling Stone* of an Archie Bell and the Drells disco LP, calling his argument "part of a general refusal to see disco partying as anything but mindless escapism when, in fact, a good case could be made for it as a vital tribal rite, an affirmation of high spirits and shared delight, a coming together to let loose that in no way ignores the problems of everyday life, but relieves them. Maybe we need a whole new aesthetics for the disco, one that includes the ritual as well as the music."[3]

In SoHo, a group calling itself the Ad Hoc Committee to Ban Discos collected eight hundred signatures toward eliminating dance clubs in the area, which would include the newly reopened Loft. At a meeting of the community planning board, the resolution to push a legislative proposal forward was approved unanimously.[4]

Harry Whitaker, age thirty-three, felt fortunate. He'd been making a solid living playing keyboards with the soul-jazz bandleader Roy Ayers (Whitaker wrote the strivers' anthem "We Live in Brooklyn, Baby" for Ayers's '72 *He's Coming* LP). But when he left Ayers to take a gig with Roberta Flack as her keyboardist and arranger, he began making real money. So he took some of it and decided to make an album.

He wasn't interested in pop songs. He wanted to create something more shape-shifting, that drew on jazz, funk, and soul but looked to the future of black music. So on January 15, Martin Luther King's birthday, Whitaker gathered a crowd of friends and family into Sound Ideas Studio on West Forty-sixth Street and recorded two songs for an LP he would call *Black Renaissance*.

The title track is a sort of free-jazz version of Marvin Gaye's "What's Goin' On." It begins with Whitaker's exploratory piano; then a deeply funky acoustic bass line by Buster Williams and the alternately smooth and shrieking tenor sax of Azur Lawrence, who had come off some time with Miles Davis's electric band. There's the sound of a police siren (or was it one of those Keds whistle rings?), and then the sound of a party, women and men jabbering and jive-talking and incanting fragments of inspirational verse in both English and Spanish—"It's a new day, a renaissance!" "*Nuevos dias!*" "Uh-huh!" "Praise—in my eyes!" "*Para los niños!*" "Can you dig it?" Then it all gets swept together in a swirl of reverb. The crowd disappears; the piano is left alone again. Buster's bass returns, slurry with glissandi but holding the groove tight. The trumpeter Woody Shaw takes the second section, smearing tones, looping into heavy echo—unusual playing from a guy generally known for upholding hard-bop tradition. Then the partygoers are back, and the cycle begins again. Dave Schnitter takes his own sax journey, and finally all the horns come together in a New Orleans–style blowout.[5]

It was a thrilling, hypnotically funky performance, the sort of music you could put on your record changer with the stacking arm up and just let play on repeat, to dance or meditate to. But Whitaker, busy with Flack, didn't have time to shop the record around, and wound up making a handshake deal with the tiny Japanese Baystate label. It wouldn't be released until '77, and then only in Japan.

A week after that session, the singer, activist, and actor Paul Robeson died. His funeral was held at the Mother A.M.E. Zion Church on 137th Street. Thousands came to the service; thousands more stood outside listening to a PA system. Joined by the congregation, the opera singer Delores Ivory Davis sang the old Negro spiritual "Oh, When I Come to the End of My Journey." Outside, the cold rain came down in torrents.

Lee Quiñones, whose tag name was simply Lee, was from Brooklyn, but he went to the High School of Art and Design in Manhattan, on Second Avenue off Fifty-seventh Street. A slim, handsome Puerto Rican kid with a modest Afro, he looked like Robert De Niro. The best graffiti writers, of which he was one, were doing end-to-ends, usually lettering their names, with various embellishments, across the entire side of a subway car. Lee was going to do the first double end-to-end. It would be called "Doomsday."

The night of January 31, he headed out to the yards where the number 6 Lexington Avenue trains were laid up. The design he had mapped out was framed by his name, LEE, in tilted 3-D block letters on the left, and a cartoon demon flanked by the word DOOMSDAY on the right, with twin heads in place of the two Os, one of them wearing a blue-gray fedora, the face obscured by shadow, with illuminated windows for eyes. Behind the letters, apartment high-rises jutted at odd angles, and in the center, spanning two cars, a rising sun. Unlike the one in Blade's Halloween end-to-end, this sun seemed malevolent, and flames lapped around the buildings like the work of some cosmic arsonist.

Next to Lee's name was a whitewashed panel, which he used for a final message, announcing that the piece was finished "on the morning of Jan 32, 1976."

When cars 9220 and 9221 began rolling toward the IRT tunnels, the familiar screech of old wheels grinding against steel track began soundtracking Lee's image of a city on fire. And in a moment, the scene was hurtling downtown.

•

The Ramones recorded *Ramones* over seventeen days in February at Plaza Sound in Radio City Music Hall. There were four songs with the word *wanna* in the title: two positive, two negative. "I Wanna Be Your Boyfriend" and "Now I Wanna Sniff Some Glue," "I Don't Wanna Go Down to the Basement" and "I Don't Wanna Walk Around with You." Two other songs, "I Don't Wanna Be Learned/I Don't Wanna Be Tamed" and "I Don't Care," didn't make the cut.

While the lyrics flirted with nihilism, the sound was as ecstatic and kinetic as any disco mix: Tommy's metronome drums, Johnny's concrete-saw Mosrite guitar, Dee-Dee's trampolining bass, Joey's weird Anglo-Queens yelp. When I saw the band at Hammerheads bar on Long Island, I had my greatest rock 'n' roll epiphany. The crowd bounded up and down, careened into one another, and chanted along for the entire fifty-five-minute set, which blasted by like an express train. I lost my shirt in the fracas, although I held on to my Levi's denim jacket, and, after finishing our smuggled-in Cuervo, wound up sucking face in the sand down on the beach with a friend of a friend of my sister's who I never saw again.

Ramones was released on April 23, and it did not set the world on fire. Produced by Craig Leon, it cost $6,400 to record—dirt cheap even by the era's standards. It sounded, appropriately, thin and metallic, with Joey barking about the "Texas chainsaw massacree" amid weird Beach Boys–cum–doo-wop harmonies, or encouraging the beating of a brat with a baseball bat over Johnny's tire-slash barre chords.

But the self-conscious primitivism was a joyride, generously tuneful. Even the absurd surliness was sympathetic, from Johnny's hilarious high-school-thug guitar break in "Now I Wanna Sniff Some Glue" to Joey's pained, geek-boy vulnerability on "Listen to My Heart." He'd been a hippie as a teenager, had made the pilgrimage to Haight-Ashbury and to Woodstock (though he got stuck in the Thruway traffic jam and never reached the concert). He often borrowed his mother's clothes during his glam phase, and made paintings using chopped-up fruits and vegetables.[6]

On the album he sings "I'm a Nazi schatze," which freaked out some people at the record label, not least Seymour Stein. In the context of the song "Today Your Love, Tomorrow the World," though, it reads as a tossed-off goof, a hollow provocation from a bunch of stoners who grew up in front of the TV making wisecracks at B-grade World War II movies. More carefully calculated was the American eagle belt buckle on the album's back cover. It was clipped out of a photo-booth self-portrait by the artist and coconspirator Arturo Vega, and the Ramones adapted it as a paramilitary-style logo, branding the band as all-American just in time for the Bicentennial.

Patti Smith and Bruce Springsteen took their musical gospels on tour to the heartland. Crisscrossing their paths were two other stars trying to sway hearts and minds: Jimmy Carter, a millionaire peanut farmer and former governor of Georgia, and Ronald Reagan, a millionaire actor and former governor of California. Reagan hated rock music; Carter had the support of his Georgia homeboys the Allman Brothers and was photographed in a Marshall Tucker Band T-shirt.

After a show in Memphis, Bruce Springsteen and Steve Van Zandt asked the cabbie who ferried them out for a late-night bite to take a detour out to Graceland. Springsteen was a serious Elvis devotee; he even wore an Elvis fan club button, partly obscured, on his leather jacket on the cover of *Born to Run*. When they got there, around three a.m., the house lights were on. Springsteen got out of the cab and climbed over the front gate.

He was about to knock on the front door when a security guard on the lawn called him over.

"Is Elvis here?" Springsteen asked.

"No, he's in Lake Tahoe," the guard said.

Springsteen explained that Elvis was his hero, and that he himself was a successful musician, that he'd recently been on the cover of both *Time* and *Newsweek*. The guard nodded indulgently and led him back out onto the street.

"You talkin' to *me*?

"You can't be talkin' to *me*."

Taxi Driver is not Martin Scorsese's greatest moment as a director, nor Robert De Niro's as an actor. But the resonance of De Niro's performance for fellow New Yorkers went deep: it's roughly two hours of watching a dude ready to snap, played out against the noir backdrop of the city viewed from a cab: wet streets reflecting Times Square's sticky nighttime neon glow, Dantesque steam clouds billowing from manholes. Scorsese enlisted the soundtrack composer Bernard Herrmann, Hitchcock's longtime collaborator, because this was a horror film: New York was the monster. (As it turned out, it was Herrmann's last work; he died shortly before the film's release in February.)

While shooting uptown, Scorsese and De Niro would eat at La Tacita de Oro on Ninety-ninth and Broadway, a counter-service Chino-Latino (wise patrons stuck with the Spanish fare) with a few tables. The men liked it. After a grueling day, they could walk in—De Niro in his Mohawk, clothes slightly blood-splattered—without anyone blinking.

Along with La Caridad on Seventy-eighth and Broadway (Rubén Blades's preferred Cuban-Chinese hangout), it was also a good, cheap place to repair after a show at the Beacon, which had become the theater of choice for sub-arena salsa bills. The Latin jazzmen Cal Tjader, Mongo Santamaría, and Willie Bobo shared a bill there in January, followed by Johnny Pacheco and Celia Cruz, reprising *Celia y Johnny* and its follow-up, *Tremendo Cache*.

Also at the Beacon that month was the First Festival of Plenas and Bombas. The main attraction was Willie Colón with his mentor Mon Rivera, a '50s bandleader who helped invent salsa's trombone-heavy vernacular and whose career had been revived thanks to *There Goes the Neighborhood*, a collaboration album with Colón. And joining them on the bill was Grupo Folklorico y Experimental Nuevayorquino, which despite the ungainly name had just recorded one of the greatest New York salsa documents.

The project was born out of a scene that had been brewing for years on Classon Point in the south-central Bronx. When the parents of Andy and Jerry González finally moved the family out of the projects and into a proper house—1963 Gildersleeve Avenue, at the center of the peninsula where the Hutchinson River and the Bronx River meet the East River—the brothers (Andy played bass, Jerry played trumpet) got the wood-paneled basement apartment. It instantly became a clubhouse for salsa musicians and Latin jazzbos of all stripes. When they weren't jamming, they were immersed in deep listening sessions at the house of their neighbor René López, a part-time musicologist and record fiend with the most astounding collection of Cuban 78s anyone had ever seen, the guy Larry Harlow enlisted to research his history-minded '74 *Salsa* LP.[7]

Concepts in Unity, produced by López, was born in this hothouse. It pushed salsa's Afro-Cuban rhythmic roots way up front, mixing Santeria bata drums and guiros into *guaguánco, guajira, plena, mazurka*, jazz, and rumba grooves without ever sounding, well, folkloric. The players shine, especially the percussionists, among them the *conguero* Milton Cardona. But the soul of the project is the trumpeter Chocolate Armenteros—a veteran of the band of Arsenio Rodriguez, the scene's godfather—whose playing is so proud and pained on "Cuba Linda" and "Choco's Guajira," it telegraphs the history of an entire culture.

Salsa had reached maximum saturation in the Latin community in the States, with labels pumping out records, good and bad, which were being exported (legally and not) around the world. Having rocked Zaire, the Fania All-Stars did the same to Japan. New York salsa was huge in Venezuela. In Colombia, a businessman named Sergio Seche with some ties to local *narcotraficantes* acquired the rights to reissue Fania material on his Melser label (he appeared to be doing quite well until his body was found in a closet, riddled with bullets).[8]

As with reggae, which *Latin N.Y.* magazine liked to call "Jamaica's Salsa," a crossover seemed just a single or album away. Or a film. Produced by Fania's Jerry Masucci and built around footage of the 1973 Yankee Stadium concert, with some overheated narration by Geraldo Rivera, *Salsa* premiered at the New Embassy on Forty-sixth Street in Times Square on March 31. Reviews were lukewarm, but it further spread the word. And so did Eddie Palmieri's acceptance of the Best Latin Album Grammy for *The Sun of Latin Music* in February.

On the business end, never Palmieri's strong suit, things were messy. He was operating without a personal manager, let alone a lawyer, and money problems continued to dog him. After the success of *Sun*, he had spent the latter half of 1975 locking horns with Harvey Averne over the Coco Records follow-up, tentatively titled *Kinkamache*, which Palmieri pledged "would extend *The Sun of Latin Music* into Africa." Chafing against deadlines and limited studio time, Palmieri abandoned the sessions midway through. Averne brought in Palmieri's band members to finish the record without him; Palmieri called for a boycott of the final product, which Averne released anyway with the title *Unfinished Masterpiece*.[9]

Like the Beach Boys' *Smiley Smile*, the record as released may have been a thin reflection of its auteur's vision. But it was still extraordinary, full of fierce grooves, breathtaking rhythm weaves, and fiery out-jazz improvising. Palmieri rejected it outright: headlining a show at the Beacon on April 2, he refused to do any of the new material. And for the Second Annual Latin NY Music Awards at the Beacon on May 16, when the record earned him statues for Best Salsa LP, Best Pianist, and Best Orquesta, Palmieri was a no-show. But with the ceremony into overtime, Palmieri's name was announced as the Musician of the Year, and suddenly there he was, strolling in from the wings, apologizing for his lateness and then humbly asking the bandleader Louie Ramirez permission to play his piano.

Palmieri sat down and launched into a virtuoso free-form improv, then led the band into "Picadillo," the Tito Puente tune he made into a jazzy barrio hit with Cal Tjader in 1966. The audience leaped up, mamboed, hooted, hollered, whistled, stomped, and clapped in clave rhythm. Other players climbed onstage; soon Palmieri was leading a jam with nearly every musician in the hall. Puente himself was there, mirroring Palmieri's riffs on timbales; Ray Barretto joined in on congas. Roberto Roena came down from the $6.50 balcony seats and grabbed his bongos, while Héctor Lavoe, who had won the Best Male Vocalist award for *La Voz*, scraped out rhythms on a guiro. Pupi Legarreta's charanga violin wound its way through the beat maze, and the crowd lost all remaining composure in the aisles.

Around the thirty-minute mark, the musicians shut it down, the MC, Izzy Sanabria, shouted *"Que viva la salsa y la musica Latina!"* and the house lights went up. People turned to one another, eyes wide, mouths locked into giddy grins, for some confirmation of the inarticulable greatness of what had just happened. How could music so transcendent *not* convert the rest of the world?

Yet the next morning, salsa remained stuck in a cultural ghetto that wasn't itself wholly supportive. The music fought for airtime and column inches in Spanish-language media like the daily *El Diario*, the AM stations WHOM and WADO, and the fuzzy, lo-fi UHF TV stations 41 and 47, which pushed higher-gloss international artists such as Iris Chacon, Raphael, and Sandro. There was a sense of conspiracy among salsa lovers that their music was seen as too Puerto Rican by the Cuban-owned media and ad agencies. (*Concepts in Unity*, indeed.) It's telling that salsa's premier radio program in New York was the Sunday-afternoon show on the jazz station WRVR 106.7 FM, hosted by Roger Dawson, an Irishman.[10]

There were other outlets: the mono AM stations WBNX 1380 ("The Only Spanish Station with the Total Salsa Sound") and WJIT 1480, and the free-form WBAI-FM, which aired *The Latin Musician's Hour* with the scholar/journalist Max Salazar, and *Latin Nostalgia*, an oldies show with Ken Rosa. The only Latin music to be heard on mainstream New York pop/rock stations was the Mexican-American Carlos Santana, who ignited arenas with his covers of Willie Bobo's "Evil Ways" and Tito Puente's "Oye Como Va."

Ray Barretto, salsa's biggest crossover hopeful alongside Palmieri, was tired of the ghetto. He played what he declared would be his last dancehall-circuit show on New Year's Eve at the Corso on Eighty-sixth Street. He planned to use the winter to figure out how to take things to the next level. By spring, he was still figuring.

> Our father, who art a cross between Miles Davis, John Coltrane, and Jimi Hendrix, hallowed be thy name.
>
> —Larry Coryell[11]

While Palmieri was banging out avant-garde note-clusters at the Beacon, Sam Rivers was hosting the Spring Music Festival at Studio Rivbea. It was essentially an extended recording session with the loft scene's best players for the producer Alan Douglas, whose adventurous boutique label had just been picked up by Casablanca Records, riding a coke-fueled, free-spending high thanks to megahits by Donna Summer and Kiss.[12] Douglas's résumé included the raw 1962 Duke Ellington/Charles Mingus/Max Roach trio set *Money Jungle*, the debut by the Last Poets, and, last year, the posthumous Jimi Hendrix sets *Crash Landing* and *Midnight Lightning*, which used the guitarist's work tapes as the basis for new recordings with the addition of session players.

The Rivbea recordings would be straightforward, although logistically tricky: to maximize the tiny space during the marathon festival, a loft platform, accessible only by ladder, was constructed overhead for the tape machines and mixer. "We'd race down the ladder," the engineer Ron Saint-Germain recalled, "fight our way to the stage to reset mikes for the next band while they were picking up their instruments, and hoped we'd get back to the machines before they actually began playing. Sometimes we didn't."[13]

The hours of tape were culled for the five-LP series *Wildflowers*, the most vivid document of the '70s loft jazz scene. The music is not inaccessible. Kalaparusha Maurice McIntyre's "Jays," which opens the first LP, is danceable funk with a flowing tenor sax journey over the top. A band led by the veteran free-jazz drummer Sunny Murray, joined by David Murray (no relation) and Byard Lancaster, plays a gorgeous "Over the Rainbow," the two saxophonists alternately doubling and unraveling the melody. On "Tranquil Beauty," Hamiet Bluiett sketches a bluesy tune on baritone sax, and is joined by the trumpeter Olu Dara, whose New Orleans–style bray gets mirrored when Bluiett switches to clarinet.

Like the CBGB festivals, the Rivbea shows presented numerous acts (twenty-eight in total, many of whom shared players) as a scene, with a shared outlook and aesthetic. Most musicians would tell you it wasn't quite like that. But the Rivbea festival put the "loft scene" on the cultural map; critics could no longer ignore the music or leave it for a yearly roundup piece. The *Soho News* announced it would begin regular coverage of the loft scene in January, and started reviewing performances nearly every week. The *Voice* followed suit. Gary Giddins had begun the year by asking the rhetorical question "Is it possible that jazz '75 could have been most impressively dominated by the late Duke Ellington and the strikingly alive Count Basie?" But he, too, began paying closer attention, with illuminating pieces on Sam Rivers, Leroy Jenkins, and others.

The sorry state of the conventional club scene also helped the lofts. A fire in December at the Blue Angel cabaret on East Fifty-fifth Street left seven people dead, so Mayor Beame and the Department of Buildings went on a cleanup rampage to save face. By early January, the Village Gate on Bleecker Street—home to the Salsa Meets Jazz series—was facing closure for code violations. And after a year of great shows, including Cecil Taylor and the Art Ensemble of Chicago, the Five Spot closed yet again. Run by a brother team, Iggy and Joe Termini, for thirty years, it was initially a tiny neighborhood bar at 5 Cooper Square, then, from 1962, a larger (200-person) venue nearby at 2 St. Mark's Place. The Five Spot had hosted some of Taylor's earliest performances in the late '50s. It had been Thelonious Monk's home base during the same period, where he often played with John Coltrane. Ornette Coleman's five-week residency there in '59 put him on the map; Eric Dolphy's stand in the summer of '61 did the same for him. Billie Holiday couldn't perform there legally after losing her cabaret card, but she would hang out during her final years—she was friends with the Terminis—and would get up onstage and sing a number if the coast seemed clear of cops. After an ill-fated detour into the food business in the '60s, the brothers reopened the club in '74, but they ran into various licensing problems, shutting the door only months after Giddins called the Five Spot "the most significant music room in this country."

In a literal and symbolic relocation, the Five Spot's final booking, a new band led by the trumpeter Ted Curson, was moved to the Tin Palace, a small club at 325 Bowery run by the poet Paul Pines, a jazz fan who used to manage the late-night East Village hub Phebe's at 359 Bowery.[14] By July, Ali's Alley would reopen with a bar and a kitchen. And other clubs began sniffing around the new school of players. The Bottom Line booked Anthony Braxton on a bill with the classical ensemble Tashi, who played Messiaen's *Quartet for the End of Time*.

In early June, following Rivbea's lead, four kindred venues staged the New York Loft Jazz Celebration. Environ, on the eleventh floor of 476 Broadway, between Broome and Grand, was a sparsely furnished space run by the pianist/sculptor John Fischer and the jazz singer Jay Clayton, also a member of Steve Reich's ensemble. The bass clarinetist Mike Morgenstern ran Jazzmania on the fourth floor of 14 East Twenty-third Street, opposite Madison Square Park, a big living room with couches, carpeting, and fireplaces. Joe Lee Wilson presided over the Ladies' Fort in the basement of 2 Bond Street, at Broadway, and a collective of players called Free Life Communications ran Sunrise Studios on the third floor of 122 Second Avenue, near St. Mark's Place. Operating mostly under the city's regulatory radar, the spaces could be as unconventional as they wanted. The musicians played as long as they wanted. Food and drink was passed around. Jazzmania did weekend "bagel brunch" gigs, and the Ladies' Fort even did a "Jazz at Dawn" program, from 6:00 till 10:00 a.m. For some fans, it began their day; for others, it ended their night.

The best of the loft players drew on jazz history and international music in different ways. David Murray and Lester Bowie were two of the most exciting players on the scene. They knew the language of '60s free jazz, its extended voicing techniques and exploded forms and breakneck tempos, but they also knew the huge mess of music that preceded it. Bowie mixed deep blues with circus-style chortling, slurs, and growls in ways that made the old tricks avant-garde again, rubbing them against whispers and shrieks that extended the language of Miles and Coltrane. Henry Threadgill, the West Coast saxman Arthur Blythe, and the New York vocalist Jeanne Lee could also traffic among traditions. Rather than choose between old and new jazz, tradition and "free," they treated the music as an ongoing conversation.

Meanwhile, two of jazz's most lyrical explorers, Don Cherry and Randy Weston, returned to New York from abroad, bringing voluptuous new sounds. Weston had been in Africa, primarily Morocco, and after two releases on Arista Freedom, he reappeared on the New York scene as a prodigal son, with a style equal parts Thelonious Monk, Duke Ellington, and Dollar Brand (Abdullah Ibrahim).[15]

Cherry had been living in an old schoolhouse on an organic farm in southern Sweden, raising his children Neneh and Eagle Eye, hitchhiking around Europe and North Africa, and practicing Tibetan Buddhism. He was a free-jazz godfather via his tenure with Ornette Coleman, and returned to New York in part to see Ornette play their old haunt, the Five Spot, in May of '75. His own band played the club in June, showing a trumpet futurist who had reinvented himself no less than Miles had on *Bitches Brew*.

But where Davis envisioned himself a psychedelic jazz-rock god, Cherry represented as a global troubadour-mystic. He performed on piano, wooden flutes, and doussin gouni, a five-string Malian hunter's harp with a calabash resonator and, attached to the neck, a riveted metal rattle that produced an insectlike buzz. He also played his signature pocket trumpet—which seemed more magically exotic than ever in this context—with a tone grown more meditative and supple.

This isn't to say his music had gone soft. His quartet here included his longtime pal Billy Higgins on drums, the muscular tenor saxophonist Frank Lowe, and the bassist Hakim Jamal. One minute Cherry would play a wooden flute in duet with Higgins, who brought soft thunder with his mallets. Then Lowe's horn would scream hot enough to peel paint off the walls.[16] (An expanded version of the quartet recorded the funky, kosmic electric-acoustic LP *Don Cherry*, later reissued as *Brown Rice*.)

Cherry didn't like playing clubs anymore—he felt the context reduced him to a liquor pimp—but he made an exception for the Five

Spot, trying to make the space as holy as he could, laying down a rug onstage, and draping a cloth wall hanging behind him decorated with the Sanskrit scale: Sa Ri Ga Ma Pa Dha Ni Sa.[17]

In the summer of '76, Cherry spent time working with students at the Creative Music Studio alongside Karl Berger, Anthony Braxton, and Kalaparusha Maurice McIntyre (who'd moved to upstate New York from Chicago in '74 at the suggestion of the drummer Jack DeJohnette, also a Woodstock resident). It was a homecoming of sorts. When Berger was a member of Cherry's Paris-based band in the mid-'60s, the trumpeter would spend hours with his ear glued to his shortwave radio, searching for international music broadcasts. One day, Cherry came to practice with a new tune.

"It's called 'Gamala Gamala Taki,'" he announced. "You just count it like three-three-two. But don't use the numbers: use the syllables."

His bandmates were puzzled, but they picked it up. Though Cherry never copped to it, Berger assumed the trumpeter had picked up the tune from a shortwave broadcast—it sounded Middle Eastern to him, Afghani perhaps, and Cherry had a photographic memory that way. The song fell by the wayside, but for Berger, the exercise of playing it blossomed into the universalizing notion that all music could be divided into units of three (gamala) and two (taki). In Woodstock, gamala taki rhythm training—group chanting sessions that arranged the words according to whatever the improvising situation called for—became the core of his teaching methodology at CMS, a principle that could connect improvisers with the musical traditions of any culture.

In March, Thelonious Monk played a headlining concert at Carnegie Hall. Except for a brief set at Newport the following summer, he'd been laying low. Was he sick? On junk? Gone mad? No one really knew. His strange, clustered chords and falling-down-the-stairs rhythms had changed jazz language, and had had a profound, if not always explicit, influence on the current scene; you could hear his sound refracted in the playing of Cecil Taylor, Randy Weston, Andrew Hill, Muhal Richard Abrams—pretty much every jazz pianist you could name with an interest in moving the music forward.

With Paul Jeffreys on tenor, Lonnie Hilyer on trumpet, Larry Ridley on bass, and his son, Thelonious "Toot" Monk, Jr., on drums, Monk played beautifully: "Misterioso," "'Round Midnight," "Evidence," "Bolivar Blues," "Rhythm-a-Ning," "Blue Monk," "Ruby, My Dear." The fifty-eight-year-old pianist even played "Just a Gigolo."[18] In his review, Gary Giddins called Monk a "great rabbi."

The Grackle came out of Brooklyn; *Cadence* was from upstate; *Bells* (named in part for the Albert Ayler composition) bussed in from Berkeley; *Radio Free Jazz* hailed from D.C. Every time you walked into a record store, there seemed to be another fanzine.

Like the musicians, music writers were adopting the DIY approach. Alongside *Punk*, there was *New York Rocker*, started by the Queens College graduate Alan Betrock, a fanzine veteran who had launched the seminal hand-drawn *JAMZ* as an undergrad back in '71, then the record collector's resource *The Rock Marketplace* in '73. Printed on newspaper stock from typewritten pasteups, *New York Rocker* debuted in January and came out monthly. It often had artists writing about themselves. In the debut, Richard Hell praised his new band, the Heartbreakers, using the pen name of his alter ego Theresa Stern, who called him "a master rock conceptualist." In the second issue, Blondie's Gary Valentine wrote about being roughed up by New York City cops and arrested, with his bandmate Clem Burke, on a weed-possession charge, and spending a couple of nights in jail, including one in the Tombs at 125 White Street. ("We didn't have any marijuana. We don't use that stuff," he lied.)[19]

In the same issue, David Byrne wrote about his band Talking Heads, his worldview ("I guess I feel a little alienated, but I don't feel like it's my pervasive attitude"), and his fondness for double-knit slacks, which he would always shrink by inadvertently washing them in hot water. He also wrote about disco songs he liked: "Kung Fu Fighting," "You Sexy Thing," and Donna Summer's "Love to Love You Baby"—"except for the long middle part where she groans," he noted. "I don't like that."[20]

> Art and culture are invented. We make them up. Otherwise,
> they don't exist.   —Philip Glass[21]

Philip Glass and Robert Wilson were rehearsing *Einstein on the Beach* five or six days a week, from 10:00 a.m. into the night, in Wilson's studio at 147 Spring Street. Glass had finished the music in November. The primary parts had been cast—including, very fortunately, the Judson Group dancer-choreographer Lucinda Childs—and they held an open audition for the remaining singer-dancers that month. More than a hundred people showed up: some of them pros, some amateurs, some kooks. Glass and Wilson chose a dozen singers for the chorus, and also found their key narrator: Samuel M. Johnson, a semiretired theater actor in his seventies who lived in Brooklyn and spent part of every day teaching himself piano.

In rehearsals, Johnson contributed two of *Einstein*'s central texts. One was the Bus Driver's story that ends the work:

> Two lovers sat on a park bench, with their bodies touching, holding hands in the moonlight. There was silence between them. So profound was their love for each other, they needed no words to express it. And so they sat in silence, on a park bench, with their bodies touching, holding hands in the moonlight . . .

The two lovers, Childs and Sheryl Sutton, a longtime Wilson collaborator, indeed sit on a bench, with a bus moving in exquisitely slow motion toward them. The music rises, thickens, and, after four-plus hours, finally ends.

No established U.S. theater or opera company would produce *Einstein*—Wilson and Glass were unknowns to opera audiences—so they planned to produce it themselves. A visit from the French minister of culture, Michel Guy, a former arts producer familiar with both men's work, led him to commission the premiere of *Einstein* for the Avignon Festival in August, followed by a two-week run at the Autumn Festival in Paris. A Venice Biennale commission followed. Now, the men had to create a touring opera production. Logistics were left to the support staff of Wilson's performance company, the Byrd Hoffman School of Byrds, which often resembled a religious cult as much as an arts organization.

Einstein was full of riveting images: a train, a rectangular spaceship, an illuminated bed that rises through the air. What did it all mean? Who knew? "Fundamental to our approach," wrote Glass, "was the as-

The New York Dolls at the Mercer Arts Center, January 1, 1973 (Photograph by Bob Gruen)

Cheo Feliciano and Héctor Lavoe at Yankee Stadium, August 23, 1973 (Photograph courtesy of Fania Records)

Bruce Springsteen and Patti Smith: bridge-and-tunnel
rock preachers, sans-serif comrades-in-arms

(Photographs courtesy of Columbia Records)

DJ Kool Herc: the King
(Photograph courtesy of Cindy Campbell)

Nicky Siano (with Michael Cappello),
opening night of the Mercer Street
Gallery, October 1974
(Photograph courtesy of Nicky Siano)

Bob Dylan and Patti Smith, 1975 (Photograph by Ken Regan)

Anthony Braxton rehearsing *Creative Orchestra Music 1976* (Photograph by Bill Smith)

The Philip Glass Ensemble, UCLA, 1977

(Photograph courtesy of Los Angeles Philharmonic/Betty Freeman Collection)

Sam Rivers and Joe Daly at Studio Rivbea, 1976 (Photograph by Tom Marcello)

Talking Heads, CBGB, 1976 (Photograph by Robert Spencer)

The Fania All-Stars (Photograph courtesy of Fania Records)

Max's Kansas City Xmas party, 1975 (Photograph by Bob Gruen)

Willie Colón and Rubén Blades, Gleason's Gym, cover shoot for *Metiendo Mano!*, 1977 (Photograph courtesy of Fania Records)

Suicide at CBGB, 1977 (Photograph by Bob Gruen)

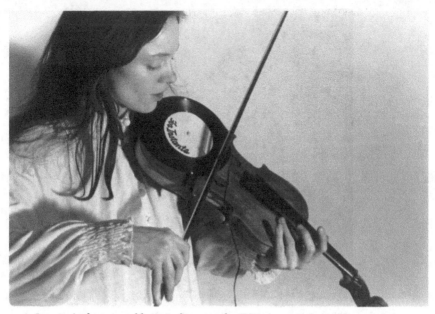

Laurie Anderson and her viophonograph, 1976 (Photograph courtesy of Laurie Anderson)

John Cale, Lou Reed, Patti Smith, and David Byrne at the Lower Manhattan
Ocean Club, 1976 (Photograph by Bob Gruen)

sumption that the audience itself completed the work. The statement is no mere metaphor; we meant it quite literally."[22]

Glass had first played this sort of aesthetic shell game when scoring Samuel Beckett's *Play* in 1965. *Play* was his first experiment with reductive/repetitive composing strategies, set against a narrative whose emotional center seemed to shift with every performance. As he worked on *Einstein*, Glass's wife, the director JoAnne Akalaitis, was directing a stage version of Beckett's *Cascando* for the Mabou Mines company at the Public Theater. Glass took time out to write the score: a cello piece to be played by Arthur Russell, a new friend of the couple's. Beckett-style obliquity was in the city air.

Aside from spoken-word pieces written mainly by Johnson and Christopher Knowles—a teenage poet-performer with a neurological disorder who Wilson met through his work with disabled students—the sung text of *Einstein* consisted solely of recited numbers and solfège syllables (*do, re, mi*). Introduced initially to aid the singers in memorizing the music, with lyrical texts to come later, they eventually *became* the sung text. At first blush, they sound hilarious. But there's a surprising power in their rhythm and melody as they set up the work's participatory tabula rasa. Like much of Wilson's work, the text and staging resist interpretation. But primarily, the nearly five-hour performance is about temporal distortion, like Einstein's notions of space-time, and to give in to the tidal surge of Glass's organ arpeggios and the choral invocations is to feel alternately suspended outside time and swept up in its rush.

As it turned out, *Einstein*'s most indelible music involved the incantations of "One-two-three-four-five-six-seven-eight," which were being rehearsed on Spring Street just as the Ramones, down at CBGB, counted off every song with "One-two-three-four!"

Rhys Chatham grew up in Manhattan. His father, Price, was a harpsichordist. Rhys took up flute and piano, studied composition at New York University, and initially threw in with the serialists. Then he began studying with the composer Morton Subotnick, whose 1967 *Silver Apples of the Moon*, commissioned by the Elektra Records subsidiary Nonesuch, was a landmark of synthesizer music (it paved the way for a slew of pop-electronic recordings, including the 1968 Top 10 hit *Switched-On Bach*). Chatham swapped ideas with the composers Charlemagne Palestine and Maryanne Archer, who were also working with Subotnick at NYU. For cash, Chatham was a piano and harpsichord tuner, and after working on La Monte Young's instruments, he began studying with him as well.

In '71, Chatham, age nineteen, became the Kitchen's first music curator and, after hearing Terry Riley perform, became a devout minimalist. His own hour-long *Two Gongs*, written the same year, premiered at the Kitchen: Chatham and his fellow experimentalist Yoshi Wada hammering nonstop on two gongs with mallets while overtone clouds billowed through the room.

Chatham spent much of the mid-'70s playing improvised music, and in '76 joined the Love of Life Orchestra as a flutist. The group was led by Peter Gordon, a composer-saxophonist from Los Angeles who used rock techniques in notated compositions. Chatham had, in fact, never been to a rock concert. So one evening in May, Gordon and Chatham— who was living with Philip Glass's sax player Dicky Landry—walked over to CBGB, where they met up with Chatham's former roommate Arthur Russell and the young percussionist David Van Tieghem to see the Ramones.[23] The club was jammed, and the noise, Chatham recalled, was glorious.[24] "I was looking for a musical voice," he told me via Skype in 2009. "I thought: 'Steve Reich uses Ghanaian music, Phil Glass uses jazz instrumentation, La Monte Young comes out of Indian music. I've got to find my own thing.' Then I heard the Ramones, and I said, 'That's my voice.'"[25]

The next day, still drunk on the sound of Johnny's buzzsaw grind, Chatham borrowed a Fender Telecaster from his friend and fellow composer Scott Johnson. More as a research project than anything else, Chatham formed a rock band, calling it Arsenal. The band lasted only a couple of performances, although he remained involved with the guitarist Nina Canal.

One evening, Chatham and Canal were fooling around on guitar in his apartment. Chatham struck the low E string and tried to make melodies with the overtones. Canal suggested Chatham make a piece out of the idea. "Rhys," she exclaimed cryptically, "it really sounds like YOU!"[26]

This was the seed of something. He spent the rest of the year trying to figure out what.

•

Steve Reich put the finishing touches on *Music for 18 Musicians* in March, and after a few more group rehearsals in his loft space on Warren Street off Church, he led the world premiere at Town Hall on April 24. The voices and bass clarinets rose and fell like waves against the granular melodies of mallet instruments and pianos, the sound dazzling. *The New York Times* allotted Robert Palmer three paragraphs to cover the performance, in a roundup of four short classical concert reviews. Palmer described "a lovely, shimmering radiance quite unlike any sound this reviewer has ever heard."[27]

Reich and his musicians went straight into the studio to record the piece for Deutsche Grammophon. The recording sounded magical: its bright mallet-drawn melodies sparkling, instantly engaging. It sounded— well, like pop, in a way. But the label, veteran promoters of European classical music, had no idea what to do with it. So the tape sat in a vault.

On Friday, April 9, Phil Ochs—who had dressed up as Elvis on the cover of his final studio LP, the comically titled *Greatest Hits*—hung himself at his sister's apartment in Far Rockaway.

The Vietnam War had ended the year before; Ochs had played a free concert in Central Park with Joan Baez to celebrate the occasion for a crowd estimated at more than 100,000. In January, Ochs moved in with his sister, Sonny. He watched TV, read the paper, took pills for his bipolar disorder, and drank. He had become a rebel without a cause.

On April 17 Patti Smith performed "Gloria" and "My Generation" on NBC's new comedy show, *Saturday Night Live*, which was rounding out its first season. President Ford's press secretary, Ron Nessan, was guest host; the episode included Dan Aykroyd pitching Bass-o-matic, and Gilda Radner, as the hearing-impaired Emily Litella, discussing "presidential erections" on "Weekend Update." It was Smith's first appearance on national television, and it was a pretty good bet that even the president was watching. Down at CBGB, the entryway TV set was tuned in.[28]

The following week, when *Saturday Night Live*'s producer, Lorne

Michaels, offered the Beatles three thousand dollars on the air to reunite there and then, Lennon and McCartney were watching together
at Lennon's apartment at the Dakota on Seventy-second Street. For a
minute, they considered grabbing a cab over to the 30 Rock studios to
accept.[29]

A few weeks earlier, Patti Smith met Fred "Sonic" Smith in Detroit.
She was leaving a preconcert party given by her label at American Coney
Island, the famous twenty-four-hour hot dog joint on the corner of Michigan Avenue and Lafayette Boulevard. The Patti Smith Group was touring the country on *Horses*. Smith was still in a relationship with Allen
Lanier and spending a lot of time with Tom Verlaine. Now Fred Smith
introduced himself. He was a former guitarist with the MC5, a tall,
quiet guy, twenty-seven years old. Patti invited him to join the band
onstage that night for "My Generation." He did, and returned to the
hotel with her, where they stayed up late. When she left the following
day, she promised to stay in touch.

The Patti Smith Group played their U.K. debut at the Roundhouse in
London on Sunday, May 16, the same night Eddie Palmieri was firing
up the Beacon and the Rivbea Festival was blowing through downtown.
It was the first of a two-night run, and the first time a bona fide New
York "punk" band had played in London since the Dolls in '72.

The show was shaky, the band spent from traveling and a hash-
baked gig at the Paradiso in Amsterdam the night before. Musically,
Kaye thought it was their worst show of the tour. But the audience,
many of whom had seen Smith sing "Horses" and "Hey Joe" on TV on
The Old Grey Whistle Test a few nights earlier—incanting verse behind
Ray-Ban Wayfarers, images of rape, murder, homosexual love, and ecstatic freedom unspooling into bedsits and tidy suburban living rooms—
were besotted. Fan mail and gifts were waiting for her backstage at the
Roundhouse; one letter read: "Marry me. I want to fuck you." Onstage
the band tore through "Free Money." In unison, the crowd of a thousand
raised their arms in the air. "Redondo Beach" had a female couple
cheering, "Yeah, tell it to them, Patti!" Kaye led a squalling tribute to
Keith Relf, of feedback pioneers the Yardbirds, who had been electrocuted two days earlier while playing an ungrounded guitar. Patti improvised over the top of the noise: "Do you feel frustrated? Do you feel like

a loser?"—intent on pushing the mob of hapless kids toward some personal revolution. They played "Horses," "My Generation," "Time Is on My Side."[30]

Viv Albertine and her art-school pal Mick Jones were there. So was Joe Strummer, singer in an R&B pub outfit called the 101ers. So was Paul Simonon. So was Chrissie Hynde, an Ohio expat who had been part of the antiwar protest at Kent State where four students were shot by National Guardsmen six years earlier. So was John Lydon.

Albertine was transfixed, above all, by the fact that Smith was wearing her hair up in a ponytail, talking about how girls shouldn't be afraid to show their faces. She and Strummer met Smith on the street afterward, when Smith was mingling with fans. In two weeks, Joe Strummer left the 101ers to join the Clash. Viv Albertine joined the Slits.

Not everyone was impressed. From the stage of the 100 Club on Oxford Street later that week, Lydon—Johnny Rotten of the Sex Pistols—weighed in. "In we go to the Roundhouse the other night," he sneered, "see the hippie shaking tambourines: 'Horses, Horses.' Horseshit!" Jay Dee Daugherty, standing in the crowd, thought, "Fuck, that was a quick fifteen minutes . . . we're fucking over already." Later that year, Lydon told a writer for *Punk*: "I don't like her. Just a bunch of [putting on a whining voice] 'Oh, yeah, when I was in high school!' Two out of ten for effort."[31]

It was the beginning of punk's war of authorship. Maybe it was partly because Rotten knew his debt, and it made matricidal sense for him to attack the New York scene first. When Lydon snarled the Pistols song "New York," he may have been, as author Jon Savage suggests, channeling Malcolm McLaren's anger at Sylvain Sylvain, who snubbed an offer from his former manager to join the Pistols in favor of a cash-grab tour of Japan with David Johansen and a re-formed New York Dolls. But when Lydon spits lines like "you're just a pile of shit" and "ya poor little faggot," with specific reference to gigging in Japan and at "Max's Kansas," the pub-fight bile seems fully his own.

Patti had a taste for internecine warfare herself. At the Marquee Club one night around the time of her Roundhouse shows, she saw the Kiss bassist, Gene Simmons. He was in England with his band for an appearance on the TV show *So It Goes*, hosted by the future Factory Records founder Tony Wilson, and was chatting up two hot groupies. Smith walked up to him, slurred some disparaging comments, slapped him in the face, and walked away.[32]

•

On May 10, the Ramones played their first Bottom Line gig, opening for Dr. Feelgood, British pub rockers who laid the groundwork for their country's punk aesthetic in the same way the Dolls did in New York— by reminding people of the joy in simple, full-throttle rock 'n' roll. It wasn't the kind of Bottom Line event Springsteen and Smith had insti- gated last year, but Warhol was there to give it an air of consequence. So was Tom Verlaine, literally taking notes, and Wayne County, uncharac- teristically dressed as a dude, characteristically causing a ruckus. It was odd seeing the CBGB gang out of their element. But then, the scene at CBGB wasn't what it had been. Competition was in the air.

Back in March, as Wayne County was onstage doing his Patti Smith parody, the competition turned violent. In a white shirt, black tie, and black fright wig, County spewed faux poetry about Jim Morrison's pubic hair floating through Parisian sewers, and howled, "Horse-shit! Horse-shit!" (because great punk minds think alike).[33]

"Handsome" Dick Manitoba, singer for the Dictators, had come to see County perform. Manitoba's band deserved as much credit for sir- ing New York City punk rock as any of the CBGB acts. They'd been together since '73. Their main songwriter and conceptualist, Andy Shernoff, had published a back-to-basics rock zine, *Teenage Wasteland Gazette*, before nearly anyone. Joey Ramone and his bandmates learned plenty about attitude and absurd humor from the Dictators back when they all hung out at the Coventry in Queens. The guys who started *Punk* magazine revered them.

But the Dictators had gotten their break early, and when Epic Rec- ords released *Go Girl Crazy* in March of '75, there was no context for what they were doing, at least not in the mainstream. The record tanked, Epic dropped them, the band split. Now they were back together, but playing catch-up with every half-assed band in CBGB.

Manitoba begins heckling County.

"Who the fuck is that? Why don't you come up here and say it, you fucking asshole!" yells County into the darkness of the club. His wig is shining under the spotlight; four or five black beauties—he can't recall how many he took—are tearing through his skull.

Manitoba keeps talking shit. This is punk rock; it's participatory. The audience response is part of the show. Like the Stooges. County hears "Queer!" He hears, "Ya fucking drag queen!" It's nothing he hasn't heard before, repeatedly, his entire adult life. He's taking in air in crazy gulps. The white light in his eyes and in his head is blinding.

Now the voice is right up near the left corner of the stage, which you had to squeeze past to get to the club's appalling bathrooms. Manitoba is still barking. Maybe he lunges at County. Nearly naked at this point in his act, his shredded dress hanging off him, County hoists up his mic stand and brings the heavy iron base down on the guy's shoulder, hard.

Manitoba sprawls backward, hitting his head on a table. He gets up, gushing blood, and hurls himself at County. David Johansen stands near the stage, aghast. The audience goes ape-shit; people jump in trying to separate the two men, or simply to cheer them on.

When fists stop flying, Manitoba is blood-soaked and can barely stand. Andy Shernoff helps him out of the club and rushes him over to St. Vincent's Hospital on West Twelfth Street, where their pal Joey Ramone once spent two weeks in the psych ward.[34]

County, also covered in blood but intact, returns to the mic. "Do you want me to quit," he screams, "or do you want to rock 'n' roll?!"

The crowd roars like Romans at lion-feeding time, and the band lurches into "Rock Me Jesus, Roll Me Lord, Wash Me in the Blood of Rock and Roll," almost as if the whole thing was part of the show.

This was something new. Sure, the city was rife with violence, and bands put up a vicious front—Patti singing about switchblades, Joey Ramone chanting "Beat on the brat / with a baseball bat!" Outright assaults by musicians, however, were pretty much unheard-of.

The upstart British bands understood the power of violence. In April, the Sex Pistols, gigging less than six months, played at a London pub called the Nashville. Word on them was getting out; John Ingham had written the first feature on the band for *Sounds*, and it lured other journalists and photographers.

The Pistols played "(I'm Not Your) Stepping Stone," and an original, "No Feelings." But the band seemed flat, the audience, full of gawkers, uninspired. The mood changed in the middle of "Pretty Vacant"— written in response to Malcolm McLaren's challenge to the band to write an anti-anthem akin to "Blank Generation"—when Vivienne Westwood, McLaren's girlfriend and business partner, decided to liven things up in the front row by slapping a girl in the face. The girl opened her mouth wide in outrage; Westwood slapped her again. The girl's boyfriend rushed in, then McLaren; then, diving off the stage with a look of delight, Rotten.

The next week, photos of the mini-riot were everywhere in the rock press. The legend had begun.

The Ramones was released in Britain the same day as the incident. But the bands felt no special kinship toward each other. The Ramones "were all long-haired and of no interest to me," Lydon wrote in his autobiography. "I didn't like their image, what they stood for, or anything about them."

On June 4, the Pistols played a small show in the upstairs room of the Manchester Free Trade Hall—the building where Dylan, performing electric with the Band, was famously called a "Judas." It was the Pistols' first gig in the city. Steven Morrissey, ex-president of the New York Dolls Fan Club, was there. So were Pete Shelley and Howard Devoto, the two converts who had booked the show, and who had recently started their own Pistols-inspired band called the Buzzcocks. So was future Joy Division member Peter Hook, who went out and bought a bass the very next day.

The same night in New York, a phalanx of second-tier CBGB bands began a long weekend of live recording sessions at the club for a multi-act album. Neither the Ramones nor Patti Smith took part—they were already under contract. Nor did Television, who were being courted by Arista, Sire, Atlantic, and Elektra in the wake of brushing off Island. Talking Heads and Blondie were on the bill, but they were close to nailing down their own deals, so they eventually bowed out of the project.

The double LP *Live at CBGB's* wound up featuring the Shirts, the Miamis, Tuff Darts, Mink DeVille, the Laughing Dogs, Manster, and Stuart's Hammer. As a layman's introduction to the New York scene, it was underwhelming. Max's Kansas City followed with its own branding compilation, *Max's Kansas City 1976*, culled from studio recordings. At this point, the impresario Mickey Ruskin was long gone, and Max's was being run by a New Jersey restaurateur, Tommy Dean. After hiring the scene-savvy Peter Crowley to book shows, Dean tried to reestablish the club as New York's premier rock dive, covering the walls with poster-sized photos of local musicians shot by County's roommate, Leee Childers. One of the best was a picture of Patti Smith with Tom Verlaine, holding his hand and looking up at the camera with a slightly guilty smirk. The club even concocted a special menu of New York Rock Drinks: the Patti Smith ("Champagne and Stout. It's been making poets horny for years"), the Suicide ("Green Chartreuse and 151 proof rum . . . on fire"), and even the Dolls ("Don't ask. Just drink it!").

Held over Easter weekend in April, Max's Festival of Unsigned Bands featured Wayne County (also the club's main DJ), Suicide (Hilly Kristal hated them), and Pere Ubu (an arty Cleveland punk band making their New York debut). The Ramones and the Heartbreakers, happy to play both sides of the street if the checks didn't bounce, also played.

So did Blondie, debuting as a polished five-piece with their new keyboardist, Jimmy Destri. People who had dismissed them as third-rate were astounded. It was especially sweet for Debbie Harry, who had been waiting tables there not long ago.

After the County-Manitoba brawl, the Dictators were banned not from CBGB, surprisingly, but from Max's, whose booker, Crowley, also managed County. Word on the street was that any band sharing a bill anywhere with the Dictators would be banned from Max's as well. Manitoba, who wound up with a broken collarbone and sixteen stitches in his head, had decided to press charges. County went into hiding, sort of: he dyed his hair from blond to black and donned a fake mustache for his next DJ stint at Max's. The police found him there and arrested him on assault charges. He spent a night in jail at the Tombs; Tommy Dean bailed him out, and helped arrange a fund-raiser for his defense expenses at Max's with Blondie, the Ramones, and others.

In the end, charges were dropped; the speed-addled County had overreacted, but he was arguably acting in self-defense. The episode stopped the Dictators in their tracks—Manitoba was wheelchair-bound for a time. The band were tagged as assholes and homophobes, and their biggest boosters, Legs McNeil and John Holstrom at *Punk*, were tarred with the same brush. The situation was fueled by Lester Bangs, who was just preparing to relocate from Detroit to New York City. According to Holmstrom, Bangs hunkered down at the magazine's offices one night and hammered out a defense of the band titled "Who Are the Real Dictators?" in which he ranted against the local "rock culture

FAGGOT MAFIA" (presumably a swipe at the Ramones manager/*Soho News* columnist Danny Fields, among others), audiences at CBGB and other NYC rock clubs (". . . THE WORST CONFORMISTS I HAVE EVER SEEN. They're worse than Maynard G. Krebs on Dobie Gillis"), and Television (who "sound like the fucking Grateful Dead").[35] The piece was never published, and things eventually settled down. But punk rock retained a homophobic taint, despite the scene's initial post-glam, anything-goes androgyny.

New York was especially high-strung that spring and summer. This was partly due to the Great Dope Famine—or, as it was known in our neighborhood, simply the Drought. There was no weed to be had anywhere. It's hard to remember, in these days of cell-phone-delivery-service characters who come to your apartment 24/7 with suitcases full of jewel-boxed hydroponic buds grown domestically, that in the '70s quality marijuana had to be imported. And for much of '76, presumably due to increased interdiction, it wasn't.

The *Soho News* ran a cover story about the weed famine in its Fourth of July issue. "Stockbrokers have lost their radar," Frank Lauria wrote. "Creative Directors can't find the hook. Disc Jockeys are at a loss for words, and Television Executives can no longer sense the pulse of the public. Manhattan's vaunted artistic turbine is sputtering lamely on stems and seeds . . . There is simply no grass to be had in fun city."[36]

With pot scarce, barrel-shaped "THC" tabs—which everyone knew were not THC but likely PCP or some dubious cocktail—flooded the market that summer. There was a brisk trade in those mysterious green and blue tabs at Cunningham Park, where we hung out. Kids also carried vials of Locker Room, an amyl-nitrate analog bogusly billed in head shops as a "room odorizer" but actually used as an inhalant that produced a debilitating head rush and loosey-goosey muscles (it was popular in bathhouses as a sex aperitif).

Less common in the neighborhood was angel dust: usually dried herbs or low-grade weed that had been soaked in a solution of PCP—chemical name phencyclidine—and then redried. PCP had been developed as a surgical anesthetic, but its side effects, which could include intense delirium and hallucinations, were eventually deemed too extreme for humans. It was reintroduced as a veterinary anesthetic in

'67 under the brand name Sernalyn, and imaginative drug dealers added it to their stock.

I took a hit of dust once from a joint passed to me at a Hot Tuna concert; it tasted like gasoline and peppermint, and made the auditorium seem like it was tumbling backward. Gary Valentine of Blondie wrote about smoking dust with his bandmates and called his high "the most gruesome two hours" of his life—he saw Debbie Harry's face as a smiling skull.[37] It was popular in the Bronx, too. It made music sound crazy, like transmissions from outer space.

Street wisdom blamed the marijuana shortage on a police crackdown both national (the Customs Bureau's vaunted "Star Trek" water-border policing program in Florida) and local. Certainly the NYPD wanted to clean things up in time for the Bicentennial celebration on July 4, when the eyes of the world would be on New York City. The attention should have inspired artists to great heights, and in some cases it did. According to the graffiti historian Jack Stewart, two B-list writers, Caine I and Flame I, pulled off the impossible in the wee hours of July 4 by covering one side of an entire eleven-car train in honor of the Bicentennial. But the first-ever full-length "worm" never left the yard: when the Transit Authority saw the grand testament to its ineffectual antigraffiti efforts, it had the cars separated, and no document of the work exists.[38]

The pair deserves credit for trying. The hoopla around the Bicentennial had gone on for so long, so loudly, it squelched most individual efforts at celebration. CBS-TV had been airing its annoying sixty-second "Bicentennial Minute" PSAs during prime time for two years already. The government minted commemorative quarters; Dr Pepper was sold in red, white, and blue bottles. And while President Ford might have been holding court in D.C., the main event was in New York.

This was Operation Sail and the International Naval Review, a maritime procession of sixteen huge sailing vessels and a few dozen warships cruising down the Hudson. It began at 11:00 a.m. The West Side Highway was shut down, and several hundred thousand people swarmed the waterfront. Some set up picnics alongside rotted-out piers; those with river views (such as Laurie Anderson, in a loft on Canal Street) threw parties. Rainy-day weed stashes were dug out and rolled up. A global fleet—including a Chilean vessel allegedly used as a seafaring prison by Augusto Pinochet, and a Soviet ship that provided the hallucinatory vision of the hammer-and-sickle flying over the Hudson to graying Greenwich Village lefties—floated by amid hundreds of private pleasure boats and rental cruisers. Cops flirted, fireboats shpritzed, the Goodyear blimp pimped. At 9:00 p.m., a $100,000 fireworks show sponsored by Macy's and choreographed by Disney blazed over the skyline.

Musicwise, there was nothing extraordinary in New York City on the night of America's two hundredth birthday. Talking Heads wrapped up a five-night stand at CBGB with Orchestra Luna. The Dictators played Club 82. The Newport Festival offered a posthumous Ellington tribute at Carnegie Hall. Studio Rivbea featured the Art Ensemble's Roscoe Mitchell, Jemeel Moondoc's Muntu Ensemble, and Sam Rivers. At the Gallery, Nicky Siano camped it up behind the turntables in patriotic drag as Lady Liberty, complete with an electric crown. The big classical event was Leonard Bernstein conducting the New York Philharmonic in Central Park's Sheep Meadow. Fifty thousand people turned out for an Americana program that was safe as milk: Schumann's *American Festival Overture*, Copland's *Lincoln Portrait*, and, of course, Gershwin's jazz-inflected *Rhapsody in Blue*. Ornette Coleman's *Skies of America* would have made a nice addition, but the celebration was not about looking forward. John Cage's Bicentennial tribute, *Apartment House 1776*, a piece of indeterminate length, melody, and instrumentation for four singers representing Protestant, Sephardic, Native American, and African traditions, wouldn't be finished for another month, and wouldn't have its premiere until the fall.

If you turned on the radio, you heard Dick Summer and Norm N. Nite on WNBC 660, broadcasting from the World Trade Center observation deck. WPLJ 95.5 played the usual rock mix; the more tie-dyed WLIR 92.7, for whatever reason, played a series of Dead bootlegs. If you wanted to avoid it all in a dark theater, there was *Logan's Run*, a featherweight sci-fi flick with Farrah Fawcett-Majors about a hedonistic future where beautiful people are exterminated on their thirtieth birthday; *The Devil Within Her*, a C-movie *Rosemary's Baby* knockoff; or *Midway*, a war drama with Henry Fonda and the tireless Charlton Heston, filmed in Sensurround, ensuring bombs and depth charges would drown out the fireworks outside the theater.

I took the E train down to Battery Park with a couple of friends. After unsuccessfully trying to sneak into office high-rises to view the ships, we bought Bud tall boys and wandered the streets with the hordes. We came upon an impromptu TriBeCa street party: some people in a second-floor loft had moved two club-size speaker cabinets into the window, and *Sgt. Pepper's Lonely Hearts Club Band* was thundering out of them. A crowd gathered, dancing and shouting along. People opened their coolers and passed around beers; some precious joints made the rounds.

As the final piano chord on side two slowly faded out, the crowd whooped and applauded. Then, the opening notes of Bob Marley's *Rastaman Vibration*, which had just come out, began throbbing from the speakers.

People booed lustily. "Turn it *off!*" shouted one man. "Nigger music!" barked another. "Beatles!" yelled another. The crowd, largely white, began bellowing in unison: "BEAT-LES! BEAT-LES! BEAT-LES!"

The DJs, with no interest in provoking a riot, faded out Marley and put on side one of *Revolver*.

Happy birthday, America.

For many, pop music still began and ended with the Beatles. When Paul McCartney played the Garden in May with his new band, Wings, on his first U.S. tour since 1966, the hysteria was profound. An organization on Long Island around this time was calling itself the International Committee to Reunite the Beatles. It sold decals of its logo—a soul-brother handshake under the words "Let It Be!"—took out newspaper ads, and held boom-box "rallies" around the city.

It's not hard to picture John Lennon, walking from the Dakota through Central Park with Yoko and baby Sean, coming upon them, shaking his head ruefully, and yelling out, "Please: let it *be*."

As payback for the Beatles, the Ramones made their U.K. debut at the Roundhouse on July 4. They were billed third, with the Stranglers and the headliners, the Flamin' Groovies, but for many they were the main event. Between a heat wave, sound-system problems, and the scale of the room—three thousand seats, far bigger than anywhere they'd played—the sold-out gig didn't go well. But an impression was made.

Afterward, Joey Ramone gave out small promotional brat-beating baseball bats.

The Sex Pistols played the Black Swan pub up in Sheffield that night; their opening act, playing their very first show, in black slacks and paint-spattered white shirts, was the Clash.

The following night the Ramones headlined Dingwalls, a pub in Camden Town. Chrissie Hynde was there. The Pistols rolled up with Malcolm McLaren, dressed like homeless street kids. Joe Strummer was waiting outside the club with Mick Jones to pay homage when the band arrived. "We're going to be bigger than the Sex Pistols," Strummer announced.[39]

Inside the club, the Clash bassist, Paul Simonon, got into a scuffle with the Stranglers bassist, JJ Burnel. When Dee Dee yelled out the first "One, two, three, four!" Strummer was right up front. So was John Ritchie, a pal of John Lydon's who also went by John Beverley (Beverley was his mother's surname), Sid Beverley, and Sid Vicious (the nickname given him by Rotten). Ritchie, notable for having recently assaulted the British music journalist Nick Kent with a bicycle chain, pogoed wildly with Vivienne Westwood. He wasn't a Pistol yet, but not long after the gig, he began teaching himself to play bass by thumping along to *Ramones*, high on speed, all through the night.[40]

British punks had started "gobbing," and the Ramones were showered with phlegm in a show of collective respect. It glistened on their leather jackets, dripped in strings from their guitar necks, sprayed off Tommy's cymbals.[41] The musicians who attended the show, and then rockers all over Britain, began playing faster after that gig.[42]

The next night, the Pistols played the 100 Club. On July 9, they had their first big London show, at the Lyceum. At one point, Rotten matter-of-factly stubbed out a lit cigarette on his balled fist. U.K. punk was on, and he was feeling no pain. If he did, it was an appealing sensation.

While London rushed on Dexedrine and methamphetamine, New York was nodding. Mexican brown heroin hit town that summer, and it was strong—around 50 to 60 percent pure, as opposed to the more heavily cut white Asian—and still cheap, at three to five dollars a bag, or twenty for a rock.

The timing, given the marijuana shortage, was remarkable. There were so many addicts looking to get clean in New York, they'd become a lobbying group: in May, over a hundred recovering junkies set up a tent city near the state capitol in Albany to protest the defunding of residential treatment centers, as taxpayer dollars were redirected into school-based prevention programs in the suburbs.[43] The Albany protestors were mobilized by Julio Martinez, a South Bronx Puerto Rican ex-junkie and salsa fan who became a drug treatment advocate and cofounder of the residential rehab facility Phoenix House.

Meanwhile, as Lower Manhattan's bargain-basement appeal grew among real estate speculators, many believed that cheap heroin was being given safe passage into certain neighborhoods via some nefarious conspiracy of power elites—since junkies, for obvious reasons, tend to be easier to evict than other tenants.

In late July, Lou Reed and John Cale reprised the Velvet Underground's "Waiting for My Man" with Patti Smith and David Byrne at a midnight jam at the Lower Manhattan Ocean Club, a new venue opened down on Chambers Street by Mickey Ruskin, founder of Max's Kansas City. It was a family gathering. Clive Davis—who had signed Smith, Springsteen, and now Reed, whose RCA contract had run its course—was there. Danny Fields, who used to comanage the MC5 with Jon Landau, was there with his pals Lisa Robinson and Lenny Kaye. Andy Warhol was there. So were Byrne's bandmates, Chris Frantz and Tina Weymouth, along with a feral-looking sixteen-year-old, Lydia Koch, who was new in town and seemed to have the hots for the wiry guitarist. (Koch would soon start her own band, Teenage Jesus and the Jerks, and change her last name to Lunch.)[44] Cale, host of the session, was playing out again after a period of laying low. He'd been touring with Smith, usually joining her for the closing "My Generation" cover.[45] Cale's drink of choice: Courvoisier and a Schaefer chaser.

The Ocean Club never took off—the location was too far south of Canal from the heart of things. And before long, the once famously teetotaling Ruskin would OD. But this night, with New York rock's past, present, and future christening his new room, he probably felt like he would live forever.

Philip Glass had been a semiregular at Max's, even played a gig there with his group once. When Ruskin sold the place, Glass remained loyal: "I followed him around," he said. "I didn't hang out as much as other people did, but I always knew where Mickey's club was, and my friends always went."[46]

Glass didn't make it to the Ocean Club that week, however. He was in France at the Avignon Festival with Bob Wilson and their "opera company" for the first full-dress performance of *Einstein on the Beach*.

There were technical issues. Kurt Munkacsi was troubleshooting a sound system with wireless headset mics, cutting-edge technology at the time. And some of the scenes were still being worked out—most critically, one in the middle of the final act, where a lightbox representing a bed slowly tilts up from horizontal to vertical, then rises, like a dream vision, up into the fly space. The trick was accomplished by two guys slowly turning a hand winch. One unsteady motion and the lightbox, suspended on cables, would begin to swing, and the spell would be broken.

Then there was the score, which was still evolving. With rehearsals going late into the night, Glass spent the days writing louder intermezzo parts to cover the scene changes. He had miscalculated: the connecting interstitials he had composed in New York, dubbed "Knee Plays," were too quiet to cover up the sound of scenery being dragged and sometimes dropped—the main reason for the intermezzo music in the first place.[47]

A bigger last-minute addition came when the singer Joan La Barbara had a diva moment. "Look," she told Glass, disgruntled, "this is an opera, I'm the soprano lead, and I don't have an aria. I want an aria!"[48]

With the clock ticking, Glass wrote one for her: a gorgeously billowing piece slotted into the light-bed scene. On record and onstage, it is *Einstein*'s most moving musical moment.

The premiere eclipsed everything else at the festival, and heralded a European tour that attracted followers as pie-eyed in their ardor as Deadheads. The nine performances at the Opéra-Comique in Paris had ticketless hopefuls clotting the sidewalk. Often they'd sneak in through the backstage area and wind up in the orchestra pit, where ushers would have to shoo them out. At times ensemble members came close to being ejected mid-performance, defending their ticketless presence in broken French.

The American premiere, slated for November, would present its own problems. But a review of the Avignon performance in the *Soho Weekly News* was auspicious. "*Einstein on the Beach* is more than brilliant, more than a masterpiece, more than mere total-theater," rhapsodized Robb Baker. "It is the first complete art statement (as much as I distrust art statements) of our times, of our schizophrenic split between mind and soul, between science and magic, between material reality and desired transcendence."[49]

With the Bicentennial and a remarkably trouble-free Democratic National Convention behind them, New Yorkers basked in a late-August glow. "This is the best summer New York has had since the '50s," enthused writer Pete Hamill. "Something extraordinary is in the air. Part of it is a sense of relief: the feds have done their worst; the financial junta has gouged large chunks out of the body of our democracy; cops, firemen, and thousands of other city workers have been laid off. We are dirtier, less charitable, less grand, and less just. But we are here. We have survived."[50]

Carter's nomination was energizing. Hurricane Belle blew fiercely through town, but did little damage. (Long Island and the Jersey Shore weren't so lucky.) New Yorkers reveled in their fabled resilience.

In the East Village, those prescient kooks the Purple People had saved the Garden of Eden, their squatter vegetable garden/art space, yet again—this time from a demolition project next door on Eldridge Street. (The city promised to hold off until harvest was over.) The Purples tended their yin-yang-shaped plot in magenta tie-dye outfits, fertilizing crops with what they called "night soil": a mixture of carriage-horse manure (collected by bicycle off the streets around Central Park) and, for spiritual good measure, their very own vegetarian feces. They worked the land devotedly, in spite of the fact that their crops—tomatoes, corn, broccoli, cucumbers, peas—were usually stolen by junkies or marauding neighbors. But as the Purple leader, the Reverend Les Ego, put it, "Life is an eternal radical transformation," and he hoped for the best.[51]

At around 1:00 a.m. on July 29, two teenage girls were shot on the street up in Pelham Bay in the Bronx. Donna Lauria was hit in the chest and killed instantly; Jody Valenti was hit in the thigh and survived. Valenti could identify the shooter only as a man in his thirties, pale complexion, about five-nine, about 160 pounds, with dark curly hair. After the shooting, she said, he turned and strode away briskly. There were no other clues, beyond what ballistics experts found out from the shell casings, which were fired from a .44 Charter Arms Bulldog revolver, an unusual weapon—a powerful, connoisseur's handgun.

The shooting made no sense. But neither did a lot of things.

A swine flu panic, triggered by the death of a military recruit at Fort Dix in New Jersey, began in September.

On Labor Day, Jimmy Carter officially announced his campaign from the front porch of FDR's house and spa retreat in Warm Springs, Georgia—the incubator of the New Deal.

Early the next morning, someone torched the Cleveland Place Bar, near Little Italy at Lafayette and Spring streets. It had been used to set a scene in Scorsese's *Mean Streets*, then closed; word was that it was supposedly reopening as a gay bar.

The next evening, a gang of young men and boys rolled through Washington Square Park with military precision. One group came off Thompson Street to the south, sweeping up to the fountain; another, in a pincer move, came from Waverly Place to the west. These guys were white, with chains and baseball bats; their targets were black or Latino. In the end fourteen people were injured, one killed. What seemed initially like a straight-up hate crime—accompanied by shouts of "Get the niggers!"—turned out to be a knottier affair, an apparent revenge move on the park's drug dealers. Many happened to be black, and most—like so many city entrepreneurs catering to tourists and bridge-and-tunnelers—were rip-off artists. The dealers, radars fine-tuned for trouble, avoided the confrontation. That left people like Marcos Mota, a twenty-two-year-old member of the Dominican national volleyball team, who was just hanging out when his skull was crushed by a bat. He died at St. Vincent's without regaining consciousness. His mother raised money to send his body back to the Dominican Republic; his team number was retired.[52]

On Friday a TWA plane leaving LaGuardia for O'Hare was hijacked by Zvonko Busic, a Yugoslavian national fighting for Croatian independence while living on West Seventy-sixth Street and working as a waiter. With his American-born wife, Julienne, and three colleagues, Busic demanded that his grievances be printed in major international newspapers, and arranged an airdrop of leaflets over New York City and elsewhere. Thirty media-saturated hours later, the hijackers surrendered in Paris after the plane touched down. No one was hurt. But the next day, a bomb planted by the hijackers in Grand Central Station exploded while a police officer tried to defuse it, and he was killed.

New York had become a symbolic staging ground for all the world's struggles. It was as if the city were so debased, it couldn't be made any worse by a couple more destroyed buildings, a few more dead bodies.

In the discos, the music was more creatively ecstatic than ever. Double Exposure's "Ten Percent," the first mass-marketed 12-inch single, was a relentless ten-minute soul jam with a cokehead bass line dressed in strings and congas. It was released by the disco adepts at Salsoul Records, and produced by twenty-two-year old Brooklyn DJ renegade Walter Gibbons. There was the zoot-suited fantasia "Cherchez la Femme" by Dr. Buzzard's Original Savannah Band, a mixed-race crew led by two weird, dreamy, intellectual kids from Bryant Avenue in the Bronx. August Darnell (who grew up in the apartments at 1503) and Stony Browder, Jr. (1621), were obsessed with '40s couture, big band jazz, and doo-wop, and they rolled it all into their disco. The song immortalized the band's Bronx-born manager, Tommy Mottola, who, per the lyrics, lived in his Cadillac, "blowing his mind on cheap grass and wine," after an especially nasty breakup. It did the same for his ex, "Miggie Bone-ee-jah," who sued the band for calling her a "whore" in the second verse.

Then came a trifecta of diva gems. The best was Diana Ross's disco coming-out party "Love Hangover"; close behind was "Turn the Beat Around" by the Broadway actress turned singer Vicki Sue Robinson; and third was "More, More, More," by the porn actress turned singer Andrea True (*Deep Throat II, The Wetter the Better*). Hot Chocolate's "You Sexy Thing" and the Ohio Players' "Love Rollercoaster" pushed beyond dance floors into the pop Top 5, as did Johnny Taylor's "Disco Lady," which hit number 1 and became the first single ever to be certified platinum, selling more than 2 million copies.

In September, *Billboard*'s second annual Disco Forum drew seven hundred industry folks with dollar signs in their eyes. Aside from those who hated it, it seemed no one could get enough of the disco sound— certainly not radio programmers, who were riding the 4/4 high-hat-driven beat like perky hookers astride weary johns. Pop acts were on board, too. Paul McCartney and Wings topped the charts in May with "Silly Love Songs," which flaunted a disco-style bass line and string arrangements. Elton John did the same in August with "Don't Go Breaking My Heart," his light-funk duet with the ex-Motown crossover hopeful Kiki Dee, followed by the Australian soft-rockers the Bee Gees with "You Should Be Dancing." More disco-pop number ones followed in September with KC and the Sunshine Band's "(Shake, Shake, Shake) Shake Your Booty" and Wild Cherry's "Play That Funky Music," an absolution for rhythm-challenged Caucasians. The parody "Disco Duck," by the Memphis radio DJ Rick Dees and His Cast of Idiots, became a candidate in October for the most irritating number 1 ever. National pop music was in the middle of a full-on cultural sea change.

Even the outer boroughs had gotten into the disco act. In its June 7 issue, *New York* magazine published "Tribal Rites of the New Saturday Night" by the British journalist Nik Cohn, which showcased the scene at 2001 Odyssey, a club in Bay Ridge, Brooklyn, that pulled a huge, hetero Italian-American crowd. The central character in Cohn's piece is Vincent, an eighteen-year-old who works days in a hardware store. Vincent was a fictional composite, but no matter: Cohn floated a prepublication copy of the piece to a friend with film contacts, and by late fall, *Saturday Night Fever* was in preproduction.

Out in Queens, the unlikely Enchanted Garden operated out of a posh converted clubhouse on the municipal golf course in Douglaston. Throwing flamboyant events—in one case, complete with fire dancers, hula girls, and a roast pig—for a mostly unfabulous, working-class, but drug-loving clientele, it was run by a pair of suits turned scenesters: the lawyer Ian Schrager and the steak-restaurant entrepreneur Steven Rubell. Neither knew much about running a disco, but they knew how to enlist talent and were quick learners. They wined and dined the Peruvian socialite/party promoter Carmen D'Alessio, a regular at David Mancuso's Loft with fashion industry ties, in hopes of bringing her into the project. D'Alessio wanted nothing to do with a club in eastern Queens, which might as well have been Dubuque. But they threw enough money her way that she acquiesced. Soon, the model turned disco diva Grace Jones and other elegant Manhattanites were taking chartered bus safaris out to the suburbs.

Nicky Siano even agreed to DJ on Tuesday nights at the club, right around the time he began romancing Steve Rubell.[53] Siano was still at the height of his powers, but he was hooked on heroin, which he had first tried for his twenty-first birthday in March. Nodding out over his turntables, he still managed to wow the dancers with his mixing. But Siano soon quit, tired of the commute, and Schrager and Rubell eventually followed him back to Manhattan, all three bound for a bigger project.

Music has the ability to induce a kind of waking dream state. But creating a hypnagogic experience for hundreds or thousands of people in a room at one time requires serious sound-science. There were plenty of professional and amateur physicists working on it in the mid-'70s. Two of the foremost were also interested in the interaction of psychedelic drugs and auditory experience.

Owsley Stanley, the fabled LSD chemist and crony of the Grateful Dead, helped create the band's fabled "Wall of Sound" PA in 1973 and 1974. It sounded amazing, but the cost and effort of transporting, setting up, and breaking down the 75-ton system—which at one point included 641 speakers driven by 48 individual amplifiers pushing around 26,000 watts of power, far beyond the state-of-the-art at the time—would contribute to the band's decision to stop touring for nearly two years.[54]

David Mancuso—whose earliest parties were called Love Saves the Day, an acronym for the LSD often dispensed in the punch bowl—remained a tireless audio explorer at his new space at 99 Prince Street. Unsatisfied with the best professional PA systems, he began buying esoteric home gear from the high-end temple Lyric Hi-Fi on Lexington Avenue between Eighty-second and Eighty-third streets, outfitting the club with custom-built Mitch Cotter turntables, Fidelity Research FR66 tone arms, and Koetsu cartridge heads (the latter about three grand a pop), which fed their signals into two Mark Levinson ML6A preamps and 16 ML2 Class A solid-state power amps. The speaker system, strung with Levinson silver audio cable at eighty dollars a meter and built around Klipsch folded-horn loudspeakers and subwoofers, was also nicknamed the "Wall of Sound," and it surrounded the Loft's dance floor, employing a delay system that created near-perfect stereo imaging all around the room. Instead of surrealistic audio effects, like the high- and low-end dropouts that his friend Nicky Siano used to enhance the dance-floor rush, Mancuso was going for ultrarealism: guitar there, drums over here, string section up there.[55]

Mancuso liked to demo his system with the quintessential hi-fi test record, the 1958 stereo Mercury recording of Tchaikovsky's *1812 Overture*, a performance by the Minneapolis Symphony enhanced with New York special effects: a recording of the Laura Spelman Rockefeller Memorial Carillon bells at Riverside Church (including the largest tuned bass bell in the world, weighing in at 40,926 pounds), and one of a muzzle-loaded bronze French siege cannon—cast in 1775, akin to the kind used by Napoleon in his 1812 Russian campaign—that was fired into specially miked woodlands up at the U.S. Military Academy in West Point.

Mancuso loved to drop Pink Floyd, Ravi Shankar, and Vivaldi into his mixes, along with one of his most beloved tracks, Chuck Mangione's 1973 "Land of Make Believe," recorded with the Hamilton Philharmonic Orchestra and the singer Esther Satterfield. An ethereal jam informed by Dizzy Gillespie's Latin-jazz work, the track dovetailed perfectly with Mancuso's hippie-utopian aesthetic. "I thought 'Land of Make Believe' was a description of the Loft," he said.[56]

Others pushed the envelope of sound in different directions. At Galaxy 21, a young French drummer, François Kevorkian, was brought in by the club owner to liven things up, literally: he set up his drums on the dance floor and played along with the records. The percussion-mad DJ Walter Gibbons—who liked to loop drum breaks using two copies of an LP, like Kool Herc and his acolytes uptown—wasn't thrilled with the new kid stealing his shine. Gibbons often turned their jams into cutting contests, spinning the trickiest drum breaks he could to see if Kevorkian could keep up. Usually he could.

Gibbons was a disco DJ obsessed with funky break beats. Joseph Saddler was a break junkie mainly plying his trade as a disco DJ, a sidekick to Pete DJ Jones, black New York's ruling club DJ, opening sets for him in clubs like Nell Gwynn's, at Forty-third and Lexington, and Harlem World. They even worked the Circle Line, which held a disco party every week on one of its Thursday-night cruises up the Hudson.

But Saddler was also building a fan base by doing his own thing, first at the park parties, then at a dive at 163rd Street and Freeman Avenue called the Black Door.[57] He had started working with Keith Wiggins, whose nickname was "Cowboy" and who rhymed on the mic like DJ Hollywood. Soon he had two other guys who wanted to get on the mic—Nathaniel Glover, a light-skinned black kid whose street name was Kid Creole, and his little brother Melvin, who everyone called Melle Mel. Mel brought in his pal Eddie Morris, a.k.a. Mr. Ness, a.k.a. Scorpio. The Three MCs became the Furious Four. Then Guy Williams—Raheim—made it the Furious Five. Why not? No DJ had a crew this big, let alone this good.

In Harlem that September, Saddler stared down the biggest room any park-party crew had ever hoped to rock: the Audubon Ballroom at 165th and Broadway, capacity roughly three thousand.

"Nigga, is you crazy?!" said Creole, eyeballing the room.

Filling it with sound would take another leap of faith. Flash's system couldn't match Herc's. But for this show he beefed it up, renting an amp so big he needed three guys to carry it, and hooking it to home-made bass bins nicknamed the "Fridgerators": monster plywood boxes, each housing four 18-inch subwoofers.

In Jamaica, bass power was the coin of the realm; sound-system crews battled for earthshaking supremacy, setting up rigs on opposite sides of a room or a yard, trading off records and routines to see who could massage people's bowels most thoroughly.

That tradition would be imported to the Bronx. But not on September 3. That was Flash's night to shine. He had gotten the amp from some Jamaican sound scientist in the Bronx. After setting up at the Audubon, he was pounding some records through a test run when the amp blew a transformer.

It was seven o'clock; the doors were opening at eleven.

So Flash and his pal Mike drive the amp up to Gun Hill Road in the Bronx, find the guy who built it, get him to swap out the transformer, and haul ass back to the Audubon. The room fills slowly at first; by one a.m. there's a line around the block. The room is packed. The sound system booms all night, and Flash debuts his new technique of needle-drop cuing, adapted in fact from his protégé Grandwizard Theodore. It's risky, but if done correctly, it doubles the speed with which he can cut from one record to another.

He nails again and again, all night long. Cowboy, Scorpio, Melle Mel, Raheim, Creole—the Furious Five—unleash new raps and choreography. On and on until the break of dawn. The entire B-boy scene is there, plus plenty of folks who aren't down but had somehow gotten word.

Flash still isn't sure, but he thinks he saw Herc that night, which would have been appropriate. Because if hip-hop was born spiritually in the rec room of Herc's apartment building back in late August '73, on this night it was born again, Flash and his crew rocking a cultural baby shower on roughly the same spot where Malcolm X was shot dead eleven years earlier.[58]

That fall, Jerry Harrison caught a ride from Harvard down to New York with Ernie Brooks, his old bandmate from the Modern Lovers. Brooks was finally moving to NYC, in part to start up a new band with Arthur Russell. Russell had kept in touch with Brooks over the phone, calling to sing him new songs. Harrison, who was finishing a degree in architecture, was coming down to rehearse with Talking Heads. The bandmembers were thinking about bringing on a fourth musician to fill out their sound, which they felt was too thin. On the recommendation of an acquaintance (the Boston musician Andy Paley), Tina Weymouth had cold-called Harrison and invited him to a Heads gig in Boston. He came. Then they asked him to come to New York to their place on Chrystie Street to play. The four went out for Chinese food, then jammed in the loft until dawn. Harrison played a Telecaster the whole time, since there'd been no room for his keyboards in Brooks's moving van.

But everyone thought he sounded great. A keyboardist who also played funky guitar was more than they'd hoped for. Harrison sat in for a couple of live gigs, and was formally invited to join. He was uncertain, still feeling the burn of the Modern Lovers' demise. Plus, he wanted to complete his degree. Finally he agreed, provided he could finish the semester up in Cambridge.

In November, Talking Heads signed a contract with Sire Records, making them labelmates with their pals the Ramones. They got a small advance, around $25,000; Harrison got $5,000 of it. David Byrne bought a small Sony Trinitron TV, so he could be a "participant in the dominant culture." He also moved out of the Chrystie Street loft and rented his own apartment, a ground-floor railroad flat on East Fifth Street. And he capped a chipped tooth.[59]

Had things played out differently, the fourth position in Talking Heads might have gone to Arthur Russell. He was a fan of the band; he had helped them get their first art-scene gig in March at the Kitchen. (The group also met Philip Glass there, who told them about *Einstein on the Beach*.) "We were friends," Byrne said of Russell. "Arthur played cello and he was part of a kind of downtown avant-garde fringe scene. But he had the distinction of also being a great appreciator of pop music. He was a big fan of Abba and of real slick Italian pop stuff, telling me how perfect they were, in terms of song craftsmanship and recording arrangement."

Russell had lots of friends and collaborators. He'd followed Allen Ginsberg to a new apartment at 437 East Twelfth Street, where the poet moved not long after his mugging on Tenth Street. (The address, also home to Peter Orlovsky and Richard Hell, was soon dubbed the "Poets' Building.") This time Russell had his own place, although Ginsberg let him run an extension cord down the fire escape into his apartment so Russell would have free electricity. Ginsberg was entertaining the dubious notion of becoming a singer, and the two played together regularly. Russell performed the music Philip Glass had written for him (though he revised it heavily, to Glass's bemusement) in the Mabou Mines production of *Cascando*, which booked a European tour after its East Village run. He also worked with Laurie Anderson in her short-lived Fast Food Band, and did some free solo gigs, singing and playing cello at Sobossek's Bar on the Bowery near Fifth.[60]

But Russell's most significant musical experience of the year, and arguably of his life, occurred in the fall, when his boyfriend Louis Aquilone began taking him out to discos. When Russell entered the Gallery, music was redefined for him. Nicky Siano recalled seeing Russell in the club pretty much every week thereafter.[61]

Salsa dancers were taking six steps over eight beats all over the city. Ray Barretto was still hoping for his great leap forward beyond the dancehalls. He was still in love with jazz. The affair began when he was a teenager in East Harlem and heard Chano Pozo's congas on Dizzy

Gillespie's 1947 "Manteca," the opening salvo of Latin jazz. It continued through the '50s and '60s as the Puerto Rican musician played with Art Blakey and Lou Donaldson.

Barretto signed a deal with Atlantic Records on September 1. His major-label debut, released in November, was *Tomorrow: Live*, recorded at the Beacon in May. It debuted a new group, built, like Eddie Palmieri's, to be as much a concert orchestra as a dance band. Barretto now had two singers, Rubén Blades and Tito Gomez. But they often laid out on compositions that were less salsa than sprawling Latin-ized jazz-funk—not unlike the fusions being dished out by the CTI label, but with more edge and *sabor*. "Slo Flo" follows a sax solo by Dick Meza, serrated with overblowing free jazz, with an Afro-Cuban chant, an abstract conga solo, and some elegant horn charts. "Que Viva la Musica," the title anthem from his beloved '72 Fania set, burns for nearly fifteen minutes with a five-minute drum descarga featuring Tito Puente—the Kool Herc of New York Puerto Rican Afro-Cuban music.

This was a big deal. Puente hated salsa, hated Jerry Masucci, and hated the Fania All-Stars, whom he dismissed as the "Funny All-Stars." He didn't think they played Afro-Cuban music properly, thought they were all a bunch of cokeheads (though he himself didn't dislike the white powder, a useful substance for musicians playing all-night dance clubs). There was professional jealousy, no doubt: over the fact that Fania's brash, pan-Latin approach had bum-rushed the Latin music marketplace, and the fact that it made Puente's friend Celia Cruz a superstar, something his '60s and early '70s collaborations with her were unable to do.

In '75, while Puente was still under contract to Tico, the label's owner, Morris Levy, added insult to injury when he sold it to Masucci. The transition did little to further Puente's career. As his close friend Joe Conzo writes in *Mambo Diablo*, while there were still road dates, Latin music's king was playing local dance clubs three or four nights a week in '76 to make his nut. He and his polished orchestra could be found regularly making brilliant music at the Corso on the Upper East Side, at La Mariposa in Washington Heights, and in the lounge of the Pan American Motor Inn on Queens Boulevard in Elmhurst, where they were the Monday-night house band.

Puente liked Barretto, however. The conguero used to play with his orchestra back in the day. Barretto was a real musician, so Puente sat in.

But for all its integrity and power, *Tomorrow* did little to expose Barretto to a broader audience.

Jerry Masucci accepted the fact that Fania couldn't create crossover hits by itself. With an eye on what his rivals at Salsoul had accomplished with their Salsoul Orchestra, he made a deal with CBS Records for the Fania All-Stars. The partnership's first release, *Delicate and Jumpy*, was not arranged by Johnny Pacheco, per usual, but instead by Masucci and Gene Page, who had scored kitsch like *H.R. Pufnstuf* and *Blacula* before making his name arranging records by Barry White and the Love Un-limited Orchestra. Traffic's Steve Winwood added some perfunctory rock guitar licks.

The results were weak, the All-Stars rhythm section (including Barretto) yoked to half-assed disco grooves and buried in overdubbed string fluff. The salsa community was appalled; the disco scene largely ig-nored it. Even the musicians hated it; the singer and *bongosero* Roberto Roena, who played on the sessions, dismissed it as "supermarket music."[62]

Yet it had been a great summer for Latin music in New York. The first official Fiestas Patronales del Barrio, a ten-day street fair imported from the Caribbean, shut down half of Third Avenue between 106th and 116th Streets in June with food booths and open-air performances. The film *Salsa* was drawing the congregation into cinemas. There was even a fleeting summit at Madison Square Garden in August, where Tito Puente's orchestra played on a sold-out bill with the Fania All-Stars. After a sharp set, Puente walked up to the promoter Ralph Mer-cado and his new boss, Jerry Masucci, and informed them he would never again open for the "Funny All-Stars." Then he gathered his troops and walked out of the arena onto Seventh Avenue to find a bar.[63]

Less than a month later, on September 3, Celia Cruz and Héctor Lavoe filled the Garden again, with Tipica '73, Barretto's former colleagues, folding synthesizer chords and Earth, Wind & Fire–style horn charts into their mix. As was often the case at salsa events, the sound system malfunctioned; it nearly ruined Lavoe's set. But he was at the top of his game, in the midst of a run in which he was sometimes singing seven days a week with his new band. True to his roots, he renewed his con-tract with Fania on October 17, despite other offers. He was still ru-mored to be shooting heroin, but for the moment he was holding it together, and everyone was hopeful.

•

At 1:30 a.m. on October 23, a couple was sitting in a Volkswagen Beetle in the Ramones' old stomping grounds of Forest Hills when a bullet came through the windshield. The woman, Rosemary Keenan, was wounded slightly. The man, Karl Denaro, had part of his skull blown off; it was repaired with a metal plate. The police launched a vigorous investigation; Keenan's dad was a detective. But no one could figure out who had shot at them, or why.

The next night on Morris Avenue and 164th Street in the Bronx, a fire broke out in the Puerto Rican Social Club—a wood-floored, second-story bar and dancehall—at the height of a Saturday-night/Sunday-morning salsa party. A locked rolling steel gate blocked the fire escape. Twenty-five people died. The fire was set by Jose Angelo Cordero, a forty-year-old married man who had had an argument with his eighteen-year-old girlfriend, who was dancing in the club. His accomplices, the ones who actually poured gas on the steps and lit the match, were two teenagers.

Luis Cedeño knew one of them from his time in the junior street gang the Baby Skulls; Cedeño had seen him douse a stray cat with gasoline once in a local schoolyard and light the fur, laughing as the creature howled. "When I looked into his eyes I saw nothing," Cedeño recalled. "No emotions, no pain, no happiness." The kid scared him.

An admirer of Kool Herc, Cedeño was trying to stay out of trouble. He would DJ around with his buddy Curtis Fisher, another Herc fan. But trouble always seemed to find Cedeño. One afternoon, his brother's basketball hit the hood of a cab, and the driver got out and beat the shit out of him. Seeing the scene from his apartment window while hanging with his girl, Cedeño grabbed a kitchen knife, ran outside in his underwear, and stabbed the man four times. Cedeño ran off, but no one in the neighborhood snitched. The guy deserved it, right?[64]

Afrika Bambaataa threw his first proper party at the Bronx River Community Center in the Bronx River Projects, at 1619 East 174th Street, on November 12. There's no record of what he played, but "Honky Tonk Women" might've been in there, along with James Brown's "I Got the Feeling," Aerosmith's "Walk This Way," the Jackson 5's "I Want You

Back," Sly's "Everyday People." The idea was to promote peace, to chill folks out.

At first, people from other neighborhoods were afraid to come to Bronx River, certain they'd be jumped. Some thought the parties were setups to lure rival gang members into a beat-down. But the Zulu Nation crew kept things cool.[65]

Frampton Comes Alive was number 1. Again. It debuted at number 191 on the *Billboard* charts in January. Then radio grabbed it and flogged it. By April it was number 1. It dipped and rebounded through the summer. By fall, it was back at number 1. My sister had the record, along with everyone else in the world, it seemed. As Wayne Campbell would recall in *Wayne's World 2*: "If you lived in the suburbs you were issued it. It came in the mail with samples of Tide."

Some of the studio-doctored live set—including "Show Me the Way," the single with the sexy robot voice that Frampton created with a talk-box effects pedal—had been recorded at the Commack Arena on Long Island the previous summer. Suburban fans swarmed Madison Square Garden in October to show their love. Lester Bangs reviewed opening night for the *Voice*:

"Even at full amplification, Peter has all the impact of a Valium getdown, unwinding solos and irrelevant words at a leisurely pace, able to make 'Jumping Jack Flash' sound like a *friendly* song, breaking off to wave back at the Beatlemaniac shrieks with fingers spread and both arms over his head like a Mickey Mouse doll."

And yet Bangs could see the appeal of a mellow love-muffin pitching woo in the pop temple-fortress, "surrounded by all the paranoia and justifiable fear and hostility and brutalization in the world."[66]

I skipped the show. I thought the talk-box stuff was kinda cool, but Frampton was annoying. The sleeve photograph of him as an immaculately stoned and blow-dried Jesus was as iconic and unreachable a beauty standard as the poster of Farrah Fawcett in an orange Danskin with erect nipples and a ceramic grin. Still, I had my shoulder-length hair streaked Frampton-style that summer—not out of a desire to emulate him, but from a desire to have the Frampton-and-peroxide-crazed girls in our Jones Beach gang run their fingers through my hair.

Seeing Springsteen was another matter. I loved his records as much as *Horses* and *Blood on the Tracks*. And having missed the '75 Bottom Line shows, there was no way that I'd miss him again. After a three-hour wait at the Ticketron counter at the Queens Boulevard Macy's, I scored a single ticket to the second night at the newly christened Palladium, formerly the Academy of Music, on the south side of Fourteenth Street down from Irving Place. My seat was dead center in the last row of the topmost balcony—I had to stand on my toes to see over the railing.

Yet the power of the band rose up. I remember being hit with vertigo during the crescendo of "Rosalita"—when the singer's tires were slashed and he almost crashed, I thought I would be sucked off the balcony and through the air into the white-light energy onstage like into the spectacular sci-fi vortex of *Solaris*, the Tarkovsky film that had opened that month. After the show, I walked down the steps to the subway feeling like I'd been baptized.

Springsteen was butch to Frampton's femme. Punk was also butch, as was Christopher Street gay culture, with its mustaches and muscle tees and black leather. Butch was big in 1976. I didn't do butch; I was too lanky and lippy to pull it off, anyway. I loved the Ramones but never bought a leather jacket; rule number one in New York City high schools was *Never wear anything someone might want to jack you for*. My uniform was a faded Levi's jacket—because any denim not branded with the little red tag was heretical—and a "Better Living Through Chemistry" T-shirt, with a smiling cartoon quaalude.

Still, all that masculine posturing made sense. In the city's civilian war zones, even tough kids felt powerless, and looking tough gave at least an illusion of power, often as good as the real thing. My masculine ideal at the time was more along the lines of Nick Drake, whose exquisite *Five Leaves Left*, released in Britain in 1969, had just now been released in the States. Brooding, poetic, handsome, gentle, fatalistic, Drake made music with a sadness so incandescent it shone like joy. Unfortunately, he had died in 1974, largely unappreciated, from an overdose of antidepressants.

In a way, Tom Verlaine was downtown's Nick Drake, albeit more high-strung and sharp-cornered. Television had grown tighter, his guitar playing increasingly expansive and mercurial. At the end of July, Television and Talking Heads played a four-night run at CBGB—a double bill of the city's two best unrecorded bands. They both sounded magnificent.

The next week, the band that spurred the CBGB scene into existence, New York rock's first best hope ever since the Dolls fell apart, finally got a record deal. As with so much in the band's career, they fretted over it. They passed on an offer from Arista that was spurred by Patti Smith (which potentially would have left Verlaine in the uncomfortable position of being Smith's less famous labelmate), and after a showcase at the label's midtown studio, they were rejected by Atlantic, because Ahmet Ertegun felt their sound was not "earth music." Sire also passed, because the group wanted too much money and on account of rumors that, because of Verlaine's dictatorial temperament, the band probably wouldn't last.[67]

They went with Elektra Records, former home to the Stooges and the MC5, now making a play for the New York scene. Verlaine wanted to make the record at Rudy Van Gelder's New Jersey studio, where Coltrane had recorded, but he was dissuaded. In October, Television went up to Phil Ramone's A&R Studios on West Forty-eighth Street to begin recording an album with the engineer Andy Johns, who'd logged studio time with the Rolling Stones but seemed unlikely, Verlaine thought, to meddle with his production ideas.

Richard Hell had also landed a record deal—for a band that didn't quite exist. He had left the Heartbreakers back in the spring and started trawling for players. One of the guitarists he found was Robert Quine, a law school graduate who, like Rubén Blades, decided not to practice. Quine was a Velvet Underground fanatic—he had hours of bootleg recordings of the band that he'd recorded himself in the '60s—who worked with Hell at the bookstore Cinemabilia, which was run by Television's manager, Terry Ork. The other guitarist, Ivan Julian, came via an ad in the *Voice*. With the drummer Marc Bell, who had been playing with Wayne County, the band rehearsed throughout the summer and fall, and cut some demos. Billed as (Richard Hell and) the Voidoids—after the name of Hell's unfinished novel—the band played its first shows at CBGB from November 18 through 20, and the demos were released the same month on Ork Records as an EP, *Blank Generation*.

Instant Records, an upstart co-run by the major-label ship-jumper

Marty Thau, didn't have much cash. But Thau figured the guy who wrote "Love Comes in Spurts," "Chinese Rocks," and "Blank Generation" was a solid bet, junkie or not. Instant had signed Blondie and had released their impressive first single, "X Offender"/"In the Sun," just as summer ended. Thau sold it to a larger label, Private Stock, for $2,500, granting it the rights to do a full album for $20,000 if it wanted to. It did. Hell later signed with Sire.[68]

In hindsight, only an idiot could have missed what was going on in the rock scene, yet major labels squirmed while the indies worked. By the New Year, Thau had sold out his interests in Instant to his partner Richard Gottehrer and started his own Red Star Records with help from Marvin Schlachter, a former co-owner of Scepter Records (with Florence Greenberg), who had just launched a new disco label, Prelude.

The first act Thau signed was Suicide. As Vega put it: "We were the last fucking apple in the barrel."[69]

The loft jazz scene was getting itself on record, too. While the *Wildflowers* sessions recorded at Studio Rivbea were still in the can, Anthony Braxton was running wild with his Arista deal. He released three LPs with the label in '76, plus another three elsewhere. The most impressive was *Creative Orchestra Music 1976*, a session for a twenty-one-piece band born in the hothouse of the Creative Music Studio in Woodstock. It included Roscoe Mitchell, the trombonist George Lewis, Muhal Richard Abrams, and Karl Berger. It also included Frederic Rzewski, the Massachusetts-born pianist-composer interested, like Braxton, in the intersection of European compositional music and improvisation. (Rzewski had just finished a masterwork of his own titled *The People United Will Never Be Defeated*, a solo piano piece of thirty-six variations based on a Chilean folk-pop song that was an anthem of the Allende era.)

The one-day recording session at Generation Sound in New York was a whirlwind. Berger recalls an exchange with Braxton during the first rehearsal:

Berger (to Braxton, pointing to sheet music): Um, Anthony, what should I play here? There are a couple of notes indicated that aren't actually on the vibraphone.
Braxton: Play as written.

Braxton was viewed with some suspicion by other jazz players, both mainstream and avant-garde. The former thought he didn't swing, the latter thought he was too obsessed with European art music. Braxton seemed like Groucho Marx, uninterested in any club that would have him as a member. But *Creative Orchestra Music 1976* was a milestone, a tightrope-walking display of Ellington-style big-band moves, parade music, free-jazz power-braying, Stockhausen bleep-bloop, and Carl Stalling cartoon effects. In *Downbeat*, it was the critics' pick for Album of the Year.

Meanwhile, Rashied Ali released *Swift Are the Winds of Life* on his Survival label. A set of very free duets with the violinist Leroy Jenkins recorded the previous fall, it was out jazz at its earthiest. Gary Giddins described the title track as "the kind of music I imagine Marc Chagall would make if he was a musician."[70] *Moon Flight*, recorded with Ali's quintet the previous summer, was well-knit Coltrane-inspired postbop. And *N.Y. Ain't So Bad* was a set with Royal Blue, whose enormous voice sounded halfway between Leon Thomas (known for "The Creator Has a Master Plan," a mantra recorded with Pharoah Sanders) and Big Joe Williams. The cover showed the singer and Ali shaking hands atop the observation deck of the World Trade Center, with Brooklyn and Queens spread out blurrily behind them.

"Moontipping," a woozy slow jam about getting high, is the record's most magical moment: Ali's scatter-groove conjuring both swing and clave without pledging allegiance to either, Royal Blue floating above. And on the title cut, stone-stepping across Ali's shifty pulse, weaving between Charles Eubanks's skittering piano chords and James Vass's steamy alto sax, Blue declares his love of disco dancing and the "hot dog town." If there's a disco beat in there, it's well hidden.

New York Ain't So Bad was Blue's only record. According to Ali, not long after the session, the singer got into an argument with a girlfriend's brother and was beaten to death with a piece of pipe, his body dumped on Third Avenue.

Of course, getting music released and getting it broadcast were two different things. A benefit concert for the Citizens' Committee to Save Jazz Radio in late November celebrated the decision of WRVR's new owners to continue their all-jazz programming. Yet most of the musicians onstage, including the Ali's Alley regulars Frank Foster and Joe Lee Wilson, would never get airplay on the station, which pushed lightweight fusions by the likes of Grover Washington, Jr., and George Benson.

The irony was not lost on Rahsaan Roland Kirk, the blind multireed player who had a contract with Atlantic but rarely heard his adventurous music on WRVR or anywhere else on commercial radio.

"I'm not a hypocrite," he said, taking the stage, "and I don't feel like playing this benefit . . . I went up to the station one day and a DJ told me I should play like Herbie Hancock. *I don't need that kind of bullshit!* Think about it. Can you turn on your radio tomorrow and hear *this* music? I'm not just talking about my records; can you hear Cecil Payne or Frank Foster or even Duke or Count Basie? Can you hear Ornette Coleman? *Can you hear Ornette Coleman!?*"[71]

Kirk delivered a beautiful set anyway, using just one side of his body—after a recent stroke, he played his tenor, indomitably, with one hand.

At about 9:00 a.m. on Friday, November 19, two forty-foot trucks carrying ten tons of equipment pulled up to the Metropolitan Opera loading dock on Amsterdam Avenue. The next evening, as the cast of Wagner's *Lohengrin* took their curtain call and the crowd walked out humming the wedding march, the Met crew began striking the cathedral set and the swan-drawn boat and prepared to hang *Einstein on the Beach*. They'd have eighteen hours to turn it around for a 6:30 Sunday curtain. In Europe, the same setup had taken three days.

Even after months of performances abroad, it was still hard to believe *Einstein* was happening here. The original idea had been to stage it over eight nights at the Brooklyn Academy of Music, where Glass had seen Wilson's twelve-hour *Life and Times of Joseph Stalin* in '73. But the scale was so huge, the production team decided only the Met could accommodate it. Plus, the idea of bringing a three-ring avant-garde spectacle to storm the uptown barricades was thrilling. When the Met agreed, thanks partly to the word-of-mouth buzz from Europe, Wilson's company reserved the Opera House for $150,000.

By October, Glass and Wilson, performing in Germany, were sweating. There was no way the whole shebang could be set up in eighteen hours, and renting the hall for a second day just to do setup was financially out of the question. The men were thinking of bailing when the Met's Jane Herman and hired gun production manager Gil Helmsley arrived in Hamburg to see *Einstein* for themselves. They were amazed. They convinced Glass and Wilson that it was doable. By the time they returned to New York, the November 21 performance was sold out, and a second was scheduled for the following weekend.

At 4:00 a.m. that Sunday, the crew began setting up Kurt Munkacsi's sound system, which accounted for five of the production's ten tons. The Met had never seen so much sound-amplification gear in its history. By the time Glass arrived at nine, haggard in faded jeans and a lumberjack shirt (he'd slept little), the system was up and tested. Around noon, the cast began a five-hour dress rehearsal. Helmsley, all Afro and belly, calmly directed backstage traffic, working the rotary phone tucked in beside the audio patch panels. The year's production costs had climbed to $863,000 by this point, and Wilson's company had managed to raise $775,000, ticket sales included. In 1976 dollars, the $88,000 shortfall was no joke. But they'd worry about it later.

The curtain rose at 6:32. Lucinda Childs and Sheryl Sutton sat at small, low desks in front of an illuminated panel. They wore loose white button-down shirts, pants with suspenders, dark Converse sneakers. A low electric organ chord billowed from the speaker stacks. It was loud, like God snoring; the seat armrests hummed. The chorus, dressed like the dancers, began incanting: "One two three four. One two three four five six. One two three four five six seven eight . . ." looping different parts of the progression, each variant conjuring a subtle emotional shift.

Gradually Childs's and Sutton's voices rose amid the chorus, and they began repeating phrases that felt randomly plucked from ad copy, pop songs, overheard conversations: "It could be very fresh and clean . . . Oh, these are the days, my friends . . ." overlapping the choral chants and recitations like the simultaneous dialogues in Robert Altman's *Nashville*. A massive plywood steam engine moved slowly forward, then backward across the stage. Around 9:30 there was a problem with the violin amp, which was quickly fixed. Otherwise, the production was flawless.

In the fifth hour (there was no intermission), Joan La Barbara sang her aria, the light-bed tilted and slowly ascended into the fly space. And in the final act, from the third tier of the "spaceship"—a giant *Hollywood Squares*–like set that Glass set himself atop, less out of ego than to assure his musicians that the rickety thing was in fact safe—the composer could see out into the maw of the opera house. The 3,000-seat

house was filled, standing room included. David Byrne, Tina Weymouth, and Chris Frantz, who Glass invited when he met them at their
Kitchen show, all made the trip up, as had many of their downtown colleagues. The curtain fell at 11:26, and the audience delivered a standing
ovation that went on and on.

At the Bottom Line, Patti Smith and band walked onstage for their
11:30 show—the last of a seven-night, two-sets-a-night run to mark the
release of their second album, *Radio Ethiopia*. It had been a good run;
Bruce Springsteen even joined her a couple of times, pounding piano on
the Velvet Underground's "We're Gonna Have a Real Good Time Together" and hollering along on the Who's "My Generation."[72]

The following Sunday, during the second performance of *Einstein
on the Beach*, Glass stood backstage with one of the Met's big *machers*,
looking out at the audience.

"Who are these people?" he asked the composer. "I've never seen
them here before."

"Well, you better find out who they are," Glass replied, "because if
this place expects to be running in twenty-five years, that's your audience out there."

Glass was a little less cocky after the performance. To help recoup
the production debt, he arranged to sell the original *Einstein* score to a
collector, and for quite some time, he funneled any extra money he
made from commissions and performances toward paying it off. Meanwhile, he went back to driving a hack. As the story goes, a well-dressed
older woman got into his cab shortly after the Met performances and
commented: "Young man, do you realize you have the same name as a
very famous composer?"

Before long, people spoke and wrote about *Einstein* at the Met as if
it were a religious experience. David Byrne talked about it for weeks.
After taking some time off, Gil Helmsley began work on his next big
production: the inauguration of the president-elect, Jimmy Carter.[73]

Glass's was not the only avant-garde opera in town. Meredith Monk's
Quarry premiered at La Mama Annex in the spring, and was re-
mounted at the Brooklyn Academy of Music on December 14 for a
three-week run. Like *Einstein*, the piece dealt with the specter of history—here, World War II and the Holocaust, its bellowing dictators and

martial chants. Its narrative logic was dreamlike and ritualistic; it combined dance, film, theater, music, and sound collage. As always with Monk, it centered on the emotional expressiveness of the human voice, hers and those in her ensemble, voices that moaned, cried out, sobbed, chanted, and consoled.

Like Monk, Laurie Anderson worked the cracks between art forms. She spent much of the year traveling, around the country and in Europe, with two large black cases full of musical instruments and electronic devices. Her performances, too, mixed music, film, storytelling, and theatrics. She enhanced her routines with her one-of-a-kind inventions, like the tape-bow violin, which used a recording head on the instrument's bridge and replaced the bow's horsehair with prerecorded magnetic tape.

When she wasn't on the road, she was living mostly upstate, in Glens Falls, at ZBS Media, a not-for-profit arts center that produced experimental radio dramas and functioned as an art commune. She'd become involved with Bob Bielecki, a sound engineer and electronics designer she'd met there in 1975 when, after her return from the Arctic, she'd received an invitation to do work at the facility.

"That changed my life more than anything else," Anderson told me in 2010 at her old Canal Street loft. "I went there to work on some stories that had sound effects. And Bob, who was the engineer, asked me, 'What kind of sound are you looking for?' And I said, 'Well, I don't know if it has a sound, but if there was sand under your contact lens, it would be the sound of it grinding against your eyeball.' The next time I come into the studio, he has these eighteen really beautiful vintage microphones set up around this piece of glass, and he's dropping grains of sand onto various materials. And I thought: 'Oooh, I'm in love.'"

When she'd finished a group of stories and songs, Anderson had them pressed onto 45 rpm records, and loaded them into a jukebox, which she installed as a sound sculpture in the Holly Solomon Gallery at 392 West Broadway. It was a logical move for a sculptor and performance artist. But she'd caught the recording bug, and knew she would need another vehicle for her sound work. She just wasn't sure yet what it would be.

"At one point, almost everyone I knew was working on an opera," she recalled. "You'd walk down the street and everyone you met would say 'How's your opera?' I guess 'opera' was just a loose way to say 'big undefinable thing.'"[74]

•

Every disaffected high school kid in America who saw it cheered, inwardly or out loud: Sissy Spacek—drenched in pig's blood after being crowned queen of the prom—setting the prom hall ablaze with her telekinetic powers in *Carrie*, howling like Satan, taking revenge on everyone who made her life hell. Adults could see their own anger projected and satisfied in cinemas, too. In the opening segment of *Marathon Man*, set in New York, an old Jew takes revenge on an old Nazi in an impressive act of road rage, forcing both their cars into a dutifully exploding fuel truck. Elsewhere in the film, pedestrians attack cars, dogs attack joggers, and a mild-mannered dude guts men with a spring-loaded bayonet blade hidden up the sleeve of his suit jacket—all with virtually no sign of the police.

In late November, the media baron Rupert Murdoch bought the *New York Post*. In a honeymoon gesture, the *Post* editors concocted a memorable cover headline to pimp a story on Gary Gilmore's mass-murder trial for the November 30 edition. It read simply: "KILL HIM." Murdoch, who would also own *New York* magazine and *The Village Voice* by January, jocularly commented, "And I haven't even laid a hand on them yet!"[75, 76]

The previous evening, a few minutes past midnight, Reggie Jackson stepped off a plane in New York.[77] Two days later, Johnny Thunders stepped off a plane in London. Awaiting Jackson was a black stretch limo and a $2.9 million contract with the New York Yankees. Awaiting Thunders was a support slot for the Heartbreakers on the Sex Pistols' Anarchy tour, alongside the Clash and the Damned. Malcolm McLaren had arranged it. The cash value of his offer, figuring expenses: basically nothing. But back home, the Heartbreakers were music biz pariahs—hopeless junkies, in most eyes—and on top of it, they'd just lost Richard Hell. So Thunders's new manager, Wayne County's old roommate Leee Black Childers, figured it was worth a shot.

The evening of their arrival, the Heartbreakers just missed watching the Sex Pistols, along with Siouxsie Sioux and other friends, introduce "punk rock" to the greater London area on the *Today* show. Summoned on short notice by their label EMI (co-owners of the show's network, Thames Television) to replace Queen, who had just canceled, the Pistols rolled into the dressing room, had a few drinks, and engaged in some banal on-air banter with the host, Bill Grundy. After Grundy (who had also had a few drinks) wound them up, Steve Jones called him a "dirty fucker" and a "fucking rotter." The broadcast aired live around 6:30 p.m., right in the middle of the dinner hour.

McLaren and the Pistols were chuckling about it on their way to pick up the Heartbreakers, who were at the airport hassling with immigration (no one had thought to arrange work permits). McLaren finally got them sorted out, then took everyone to a burger joint on Fulham Road called the Great American Disaster.[78]

By the next morning, British punk had transmogrified from underground music scene into national media scandal. Jerry Nolan, chronic insomniac, was wandering the streets when the morning papers hit, and he brought a stack back to the hotel. The incident got front-page billing. The *Daily Mirror*: "THE FILTH AND THE FURY!" Murdoch's *Sun*: "ROCK GROUP START A 4-LETTER TV STORM." The *Evening Standard*: "THE FOUL MOUTHED YOBS."

Grundy was suspended, and most of the Sex Pistols' tour dates were canceled by promoters or banned by municipalities that feared rioting. The few that took place were sparsely attended, or filled with more gawkers than fans. Moral guardians were out in force; a show in the Welsh village of Caerphilly was blockaded by a local church choir singing hymns. When the tour ended on December 22, all parties were broke, exhausted, and more or less infamous. EMI kicked the Pistols off the label.

The Heartbreakers stayed on in London, crashing with a wealthy fan, determined to parlay their cred into money, fame, and dope (or at least methadone). Knocking around South Kensington one day, posing for snapshots with Childers, they looked less like punks than reformed glams in their Salvation Army winterwear, all in stacked heels but Walter Lure, who towered over the rest of the band even in flats. They had Christmas dinner with the Pistols, the Clash, and the Damned at the journalist Caroline Coon's house, eating Christmas pudding and listening to old Jim Reeves records.[79]

Back in New York, another Heartbreakers debuted at CBGB. Billed as TOM PETTY AND (THE HEARTBREAKERS) FROM MIAMI, FLORIDA, they were on tour to promote their debut LP, which had ABC Records behind it. Still in search of a record deal in cold, gray London, Thunders and Nolan decided to rename their band the Junkies.

•

As the year wound down, Stevie Wonder's *Songs in the Key of Life* was rotating on turntables in discos and living rooms. In particular, "Sir Duke"—Stevie's tribute to the late jazz genius and fellow pianist-composer—got people dancing, twirling, kissing. *Dr. Buzzard's Original "Savannah" Band* and Donna Summer's *Four Seasons of Love* and *A Love Trilogy* also split the difference between disco's beat utilitarianism and the art of album making, serving as a soundtrack for holiday parties where revelers stared up their own nostrils in coke-mirror reflections.

After getting beaten by Daniel Patrick Moynihan in her bid for the Senate in November, the ex-congresswoman Bella Abzug decided to run for mayor. "Bella Abzug is the quintessential New Yorker," wrote the smitten Vivian Gornick. "Brash, vulgar, inventive, courageous, energetic, possessed of a street-smart sense of the politicalness of life and a hungry, cocky desire to beat the system."[80]

The same could be said of Patti Smith, who already was mayor of New York below Fourteenth Street. *Radio Ethiopia* got mixed reviews, but they didn't slow her down. She rang out 1976 headlining a New Year's Eve show with John Cale and Television at the Palladium. Tickets were $9.50. Wayne County, a free (wo-)man, played Max's. The night before, David Johansen and Sylvain Sylvain, now calling themselves simply the Dolls, shared a bill with Blondie, whose self-titled debut came out on December 27.

The upscaled Ali's Alley on Greene Street was booked solid all month: Ornette Coleman's fierce electric guitarist James Blood Ulmer led the Music Revelation Ensemble; Muhal Richard Abrams, finally relocated from Chicago, lead a quintet with the baritone sax man Hamiet Bluiett; the great multiculturally minded pianist Don Pullen played, as did Sonny Murray's new band. Ali led his own band there New Year's Eve.

On screens, a new King Kong plummeted from the top of the World Trade Center, and Rocky fought his way up the steps of the Philadelphia Museum of Art. Gimbel's advertised "television tennis," the first home video game, at $69.95—not bad compared to Sony's Betamax video recorder, introduced earlier in the year, which cost more than $1,000. At the time, less than one-tenth of 1 percent of TV viewers had a VCR. Still, in an effort to protect their interests, Universal Studios had teamed up with Disney to sue Betamax out of existence. Dreamers predicted that in less than ten years, compact computers might be available to home consumers for as little as five hundred bucks.[81]

1977

LA RESURRECCIÓN

No Elvis, Beatles or the Rolling Stones
In 1977
—The Clash, "1977"[1]

A knife, a fork, a bottle and a cork
That's the way we spell New York
—Dillinger, "Cocaine in My Brain"[2]

Larry Harlow, the Jewish Marvel, got into the elevator at 1440 Broadway, at Fortieth Street, and pressed the button for the twenty-fifth floor. He was heading up to La Tierra Sound to begin recording his crowning statement as a salsa musician—something even greater than *Hommy* at Carnegie Hall in '73. This time, he didn't need to skitch a ride off a British rock opera.

La Raza Latina was a four-part suite depicting Latin music's evolution, from Africa (Part 1), through Cuba and the Caribbean (Part 2), to the New York big bands in the '50s and '60s (Part 3), and into the future (Part 4). How to imagine the latter? Just as he had studied 78s while making his *Salsa* LP, Harlow looked again to Cuba, this time for new sounds. Sitting in front of his shortwave radio day and night, as Don Cherry often did, he listened in on Cuban broadcasts— which, given the U.S. cultural boycott, were like transmissions from another planet. He came across a group called La Orquesta Cubana de Musica Moderna, who had turned Gershon Kingsley's Moog synthesizer composition, "Popcorn" (an international hit for Hot Butter in '72), into a dizzying, guitar-fuzzed rumba. The bandleader's ideas began to flow.

Harlow gathered thirty players into the studio, including his old bandmate in Ambergris, Elliott Randall, best known for his indelible, intensely rhythmic guitar soloing on Steely Dan's '72 hit "Reeling in the Years." Harlow brought in the singers Nancy O'Neill, Ada Chabrier, and Rosa Soy, part of the all-girl salsa group he was working with, Latin Fever. For the leads, he brought in Rubén Blades, the mailroom kid he had encouraged and with whom he felt a kinship. Figuring the album needed to be baited with a single, Harlow wrote a stand-alone song called "La Raza Latina," which he gave to Nestor Sanchez—"El Divino Albino" to Harlow's "El Judio Maravilloso." On Latin radio, it was a hit. And when people heard the album, they would understand how profound this music dismissively called "salsa" truly was, and how deep was his love for it. The next time one of his crotchety *alte kakker* relatives asked him what he was doing with his life, he would show them this.

The cover of the January 17 *Village Voice* featured a close-up of the singer with the headline "Christgau Joins Patti Smith Cult." The paper's chief critic called her New Year's Eve gig at the Palladium the best concert of 1976, but he also thought Smith was in trouble. "She's caught in a classic double bind," he wrote, "accused of selling out by her former allies and of not selling out by her new ones."[3]

That concert was supposed to be broadcast live on WNEW-FM. But after Smith said *fuck* on the air in November—in a live interview with the soft-rock singer Harry Chapin during the station's annual Hungerthon fundraiser, and after a specific plea to rein in her language—the station management backed out. Earlier in the year, she'd also run afoul of WBCN in Boston for cursing through a live interview, and fell out with the owners of the Bottom Line after being accused of acting abusive toward the staff during her run in November.[4] Her first U.K. tour played to mixed reviews, especially in London, where the punk scene had soured on her in the wake of *Radio Ethiopia*. At an antagonistic press conference, she threw food, then jumped on a table and announced, "I'm the field marshal of rock 'n' roll. I'm fucking declaring war!" before storming out of the room.[5] And her romantic life remained complicated: she'd bought an apartment with Allen Lanier at 1 Fifth Avenue—just downstairs from Sam Wagstaff's penthouse, where Mapplethorpe shot the *Horses* cover—and was continuing a relationship of sorts with Fred "Sonic" Smith via phone and mail.

Nevertheless, the New Year began onstage at the Palladium among family: Television and John Cale played magnificently, and the Patti Smith Group raged. Fans rushed the stage, two women removed their tops, and both Smith and Ivan Kral smashed their guitars at the end. Even David Johansen, who was working on his debut solo album, blessed the proceedings, blowing harp on "My Generation," no doubt weighing the sentiment. Backstage, Smith had a belated birthday celebration, swigging champagne and flinging cake. She had just turned thirty.

The Patti Smith Group began the U.S. leg of the *Radio Ethiopia* tour in Florida in January, opening for Bob Seger, who had just hit it big with *Night Moves*. Despite the Detroit street cred Seger shared with Fred Smith and Iggy Pop, the pairing—arena-scale heartland rock and club-scale NYC art punk—was a dubious idea. But Smith and Kaye were determined to take her message wide. And if anything, the lukewarm reviews for *Radio Ethiopia* and the antagonism she had encountered on the U.K. punk scene only steeled her resolve to transcend it. On the first night, in Hollywood, Florida, the band was not well received. On the second night, January 26, in Tampa's six-thousand-seat Curtis Hixon Hall, the largest venue the Patti Smith Group had ever played, the field marshal was prepared for battle.

The second song was "Ain't It Strange." The *Radio Ethiopia* version is an abstracted reggae groove that gradually accelerates as Smith howls and sputters, speaks in poetic tongues, scat-sings gibberish, spits phonemes like a free-jazzer, and reaches for a gold-ring epiphany just beyond her grasp. Live, the song had become a shamanic ritual, Smith spinning like a Sufi, Kaye engaging her in what he called a sort of "ballet" during the song's shape-shifting second half. At one of the November Bottom Line shows, Smith chased Kaye through the crowd during the song, walking across tables, knocking over drinks.

Tonight, in front of several thousand nonbelievers, Smith needed to go from 0 to 60 fast. As the song accelerated, she yelled, "C'mon God, make a move!"—a fleeting moment in the song's stream-of-consciousness spiel. She began her dervish twirls, around and around. Then she reached for her microphone, tripped over a monitor at the lip of the stage, and fell backward.

Her brother Todd, part of the road crew, tried to catch her. But there was no time. She dropped down fourteen feet from the stage onto a concrete floor, landing on her neck and hitting her head. By the time the paramedics reached her, she was in a pool of blood.

"It was like a Bugs Bunny cartoon," she said later, "when he walks over a cliff into midair and just keeps on walking until he realizes there's nothing there.[6]

Smith wound up at Tampa General Hospital with cracked vertebrae and broken bones in her face; she got twenty-odd stitches to close up cuts in her head. She was flown back to New York after two days, and when she got back to her new apartment she was seeing double and could barely walk. Her doctors doubted she'd perform again. One recommended spinal surgery; another, rigorous physical therapy. She chose the latter.

In between therapy sessions, she hung out in bed, smoked pot, swallowed Percodans, and returned to writing poetry. A small altar in the corner of the bedroom displayed a photo of Rimbaud, a first edition of *Naked Lunch*, and a set of rosary beads. Before leaving for the tour, she'd signed a five-thousand-dollar contract for what became the poetry anthology *Babel*. The cash came in handy. All of a sudden she was out of work: she had blown most of her savings on the apartment, and royalties from *Radio Ethiopia*—which she was now unable to promote— were not looking good. Kaye and his bandmates, meanwhile, hit the long lines at the unemployment office.

Smith held court for friends, including Lisa Robinson and Legs Mc-Neil (the latter would often shoot pool with Allen Lanier down at Julian's pool room on Fourteenth Street, located in the same building as the Palladium, which allowed discreet brown-bagging). Richard Hell would come by to talk and collaborate on poetry for a book that was never realized ("We'd pass the typewriter back and forth," he recalled).[7] Springsteen paid a bedside visit, and the two listened to favorite old 45s.

Smith had no choice but to cancel her show at Nassau Coliseum on Saturday, February 5; she was slotted as the middle act between openers the Ramones and her boyfriend's band, Blue Öyster Cult—which had just hit the hard-rock big time with the FM radio staple "(Don't Fear)

The Reaper." (The album, *Agents of Fortune*, featured a cameo by Smith on "The Revenge of Vera Gemini.") Their show featured smoke machines and a brand-new, sixty-thousand-dollar laser light show that dwarfed all that had come before.

Smith also had to miss Robert Mapplethorpe's great artistic coming-out party the same night. Her soul mate shuttled between the openings of two simultaneous one-man shows: *Portraits*, with images of Princess Margaret and Arnold Schwarzenegger (whose film *Pumping Iron* was still in theaters), at the Holly Solomon Gallery, and *Pictures*, the debut of his explicit S&M/B&D photos, at the Kitchen.

Mapplethorpe had booked the after-party in the restaurant One Fifth, in the lobby of Smith and Wagstaff's apartment building, hoping Smith would make an appearance. But she was still unable to walk, and declined Mapplethorpe's offer to rent her a wheelchair. He spent the evening taking the elevator up and down between the party and her apartment. "I'm a success!" he declared to Smith, who was in bed eating a bowl of couscous with a gray sombrero covering her stitches. She smiled. Stoned on champagne and whatever else, he gathered his friend in his arms and tried, unsuccessfully, to carry her to the elevator.[8]

The Ramones had canceled their holiday gigs and, worse, postponed the promotional tour for their second album, *Leave Home*, after Joey was hospitalized for a foot infection, the result of a cut he got stumbling shoeless around Arturo Vega's loft.

Playing catch-up after their set at Nassau Coliseum that night, they barreled back to the city to play two sets at CBGB. Opening for them was Suicide, the band that had played the room before everybody, back when it was Hilly's on the Bowery. It was their return after a long feud with Hilly Kristal, who never liked them. The inventors of punk's Theater of Cruelty had spent the past few years refining their approach, yet they were still devoted headfuckers. "The crowd hated us," recalled Vega, "they booed the shit out of us."

Suicide played a short set and got offstage. But the Ramones, who had gotten lost in the Coliseum's parking lot, were still stuck in traffic on the Long Island Expressway, and the normally mellow Hilly was freaking out. He shouted that Suicide hadn't played long enough, and ordered them to play another set. "I could not believe the look on his face," said Vega. "It was red, the veins in his neck were sticking out."

When the band took the stage again, the boos were deafening. "I can't hear you," Vega said. Then he took out a knife and drew the blade across his face.

People stopped booing.

Cheek bleeding, chain in hand, with Martin Rev generating a synthesized turbine roar behind him, Vega jumped off the stage into the crowd. "You would see waves of people go backwards," Vega said. "Everyone thought I was a total lunatic."[9]

Suicide would soon record their debut at 914 Studios up in Blauvelt. For all their aesthetic differences, Vega trafficked in the same romantic hood-rat highway-rock mythology as Springsteen; he just twisted it up differently. On "Ghost Rider," he conjures a biker, breathing heavily through a distortion circuit: "He's a-screamin' the truth / America America is killin' its youth!" On "Rocket USA," someone speeds down the road: "Gonna crash / Gonna die!" On "Cheree": "My comic-book fantasy / I love you."

The band's equipment was Marty Rev's carload of electronic junk, including a beat-up Farfisa and a transistor radio good for ambient noise and feedback. Craig Leon, a twenty-five-year-old who had worked on the Blondie and Ramones debuts, had the idea to run Vega's voice, along with some of Rev's keyboards, through an early Eventide digital-delay pushed to the distortion point, a technique he'd learned from the Jamaican producer Lee Perry during a Bob Marley session. The effect was terrifying.

More terrifying was the record's centerpiece, "Frankie Teardrop." Vega based the song on a newspaper story he'd read about a young guy who lost his factory job and, unable to cope, killed his wife, his kid, and then himself. Vega recited the narrative of a twenty-year-old's crash-and-burn, interspersed with bloodcurdling shrieks, over breathless drum-machine patter and a menacing electronic drone. Lou Reed once said he wished he'd written it.[10]

Back at CBGB, the Ramones finally arrived, and Suicide survived to make their record.

•

Earlier that same night, Willie Colón had played Madison Square Garden on a bill dubbed "Salsa's Perfect Combinations." The headliners were Johnny Pacheco and Celia Cruz with the Cuban singer-bandleader Justo Betancourt and pianist Papo Lucca. But the real news was the debut of Colón with Rubén Blades. Blades was not an unknown: he'd recorded with Barretto and Harlow; he had done "El Cazangero" with Colón on *The Good, the Bad, the Ugly*.

But this was different. Colón didn't just want a singer, he wanted a collaborator, like his troubled former partner Héctor Lavoe. Those were big shoes to fill. Salsa fans loved Lavoe; his work with Colón defined early New York salsa. Blades was not a singer like Lavoe. His plainspoken tenor was more like that of Cheo Feliciano, whose style he initially copied. Blades was a songwriter, too, and while he could play the romantic lead, his political conscience drove his work. Colón encouraged it. In Blades, not a Nuyorican but a Panamanian versed in the wider world, he saw a singer who was interested in more than simply being El Rey de Nueva York.

They'd just recorded the first fruit of their partnership, *Metiendo Mano!*, to be released later that spring. The LP opened with Blades's "Pablo Pueblo," a story-song about ghetto hunger and poverty in the shadow of sham politics that Colón caps with a tuba solo. "Plantación Adentro" was penned not by Blades but by the New York journalist turned songwriter Catalino "Tite" Curet Alonso, with the sort of historical-social commentary that would define Blades's own writing. He debuted it at the Garden, articulating the intro to make sure the song's genocidal context was clear. Addressing the audience as "camará"—"comrade"— Blades sang about shadow people and murder amid "la la la's," Afro-Caribbean drums, and chortling trombones in Colón's shape-shifting arrangement, which included a disco-pop break foreshadowing Michael Jackson's "Wanna Be Startin' Somethin'" and some samba-style rhythms signaled by a Brazilian cuíca. A dance group, Los Bailarines de Latinoamérica, enacted abstract impressions of plantation life.[11] It was not the usual "Baile!" business.

Neither was Colón's soundtrack to *El Baquine de Angelitos Negros*, a "symphonic salsa" composition written as the score for a salsa ballet on public television. With no vocalists and no singles, it sold very few copies, yet it contained some of the most exciting music of the bandleader's career, with all sorts of riveting arrangements and solos (see Yomo Toro's cuatro and Alfredo de la Fé's violin on "Son Guajira del Encuentro"). Colón also managed to complete a saucy collaboration with Celia Cruz titled *Only They Could Have Made This Album*. Creatively, it was shaping up as his best year since his days with Lavoe.

Things were also going well for Eddie Palmieri. Though still feuding with Harvey Averne's Coco Records, he managed to land a half-million-dollar deal with Epic. He began work on his first major-label project, *Lacumi, Macumba, Voodoo*, his own dig for salsa's Afro-Caribbean and Afro-Brazilian roots.[12] His coproducer was the drummer Bobby Colomby, a founding member of the jazz-pop band Blood, Sweat & Tears, whose musical interests were broad: he was the uncredited drummer on *Church of Anthrax*, the record John Cale made with his fellow La Monte Young associate Terry Riley after leaving the Velvet Underground. Palmieri and Colomby spent lavishly, hiring dozens of musicians, including Eddie's older brother Charlie, Chocolate Armenteros, and their favorite jazz-fusion players: the trumpeter Jon Faddis, the guitarists Steve Khan and Hiram Bullock. Palmieri conjured disco ("Spirit of Love"), danzon and rumba ("Colombia Te Canto"), contemporary classical composition and free jazz ("Mi Congo Te Llama"). Recording in CBS's fully loaded Studio B on Fifty-second Street, where Miles Davis recorded *Bitches Brew*, Palmieri finally had the resources to channel the swirl of music he heard in his head.

Things were not going so well, however, for Héctor Lavoe. By most reports, his drug use was out of control. But he somehow hadn't hit bottom yet.

On January 29, the successful twenty-two-year-old Puerto Rican/Hungarian comedian Freddie Prinze, star of the hit TV show *Chico and the Man*—born and raised in Washington Heights and at that moment the most famous Puerto Rican entertainer in the world—shot himself in the head in Los Angeles after a phone conversation with his estranged wife. Colón and Blades began their Garden set by asking for a moment of silence in his memory.

Casanova Fly and DJ Disco Wiz—a.k.a. Curtis Fisher and Luis Cedeño—challenged Kool Herc to a sound-system battle at the Webster Police Athletic League gym. The sixteen-year-old Cedeño used to box there, hoping to succeed in the ring like his hero Roberto Durán. The duo got their asses kicked by the king at first, but held their own, and earned respect from Herc's crowd. It was their coming-out party.[13]

The Grandmaster Flash/Herc face-off was a by-product of another battle: Herc versus Flash's mentor, Pete DJ Jones, booked at Herc's home base, the Executive Playhouse, a dimly lit, fairly sketchy place at the intersection of Mount Eden and Jerome avenues, just below the elevated platform on the IRT number 4 line. Jones played to an older, tonier crowd than Herc's, and on the turntables, they were apples and oranges. The idea was to pack the house with two big names who weren't going to encroach much on each other's turf. Everybody gets paid; everybody goes home happy.

It might have worked out that way, except it didn't. As Mark Skillz described it in *Wax Poetics*, two of Herc's break dancers—the brothers Keith and Kevin Smith, known as the "Nigger Twins"—had some beef with him. They were part of the DJ's performance crew, collectively known as the Herculoids (alternately, the Herculords). When the twins ran into Jones a week before the battle, they wrote out Herc's exact playlist for the challenger in a fit of revenge. The night of the event, Jones got on the decks first and played every song on the list, in order. "It sounds like I'm listening to a tape of myself," Herc muttered into the mic at one point. But he just dug deeper into his record crate, playing to his home advantage. When Jones got back on the decks, he played his usual mix, which didn't especially move the crowd. But he'd come with young backup DJs: Lovebug Starski and Flash.[14]

Kool DJ AJ, a devoted Herc fan, saw and heard Flash for the first time that night. When it was over, by AJ's measure, the audience had found a new hero.

The wildest disco record of early '77 was *Love in C Minor*, a French import LP by the Paris-based Jean-Marc Cerrone, a one-man band and teenage Club Med talent booker. The cover showed the artist in a bathrobe with a naked woman draped over his shoulder; the title track was a sixteen-minute account of three ladies picking up a dude in a club and moaning through a spirited four-way. David Mancuso was among the first to nab a copy, of course, and it became a Loft staple. By February it got a rush U.S. release by the Cotillion label, which wound up going head-to-head with a lukewarm cover version by Heart and Soul Orchestra, an outfit overseen by the WBLS program director Frankie Crocker. The disco market was so lucrative, anything that started popping was jumped on and replicated.[15]

The result, increasingly, was a globalized genre. In January, New York DJs got their hands on *Ojah Awake* by the Anglo-Nigerian group Osibisa, and *Tropical*, a domestic compilation by the Brazilian hero Jorge Ben. The latter included the great "Taj Mahal," a samba-funk jam that spawned two significant disco covers: one by France's Crystal Grass (brainchild of Cerrone's partner Alec R. Costandinos), and another by Rod Stewart, who remade the song as "Da' Ya' Think I'm Sexy" without crediting Ben (the Brazilian singer later sued, and won). But like so much international commerce, the business of disco coursed through New York whether the music was being made there or not.

The business of sex was coursing through New York, too, as always. And it was reaching new highs—or lows, depending on your sensibilities. A double-chinned forty-something former McDonald's manager from Brooklyn named Larry Levenson—a recent convert, along with his girlfriend, to the joys of "swinging"—decided to open a swinger's club in Manhattan. Initially, he and his business partner (whose day job was running a collection agency) rented a brownstone on Eighty-sixth Street. Then they moved their parties to a health spa off Gramercy Park, which they rented Wednesday, Friday, and Saturday nights after the spa crowd went home. Aspiring swingers had to call Levenson at 646-1169; he personally screened them. The event was named Plato's Retreat.

At the Gramercy spa, there was a heated pool, a small dance floor, disco music, and padded gym mats. Admission was twenty dollars per couple; single women were charged eight; no single men were admitted. Towel rental was fifty cents, and there was a nonalcoholic open bar. Soon, the weekend crowd was topping two hundred. Many people stayed dressed, hanging out and watching. Others stripped partly or fully, shaking what they had on the dance floor. By the wee hours, a couple dozen couples were usually fucking enthusiastically on the mats and in the pool. Occasionally groups of three or four would develop. But mostly it was one-on-one, straightforward, wholesome American sex. Women could do as they pleased. But Levenson made it a house rule that absolutely no male homosexual activity was allowed.[16]

Of course, Plato's was just taking its cue from the gay bathhouses and back-room bar scene, thriving for years, which by now had evolved toward full-on fantasy spaces like the Anvil, the Mineshaft, and the Toilet. In January, in the wake of the murder of a Chinese drag queen/back-room boy named Toni Lee, found in his MacDougal Street apartment bound to his bedposts and strangled, the *Voice* ran a notorious piece by Arthur Bell on the S&M club scene. He described a tour of the Mineshaft, where he encounters "the rack" and viewed

> a long haired gentleman stretched and strung. Cries of ecstasy leave his lips as the passing parade sticks hands, wrists, elbows up his rectum. At the foot of the bar, a pleasure-seeker splashes around in urine the way a child would smear wet sand on his face and stomach at the ocean's edge. "We have a hot mouth here," shouts the bartender with barkerlike intensity. "This man is waiting for your pissloads. He has taken 32 pissloads this evening. Free beer to those who piss on him!"[17]

At a time when job protection, housing rights, and partner rights were routinely denied, plenty of gay men wondered if this indeed represented liberation. But the parties rolled on.

Mayor Beame had ordered a police raid on some of the city's porn landmarks in March, with news media in tow. He began at the gay cruising intersection immortalized in the Ramones' "53rd and 3rd"—a song Dee Dee Ramone may or may not have written from experience. The nearby strip club Jax 3-Ring Circus was shut down. Beame and the police were heckled by passersby who felt the officials could be making better use of their taxpayer-funded time. Within hours, Jax had a court order permitting it to reopen.

Beame's effort was laughable. The city was beyond his control.[18]

Today people are buying brownstones in Brooklyn. Instead.

The full-page ad for the Brooklyn Brownstone Fair in October 1976 announced that Brooklyn had more nineteenth-century brownstones than any city in the country. Bargains abounded—you could get a grand two-family in Park Slope for around $70,000. And there were signs of cultural life, too. In March, a six-hundred-seat club called Smucker's Cabaret opened across Flatbush Avenue from the Brooklyn Academy of Music at 378 Schermerhorn Street—the first Brooklyn club with top-shelf, new-era talent. One week in April featured shows by Eddie Palmieri, Sun Ra, and the disco queen Vickie Sue Robinson.

Overall, though, the borough was as much a mess as the rest of the city. South Williamsburg had a thriving heroin street trade, brown rock available neatly packaged in glassine envelopes branded with colored tape. Harrison Avenue near Union Avenue was a hot spot, kids retrieving dime bags for buyers from trash-can stashes. In the Polish Northside community a dozen blocks up, kielbasa business was brisk on Bedford Avenue. But along with generic recession troubles, the neighborhood was a civic battleground. In '73, families were evicted from their homes on North Third and Fourth streets to allow expansion of the S&S Corrugated Paper Box Machinery Company. And in '75 the city closed Engine Company 212 at 136 Wythe Avenue. Some heroic locals seized the engine and the building, renaming it "People's Firehouse #1" and beginning a long fight with City Hall. But operating it was another matter. The neighborhood lost a hundred homes to fire in little more than a year.[19]

And there were the subways. Height similarities notwithstanding, Beame was no Mussolini, and the trains did not run on time. Wild delays were the norm, and rarely announced. Trains were often shortened, meaning you might sprint down the stairs to find the train doors closing on the end car halfway down the platform. There were 2,971 purses snatched in the subways in '76, 5 rapes, 5 homicides, 145 felonious assaults. Operating hours for booths were shortened, and lines long, so you had to stock up on tokens, fifty cents each. Stations stank of garbage. People smoked freely and flicked their butts onto the tracks; tunnel fires were common. The trains were old, maintenance was sketchy. At its best, graffiti actually helped more than hurt.[20]

In March the *Voice* ran a cover story titled "Why We Hate the Subways," and everyone had their own tales. Me, I'd been mugged on trains a few times, twice at knifepoint, coming home from Manhattan shows alone at night. But the worst was in May, when I was stuck on a broken-down E train for an hour en route to the Port Authority Bus Terminal to meet a girl I was cross-eyed crushed-out on. She had tickets to see the Grateful Dead five hours north that night, at Cornell University's Barton Hall. When I finally arrived, the girl and the bus—the last Ithaca run of the day—were gone. I was more upset about missing the girl. But in time, via magnetic tape, Barton Hall 5/8/77 would enter Dead lore as arguably the single greatest show the band ever played.

Fucking subway.

Television's *Marquee Moon* was released by Elektra Records on February 8. As with Smith's *Horses*, the cover was a photo by Robert Mapplethorpe, though you wouldn't guess it at first glance (the original shot was processed via color Xeroxing). To celebrate the album's completion, Verlaine treated himself to a London vacation, his first-ever visit. At a Notting Hill Gate newsstand, he saw the February 5 issue of the *NME* with his band on the cover. The review was a two-page spread. The critic Nick Kent called it "a 24-carat inspired work of pure genius."

Notwithstanding the U.K. music press tradition of hyperbole, this was deserved praise. Clinton Heylin, author of the excellent U.S. punk history *From the Velvets to the Voidoids*, calls it "probably the most dramatic debut of any American rock band," true enough depending on your definition of *dramatic* and whether you consider *Horses* or *Are You Experienced?* the debut of "bands." By any measure, this was a great rock record: razor-blade attitude, blunt heartache, indelible songs, breathtaking guitar playing. It certainly rivaled *Horses* and *Ramones* as the most perfectly realized record to come out of the CBGB scene.

Figuring he should maybe call up the London office of Elektra, which had no clue he was in town, Verlaine found them startled that he'd been there all week, sightseeing by himself and chain-smoking (he had a two-pack-a-day habit) when he could have been doing press to promote the record.

Back in the States, meanwhile, Television's debut was apparently no big priority for Elektra. One can imagine the marketing meetings. What the hell is this record? Punk rock? With guitar solos and ten-minute songs? Art rock? With no synthesizers or oversized drum kits? Why is the band called Television, anyway?

In March, the band was back onstage at CBGB. But now the audience was full of famous people who'd come down to the Bowery by town car. At one set, Linda Ronstadt, Paul Simon, and Peter Gabriel showed up. Champagne was sent to the "dressing room," a six-by-nine storage space of graffitied plywood and plasterboard. Gabriel was smitten, and invited the band to be the openers for his debut U.S. solo tour. They accepted. The catch: the tour started in a few days. In many cases it was too late to advertise the band in advance, so Television faced a crowd of Genesis fanatics expecting a whole night of their hero Gabriel, who had recently left the band.[21]

For all of the musical kinship between the acts, the upshot of the pairing was inescapable: it was a showdown between punk and prog rock. Even the hometown show at the Palladium was a battleground. I'd woken up at dawn to wait outside the Ticketron outlet at Macy's on Queens Boulevard and scored fourth-row seats—the best I'd ever had for a show. The band came out to scattered applause and a chant of "GAY-BREE-ELLLL" that persisted thoughout the set. Verlaine looked all business; Lloyd smirked tightly. Verlaine started into the tick-tock rhythm of "Prove It," spitting out the title refrain amid guitar spirals like he was arguing with the crowd, taunting them, yelping "Just the facts!" like Dylan shouting "I don't believe you, you're a liar!" to a heckler at Manchester Free Trade Hall in 1966 before tearing into "Like a Rolling Stone." "Venus" was violent and spiky, more Georges Braque than Alexandros of Antioch; "Marquee Moon" was accelerated but incandescent, notes stabbing like knives, then twisting to open the wound wider. The crowd, fans of Gabriel's theatrics with Genesis, was unimpressed with the four guys who pretty much just stood onstage, unsmiling, playing their instruments. The boos and chants competed with the cheers and finally overwhelmed them. Verlaine flipped off the crowd with his spindly middle finger and left the stage.

Television headed off for their debut U.K. tour, followed by Blondie, who were their opening act. There was no love lost between the groups. Television were surly and standoffish. On top of it all, Chris Stein and Debbie Harry had to see their former bassist, Fred Smith, who Television had poached two years prior. At one point, Richard Lloyd and Blondie's keyboardist, Jimmy Destri, got into a fistfight.

Television's sets were received rapturously, though some critics complained that they could seem "icy" onstage. Blondie toughed it out, working through songs from their debut LP until each one was airtight. Debbie Harry, now a peroxide blonde in front, still a brunette in back, strutted across stages in short skirts and thigh-high boots, a street-urchin Shirelle shimmying to hopped-up garage-rock tunes. She came on tough, but icy she was not. The catcalls were always enthusiastic, even from the most jaded crowds.

The Ramones, as it happened, were touring Britain and Europe, too, with Talking Heads as openers. Blondie caught the double bill of their pals in Glasgow the night before their tour with Television began. The show was great; the audience jumped up and down so hard during the Ramones set, the floor of the Strathclyde University student union hall felt like a trampoline. Throughout the tour, crowds stared in rapt fascination at the Heads—wiry Byrne with his yelping vocals and mental-patient moves, tiny Tina with her boyish bob and gigantic bass—then went wild pogoing and gobbing on the Ramones. In Tampere, Finland, an Elvis impersonator opened the show, providing some historic perspective.

Offstage, the groups shared a bus and tried to be civil. Talking Heads were mostly happy tourists despite the low-budget travel and crappy venues with dubious wiring. In Lyon, David Byrne was nearly electrocuted by a faulty microphone during a soundcheck; the shock knocked him to the floor for ten minutes. In London, the group played a small headlining gig of their own, at the Rock Garden in Covent Garden on May 14. Brian Eno saw the show and was fascinated. He invited the band to lunch the next day, and afterward they hung out at his Maida Vale apartment. Eno put a copy of Fela Anikulapo Kuti's *Afrodisiac* on the turntable; the Nigerian group's rhythmic web—which Eno described as "the future of music"—amazed his guests.

Johnny Ramone, a grouch under the best of circumstances, hated Europe. The accommodations were glorified youth hostels, and the food was alien. He had tantrums over lettuce (it wasn't iceberg) and over the James Brown tapes Tina Weymouth played on the bus; he refused to get off the bus at Stonehenge to see "a buncha rocks." Otherwise, Johnny spent the trip berating the stage crew and slapping his girlfriend around, according to Joey's brother Mickey Leigh, who was by then ready to quit his job as the Ramones' roadie. But the band was received as low-life royalty. They headlined London's Roundhouse, after their Fourth of July, third-on-the-bill opening slot the previous year. "Guys from the Pistols, the Clash, the Damned, and other future legends were filching our after-show beer from the coolers," Leigh recalled, "exactly what we would have been doing if it were the other way around."[22]

Marquee Moon made it to number 33 on the British charts. But

Television still came home broke, the tour profits supposedly tied up among venues and booking agents. The LP never cracked the U.S. charts. By summer, the band was selling off their stage gear to make rent.

The Heartbreakers were still in London, trying to get an album together. They had signed a sketchy deal with Track Records, a small label run by Kit Lambert, the drug-loving onetime manager and creative guru of the Who, which promised them a £50,000 advance. Johnny Thunders's baby mama, Julie Jordan, flew over with little Vito and Johnny Jr. and set up a communal home of sorts for him and the band. They began recording in February. Their debut would be called *L.A.M.F.*, shorthand for *Like a Motherfucker*.

Thunders and Nolan found the necessary dope connections and began modeling their lifestyle for their London peers. Twenty-two-year-old Viv Albertine, guitarist for the Slits and girlfriend of the Clash's Mick Jones, was introduced to heroin by Thunders, who she began seeing on the side. He stuck a needle into her arm—given his habit, other sorts of penetration could be difficult—but he didn't make a convert. Even her arm rejected the experience; it turned black-and-blue, and she had to wear long sleeves for a week so her mum wouldn't notice.[23]

Jerry Nolan claimed he turned Johnny Rotten on to heroin (Rotten won't say). Assuming it happened, one wonders what Nolan thought at the moment he injected the young punk rocker. The Heartbreakers postured like street toughs in the U.K. press. It's easy to imagine Nolan gripping the hypodermic's finger flange and pushing the plunger into the pasty, scrawny Rotten as if he were pulling a zip-gun trigger.

New York had arrived in London. Back in New York, the cover of *Punk* featured the Sex Pistols.

On Friday, February 18, Kiss finally played Madison Square Garden. It had long been their dream. The drummer, Peter Criss, raised George Peter John Criscuola in Greenpoint (where he was pals with Nolan, who beat him out for the Dolls' drum stool), would always say, "Let's kick ass like we're playing the Garden," to psych his bandmates up for a show. For rockers growing up in the boroughs, the Garden was St. Peter's

Square. Finally, tonight, here they were, thirty-some blocks and three years from opening that show for Wayne County at the rivet factory on Bleecker Street. Fully costumed in studs and leather, faces painted spectacularly, they rocked tandem guitar lines in the dry-ice clouds in front of a strobing fifteen-foot-high light display of their band logo, which was also stenciled and silkscreened on the T-shirts and jackets of half the kids in the audience.

The same day, in Lagos, the commune of Fela Anikulapo Kuti was raided by a thousand Nigerian soldiers, who beat him, raped many of the women there, and threw Fela's mother from a second-story window; she died from her injuries. Pictures from the period show her in Malcolm X eyeglasses sitting next to her son, whose music, on LPs pressed in Africa and in Europe, had found its way to progressive DJs like David Mancuso and Afrika Bambaataa. *Zombie* was Fela's first LP to get a proper U.S. release. It was widely thought to have spurred the attack: the lyrics of the title track are about a soldier and clearly aimed at the ruling military junta. In some places, talking shit in a pop song is no joke.

Near the end of the month, Keith Richards was busted in Toronto for possession of nearly an ounce of junk and a few grams of cocaine. Heroin's rock 'n' roll poster child had been strung out for years, on and off. Now it looked like he was finally going to jail. Or else, possibly, he was going to die.

Arthur Russell was rehearsing a new rock band, the Flying Hearts. He was also soaking up disco and composing art music. The latter included *Instrumentals*, an epic mixed-media project with his Buddhism teacher/photographer Yuko Nonomura that used improvisation and repetition. He envisioned it as potentially forty-eight hours long.[24]

The Flying Hearts included players Russell had worked with for years: the bassist Ernie Brooks; the percussionist David Van Tieghem, a Harry Partch fan who built rhythms using balloons, brake drums, Pop Rocks, transmission housings, and vibrating dildos; the trombonist Peter Zummo, a recent Wesleyan grad who studied with Sam Rivers; and Peter Gordon, whose Love of Life Orchestra sometimes featured Russell.

In March, the group made its live debut, minus horns, at the Other End on Bleecker, opening for Russell's neighbor Allen Ginsberg, then followed it up with a gig at the Lower Manhattan Ocean Club. Russell's friendship with Talking Heads got him invited to play cello on a take of "Psycho Killer" during the sessions for *Talking Heads: 77* (the band ultimately went with a different version for the album). By summer, as Talking Heads were finishing their record, Russell would go into a studio with the Flying Hearts to make some arty pop music of his own.[25]

"Can Salsa Escape the Cultural Ghetto?" asked a headline in *The New York Times*. Answering the question, Robert Palmer was guardedly optimistic, citing the Fania All-Stars crossover bid *Delicate and Jumpy*, Ray Barretto's major-label debut *Tomorrow*, and his favorite of the batch, *Lo Dice Todo*, the second LP by Grupo Folklorico y Experimental Nueva-yorquino.

Carlos Santana, still the nation's most successful Latin crossover artist, came to town in March. While his band's early recordings became FM rock staples, the guitarist had since connected (along with the jazz-fusion star John McLaughlin) with the guru Sri Chinmoy, and in the early '70s became Devadip Carlos Santana, slipping off his Latin-rock guitar-hero crown and losing a big chunk of his audience, especially Latinos. But he had a new record to promote, *Amigos*, with a minor radio hit ("Dance Sister Dance"), and the idea was a "return to the roots."

The big event was not Saturday night down at the Palladium but Friday night up at the Roseland Ballroom, where he co-headlined with Tito Puente. The pair had never shared a stage before, and as a rule—his recent set with the Fania All-Stars notwithstanding—Tito Puente shared top billing with no one. But this was the Roseland Ballroom on Fifty-second Street, one of the city's legendary dancehalls. It beat playing clubs. Plus, Santana's promoter, Bill Graham, was an old friend of Puente's. Business, after all, was business. Not long after the West Coast band turned Puente's "Oye Como Va" into a hippie rock hit in 1970, Puente received a royalty payment, which he barely looked at, and brought to the bank with some other checks. As Puente told it, he scribbled $35 on the deposit slip, but the clerk had to correct him: he'd left three zeros off the number.

There was a battalion of bouncers at Roseland, and at a steep fifteen dollars a ticket, the crowd was a bit on edge. "This is the toughest audience in New York," wrote Pablo "Yoruba" Guzman, a former Fania

hype man turned media maverick who had recently signed on as program director at listener-supported WBAI-FM, the city's most reliably
radical radio station. "A night out for this crowd represents two weeks
pushing garment racks on Seventh Avenue or a week hustling loose
joints. When they come to party, they ain't playin': the shit is *serious* . . .
A band could literally get taken apart."

But weed was smoked; rock fans clapped in clave, salsa dancers
found grooves in feedback, and the event went off beautifully. Puente's
second set peaked with a collaborative, off-the-hook "Oye Como Va,"
Santana sitting in.

On April 24, Héctor Lavoe went to see the Argentine superstar Sandro
(a.k.a. "El Elvis Argentino") at the Felt Forum. The next night, he gigged
at a joint called the Colombian Club in Elmhurst, apparently stoned to
the gills, talking to himself onstage. The next day, he was admitted to
Creedmoor Psychiatric Hospital in Queens Village, the same facility
where the pianist Bud Powell and a teenage Lou Reed got electroshock
therapy.

Few in the salsa world knew what had happened, and those who
knew weren't talking. *Latin N.Y.* published a full-page essay, "What
Happened to Héctor Lavoe?" in its July issue. It speculated that Lavoe
had become a medium of a Santeria cult, that he was in Puerto Rico
seeking spiritual consultation, or drug rehab, or both. It encouraged
fans "to send him some get well notes and cards to make him feel loved
and wanted and respected," giving the address of his manager, Ralph
Mercado.

The era of thirty-day Malibu rehab vacations with well-honed media campaigns were still a ways off.

In February, four FALN bombs went off simultaneously, two in Chicago and two in New York. In March, two more exploded in New York.
On Saturday, April 9, the script was changed when three bombs went
off simultaneously in the evening, around 8:45, in three midtown department stores: Bloomingdale's, Macy's, and Gimbels. Remarkably, no
one was injured. On the morning of August 3, Charles Steinberg was
not so lucky. He was killed by a bomb explosion at the Mobil Building

on Forty-second Street. Five others were injured. The bomb had been tucked into the cone of an umbrella in the company's employment office. After a tip was called in to the *New York Post*, one of the group's trademark communiqués taking credit for the bombing was found in Central Park.

Rubén Blades read the paper and shook his head. No one he knew, Puerto Ricans included, was down with this sort of terrorism. As someone who recently fled a military dictatorship, the idea of using violence as a political tool had zero appeal.

After much paperwork, Celia Cruz became an American citizen, roughly seventeen years since she had left Havana. Walking out of the federal courthouse on Cadman Plaza in Brooklyn after the swearing-in ceremony, she began screaming, shrieking, with joy. A cop came over to see if she was all right. She told him she was. Yes, indeed, she very much was.[26]

Peter Brown's spectacular 12-inch "Do You Wanna Get Funky with Me?" with its calibrated builds and tantric-orgasmic coda of "I'm burning up!" came out in April via the Miami producer Cory Wade, already riding high on disco playlists with T-Connection's anarcho-sexual "Do What You Wanna Do." It was a hot month for disco culture. From Dayton, Ohio, came "We're So Hot" by Sun, a funk band in the tradition of hometown neighbors Zapp, Slave, and album-cover conceptualists the Ohio Players (whose honey-dripping nude cover model nearly died during the photo shoot for their *Honey* LP when the sticky stuff dried under the Klieg lights and sealed off her pores). Nicky Siano was banging "We're So Hot" at the Gallery; so was a nineteen-year-old named John "Jellybean" Benitez, DJing at Experiment 4. Both versions of Cerrone's "Love in C Minor" continued to drive dance floors, as did "I Need a Man," a Tom Moulton production sung by Grace Jones that was an instant anthem among leather dudes at the Anvil.[27]

But the most significant record that spring—arguably, the most consequential record in the history of club music—came from Düsseldorf, Germany. Kraftwerk's "Trans-Europe Express," which DJs played straight into its presegued follow-up "Metal on Metal," sounded unlike anything else with its chugging mid-tempo synth drums, processed vocals, and zero-gravity vibe.

"Trans-Europe Express" was so strange that even Vince Aletti, disco's most knowledgeable critic and a man of eclectic tastes, qualified his praise in his April 23 column in *Record World*. "Not exactly light entertainment, but quite incredible, especially on a powerful system," he wrote. "Highly recommended for freaky crowds, otherwise a little too off-the-wall . . ."[28] Nevertheless, adventurous DJs ate it up: Richie Rivera at the Anvil, the pioneering boys-club buster Sharon White at Sahara, Jorge Wheeler at Siglo 21 in the Bronx.

Afrika Bambaataa didn't report his playlists to *Record World*, as his "club affiliations" were still school yards, parks, and housing project rec-rooms. But he pounded the record for hardscrabble, funk-fiending blacks and Latinos, who found themselves getting down to stiff electro beats made by white Germans chanting in a robotic monotone to the rhythm of a sci-fi subway.

The sixteen-floor high-rise at 254 West Fifty-fourth Street (New York City Building Inspection Number 1024843) had a very musical history. Its ground floor was once the Gallo Opera House, which opened on February 7, 1927, with a production of Puccini's *La Bohème*. It later hosted *The Tonight Show*, the soap opera *Love of Life*, and *Captain Kangaroo* as a CBS television studio. Until recently, the upper floors had been home to the offices and recording studio of Scepter Records, where the Shirelles jump-started the girl-group craze, where Lou Reed and Andy Warhol recorded *The Velvet Underground & Nico* in 1966, and where Tom Moulton was hired to create the first disco remix. The spirit of all this history, in one way or another, informed Studio 54, which opened in the former opera house on April 26.

Studio 54 was less about cutting-edge music than star-fuck fabulousness. Steve Rubell and Ian Schrager had come ashore in Midtown, washing their hands of the Enchanted Garden in Queens; the party promoter Carmen D'Alessio helped bring in design pros to overhaul the space, which could hold two thousand people. The tab ran around $700,000. The stage was the dance floor—because everyone wants to be onstage—and famously, outrageously, against one wall, a gigantic prop coke spoon mechanically tipped up into the nostril of the man in the moon. Music would be provided by Richie Kaczor, a Sanctuary veteran whose mixes never got too weird.

On opening night, the first song played was "Devil's Gun" by the Detroit R&B outfit C.J. & Co., a giddy funk jam with the reprise "FEE-FIE-FOE-FUM." The crush outside pretty quickly became impenetrable. Bianca Jagger made it in; Mick didn't (Keith Richards, out on bail from his Toronto bust and coming off a rehab stint, was laying low in New Jersey). Donald Trump pushed through the crowd. Frank Sinatra was S.O.L., ditto Henry Winkler—the Fonz!—and Warren Beatty. Cher was on the dance floor with Margaux Hemingway. Brooke Shields, an eleven-year-old model with the Ford agency, was being escorted around the club by a British journalist named Robin Leach. Outside, a guy with a plastic bottle full of quaaludes started passing them around, and before long the beautiful people that had been shut out had their own groping party/orgy right there in the street: shirts up, dicks out.[29]

Things were slow the next few nights—unnervingly slow. Then D'Alessio hit on the idea of throwing a birthday party for her pal Bianca: a really big birthday party. Bianca went along with it, and it was scheduled for May 2. Nicky Siano had been hired as a midweek DJ, and he played "Sympathy for the Devil," from the only Stones record he owned. Bianca—in a red chiffon Halston gown—rode into the room bareback atop a white stallion, led by naked footservants daubed in gold paint. It was celebrity decadence as staged photo op, and while there were only around a hundred people in the club, the photos filled the coveted centerfold of the *Daily News*, and later circled the globe, cementing Studio 54's reputation as the most exclusive, spectacular disco in the world.

Its exclusivity turned many people off, beginning with the red rope, above which weasel-faced Steve Rubell declared yea or nay to aspiring patrons. A friend and I stood on line one night as a joke, laughing as people jockeyed for position, assuming we wouldn't be ushered in (we weren't). The Loft's David Mancuso went and was appalled: it was a perversion of everything he held true about the brotherhood-and-equality-promoting magic of music and collective dancing. It hardly mattered that D'Alessio was one of the Loft's biggest fans, and learned many of her lessons from Mancuso.

Siano, however, with a remarkable negative capability for moving between the underground and the commercial, saw Studio 54 as the logical culmination of everything that New York club culture had started at the beginning of the decade. "It was just a large version of that little lamp in the corner of the Loft that was turned on and off," he said.[30]

Siano's honeymoon with the club was brief. His taste for heroin was derailing him; by summer, he got the boot. His final transgression the night he was canned: playing Kraftwerk's "Trans-Europe Express."

Larry Levan lived in an unfinished garage space on King Street west of SoHo. He and the promoter Michael Brody had begun hosting parties there—construction parties, they called them—to help raise the money to create a club that, unlike Studio 54, would *truly* be a large version of Mancuso's Loft. It would take a year. But the Paradise Garage would become the world's second most famous disco.

On May 13, Casablanca released Donna Summer's *I Remember Yesterday*. A concept album about musical evolution, not unlike Larry Harlow's *La Raza Latina*, it ends with a song that is ostensibly the future: "I Feel Love." Summer cooed "Love to Love You Baby"–style over a chugging track made up entirely of synth beats and arpeggiated chord washes, a yin to Kraftwerk's yang. New York DJs loved it instantly. As unprecedented as "Trans-Europe Express," it became just as essential, an electronic dance music template. Blondie covered it live, fairly faithfully, with Chris Stein adding Santana-style guitar licks. After hearing it in Berlin, Brian Eno rushed into the studio where he and David Bowie were working on *Heroes*, waving a copy of the record, raving that it would change the sound of club music "for the next fifteen years" (Eno was fond of grand statements). One can imagine the record spinning while the two Philip Glass fans listened to its hypnotic repetitions, the sonic possibilities blooming in their minds like flowers in a stop-motion film.[31]

In Florida in January, the Dade County legislature had passed a gay civil rights amendment. Outraged at the decision, Anita Bryant—a 1959 Miss America runner-up turned small-potatoes actress and TV-ad spokeswoman for the Florida Citrus Commission—was reborn as a Leviticus-quoting activist, appearing on *Good Morning America* and *The Phil Donahue Show* to spread the word that homosexual activity was immoral. Spearheading an effort to reverse the decision, she helped gather eleven thousand signatures, enough to force a revote. The decision was made to put the issue to the public.

Around the country, gays and their supporters wrote letters denouncing Bryant to the Citrus Commission, and flaunted T-shirts declaring ANITA BRYANT SUCKS ORANGES. Meanwhile, in Florida, you could buy KILL A QUEER FOR CHRIST bumper stickers. In Miami, not long after watching Bryant on the *Donahue* show, a despondent twenty-eight-year-old activist in the Dade County Coalition for the Humanistic Rights of Gays shot himself in the forehead.

On June 7, a special election repealed the amendment; gay bars around the country removed screwdrivers and other orange-juice drinks from their menus.

A few days before the vote, on May 25, the Everard bathhouse in New York, a city that had yet to pass a gay civil rights bill, burned down. A notoriously seedy joint at 28 West Twenty-eighth Street that had been host to gay men's assignations since the '50s, it had been set alight by arson a number of times. The owner had been planning to get a sprinkler system installed the week after the fire.

Nine men died. One was Jimmy Stuard, DJ at 12 West, who would go to the Everard in the wee hours after his set ended, mainly to sleep in the cubicles, which could be locked from the inside. One of his last playlists, published in *Record World* in April, included T-Connection's "Do What You Wanna Do" and Denise LaSalle's "Freedom to Express Yourself."[32]

The community responded to the bathhouse's demise with mixed emotions. "I hated this place," one patron told a reporter the morning after the fire. "Why did I go? I'm gay."

"A New Life for the Bowery," a *Times* headline announced. Writer Robert Palmer watched hundreds of kids milling around CBGB at 315 Bowery while a new rock club, Great Gildersleeves, was about to debut down at 331. Meanwhile, jazz bubbled at the Tin Palace (325 Bowery), the Ladies' Fort (2 Bond Street), and Studio Rivbea (24 Bond). After a show, you could munch out at the Tin Palace, Phebe's, or Ali's Alley on Greene until three o'clock most mornings; the Kiev on Second Avenue and Seventh was open for mushroom barley soup and challah French toast 24/7. If all you could afford was an egg cream, there was always the Gem Spa at Second and St. Mark's.

Two days later, the *Sunday Times Magazine* ran a piece by Stanley

Crouch: "Jazz Lofts: A Walk Through the Wild Sounds." Crouch wrote of adventurous music; of international talent scouts on the prowl; of the scene's history, including the 1972 Newport Jazz counterfestival that drew the attention of grant-givers; and of the homey ambience, with Sam Rivers's daughter selling four-dollar tickets at the door of Studio Rivbea, and the chef at Ali's Alley serving up fish and greens on paper plates while Muhal Richard Abrams played to a full house at one in the morning.

"You must watch the term 'loft jazz' because it's too limiting," Abrams told Crouch. "We didn't come to New York to play in lofts; we came to make a living. But an audience can start, and grow until it gets too big for the lofts and the music moves to another level. That's what we're interested in."[33]

The five-LP *Wildflowers* series, recorded at Rivbea the previous spring with most of the major players, was finally released. David Murray, now twenty-two, released a pair of debuts: *Flowers for Albert* on India Navigation, and *Low Class Conspiracy* on Adelphi. The latter opens with a seven-minute tenor solo, abstract and scalding, recorded live at the *Wildflower* sessions, before moving into more conventionally swinging territory. Murray's roommate and collaborator Crouch sang his praises in the LP's liner notes; Gary Giddins at the *Voice* called *Conspiracy* "the most impressive debut (or semi-debut) I've heard in years."

Groundbreaking earlier records were rediscovered. Julius Hemphill's *Dogon A.D.*, the opening salvo from the St. Louis Black Arts Group that the saxophonist had self-released in 1972, was reissued on the Arista Freedom label. The drummer Phillip Wilson (who also played on the Murray LPs) builds muscular rhythms under Hemphill with the cellist Abdul Wadud; the title track, with Baikida Carroll's searching trumpet and Hemphill's sharp alto, stomps with funk-rock power in a completely different way than that of the fusionists. Like many of the St. Louis and Chicago émigrés, Hemphill made music that looked back to early blues, spirituals, field hollers, New Orleans jazz, and R&B honkers as well as latter-day Coltrane.

One of the greatest expressions of this aesthetic debuted at the Tin Palace in February. The previous summer, the New Orleans alto Kidd Jordan came north to check out the loft scene. He invited Hemphill, along with his fellow St. Louis horn players Oliver Lake and Hamiet

Bluiett, down to Southern University in Baton Rouge to play a show. Back in September 1974 they'd recorded a sax quartet with Anthony Braxton, sans rhythm section, titled

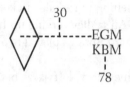

(alternately, *Opus* 37) that wound up on Braxton's Arista debut, *New York, Fall 1974*. At Southern University they revisited the idea with David Murray replacing Braxton. The audience literally danced in the aisles ("We hit," said Bluiett). Among the young local musicians Murray met at a workshop the group hosted that afternoon were two brothers who were already impressive players: Wynton Marsalis, fifteen, and Branford, who was about to turn sixteen (their dad, Ellis, was a pianist who had worked with Jordan).

The four New York sax players decided to form an ongoing unit. They called themselves the New York Saxophone Quartet, got threatened with a lawsuit by a classical ensemble who'd already claimed the name, then rechristened themselves the World Saxophone Quartet. At the Tin Palace in February they opened with a flute quartet, then picked up their horns and blew the house down, four Gabriels announcing a party on Judgment Day. On *Point of No Return*, a live set recorded in June at the Moers Festival in Germany, the energy crackles like chain lightning. It was jazz with ricocheting second-line flavor and an invisible rhythm section, swinging no less for it.[34]

Old-school artists started sniffing around the lofts as well. Dave Brubeck and his loft scene–loving sons arranged a gig for their band Two Generations of Brubeck at Environ in April, the same weekend the South African pianist Abdullah Ibrahim (the former Dollar Brand) played; the vocalese pioneer Eddie Jefferson wowed crowds at the Ladies' Fort during the New York Loft Jazz Celebration in June.

And the core of loft players was growing. The spring's jazz highlight was a four-day concert series at Columbia University's Wollman Auditorium, "Chicago Comes to New York." It was organized by the

AACM—now about 150 players strong, split among Chicago, New York, and elsewhere—and Taylor Storer, a student broadcaster at the university's WKCR-FM, source of the city's most adventurous jazz radio. A rented bus brought players east from the Windy City, and the station devoted ninety hours of programming to accompany the shows, playing every AACM-related record it had, along with unreleased tapes and many interviews. *The New Yorker*'s Whitney Balliett thought the festival and the broadcast "revealed a determination to bring into being a new and durable music—a hard-nosed utopian music, without racial stigmata, without clichés, and without commercialism."

The shows included a virtuosic, often funny solo set by the trombonist George Lewis, who (Balliett declared admiringly) "could easily have made the Ed Sullivan Show"; and one by the trio Air that "suggested the feckless, churning ensembles of Ornette Coleman at the Five Spot in 1960." Another standout trio featured Braxton, Leroy Jenkins, and the trumpeter Leo Smith. The weekend ended with a single ninety-minute piece by the AACM Orchestra, led by Muhal Richard Abrams, including virtually every musician in the festival. Only four hundred or so listeners actually turned out for the shows, but as Balliett concluded, "such events are carried by the wind, and in due course take hold."[35]

It's true that Balliett—along with Giddins, who had ratcheted up his coverage of the loft scene—was coming late to the table. But it was true, too, that the music had finally reached a creative critical mass. By the summer, even the mainstream media was crowing. *Newsweek* ran a cover story that declared "All of a sudden, *le jazz* is hot," and featured Abrams, Braxton, and Sam Rivers alongside Herbie Hancock and Miles Davis. And the British writer-photographer Valerie Wilmer published *As Serious as Your Life: John Coltrane and Beyond*, the first jazz book to make a case for the new-school aesthetic evolving in the New York lofts. The future, to paraphrase the title of an old Ornette album, was apparently now.[36]

Miles Davis's birthday, May 26, began with an unusually early traffic jam at the Holland Tunnel. Not far away from the Manhattan end, someone was scaling the World Trade Center. It wasn't Philippe Petit, the man who had walked a cable between the towers in the summer of '74 and now had a studio apartment in its shadow. The climber was George Willig, a twenty-seven-year-old toymaker from Queens who planned his climb for a year, fashioning customized climbing clips that fit into the window-washing tracks on the South Tower. A crowd, including Petit and many hapless police officers, watched his climb, which took three and a half hours to complete. He was arrested when he reached the top.

As with Petit's wire walk, it was tempting to read the act not solely as a lone nut-job's challenge to architectural topography but as an act of gentle artistic terrorism, the Common Man challenging the System. In one account of the climb, the World Trade Center was described as a "rapacious symbol of capitalist greed and rich people's power."[37] Mayor Beame had Willig released after fining him one cent for each floor he scaled, for a total of one dollar and ten cents.

The night after his climb, Willig and Petit and an entourage had dinner at Windows on the World atop the North Tower. They raised a champagne toast "to the people looking up."

In an effort to pay off the *Einstein* debt, Philip Glass arranged for a recording of the opera. He scared up some grant money to cover costs, reconvened the cast (with the Brooklyn violinist Paul Zukovsky replacing Bob Brown, who had decamped to Germany), and headed into Big Apple Studios on Greene Street, run by his associate Michael Reisman. Glass shaved some repetitions off certain sections, since the composition no longer needed to conform to Wilson's slo-mo choreography. Still, when they finished, they had a master tape nearly three hours long. The music sounded great, but producing for international distribution what would have to be at least a four-LP set was beyond the scope of Glass's indie label, and he couldn't find a single record company interested in putting it out.[38]

Music for 18 Musicians had made Steve Reich a star. He premiered it in London in January (there was no score for the complex piece; his ensemble had memorized it from two years of practice). Frustratingly, the recording he made for Deutsche Grammophon remained unreleased.

As it happened, another German label came to the table: ECM, the Munich-based jazz label run by Manfred Eicher, a producer who had made a name and some real cash in 1975 via Keith Jarrett's *The Köln Concert*, which moved the kind of numbers usually associated with pop records. *Music for 18 Musicians* was far from jazz, but Eicher took recorded music seriously and packaged it beautifully, and both men could see Reich's work appealing to audiences that were scooping up Jarrett's meditative, prismatic solo piano recordings. And for Reich, the former John Coltrane obsessive, there was surely some pleasure in the idea of his music coming out alongside modern jazz recordings.

Now, having consolidated his studies of Ghanaian and Balinese music, Reich decided to explore a tradition somewhat closer to home, at least spiritually: Hebrew cantillation. So in June, he and his wife, the filmmaker Beryl Korot, went to Israel, where he drank tea with a sixty-something Yemenite Jew who sang for him—"through his nose in a totally authentic 1,500-year-old-tradition." Reich thought this singer sounded fantastic, and recorded him. Parsing the melodic logic of the recordings would preoccupy him for some time.[39]

Other downtown composers were getting their music out, too. One Ten Records, a newly formed indie label, debuted with a double LP titled *Airwaves* featuring Meredith Monk and the first commercially available recordings by Laurie Anderson. *New Music for Electronic & Recorded Media: Women in Electronic Music—1977*, assembled in the spring by the Bay Area composer Charles Amirkhanian, also included tracks by Anderson, along with some by Laurie Spiegel, a classical guitarist and banjo player who founded the computer music studio at New York University and made gorgeous recordings of minimal, computer-generated melodies.

With help from Bob Bielecki and the producer Roma Baran, an acoustic-guitar player who grew up in Montreal playing with Kate and Anna McGarrigle, Anderson made recordings that were part performance-art narrative, part futuristic folk music. On one track she plays with the phrase *Ethics is the aesthetics of the future* on her tape-bow violin. "It's Not the Bullet That Kills You—It's the Hole (For Chris Burden)" is a reggae-tinged, harmonica-sweetened hoedown with Anderson playing some impressively raw fiddle licks. But it's her storytelling that sticks. On "Is Anybody Home," she begins a tale about her loft space on Canal Street near the Hudson River, from which she watches boats go by, imagining that the ships are motionless and that "all of Manhattan has become unanchored, and is slowly drifting out to sea."

One Saturday morning in June, a stream of curious concertgoers marched up the stairs to Meredith Monk's loft on West Broadway, where she served them coffee and fresh-baked bread. Then she sang for them. The program was *Songs from the Hill*, a group of wordless solo vocal pieces she had written over two summers on a hill in the desert near her sister's place in New Mexico. The music was ecstatic, hypnotizing in its displaced beauty. Yet a pedestrian passing below Monk's window—hearing "Insect," with its groaning glottal attacks; or "Descending," all squeaky "ee-ee-ee's" and "na-na's" and ambulance-siren "oh-wee-oh-wee"s; or the breathtaking, hilarious, ornithological "Bird Code"—might have figured there was an insane asylum on the floors above.

Monk sometimes wondered whether the stuff she was making was really music or art at all. But fellow musicians encouraged her to voice the odd sounds she heard in her head. Sam Rivers was one. "He made me feel like I wasn't crazy," she said years later, laughing out loud just a little crazily.

On April 4, the Symphony no. 3, op. 36, also known as the *Symfonia pieśni żałosnych* (*Symphony of Sorrowful Songs*), premiered at the Royan International Festival in southwestern France. It was written by Henryk Górecki, a Polish composer who, like Glass and Reich, had been trying to reimagine modern Western classical composition using traditional music sources—in this case, Polish folk songs—simplified melodies, and repetition. The hour-long piece, written for soprano voice and orchestra, is hushed, with moments that swell to magnificent, breathtaking heights. It sounded like nothing else. Critics trashed it; one described it as dragging "through three old folk melodies (and nothing else) for an endless 55 minutes."

Patti Smith was booked for a show at CBGB on Easter Sunday, April 10. It sold out instantly. It was billed as "La Resurrection."

The injured singer had been relentless with her physical therapy in preparation. As she and her band had been out of work for months, everyone was asked to pay the six-dollar cover at the door, even Arista's

Clive Davis (who was not amused). Cleveland's Dead Boys and England's Damned—spawns of punk seed scattered—played a matinee show. Around dinnertime, William S. Burroughs read. Then the Patti Smith Group played. The singer performed with a neck brace, and made a show of yanking it off mid-set. Thurston Moore had taken the train in from his parents' house in Connecticut. He stood in the packed room, neurons popping like flashbulbs.

A few weeks later, Smith was onstage at CBGB again for the first of two *Punk* magazine benefits. The second night's bill featured Blondie, Richard Hell and the Voidoids, the Dead Boys, the Cramps, and, as unlikely headliner, *Punk*'s star writer, Lester Bangs, in his own attempt at artistic rebirth. Bangs had been a friend of Smith's; he championed her debut LP in *Creem*, then fell out of favor when he criticized *Radio Ethiopia*. (Robert Christgau rejected a harsh review he wrote of the album for the *Voice* on the grounds that it smacked of "resentment, and that's not a pretty thing in anybody.") Still, Bangs admired Smith's transformation from poet and rock crit to rocker, and figured he could do the same. He wasn't entirely new at it: in Detroit in 1974, on a dare from the J. Geils Band, he took his electric Smith-Corona onstage and type-jammed along to "Give It to Me," then smashed his machine à la Pete Townshend.

At CBGB, he was the lead singer. The band was Smith's drummer Jay Dee Daugherty, Fred Smith of Television, the Dictators' Andy Shernoff, and several members of Blondie. Bangs hollered out "Wild Thing" and a long "Sister Ray." Slurring and squealing like a drunk Richard Hell, he made a decent rock singer. Terry Ork offered to put out a single, so Bangs wrote some songs and recruited a band, including Daugherty and the Voidoids guitarist Robert Quine. When Ork ran out of money, Bangs's drinking buddy, John Cale, and Smith's ex-manager, Jane Friedman, came to the rescue, releasing "Let It Blurt" backed with "Live" on their new label, Spy.

With the record finished, Bangs and friends played a three-night stand at CBGB in June. When the run was over, the front man was told that his bar tab canceled out the band's earnings.[40]

After *The Dictators Go Girl Crazy!* bombed, the band had broken up, re-formed, and been sidelined while Manitoba healed from his dust-up with Wayne County. Now they'd gotten another shot. Signed to Asylum Records in the midst of the County brouhaha (proving again that there is no such thing as bad publicity), they recorded *Manifest Destiny*, an attempt at a straightforward hard-rock record, dialing back the juvenile delinquent humor of their debut. As a commercial move, it failed. But the LP's final track, a cover of "Search and Destroy" from the Stooges' *Raw Power*, was pure punk rock, a reminder that the Dictators deserved as much credit for inventing the music as any New York band.

Led Zeppelin played Madison Square Garden in June. I'd been shut out in '75, so to make up for it I went twice, to the first and last nights of a six-night run. I got great seats for the latter, and my friend and I smuggled in a pint of Southern Comfort. The show was monstrously loud, the music huge, John Bonham's drumming superhuman. The scale was awesome, and at points—"Kashmir," with its scimitar guitar line cutting through the dark arena while an illuminated mirror ball rotated slowly overhead—the show was thrilling. At other points—like the familiar "Whole Lotta Love/Rock and Roll" closer—it felt stale, a remake of something that had lost its original meaning.

I was also struck by how *old* the band looked. These guys were what, in their thirties? They were grown-ups. I mean, what the fuck?

By the time Johnny Thunders had gotten off a flight from London at Kennedy Airport on the night of July 13, the entire city was blacked out. Generators kept utility lights burning inside the terminal; outside, beyond the line of cabs, New York was invisible. There was no skyline. There was no telling what was going on downtown. The streets were illuminated only by headlights and revolving cop-car beacons.

The Heartbreakers had just landed a hit single in Britain with "Chinese Rocks," and they'd finished an album, which needed remixing and an American distributor.[41]

But right now, Johnny needed a fix.

Casanova Fly and Disco Wiz had set up their sound system earlier in the evening at 183rd Street Park. They were prepared for a battle, and if they were outgunned, they wouldn't be outsmarted. The Master Plan Crew—basically one kid, DJ Eddie, with no skills and a bunch of weak-ass disco records—had challenged them many times, and they'd finally agreed. Eddie had big Cerwin-Vega speakers and a serious amp, but he didn't know the science of funk.

Caz and Wiz let him go first while they fiddled with their own gear—essentially Caz's home stereo system—on the opposite side of the park, hooking it up to an extension cord they'd wired into the lamppost. As night fell, it was still near 90 degrees and sticky. Wiz was worried about their amp blowing in the heat. The crowd was getting thicker. People brought coolers with forty-ounce bottles of malt liquor; you could smell the acrid scent of dust being smoked.

When it was Caz's turn, he slapped the Incredible Bongo Band's "Apache" on the turntable and let it rip. The conga beats ricocheted around the park, everybody in the park shouted their approval, and Caz knew that Eddie was finished. He cued up his second record for the one-two punch: Pleasure's "Let's Dance." "Let's make it fuh-fuh-fuh-fuh-fuh-fuh-fuh-FUNKY!!" the singer chanted over a churning wah-wah riff. Then the drums crashed in, and the horns, and the kids who came to hear Caz and Wiz were going bananas.

And then the beats started slooooooooooooooowing down, until they stopped dead.

Time stretched out. The streetlight they were plugged into went dark; then the other streetlights around the park perimeter, one by one.

"What the fuck did we just do?!" Wiz yelled. You could barely see your hand; there was no moon.

The crowd in the park muttered and laughed, shouted, looked around. There were no lights in any of the apartment buildings.

Somebody asked the time; a guy with a glow-in-the-dark watch said it was 9:40.

Then someone else yelled: "Hit the stores!"

Others repeated the cry.

People started running toward the shopping strips on Jerome Avenue, West Tremont Avenue, Grand Concourse. One group decided to start the looting with Caz's sound system. Caz and Wiz both pointed handguns at the fans they had just been playing records for.

"Go *that* way, motherfuckers!!" instructed Caz, pointing out of the park.

Caz asked Wiz and their crew to pack up the gear, then dashed off, saying there was something he had to get. As Wiz tells it in his book *It's*

Just Begun, Caz came back fifteen minutes later with a single item: a Clubman Two mixer that he'd been eyeing at a local shop for quite a while.

Battery-powered radios were the only information source, and people gathered around them. WNEW-FM came back on the air around eleven. Scott Muni had walked from the station's studios on Fifth Avenue and was broadcasting from its transmitter site in the Empire State Building. "I have a small microphone here, and, uh, a small turntable," he said, in the same consoling, foghorn baritone that talked down the hostage-taking Deadhead Ray "Cat" Olsen two years earlier. "Just a little setup where we are able to talk to yuh and tell yuh we are back on the air after many hours of absence. Not due to anything else other than another historical event for New York City that'll be written about and talked about and motion pictures made about. Albums. And no doubt there'll be a song—someone right now is writing the song, or already has written it.

"If you would like," he added, "I think it might be a nice idea to tell some of your friends, since we are sort of a family, if you would talk to your friends, give 'em a call, since telephones are working, and say 'WNEW is back on the air.'"[42]

Looting of shops went on wholesale in the poorest areas of the Bronx, in East Harlem, in Bushwick and Brownsville. Elsewhere, other dramas unfolded. When the lights went out at Caesar's Retreat in midtown, the porn star Annie Sprinkle was in the middle of a blow-job-for-hire. At CBGB, the Shirts were on a bill with the Romantics; Hilly canceled the show, so guitarist Artie Lamonica and bassist Bob Racioppo hung out and drank his beer by candlelight. The cast of *Beatlemania* led a sing-along with acoustic guitars up at the Winter Garden in Times Square; a harpist for the Canadian Ballet plucked out the notes to "Dancing in the Dark" up at the Met. On the side blocks off Christopher Street, naked men fucked against parked cars.

The newspapers, which had gone to press with their Thursday-morning editions, scurried to pull together supplements. *The New York Times* dug out some old propane lamps left over from the '65 blackout and sent runners over to Holy Cross Rectory on West Forty-second to scare up candles; as the newsroom still had plenty of manual typewriters, editors and writers kept right on typing. Outside the *Daily News* building, also on Forty-second Street, a film crew was shooting *Superman* with diesel generators; after some pleading, the *News* staff borrowed some lights from them and ran wires up to their seventh-floor editorial offices.

On Seventy-seventh Street and Lexington Avenue, power mysteriously returned to the music writer Paul Nelson's apartment and other buildings on his block after just a few hours. He and Lester Bangs, who had hiked uptown, listened to the new Sex Pistols single, "Anarchy in the U.K.," over and over. Then they went up to the roof and watched buildings burn uptown and across the river.

Bruce Springsteen and the E Street Band had been at the Record Plant on Forty-fourth Street when the power went out. They muttered curses, then accepted the rare gift of a night off. Springsteen and Jon Landau left the studio and walked, the city lights extinguished around them. But they barely noticed: they were deep in conversation about the record that was finally getting made.

Down the block from the Record Plant, at Sardi's, David Murray had been eating dinner with Ntozake Shange—his new wife—and some friends. Shange's *For Colored Girls Who Have Considered Suicide When the Rainbow Is Enuf*, an experimental poetry-theater piece that premiered at Studio Rivbea and wound up being produced at the Booth Theater, had been nominated for a Tony Award for Best Play, though it lost to Michael Cristofer's *The Shadow Box*. Still, the couple was on top of the world. They had met last year, fallen in love, and were married on July 7—7/7/77—in Berkeley, California, Murray's home turf. Back in New York, dining in the restaurant where Brock Pemberton had conceived the Tonys back in 1946 in tribute to his late wife, Antoinette, the newlyweds were getting ready to leave for a honeymoon in Hawaii. When the lights went out, they settled their tab, made their way out to the street, and wandered downtown, sated.

Meredith Monk had been watching *Annie Hall* at a midtown theater with a friend when the film sputtered to a halt. They headed back toward her loft in TriBeCa. Elsewhere downtown, Robert Quine, the dominatrix Anya Phillips, and Lou Reed's future wife Sylvia Morales played Monopoly by candlelight.

In Long Island City, Chris Frantz, Tina Weymouth, David Byrne, Jerry Harrison, and some friends were barbecuing hot dogs and hamburgers on the roof of Frantz and Weymouth's loft building, 9-01 Forty-fourth Drive, at the corner of Vernon Boulevard, right off the East River. They were taking a night off from recording their album; a cool breeze was wafting in off the water. Frantz was looking at the Manhattan skyline when the lights uptown suddenly cut out, then the lights of midtown; in a few moments, Lower Manhattan went dark, too. In their neighborhood, strangely, the electricity stayed on. So they all finished dinner.

The subways were out, but the *Soho News* photographer Allen Tannenbaum was able to grab a PATH train to New Jersey in the wee hours of the morning, and shot the unplugged skyline across the Hudson River as dawn broke.

Roberta Bayley, a photographer who occasionally worked the door at CBGB, had been afraid to leave her apartment on St. Mark's. But the next day she met up with *Punk*'s John Holmstrom and headed over to Chris Stein and Debbie Harry's apartment on Seventeenth Street, where Iggy Pop, just back from Germany, played them tracks from *Lust for Life*, which he'd recorded with David Bowie at a studio near the Berlin Wall. "He sees the stars come out tonight / He sees the city's ripped backside," Iggy sang on "The Passenger," his voice pulsing through the living room speakers.[43]

In Queens, my friends and I had been hanging out in the center of Cunningham Park when the streetlights ringing the field flickered out in rapid sequence, like arcade lights on an amusement park ride. We had wandered the darkened neighborhood, stopped in to grab some bialys from Leroy at Turnpike Bagels, and tried to scam some free beers along the strip of bars on Union Turnpike near Utopia Parkway. No luck: the strip was full of uniformed cops, who, as far as I could tell, were treating the blackout as a night off. Fresh Meadows was a middle-class neighborhood; there was no trouble at all. The next morning, Union Turnpike was deserted, the traffic lights colorless. I walked down the middle of the street, my dream of being Charlton Heston in *The Omega Man* suddenly made real.

Power was restored citywide that evening, Friday, July 14. Most of us picked up our lives as we had left them. But quite a few kids across the Bronx and elsewhere were wiring up brand-new sound systems—determined, now that they had the gear, to learn how to DJ.

•

Arthur Russell went up to CBS Studios on Fifty-second Street to cut some demos for John Hammond. The Flying Hearts had turned into a real band. On one of the tracks, "What It's Like," Russell spoke over a slow vamp, recalling Patti Smith's "Piss Factory" and Lou Reed's "Coney Island Baby" in its confession-booth storytelling. "In Iowa, in the tall grass, there is a couple," he began, setting a scene in his home state, describing a girl and a young preacher brought together, then separated by their love of the Lord. Then Russell bursts out singing, slightly flat but flush with emotion, shifting into the first person ("I feel like I ache all over!") with gentle Stax-style horns cushioning his lament.

In May, an expanded version of the Hearts played Russell's minimalist composition *Instrumentals* at the Experimental Intermedia Foundation on Centre Street. It was a shorter performance than the composer's idealized forty-eight-hour one. Still, it got a glowing review from Robert Palmer in the *Times*.[44] The Hearts played Russell's pop songs at the Village Gate, between a Patti Smith poetry reading and a set by Talking Heads. Larry Saltzman, the band's guitarist, felt the Hearts blew the Heads off the stage, though bassist Ernie Brooks wasn't so sure.[45]

Russell had also convinced Nicky Siano, who was looking to break into production, to fund a collaborative 12-inch disco single from his Gallery nest egg. The composer began working on the track at Brooks's spacious new loft space in Long Island City. Russell rehearsed a single bass riff so incessantly that the downstairs neighbors, Chris Frantz and Tina Weymouth, began complaining. (David Byrne would wind up playing guitar on the track.) It was like Russell was a radio receiver, tuning in all of the city's sounds and simultaneously sorting out the frequencies.

Hammond, officially "retired" but still at Columbia, thought the sessions went well. He told Russell that history would remember John Hammond for having discovered "Billie Holiday, Charlie Christian, and George Benson, and then Dylan, Springsteen, and Arthur Russell."[46]

Bruce Springsteen finally cut himself loose from his manager Mike Appel on May 28. For more than a year he had been legally barred from recording a follow-up to *Born to Run* as he wanted, with Jon Landau producing. He used the time to tour hard and write new songs. One that he'd begun playing live was a ballad called "The Promise." Though Springsteen resisted the interpretation, most people heard it as being about his falling-out with Appel, his champion from the beginning: "When the promise is broken, you go on living / But it steals something from down in your soul," Springsteen sang, before incanting the title of *Born to Run*'s "Thunder Road" like a funeral threnody near the song's end.[47]

The night the lawsuit was settled, Springsteen and Steve Van Zandt drove from New York to Philly to see Elvis Presley at the Spectrum. Springsteen had been obsessed with Elvis since his teens. But the lawsuit got Springsteen thinking anew about Elvis's career and how badly it had gone off the tracks, in part due to corrupt management. At this point, Springsteen was living on a farm in Holmdel, New Jersey, and when he wasn't on the road, he'd visit old haunts, not wanting to lose touch with his roots. The previous week, he'd been drinking at the Stone Pony in Asbury Park and had joined his old friend Bob Campanell and the Shakes onstage; Bruce borrowed a guitar and led the band in a letter-perfect "Jailhouse Rock," hip swivels and all.[48]

For the Philly concert, Springsteen and Van Zandt didn't call in any VIP favors; they got their tickets and sat in the crowd with the rest of the fans. The evening should have been a party, a celebration of Springsteen's freedom. But Elvis was a mess, nearly a self-parody. The performance was so disappointing, the two musicians barely said a word to each other on the drive home.

In July, Springsteen finally hunkered down for the album sessions at the Record Plant with Landau and Jimmy Iovine. Bruce and Miami Steve set up a shrine to Elvis, and were passing back and forth an advance copy of *Elvis: What Happened?*, a tabloid warts-and-all bio by the *New York Post* columnist Steve Dunleavy.

Presley died on August 16. Methaqualone, the drug that helped kill the New York Dolls drummer Billy Murcia, was in his bloodstream, along with codeine, morphine, Valium, and more. In London, Malcolm McLaren was speaking to the journalist Charles M. Young for a *Rolling Stone* cover story on punk rock when he got a call about Presley's death. "Too bad it couldn't have been Mick Jagger," he quipped.[49] John Lennon—who, like Springsteen, had worshipped Elvis as a young man—told a journalist, "He died when he went into the army."

Lester Bangs was drinking beer with a friend on a Chelsea fire escape when he heard the news. He did a casual survey of the neighbors and was disturbed that no one seemed to care. A guy at the meat market told him a story about taking his wife to see Elvis in Vegas in 1973: "We paid fourteen dollars a ticket, and he came out and sang for twenty minutes. Then he fell down. Then he stood up and sang a couple more songs, then he fell down again.

"Fuck him," the man concluded.

Bangs wrote a cover story for *The Village Voice*. He credited Elvis's hips as sparking societal upheavals of the '60s, then spun outward to lament the state of pop culture and the current unfashionableness of love. The King, indeed, had been dead for quite a while.[50]

Johnny Thunders, whose mother bought him a plastic toy guitar after he was wowed by Elvis on *The Ed Sullivan Show*, heard the news about Presley on the drive back from his wedding reception. (An Italian Catholic, he married his baby mama, Julie Jordan, in a civil ceremony.) Two days later, the Heartbreakers began a sold-out three-night stand at the Village Gate. The band was heralded with a full-page ad in the *Voice* announcing "the HEARTBREAKERS in their ONLY NEW YORK APPEARANCE before they return to Europe!" alongside a photo of a beehived blonde hiking her skirt up to her garters.

"Anarchy in the U.K." blared from the jukebox opening night; Thunders sang "Jailhouse Rock" with the rockabilly throwback Robert Gordon. Offstage, he chatted with his old comrade David Johansen. Debbie Harry gave him a kiss on the cheek.

Soon the band was back in London, trying to finish *L.A.M.F.* The recording sounded terribly muddy; Jerry Nolan had tried remixing it himself, to little avail. The standout track was "Chinese Rocks," a song credited to Dee Dee Ramone, Johnny Thunders, Jerry Nolan, and Richard Hell that had been bouncing around for a while. Dee Dee wrote it, in fact, but the rest of the guys made it the de facto anthem of New York City junkie rock.

The weekend the Heartbreakers played the Gate, the local PBS affiliate Channel 13 aired *El Baquiné de Angelitos Negros*, with music by Willie Colón. The story line of the salsa ballet drew on the tradition of the baquine, the special wake held for a dead child, whose innocent soul is believed to transform immediately into an angel.

Business practices at Fania, an operation short on innocent souls, remained dubious from the point of view of its musicians, most of whom were paid flat fees for their albums with no royalty structures, though Jerry Masucci might set up his biggest earners with a car or a company credit card. But the money was still flowing, so no one wanted to rock the boat—just as it was back when Joe Bataan tried to organize a sit-in.

At the end of July, the label held its most dazzling blowout yet at Madison Square Garden, headlined by the Fania All-Stars, emceed by DJ Roger Dawson and *Latin N.Y.*'s editor, Izzy Sanabria, whose magazine, with help from Fania ad revenue, boasted a circulation of forty thousand salsa fiends. The crowd included a large number of them, and the presentation was all mainstream rock 'n' roll flash. Roberto Roena flew into the air on wires. The pianist Papo Lucca, in a shtick probably borrowed from the same production company used by Emerson, Lake and Palmer, played a piano that spun in midair.

The revelry continued backstage. Pete "El Conde" Rodriguez, the Fania veteran who sang on the label's first official release back in '64, sang with the All-Stars that evening. At one point during the after-party, as Jerry Masucci was holding court in a dapper white suit, Rodriguez stepped up to him, raised a pistol, pointed it at his temple, and pulled the trigger.

Women screamed. Masucci bent down, holding his head.

But the gun had fired only blanks. Rodriguez borrowed it from the timbales player Nicky Marrero, who performed that night as a mariachi gunslinger with a huge sombrero and a pistol belt. When Rodriguez fired it, some of the flash powder hit Masucci and burned him around his eye, though not seriously.

The "joke" said plenty about relations in the Fania family.

Héctor Lavoe was about to be released from Creedmoor. He seemed to have made the best of his time in the hospital. He made friends with fellow patients. A picture of him with his pianist, Gilberto Colón, in June on the hospital grounds showed him relaxed and smiling. In late August, he was sent off with a prescription for antidepressants. His wife, Puchi, picked him up. He looked good, healthy.

Two weeks after his release, he walked onstage for a headline set at a sold-out Madison Square Garden. The crowd had been chanting his name all night. Lavoe sang the hell out of "Mi Gente," the audience joining in. He also introduced the audience to a new song, written by Rubén Blades, "El Cantante"—a showstopper about a singer whose life offstage is filled with sorrow.

The next morning, he and his band flew to Venezuela for a series of gigs. The unspoken rule was that Lavoe should never be left alone, and he wasn't. The shows went well. Lavoe returned home to his old life with Puchi and their son, Héctor Jr. Willie Colón even invited him into the studio for a one-off reunion album.

Armed with their brand-new mixer, Casanova Fly and Disco Wiz took on the mighty Afrika Bambaataa at a sound clash that fall at the Police Athletic League gym on Webster Avenue. The duo began their set with Queen's "We Will Rock You."

As it thumped through their still-modest sound system, Bambaataa's MC, Mr. Biggs, got on his mic and shouted:

"CASANOVA! WE CAN'T HEAR YOU! TURN UP YOUR SYSTEM!"

They pushed the volume up to the max.

"CASANOVA!" Biggs bellowed, "WE STILL CAN'T HEAR YOU! THIS IS WHAT IT SOUNDS LIKE . . ."

Bambaataa had cued up the same record on his vastly superior rig, and the beats thundered over Caz and Wiz like Godzilla stomping on Tokyo.

There was nothing for them to do but unplug their system and call it a night. But they stuck around, hanging out with Bambaataa, proud to have at least had their shot.

That year, Bambaataa helped assemble a dance crew called the Zulu Kings: they included his boy Pow Wow, who would also rock the mic with rhymes; Kusa, Amid, Aziz, and Zambu. (Zulu Nation members who didn't have Africanized names from birth adopted them.) The dancers had been studying Kool Herc's dancers—the Nigger Twins and Clark Kent—and their comic moves, which included *Monty Python*–style funny walks, Charlie Chaplin penguin-stepping, and assorted pantomime riffs. But the Kings had a more serious demeanor, more like

Olympic athletes trained on a school-yard blacktop: they'd execute high-speed footwork, often with one knee in the air (from the Good Foot, a dance older gang members showed off back when Bambaataa was with the Black Spades), then drop to the ground and spin on their tailbones. The funk dance crews that lived for the rhythm breaks in songs—wholly distinct from disco dancers—were called break-boys or just B-boys, a term that also signified their territory (Bronx) and echoed an older term, "boi-oi-oingers," from the cartoon sound effect the rubbery dancers conjured.[51]

At Goose Pond Park next to Jamaica High School in Queens, as the winter thawed, the white kids would sit on one side of the pond smoking cigarettes and joints while, across the way, the black kids with their boom boxes did the same. They'd blast WBLS, or cassette tapes of funk, disco, and fusion jams. Across the divide, all heads nodded to the beats.

The previous year, Sal Abbatiello's dad, Al, opened a club at 167th Street and Jerome Avenue in the Bronx, not far from the Executive Playhouse. He called it Disco Fever. It didn't do booming business. After hours, when the main DJ ended his set, the night manager, Sweet G Godfrey, got on the turntables to close things out, and he'd do a little smooth talking and rhyming on the mic, calling out people in the crowd. One night Sal was there, and he was impressed. When G got on the mic, the room energy spiked—people were hollering and dancing, even though it was near dawn. Afterward, they got to talking, and G agreed to give Sal a crash course on local DJing.

They went to see DJ Hollywood at Club 371, who had his dancing girls and his DJ partner, Junebug. Abbatiello was blown away by Hollywood's star power, his microphone spiel, and especially his adoring crowd, who shouted along with his routines. But Club 371, off Webster Avenue, was posh; it was where Manhattan DJs came to play, where the serious gangsters hung out. Hollywood was getting five hundred dollars a night, minimum, and driving a Cadillac. Sal couldn't afford him.

Then Sweet G took Abbatiello to see Grandmaster Flash do a park jam, with his quick-cutting turntable tricks and his emcees. Abbatiello thought Flash was even more amazing than Hollywood. He couldn't afford Flash, either, really, but he promised him a weekly gig—something he'd never had—at fifty dollars a night to start, and more if things worked out. Flash agreed, ultimately getting an extra twenty-five for his MCs. Abbatiello papered the neighborhood with flyers: a dollar at the door, dollar drinks, showtime 1:00 a.m.

In the early morning hours of Wednesday, August 15, Grandmaster Flash made his Disco Fever debut. About five hundred people showed. Flash drove them crazy; same thing the next week, and the next. Word was out. The crowds, mostly teenagers, began getting a little unruly. So Abbatiello changed the door policy to subsidize the cost of increased security: it was now a one-dollar cover for everyone wearing shoes, five if you were wearing sneakers.

Shoes?

Most kids paid the extra money.

The scene stayed wild. People openly razored out coke on the tables and fired up pipes filled with dust. The club was on the second floor with a cashier booth at street level. Whenever the police paid a visit, the cashier flicked a switch that triggered a light in the DJ booth, and someone would announce "code blue" through the PA. Voilà: by the time the police made it up the stairs, all illegal substances had disappeared.

Of course, the police must have been grateful for Disco Fever. Anyone who could remove five hundred teenagers from the late-night streets of the South Bronx and keep them amused was doing the community a great service.[52]

Jorge Pabon and his twin brother, Pete, were twelve years old when they rode their Apollo five-speeds from el barrio on East 123rd Street over the Third Avenue Bridge to check out a jam at the Betances Houses in Mott Haven. The Wicked Wizards were hosting, and one of them was dating the Pabons' older sister, Noemi, so the twins hopefully wouldn't have any trouble.

The sound system, plugged into a lamppost, was booming, the MCs hollering into echo delays. But what really wowed them were the dancers. They'd seen up-rocking street crews before in Spanish Harlem— the Savage Samurais, the younger Floor Master Tops—but this was another level. Huge Afros wobbled as dancers spun precisely in bell-bottom Lee Rider denims, baseball caps, and layered tube socks with multicolored stripes, like team colors. It turned out kids were busting moves like this all over the city, steps learned perhaps from the Nigger Twins or the Zulu Kings, then flipped, embellished, and passed around. Girls were even getting into the act: there was talk of a dance crew called the Zulu Queens.

This was the summer that Jerry Dee Lewis—a.k.a. JDL—rocked a mic for the first time. Up until then he'd rhymed with buddies in the street, banging out beats on the hoods of parked cars (or abandoned ones, the safer option). He went to every jam he could, no matter how late or how dangerous the neighborhood, to study the only serious MCs that existed: Flash's Furious Five, Busy Bee Starski, and JDL's future partner, Casanova Fly. JDL's mom would frequently kick his ass for missing curfew. But it was worth it.

His debut night was a jam with DJ Whitehead and Dr. Pepper at the Junior High School 82 playground at Tremont and University Avenues. He came with his neighborhood rhyming crew, including Butch Kid, who had the records, and they all hung back for a while. Once the party got simmering, around nine o'clock, JDL slipped under the ropes and asked Whitehead if he could get on the mic. Butch Kid gave the DJ some records: Pleasure's "Let's Dance," James Brown's "Funky Drummer," Juice's "Catch a Groove," "I Can't Stop" by John Davis and the Monster Orchestra. Also in the stack was "Take Me to the Mardi Gras," a Paul Simon cover by the avant-gardist turned smooth jazz kingpin Bob James that had an awesomely funky drums-and-agogô-bell intro. Eventually, among hip-hoppers, the song would be known only by its nickname: "The Bells."

JDL spat like crazy, shouting out Whitehead and friends in the crowd, freestyling, hurling every haymaker he knew, rhyming "one" with "fun," "two" with "boogaloo flu," and "rock 'em well y'all" with "so swell y'all." Afterward, folks congratulated him, and said he was nice on the mic. "Orgasmic, to the tenth power," was how JDL described it.[53]

Outside the Pine Hill Towers apartments in Yonkers, Detective John Falotico held his service revolver up to the driver-side window of a cream-colored Ford Galaxie and asked the suspect to step out of the car. In a duffel bag in the backseat was a Commando Mark III rifle; in the front seat, in a brown paper lunch bag, a .44 Charter Arms Bulldog revolver. In the glove compartment was a letter addressed to the Suffolk

County Police Department pledging a forthcoming visit by Son of Sam to a disco in the Hamptons.[54]

Son of Sam's shooting spree had begun the previous July, and folks in the Outer Boroughs, where the murders had occurred, had been in a state of panic all summer. But it wasn't until he mailed a letter to the *Daily News* columnist Jimmy Breslin on May 30, and Breslin and the *News* printed most of it, that the fear spread citywide.

The letter began:

> Hello from the gutters of N.Y.C. which are filled with dog manure, vomit, stale wine, urine and blood. Hello from the sewers of N.Y.C. which swallow up these delicacies when they are washed away by the sweeper trucks. Hello from the cracks in the sidewalks of N.Y.C. and from the ants that dwell in these cracks and feed in the dried blood of the dead that has settled into the cracks.

The author praised Breslin's writing, pledged further killings, and wished luck to the detectives hunting him, whom he promised to buy new shoes for when he was caught. His name was David Berkowitz. He signed the letter "Son of Sam."

There had been two more shootings that summer: one in late June outside the Elephas disco in Bayside, Queens, a final one in Brooklyn on July 31. Business in Outer Borough discos had withered in light of the attacks. The night of the Elephas shooting, the club was near empty; on the anniversary of the first shooting, July 29, there were just twelve fearless partiers at the Enchanted Garden, Steve Rubell's former Queens hot spot.

Kids came armed to street jams in the South Bronx, boasting that Son of Sam wouldn't dare fuck around in their neck of the woods. Manhattan clubbers watched their backs, per usual, but didn't sweat it much; the .44 Caliber Killer worked in the Outer Boroughs, a million miles away.

Even out in Queens, those of us not going to discos didn't think too much about it. Guns were rare in middle-class Flushing. Knives less so. In September, as I tromped down the long concrete stairway of Jamaica High School with my friend Patty toward Goose Pond Park, a lanky Hispanic kid came bounding up the stairs toward us, clutching his neck. When he reached us, he let his hands drop. His neck was covered in blood, and there was a U-shaped gash under his chin.

He paused and looked me in the eye, his right hand out like a gesture of supplication or inquiry. Then someone behind him shouted, "Run, motherfucker! Go to the office! Go to the fucking office!"

The kid darted past us toward the school.

I don't remember feeling scared, or any more scared than usual. Violence was everywhere; you just kept your eyes open and tried to side-step it.

Over the summer, *Rolling Stone* magazine pulled up stakes in San Francisco and moved to New York City. It's a wonder they waited so long. Their new editorial offices were at 745 Fifth Avenue, just off Fifty-eighth Street, with a terrace overlooking Central Park.

By fall, 1977 was looking like the most successful year in the history of the music biz. Disco was why. At the annual Disco Forum conference at the Americana Hotel, the hungry and the giddy talked about a $4 billion industry—bigger than films and television, behind only organized sports as a cultural cash cow. At night, conference-goers got down to Meco's disco take on the *Star Wars* theme, Peter Brown's "Do You Wanna Get Funky with Me," and "Bourgie Bourgie" by Ashford and Simpson. No doubt they also heard "Dance, Dance, Dance," an impressive debut single by a group of New York session players calling themselves Chic.

Then there was Donna Summer's awesomely cheesy cover of Serge Gainsbourg's porn-pop classic "Je t'aime moi non plus"—fitting, as Summer's "Love to Love You Baby" owed plenty to Jane Birkin's vocal orgasm on the original "Je t'aime." The song's bilingual fuck-me promise seemed to encapsulate disco's globalized brilliance as other regional hits were remade as jet-setting pop: two other notables that fall were Samba Soul's disco mix of Jorge Ben's "Chove Chuva/Mas Que Nada," and Grace Jones's cover of Edith Piaf's signature "La Vie en Rose."

The next generation of dance DJs were also making themselves heard. Larry Levan's construction parties were rocking 84 King Street. Meanwhile, his old bathhouse pal Frankie Knuckles, who had been looking for steady work since the Continental Baths closed, had relocated to Chicago. The move was spurred by an invitation from Robert

Williams, a devotee of the Loft who was trying to spark a Windy City club scene with a similar spirit. The two became partners in the Warehouse, a club at 206 South Jefferson Street where Knuckles would spin from midnight to noon the next day, taking breaks in the morning hours to hit the dance floor himself.

Things were changing for the old guard in New York. While devotees still turned out to hear Mancuso at the Loft, the Gallery had fallen off. Joe Siano gave his junk-loving younger brother an ultimatum: Get your shit together or I close the club. "Just close it, see if I care!" was Nicky Siano's response. And that was that.

The crowds came back in the final weeks, but it wasn't the same. On the last night, the club packed to the gills, Siano tried an old trick: during the part of Vickie Sue Robinson's "Turn the Beat Around" when the singer goes "rat-tat-tat-tat-tat on the drum," he cut the volume so the diehards could shout the line. But no one did.[55]

Inspired by Nik Cohn's fictionalized *New York* magazine story "Tribal Rites of the New Saturday Night," *Saturday Night Fever* finished shooting in Brooklyn over the summer, mostly in Bay Ridge and Bensonhurst. It would present a much different vision of disco culture than the one born in the Loft and the Gallery.

In the same hotel that hosted the Disco Forum revelers, Mayor Beame was having less fun in the wee hours of September 9, watching the primary returns in a twentieth-floor suite. For the first time in more than half a century, New York Democrats had dumped an incumbent to nominate a new candidate.

There was no way for Beame to salvage his rep in the wake of the blackout rampages and the fiscal crisis. His blame in the latter was magnified tenfold by an SEC investigative report that hit ten days before the primary that basically said that he had countenanced the fiscal shell games that caused the crisis.

Ed Koch—a hybrid liberal-cum-social-conservative campaigning on a pledge to bring back the death penalty amid the Son of Sam fallout, among other tough talk—got the nomination. On his arm during the campaign's final leg was Bess Myerson, the fifty-three-year-old Bronx-raised Miss America (crowned in 1945, its first Jewish honoree) turned commissioner of consumer affairs. She was an old-guard New York City celebrity, and also an effective parry for those questioning Koch's sexuality. Rumors were circulated, all false, that they were a couple, perhaps thinking of marriage. Meanwhile, an anonymous campaign had bubbled up in the Outer Boroughs around the election bid of New York secretary of state Mario Cuomo. Its catchphrase, whispered in bars and printed on flyers, was "Vote for Cuomo, Not the Homo."

In the end, Koch beat Cuomo by less than 1 percent (Beame trailed Cuomo by less than 1 percent). Koch won a runoff two weeks later more decisively. Bella Abzug came in fourth. The band at her primary-night reception began the evening with the theme to *Rocky*. It ended it with "Eleanor Rigby."[56]

Beame cried as he admitted defeat. His wife hugged him, both to console him and to deflect attention from his tears. The author Jonathan Mahler wrote: "He was no longer an easy object of derision, a pint-sized emblem of the city's failures, but rather a dignified civil servant, the embodiment of a vanishing New York, a New York in which the sons of socialists overcame poverty and then quietly devoted themselves to making the city a better place to live, where the Democratic Party machine (however corrupt) and the labor bosses (however power-hungry) always took care of their needy constituents."[57]

On October 5, Jimmy Carter took a detour to the South Bronx during a visit to address the U.N. in Manhattan. Although most New Yorkers saw their new president as an improvement over Ford, he was never really embraced by the city—though he won New York State in the election, the born-again Southern Baptist and fiscal conservative had been rejected in the '76 Democratic primary (in favor of Senator Henry Jackson from Washington State).

On this fall day, followed by a phalanx of international media, his motorcade drove along the Grand Concourse, and stopped near the decimated Charlotte Street. There, the entourage walked along a two-block stretch of rubble, the remains of apartments, and paused for a photo op. Mayor Beame, already written out of history, followed behind the president like a small dog. That night, in living rooms across the nation, the South Bronx became the archetypal inner-city slum.

The World Series began at Yankee Stadium a week later: Yankees versus Dodgers, a reprise of the great rivalry of mid-century New York, when the Dodgers were based in Brooklyn. During game two, a fire started in an abandoned elementary school not ten minutes from Charlotte Street, and grew into a five-alarm blaze. "There it is, ladies and gentlemen," the ABC sports commentator Howard Cosell pointed out, "the Bronx is burning." On October 18, during game six, Reggie Jackson pounded three balls into the stands, one each off the first pitches of his three times at bat. The Yankees won the game and the series, and the mainly black and Hispanic neighborhood basked in Jackson's shine, even if the team's ticker-tape victory parade took place on lower Broadway.

As a parting gesture in legacy repair, Beame pushed his support staff for a special report on the area, which was published in December: *The South Bronx: A Plan for Revitalization.* The revitalization was very slow in coming.

Meanwhile, Grandmaster Flash kept up his gigs at Disco Fever; his MCs polished their rhymes. Casanova Fly and Disco Wiz perfected their attacks on the Clubman Two mixer. One night Kool Herc tried to break up a scuffle at the door of the Executive Playhouse—which had just recently been renamed the Sparkle—and was stabbed four times: three times in the side, once in his hand.

Herc survived, but he was laid low for quite a while.

Bruce Springsteen and the E Street Band began a marathon recording session at the Record Plant on September 30; by the wee hours of the following morning, they had filled four reels of two-inch tape, which Jimmy Iovine stacked up in boxes next to the mixing desk.

There was a lot to record. Springsteen had written seventy songs during the lawsuit period, the lyrics scribbled in the spiral-bound notebooks he always carried with him. The song selection for his fourth album was changing from day to day. Just as Larry Harlow studied Cuban 78s, Springsteen and Landau pored over the early scrolls of rock and pop: Phil Spector's girl groups, the British Invasion bands, Stax R&B. Some of the new songs were direct homages: "Sherry Darling" and "Ain't Good Enough for You" were doo-wop–flavored goofs as catchy as mid-'60s AM radio singles. On "The Little Things My Baby Does," Springsteen went for Roy Orbison–style vocal drama. When he wrote "Fire," a perfect Elvis Presley manqué, it was with thoughts of submitting the song to Presley's management for the King to record. That was out of the question now. For a dark ballad titled "Come On (Let's Go Tonight)," Springsteen wrote the line "The man on the radio said Elvis Presley died."

In the two years that had elapsed since *Born to Run*, however, New York City rock had become "punk rock," and the music was being mirrored back from Britain. Springsteen was especially struck by the Clash, whose first singles came out in the spring: "White Riot" and "Remote Control." (The even better "Complete Control" arrived in September.) He admired how stripped-down they were, their power and conviction, their seriousness. He had no interest in punk's nihilism and romance with decadence, spent no time in CBGB. But he wasn't interested in making an oldies record, either. Springsteen had turned twenty-eight in September. The image of Elvis—bloated, spent, nearly irrelevant, dead at forty-two—haunted him.

He thought about the guys he grew up with. They weren't rock stars; they were holding down shitty jobs with kids to support and dreams that were largely shut down. There but for fortune . . . These were his roots, this was the audience he cared about—not a bunch of slumming junkie New York City bohemians. How might Woody Guthrie have handled being a superstar? What if Phil Ochs had become as big as Elvis? The question for Landau and Springsteen, in the wake of *Born to Run*'s megasuccess and the collapse of the singer's relationship with Mike Appel, was not just how to present Springsteen as an artist. It was how to protect his soul.

No longer did the singer's characters represent mainly as hustlers, hoodrats, and hungry hearts crossing between Jersey and Manhattan. As the new songs evolved, those regional signifiers dissolved as the cars headed south into farm country, north and west to the rust belt. "The Promised Land" begins in the Utah desert. Other songs could be set anywhere from Tuscaloosa to Bakersfield, eastern Long Island to Louisiana. "Badlands," which begins by announcing that there is "trouble in the heartland," was about "workin' in the fields 'til you get your back burned." "Come On (Let's Go Tonight)," about life in a factory town, tried to capture some of the fatalism of Hank Williams. It also made Springsteen think about his father, who lost his hearing while employed in a canning factory.

As a voice, Springsteen was morphing into an Everyman for America's New Depression. It would be by this new record—not *Born to Run*, for all its success and accolades—that his persona would be defined: not as a heroic, dreamy street punk, but as a heroic working-man with a sound moral compass. The kind of persona a musician could become an adult in, mature in, and not devolve into a self-parody.

Jimmy Iovine was a producer now. No big surprise: he was an ambitious guy. He had begun work on Patti Smith's third record at the Record Plant, working in the studio next door to the one that Springsteen and the E Street Band were holed up in. Sometimes, Iovine would be darting back and forth between sessions in the two studios, producing Smith while engineering for Springsteen. Iovine had always imagined that the two musicians might collaborate on something. They were friends, came from similar backgrounds. Listening to Bruce sing about hardscrabble working folks, Iovine thought about Patti's first single, "Piss Factory."

Springsteen and Landau's vision of the new album had become so laser focused, it seemed like all the catchiest songs—the fun ones, the romantic ones—were being abandoned. Iovine asked Springsteen if he had something that might work for Patti's voice. Bruce had the beginnings of a love song that he thought might be something. It was unfinished—just a chorus, really—but he gave Iovine a demo cassette, and Iovine passed it on to Smith.

She listened to it over and over one night, alone, in her apartment at 1 Fifth Avenue. She was waiting for a call from Fred Smith. "Love is a ring, the telephone," she wrote. Her romance with Tom Verlaine had passed, her relationship with Alan Lanier fading as their paths forked. She finished the lyrics quickly that night, and brought them into the studio the next day, where Lenny and the band worked up an arrangement. The song, "Because the Night," fused Springsteen's earthy physicality ("Because the night / Belongs to lust") with Smith's mystic ecstasy ("love is an angel disguised as light").

The song was amazing, no doubt; it was arguably as great a song as either Springsteen or Smith had produced. If her band was going to have a hit, this would be it. Patti suspected that the collaboration with Springsteen might strike some of the downtown crowd as a sellout. But she'd heard that accusation before and, at this point, couldn't care less.[58]

•

Richard Hell and the Voidoids began a British tour in October, opening for the Clash. They came offstage most every night covered in spit. Hell was junk-sick for much of the trip, despite visiting his connected pals Johnny Thunders and Jerry Nolan in London whenever he had an off day.[59] He was pissed that the Voidoids debut hadn't been released in Britain yet, and while he was very proud of it, he was—after forming three extraordinary bands in four years—ready to throw in the towel.

"It's completely clear that I've lost interest in rock and roll," he wrote in a diary entry dated November 1, in the hardbound journal Patti Smith gave him back in '74. "I think I've learned this much—that ambition for public acknowledgement of my abilities is utterly foolish. It constituted a lot of my incentive for entering r&r and I've received enough of it to know it's entirely hollow."

Still, the shows were hot. Lester Bangs, working on what became an epic, three-part Clash feature for the NME, thought the Voidoids never sounded tighter, and praised Bob Quine's astonishing guitar playing in the essay, noting Quine's obsession with the electric-guitar sounds on Miles Davis's *On the Corner* and *Agharta*. (Of course, Quine was Bangs's guitarist, too.)

As for the Heartbreakers, the bond between Johnny Thunders and Jerry Nolan had crumbled, between the stress of nonsuccess and the debacle of the *L.A.M.F.* recordings. The album, muddy sound unimproved, was released to mixed reviews. Nolan quit the band, rejoined for a few gigs, then left for good. The Sex Pistols' Paul Cook sat in on drums for one show; Terry Chimes, the Clash's first drummer, auditioned for the gig and got it. The new Heartbreakers played a couple of shows, then went into the studio to make demos on December 17. They tracked "Too Much Junkie Business" and "London Boys," a sneering answer song to the Sex Pistols' New York Dolls–baiting "New York" on *Never Mind the Bollocks, Here's the Sex Pistols*, which had been released in Britain in October. When Thunders's bandmates left town for the holidays, the band drifted into limbo.

On Christmas Day, the Pistols played two shows at Ivanhoe's in Huddersfield, Yorkshire, a few hours north of London. The first was an afternoon show for needy kids—young teens from broken homes, those whose parents were on strike or otherwise unemployed. Sid Vicious stepped to the mic and sang two Heartbreakers songs: "Chinese Rocks" and "Born to Lose."[60] His band was scheduled to begin its first U.S. tour in a matter of days.

Talking Heads: 77 had been released on September 16. It was a pop record, sort of. The first song, "Uh-Oh, Love Comes to Town," sounded like an old Motown number. David Byrne yip-crooned, "I'm not the people that you read about in books." There were steel pan fills. The songs were short, minimally apportioned, full of hooks. Unlike the Ramones' debut, there was space, air around the instruments. The rhythms were spasmodic. It was the sound of a panic attack massaged into a way of life—alternately (often simultaneously) funny, scary, ecstatic. "Psycho Killer" was actually a pretty good dance track.

Chris Frantz and Tina Weymouth had gotten married over the summer—Byrne sent a photo of the newlyweds to the *Voice*, which actually ran it, just like a *New York Times* wedding announcement. The band played the mandatory Bottom Line record-release show on Thursday night, October 27. With Jerry Harrison on second guitar, the group looked almost like a normal rock band. Byrne declared from the stage: "It sure is fun to be here!" Roy Trakin from the *Soho Weekly News* was both exhilarated and disturbed at how commercial-sounding the band had become. It sounded to him like the '80s had already begun.

Talking Heads toured colleges around the northeast through the fall; at some shows, the crowd would heartily sing along with the "tweet tweet tweet's" on "Love Goes to Building on Fire." (Released back in February as their debut single, it was left off the LP.) In December, the Heads did a two-week stretch of gigs in California. When they came home later that month, they pondered how to approach their second album.

They already had a stash of songs. One was called "Warning Sign," a fast, funky number that they'd demoed back in '75 using the sound of a zipper as percussion. Another, called "Stay Hungry," which featured Jerry Harrison on disco-style wah-wah guitar, had been recorded for *Talking Heads: 77*, but was ultimately held back. The album's coproduction team—Tony Bongiovi and Lance Quinn—was great in theory: they were industry hit makers, and Bongiovi's track record with the Disco Corporation of America (the production team behind Gloria Gaynor's

'74 remake of the Jackson 5's "Never Can Say Goodbye," among other club hits) impressed the Heads, who saw themselves as a dance band, albeit a high-concept one. Bongiovi also produced the Ramones' *Leave Home*. But Talking Heads didn't vibe with him, and they had other things in mind.

Brian Eno had finished work on David Bowie's *Heroes* album, left West Berlin, and moved into an apartment on Eighth Street. His pal Robert Fripp had gotten a place on the Bowery earlier in the year. Back in May, when Eno was crashing on his couch, the two took Bowie to see an unsigned midwestern band called Devo at Max's Kansas City. Eno would stroll Lower Manhattan like a native New York flaneur: he might see Philip Glass eating fries at Phebe's, chat a bit, then drag him to CBGB. There, he might run into David Byrne, and head off with him for a nightcap. He liked this town.

Eno had completed a new album of his own, *Before and After Science*. The title of its most frenetic song, "Kings Lead Hat," was an anagram for "Talking Heads." He'd written it in hopes that the band might play on it. It didn't work out due to scheduling. But during a discussion one afternoon at Tina and Chris's place in Long Island City, which was also the group's rehearsal space, Talking Heads and Eno decided to work together on the Heads' next record.

Chris and Tina's building was a hive of musicians. One day, Eno met their upstairs neighbor, Don Cherry, and tried to convince Cherry to use more repetition in his solos. Cherry was as interested in rock music as he was in any other world folk music. Last December he'd been invited by Lou Reed, a devoted fan of the classic Ornette Coleman Quartet, to sit in on a show Reed was doing at the Roxy Theater in Los Angeles. They exploded Reed's New York City punk dramas into jazz-funk journeys: one minute the music sounded like Springsteen's "Rosalita," the next like Miles's "Bitches Brew."[61]

Arthur Russell was still working on his dance single with Nicky Siano, who bankrolled a November session at Sundragon Studios, up on the eighth floor of 9 West Twentieth Street (where Talking Heads recorded their debut). Russell marshaled a disco-funk army under the name Dinosaur: two drummers, two bassists, and two electric guitarists, including Byrne, who riffed off the scratchy guitar style on the Fela Kuti records Eno had introduced him to. Siano coached the Latin singer Myriam Valle in disco-diva dramatics; Russell sawed away on his cello.

"Kiss Me Again" was busy, bizarre, and brilliant, a totally decentered thirteen-minute composition where cello and bass lines, congas and kick drum, verses and choruses, move in and out of the spotlight like bodies spinning around a dance floor. Siano played an early mix on one of his final nights at the Gallery, and the crowd loved it; he gave acetates to friends, who returned with similar reports. But Russell, a perfectionist in disco now as in everything else, felt the recording could be better. He decided to keep reworking it.

As his disco fascination grew, he lost interest in the pop music of his Flying Hearts project. In the Poets' Building at 437 East Twelfth Street, where he'd occasionally see his neighbor Richard Hell, he'd open a window and, on the rare moments that he didn't have his headphones on, he'd listen to the swirl of street noise. Often it included a sound system battle between the Puerto Rican kids blasting salsa from boom boxes and the Italian family next door blasting opera on their stereo. Russell would trip out on the cacophony. The world of sound was dizzying, truly limitless.[62]

Rhys Chatham had finally worked out the idea with the low E-string drone that he and Nina Canal had hit on last year. He conceived a piece for two guitars, his and Canal's, thrumming with overtones, with their friends Peter Gordon and Robert Appleton playing sax and drums, respectively. They tried it out at Franklin Furnace, the downtown art space at 112 Franklin Street, below Canal Street off West Broadway. Chatham's friend Glenn Branca, who played guitar in a rock group called Theoretical Girls, was in the audience. Branca liked the piece a lot. Chatham wasn't done with it, though. He wasn't sure about the sax. Maybe he needed more guitars?

Martin Scorsese followed up *Taxi Driver*'s dirty realism with *New York, New York*, a tribute to the golden era of movie musicals and the city. Instead of shooting on the streets, Scorsese worked up a pristine simulacrum of New York on soundstages to tell a stylized, doomed-love story about two musicians. Released in June, the film was a box office bomb but a brilliant artistic train wreck, a testament in part to Scorsese's manic cocaine use.

The high point is Liza Minnelli's performance of the song "New York, New York," written for her by John Kander and Fred Ebb, show-tune writers best known for *Cabaret* and *Chicago*. As a nightclub pianist pecks out the major-chord melody near the film's end, Minnelli's character lays into the lyrics with desperate intensity, channeling the song's determination-in-the-face-of-heartbreak with the method-acting mania that her costar Robert De Niro would tap in Scorsese's next film, *Raging Bull*. "Come on! Come through! New York, New York!" she sing-shouts at the climax, changing the final line from the more passive "It's up to you, New York, New York!" as if she were trying to slap a nodding junkie back to consciousness.

After a screening, the *Voice* critic Andrew Sarris noted, "The audience applauded when Liza sang 'New York, New York' as if they were bombed-out Britons in 1940 cheering a rendition of 'There'll Always Be an England' or 'When the Lights Go On Again.'"

The city's other cinematic suitor, Woody Allen, had also made a doomed love story about artists, and it, too, ended with the female lead singing a wishfully romantic song. When Diane Keaton's Annie Hall sings "Seems Like Old Times," it feels as much about New York as about her relationship with Allen's Alvie Singer. The film was shot on location around a city that, aside from the occasional joke about Central Park muggings or apartment bugs, was mostly scrubbed clean, a hyperventilating intellectual's ideal; the biggest threat to anyone is Keaton's midwestern-shiksa driving. "Don't you see the rest of the country looks upon New York like we're left-wing Communist Jewish homosexual pornographers?" Allen tells Tony Roberts after a game of tennis, exasperatedly explaining why President Ford told the city to drop dead. "*I* think of us that way sometimes, and *I* live here!" In the end, though, there is no choice; even Annie comes back to her senses, and to the city, after a fling with California.

On other screens across the city, light sabers flashed in the name of honor and righteousness. Kids from the boroughs, dressed in goth drag, took the subway to West Fourth Street every Friday and Saturday to midnight showings of *The Rocky Horror Picture Show*, hurling rolls of

Scott toilet paper when the character Brad exclaims "Great Scott!" and singing along with the sweet transvestite from Transylvania. The screenings had been taking place there every weekend since April 2, 1976.

Kids got stoned in basement bedrooms and watched *The Gong Show*, a hit in its after-dinner 7:30 time slot. Down the block from my house, at the Mayfair Theater off Utopia Parkway, X-rated films began flickering again. Back in the spring, the screen had gone dark when the theater's owner decided to turn it into a rock 'n' roll club. When local residents got wind of the venue's transformation into the Mayfair Music Center, they dialed their community liaisons at Borough Hall and got out on Fresh Meadow Lane with placards. The Mayfair managed just six shows, booking Long Island faves like the Good Rats and Stanky Brown, before everyone decided a porn house was less trouble.

The kids who hung outside Manny's candy store were pissed. But what could they do? "The lady who lives next door to me said if the place got going there'd be drinking and kids stoned in the street," said one young man. "I felt like saying, 'Hey, lady, what do you think we do now? There ain't nothing else to do around here.'"

The marijuana famine was over. For the big Dead show in Englishtown, New Jersey, on September 3—the biggest concert in the state's history to date, with more than 100,000 heads decending on the dusty field of Raceway Park—my friends were well stocked. In downtown Flushing, the Jolly Joint was selling bongs for half price. A company called Correct Count in Mineola advertised custom-made carrying cases for their Ohaus 750S triple-beam scales, along with Easy Bagger scoops "to bag your ounces within seconds." In Manhattan, a seven-year-old named Jackie sold loose joints outside the subway entrance at Seventy-ninth and Broadway.

Angel dust was still popular, although it was getting bad press: some users apparently ran around naked and deranged, others flipped out and stabbed people. Cocaine was still in its pop-honeymoon period, but heavy users discovered the toll it took on the nasal linings. Some savvy entrepreneurs began marketing a device called a Sno-blower: a six-inch piece of glass tubing with a rubber bulb on one end and a small scoop on the other, designed to shoot cocaine directly into the back of the throat. It was legend that Stevie Nicks—who performed two sold-out nights of the *Rumours* tour at Madison Square Garden with Fleetwood Mac a couple of weeks before the blackout—had an assistant/roadie use a similar device to blow coke up her ass before shows, so as to save her golden voice. Nicks has vehemently denied it.

By the year's end, intrepid cocaine fiends took a great leap forward, starting a mini-fad: they began smoking it.[63]

Sire Records released *Rocket to Russia* on November 4. The Ramones' third record, and second that year, had more varied and arguably better songs than the first two: a great buzz-saw version of the Beach Boys' "Do You Wanna Dance?," a cover of the Trashmen's demented "Surfin' Bird," Dee Dee's Queens anthem "Rockaway Beach," and, best of all, Joey's "Sheena Is a Punk Rocker," released over the summer as a single—their catchiest song yet, a celebration of a disco turncoat with a declaration that "New York City really has it all!" Robert Christgau gave them their first "A" grade. In the *Soho Weekly News*, a Sarah Lawrence student named Ira Kaplan argued: "So what if the albums all sound the same? Did you complain about *Something New* or *Rolling Stones Now?*"

Sire took out full-page ads for their four new releases: *Rocket to Russia*, *Blank Generation*, *Talking Heads: 77*, and *Young, Loud and Snotty* by Cleveland's Dead Boys. Together with *Marquee Moon* and *Blondie*, the New York underground had finally arrived on record.

Yet it already seemed a bit pale compared to what was happening in Britain. *Never Mind the Bollocks, Here's the Sex Pistols* got its U.S. release on November 10. The West Coast critic Greil Marcus, writing on *Rocket to Russia* in the *Voice*, argued, "at this point, the group's music does not compare to Alice Cooper's 'Eighteen' or just about anything by the Clash or the Sex Pistols."[64]

On November 19, the Ramones played the Capitol Theater in Passaic, New Jersey, with Talking Heads opening. An old vaudeville house built in the twenties, it had 3,200 seats, a big venue by the two groups' normal standards. While the Heads played, Joey sat backstage breathing in steam from a jerry-rigged teakettle—part of his regular preshow regimen, along with drinking endless cups of black coffee. As he sat with a towel draped over his head, the foil cap on the jerry-rigged spout popped off, and his face and neck were blasted with boiling water.

Joey screamed, covering his face with his hands.

"SHIIIIIIIT! SHIT!"

His brother Mickey pulled his hands away to see. His face and lips were already beginning to blister; it looked like his flesh was peeling off.

With about an hour before the band's set, their manager, Danny Fields, got Joey to a local ER. They returned to the theater, Joey's face covered in ointment, where he delivered one of his greatest shows ever dripping in whiteface, the cream melting under the heat of the spotlights. The next day he was admitted to the Cornell Burn Center up on East Sixty-eighth Street.

Rocket to Russia peaked at number 49 on the *Billboard* album charts. Tommy Erdelyi quit the band soon afterward, deciding life would be better lived as a producer than as a touring drummer.

Suicide's debut didn't get within a country mile of the charts, but it was more terrifying than any American punk record, and most British ones. The band played a record-release gig at CBGB the first weekend in December. On a recording made of the show, Alan Vega shouts "OH JESUS!" over a primitive drum-machine beat similar to the one used on William De Vaughn's '74 soul classic "Be Thankful for What You Got." Then Martin Rev starts the turbine-grinding rhythm of "Frankie Teardrop."

"SHUT THE FUCK UP!" Vega howls at the heckling crowd. "IT'S ABOUT YOU!! YOU'RE ALL FRANKIES!" He gives a bloodcurdling reading of the multiple-murder ballad, then segues into a shivering, Elvis-style cover of Jackie DeShannon's "Put a Little Love in Your Heart." It was sort of a cover, anyway, Vega chanting the title in between screaming into a Roland Space Echo delay unit.

The next summer, Suicide would tour with both the Clash and Elvis Costello. One night Vega was punched in the nose and performed with his face smeared in blood. Another night in Brussels, the crowd stole his microphone, threw chairs, and, after a ferocious set by Costello, had to be dispersed by the local gendarmerie with tear gas.

"Each year a special motion picture comes along that touches something within everyone, everywhere," read the ad copy. "This year, *Saturday Night Fever* is that special movie."

Opening wide on December 16 in time for the holidays, *Saturday Night Fever* was disco's peak, and everybody knew it. And yet, paradoxically, the movie was less about the music's joyfulness than about disco culture's emptiness. John Travolta, a kid from Englewood, New Jersey, who did time on Broadway before landing a sitcom role as the Brooklyn high schooler Vinnie Barbarino in *Welcome Back, Kotter*, played Tony Manero, a version of Nik Cohn's composite. When Tony walks away from the disco world for the "real" one, you realize you're watching an escapist movie moralizing about escapism.

Yet the soundtrack album wound up under several million Christmas trees, and discos played its songs for tireless Tony Maneros around the world.

On Intervale Avenue in the South Bronx, PS 54 had been sitting in ruins since it closed. And like PS 3, whose burning image on live TV occasioned Howard Cosell's famous aside in October, it had become a playground for bored arsonists. A message needed to be sent, so the city made plans to demolish it with dynamite early the next year. A contractor in Towson, Maryland, won the job, for which he would be paid $200,000.[65] A wrecking ball might have sufficed, but there was something about dynamite that befitted the borough's war-zone spirit.

Public schools that were still unexploded were struggling. Music and art education had largely disappeared. Back in the late '60s, there were around 650 art teachers in the New York City public schools. By '77, there were fewer than 250, roughly one for every thousand students. In '73, the one-year fine art requirement needed for a high school diploma became a one-semester requirement, often met with an "art appreciation" class. It was not uncommon to graduate from a city high school with no fine or performing arts education at all.

The graffiti master Lee Quiñones was fortunate enough to go to Manhattan's High School of Art and Design. And all year long, he'd been planning the follow-up to his double-car piece in 1976: a full-train worm. If the story of Caine I and Flame I's Bicentennial worm was even true, it never left the yard. For all intents and purposes, Lee's would be the first.

On Saturday, December 10, in the early evening, the Fabulous Five—as Lee and his crew were known—were hanging out with some girls on Staten Island. People were already getting drunk, but Lee was obsessed with attempting the worm that night. He and Mono had been shoplifting spray paint cans for days, visiting hardware stores all over town, wearing coats with baggy sleeves and big pockets. They left the party, met up with Slave I at Lee's house, packed 110 cans into shopping bags, and ran to catch the ferry.

By nine o'clock or so, they'd found a ten-car IRT number 4 train parked in a Brooklyn layover. They spread out their paint cans on the ground and got to work.

Moving at an incredible clip, they had three cars finished when Mono whispered loudly, "Move! MOVE!" Flashlights were coming down the tracks.

Slave I, fast as hell, was gone in an instant. Mono stumbled but kept running. A train pulled into the yard; Lee cut under a stationary car and nearly got hit. "Motherfuckers, we got you now!" they heard a man yell. Eventually, the two found their way to the opening in the security fence and headed toward the subway. They'd left behind all their paint, along with Lee's camera.

The next day, they found out that the men with the flashlights weren't cops. It had been Slug I and Doc 109, who had followed them to Brooklyn just to fuck with them. Motherfuckers! Mono and Lee were pissed. But it was only Sunday; most likely the train they were working on wouldn't be back in service until Monday morning. So the four of them returned (Slave I bowed out) and worked through the night, putting the finishing touches on their worm just as the sky began to lighten.

The centerpiece was a car by Lee: the crew's name, FABULOUS FIVE, in pale blue block letters with beige shadowing, with an impressively accurate Mickey Mouse head between the two words, gloved hands reaching up in victory, thumbs pointed upward just above the car windows. The final two cars were a holiday card: a scene of winter in the city, white shpritzed snowflakes falling against a deep-blue sky, with Santa and his reindeer, and a snowman sentry on either end. Each man wrote his tag in fat blue 3-D letters, and at the end were two scrawled messages: MERRY CHRISTMAS TO NEW YORK and WE HAVE FINALLY SUSCEEDED . . .[66]

On Monday morning, the masterpiece rolled out of the yard on the side of an IRT number 4. Lee had gone home to clean up, then headed toward Manhattan to see the train in action. He got off the ferry and walked to Brooklyn Bridge Station near City Hall. Some fellow writers, early risers, had seen it pass through on its way up to the Bronx. Lee had just missed it.

He jumped on the next train and rode it to the Bronx, getting off at Intervale Avenue, the elevated stop off 163rd Street. It was freezing. Lee waited. He noticed two cute girls. And then he saw his train coming down the track, sunlight glinting off the sides.

"There it goes!" he yelled. He began taking pictures. The train approached slowly, cars wobbling from side to side. "It's coming, it's coming!" he said to the girls.

"What's coming?"

"Look at that train!"

"Oh my God!"

The train traveled back and forth across the city for the rest of the day, from Woodlawn in the Bronx, through the Upper East Side and Grand Central Station, to Union Square and Wall Street, then Atlantic Avenue in Brooklyn and New Lots Avenue, the end of the line. Then the MTA separated the cars. For some reason, they kept the holiday-themed double car together; it ran all winter long, through spring, and into the following summer.[67]

Héctor Lavoe was finally slated to record his third solo record after nearly three years of "taking it easy," as his pianist and bandleader Gilbert "El Pulpo" Colón put it. La Tierra Sound Studios was booked for three days, December 20–22. Willie Colón would be producing. With a touch of black humor, the record would be called *Comedia*.[68]

The most remarkable song that came out of the sessions was "Bandolera," a dance number with an extended piano solo by El Pulpo—all muscular, shape-shifting, jazzy elegance, with folk song references played against a punishing *montuno* to rival anything Eddie Palmieri recorded. Lavoe encouraged lengthy solos: the other musicians could cover for him when he was too high, or needed to slip offstage to get high. He always had sidemen with chops.

Lavoe's lyrics are an extended threat to beat the shit out of a deceitful lover. "Pau! Pau! Pau!" the backing vocalists sing, echoed by three horn jabs like gunshots, or an explosion of balled fists. Some listeners, women especially, were outraged. Yet the song was a club hit.

The record's centerpiece was "El Cantante," written by Rubén Blades. One version of its creation myth has Héctor, performing at the Corso, inviting Blades onstage, where he sings "El Cantante" and then announces he is giving the song to Lavoe. According to Blades, Willie had asked if he had any new material that might work for Héctor, and Blades offered up the song. Its operatic sense of tragedy was more suited to Lavoe's life experience than his own, and he figured Lavoe would sing the hell out of it.

He did. The night it was recorded, the singer was late, as usual. As the story goes, Lavoe finally rolls in with two sketchy-looking pals, apparently fresh from a Lower East Side drug run. He asks for the lights to be dimmed, and has the studio assistant fix a small flashlight on his music stand. Lavoe pulls a crumpled lyric sheet out of his pocket and sings of his hidden sorrow, like Smokey Robinson did in "Tears of a Clown."

He nails it on the first take. And out he floats, back to the streets.[69]

At Brooklyn College earlier that month, a four-day conference titled "The Phonograph and Our Musical Life" commemorated the hundredth anniversary of the birth of audio recording—the day Thomas Edison's recitation of "Mary Had a Little Lamb" was captured on a piece of tinfoil. John Cage complained that modern recordings sounded too perfect. "You lose any sight of the fallibility of humans," he said in his opening remarks. There was a discussion of "digital recording," which was being developed by a computer scientist named Thomas Stockham at the University of Utah. Stockham made his name, and began his journey into digital sound, as leader of the research team investigating the eighteen-minute gap on the Watergate tapes (his conclusion: the erasure was not an accident).[70]

On the Bowery, CBGB's success was becoming a problem. Its legal capacity was 150; Hilly Kristal usually capped things at around 450. He'd begun getting visits, and citations, from fire inspectors; guys from the buildings department and the health department had come by, too (the latter told him to banish his incontinent saluki, Jonathan).

One solution was to open another venue. On December 27, the CBGB Theater, at 66 Second Avenue, hosted its first show. Talking Heads headlined; the Shirts, now managed by Kristal, were opening. While their singer-cum-actress Annie Golden spent the day on the film set of *Hair*, the guys in the band came in to help Kristal spruce the place up.

They did what they could. Formerly known as the Anderson Theater, it had been a popular Yiddish vaudeville hall in the '20s and '30s,
with a brief stint as a Spanish-language movie theater in the mid-'50s,
when it was called the Antillas. In the late '60s it was a kid sister to the
Fillmore East up the block at 105 Second Avenue. Janis Joplin played
her first New York gig in the Anderson; the Grateful Dead played there
in 1970, a show underwritten by the neighborhood chapter of the Hell's
Angels. The Cockettes, the psychedelic San Francisco drag troupe, gave
a handful of performances there in November '71 for an audience including Andy Warhol and John Lennon, just weeks before the New York
Dolls would play their first gig.[71]

A dump back then, the Anderson had been unused for years, and
was now a total wreck. The basement was flooded; the boiler was virtually nonfunctional. The electrical system was shot as well. Kristal
brought in lights, a sound system, and a noisy diesel generator; the
power draw was such that whenever the spotlights were turned up, the
sound level dropped. There was mud on the floor of the entrance hall,
standing water in the men's room, fabric peeling off the walls. When the
bands hit heavy bass notes, soot rained off the old chandelier onto the
soundboard. The room could legally hold around 1,700 people. Opening
night packed in around 2,000. The upside, since it was a frigid night
and the place had no heat, was that the crowd could huddle together for
warmth.

It was the Bowery's DIY aesthetic blown up to semi–big time. Talking Heads played a valiant opening-night set, running the songs from
their debut through a crappy sound system. The following night, a show
by the Dead Boys and the Dictators imploded when the former's Johnny
Blitz stormed offstage after two songs, bitching about the sound and
overall shitty accomodations.

Three shows by the Patti Smith Group capped the opening week.
Richard Hell and the Voidoids, back from the grueling Clash tour, was
the opening act. On the second night—December 30, Smith's thirty-
first birthday—Bruce Springsteen came out to play guitar and sing
backup for her. They played "Because the Night" together, the first time
the song had been performed live by either of them. Then the fire marshal came onstage and closed the place down. It reopened for Smith's
third show, on New Year's Eve.

Then, nothing. Kristal rented it out to a flea market/record show operator for a number of weeks. A few months later, falling behind in the mortgage after sinking a bundle into repairs, he went into foreclosure on it.

Snow fell over Manhattan on New Year's Eve. It dusted the canopy of CBGB, where the Shirts were headlining. While Smith played her final night on Second Avenue, Springsteen was back in Jersey, guesting at a Southside Johnny show at the Capitol Theater in Passaic. Willie Colón and Rubén Blades were playing for four thousand people at La Hacienda Villa in Lima, Peru, the first big-name salsa show in the city's history. The Ramones were back in London, headlining a show at the Rainbow Theater that was being recorded—hopefully, if things worked out, for a live album.

Rashied Ali played with his quintet under his apartment at Ali's Alley. Art Blakey was at the Vanguard; Joe Lee Wilson was at the Ladies' Fort. Levon Helm came down from Woodstock to play at the Palladium with the RCO All-Stars, a supergroup featuring his fellow southerners Dr. John, Booker T., and some MGs. At the Minskoff Theater on Forty-fifth Street at Broadway, the American Symphony Orchestra was playing "A Star Wars Laser Concert."

The Sex Pistols, who'd initially planned to play Madison Square Garden and *Saturday Night Live*, were slated to play New Year's Eve in Chicago. But visa problems had them grounded in England.

New Year's Eve rarely works out according to plan.

Studio 54's first year-end bash was a disaster. Celebrities don't go out in public on New Year's Eve, even to Studio 54. The club was packed with "the bridge and tunnel people," as the *Soho News* columnist Bob Weiner sniffed, and they were stoned to the gills. Grace Jones's debut, *Portfolio*, produced by Tom Moulton, was one of the year's great disco albums. But her 3:30 a.m. set, by Weiner's measure, only proved that "she can't dance, sing, or move."[72]

Some vital music did come out of the evening. Jones had wanted Nile Rodgers and Bernard Edwards of Chic to produce her next record, so she invited them to the show. Somehow their names didn't make it onto the guest list. Despite being two of New York's hottest disco producers—whose single "Dance, Dance, Dance" would be spun tonight in clubs all across the city, Studio 54 no doubt included—they could not convince the gatekeepers to let them past the velvet ropes. So they gave up and trudged back to Rodgers's apartment on Fifty-second Street, picking up some champagne on the way. They got home, sparked a joint, cut up some lines, and began to jam. Rodgers started rapping "Fuck Studio 54! Fuck you! Fuck off!" over their riffs. Eventually a killer groove settled around the phrase "Ahhhhhhhhh, fuck off!"

Upon later consideration, "fuck off" became "freak out," and a career-making song was born. When they recorded "Le Freak," Rodgers and Edwards gave a shout-out to the club that dissed them: "Just come on down to 54," the verses went, "Find a spot out on the floor." The following New Year's Eve, "Le Freak" was the number 1 song in the country. By that time, Rodgers had received a VIP admission card to Studio 54. But it meant less than it would have the year before.[73]

Maybe the best music made in New York City on New Year's Eve 1977 was played in the afternoon, for a few dozen listeners, at Mickey Ruskin's Lower Manhattan Ocean Club.

David Murray had been playing relentlessly over the past year, as would any cocky twenty-two-year-old whose debut records had critics calling him the greatest young player in jazz. His marriage to Ntozake Shange, though, was over. It had lasted three months. They were artists; they served their muses. And as Murray would testify, there were many beautiful women in New York City who loved the sound of his saxophone.

This afternoon, along with his usual rhythm section of Fred Hopkins and Phillip Wilson, was Lester Bowie. A classic modern quartet like that of Ornette Coleman, it was a rare meeting of the two most gifted horn players associated with the loft-jazz scene. The show was billed as "The Last," a reference to it being the last of the year's afternoon jazz gigs—gigs, like the regular Sunday sessions at Tin Palace, that had become important showcases, think tanks, and networking centers. The show was being recorded, and the mood was relaxed; the sun hadn't yet set, the evening still a while away. Murray's circle of friends were in the audience, Shange among them.

Listening to that recording now, you hear the musicians count off "Nevada's Theme," a boozy waltz with a slow-mo swing, the horns weaving a theme, then unraveling it. Murray is an intense player; when he works the tenor's lowest register and unfurls his puffy Ben Webster lines, he can be very romantic. But it's possible he never sounded this playful and straight-up joyous. On "Bechet's Bounce," another Murray original, his squeaky, dancing, clarinet-like soprano lines are nearly stand-up comedy. When Lester leaps in, you hear jazz history tumble out: in circus-tent brays and Dixieland chortles, New Orleans brass band jostling, be-bop hard-charging, and the smeared squawks and water-on-a-hot-skillet sputters of modern technique. After all, making music is never about "inventing" the "new": it's about the past reemerging in the present, becoming again, like the Buddhist concept of *punarbhava*. Old Cuban 78s pumping through Willie Colón's trombone. The Ramones channeling the Trashmen. Grandmaster Flash piecing together the breaks.

Murray and Bowie work their way through two compositions by Lawrence "Butch" Morris, a cornet player whose writing would become a pillar of Murray's repetoire. On "Obe," Bowie uses far-out voicings to dig into deep emotions; he plays the blues, floating over swift rhythms, above the fray, gradually slowing his phrases down until, around the six-minute mark, he's reduced his horn to the sound of a human voice, ageless, crying through brass tubing, and then slower still, until all that can be heard is the sound of breath being drawn, as if he were playing a deathbed scene.

Then Bowie comes back again like a boxer rising shakily up off the mat, Wilson hitting the cymbal bell like a ref ringing off a new round. Bowie jabs and weaves. Murray comes in fast, and they spar, heat high. Then it's tag-team; Lester lays out, and Murray pushes out shivering, fat honks, hyperkinetic squiggles of exploded thought. Maybe he's looking across the room at his ex-wife. Maybe not. It's the sound of someone hell-bent on expressing the inexpressible. A musician fighting for his life as a way of life.

And then Murray skids down into a sultry, voluptuous tone, which becomes a breathy come-on, then a ballad. The fight's over; the players sway in tandem. This song is called "Let the Music Take You." And so it does.

EPILOGUE

Now, y'know, kids'll find some other club. They'll need some-
place to play and they'll . . . Yeah, yeah, 'cause that's what's
supposed to happen. This place is not a fuckin' *temple*; it's just
what it is. And the greatest thing about it, and the best way it
can serve the people, is just show an example of what ya can
do. Ya just get a place, some crappy place that nobody wants,
where ya got one guy that believes in ya, and ya just do your
thing. And anyone can do that, anywhere in the world. Anywhere. Anytime.

— Patti Smith, onstage at CBGB at the club's final night
of live music, October 16, 2006

And although the legend goes
We birthed this flow
But who the fuck are we?
Nobody knows
— Luis Cedeño, a.k.a. Disco Wiz

You're still the one pool / Where I'd happily drown.
— LCD Soundsystem, "New York, I Love You
but You're Bringing Me Down"

In October 1978, Frank Sinatra unveiled his version of "Theme to New
York, New York" at Radio City Music Hall. People loved it, and he recorded it in 1979 for a lavish, foil-trimmed box set, *Trilogy: Past Present
Future*. The song became his latter-day signature, and the city's, too—
to an extent that it's hard to recall a time when it wasn't.

Thirty years later, the Yeah Yeah Yeahs played their chiming, churning "Maps" in the same hall. "It's time for a New York City love song!" bellowed Karen O—a Jersey-bred, NYC-schooled rock heroine, like Patti Smith and Debbie Harry before her. "This song was written for *you*, New York City!" The crowd sang along heartily, repeating the hook— "Wait: they don't love you like I love you"—over and over and over.

With the twenty-first century under way, New York's music scene was seething again. The *Village Voice* Pazz & Jop Poll, conducted annually among national journalists since Robert Christgau created it in the '70s, calculated that NYC-based or -nurtured talent made half of 2009's top twenty LPs: Animal Collective, the Yeah Yeah Yeahs, Dirty Projectors, Grizzly Bear, Raekwon, Mos Def, St. Vincent, Maxwell, the Pains of Being Pure at Heart, and the by-then scene elders Sonic Youth. Critics voted "Empire State of Mind," a New York City love song by Brooklyn's Jay-Z and the Manhattan-bred R&B singer Alicia Keys, single of the year. "I'm the new Sinatra," Jay raps, "and since I made it here, I can make it anywhere."

The concentrated vitality of the '70s music scene diminished in the '80s and '90s as the city revived economically and Manhattan's downtown artist ghetto became a high-end playground and marketplace, driving nascent musicians elsewhere. But the creative impulse never faded, and some of the most visionary fusions were ahead. There was the jazz-punk-funk-disco mixing of the late '70s and early '80s that rose up in Manhattan venues like the Mudd Club, Tier 3, and the Knitting Factory; on indie labels like Ze and Celluloid; in acts like Defunkt (led by Lester's trombone-playing brother Joe Bowie) and Ronald Shannon Jackson's Decoding Society (led by Ornette Coleman's onetime drummer); on records like *No New York*, the Brian Eno–produced compilation that christened the thrillingly dyspeptic no wave scene. And there was hip-hop's golden era in the late '80s and early '90s, which occurred farther afield, from the crime-plagued Queensbridge Houses in Long Island City (Marley Marl, Nas) to suburban Long Island (Public Enemy, De La Soul). Other New York scenes sent spores elsewhere. Punk was reborn in Seattle; disco in the U.K. and Europe. And on and on.

•

After scoring her big hit in 1978 with "Because the Night," Patti Smith bought her mom a big fridge stocked with Omaha Steaks and, after 1979's *Wave*, moved to Detroit with Fred "Sonic" Smith of the MC5 to raise kids. Television split in 1978 after their second album sold even more poorly than the first. The English guitar guru Robert Fripp—by then living in New York and playing recitals with Steve Reich–style tape loops at the Kitchen—made an unsuccessful pitch to re-form Television with himself as lead guitarist. (He'd go on to record with Blondie and Talking Heads.) The original Television lineup eventually re-formed for a pretty decent comeback LP in '92; they've performed infrequently since.

The Ramones, despite starring in the 1979 B-movie *Rock 'n' Roll High School*, remained cult heroes to the end, even as they headlined stadiums in Brazil and posthumously made the cover of *Rolling Stone's* Japanese edition.[1] Joey died of lymphoma in 2001, Dee Dee of a heroin overdose in 2002, Johnny of prostate cancer in 2004. Tommy, who quit the band in '78 to work as a producer, moved upstate to the Woodstock area, where he plays bluegrass mandolin with his wife in a band called Uncle Monk.

Though they were beloved, the Ramones seemed plagued by bad luck. After crossing paths with Bruce Springsteen following a show in Asbury Park in 1978, Joey asked Bruce if he might write a song for the Ramones, hoping it might do for them what it did for Smith. Springsteen wrote one the same night. But when his management team heard the song, "Hungry Heart," they convinced him to keep it. Not wanting to break his record's sober tone, Springsteen had given away the most radio-friendly songs from the *Darkness on the Edge of Town* sessions to other artists. Some, like Smith and the Pointer Sisters, who recorded "Fire," had major hits with them, while *Darkness*, brilliant as it was, didn't earn Springsteen a single hit. He didn't want to repeat the cycle.[2]

After about ten years of music-making, Richard Hell returned his attention to the writing life he shelved after Tom Verlaine convinced him to pick up his Danelectro bass. Wayne County began taking hormones, got a nose job, changed his name to Jayne, and relocated to London, taking her place as a punk rock forebear. She decided against a full sex-change operation. "I'm happy in between the sexes," County wrote in her autobiography, *Man Enough to Be a Woman*. She has been living a fairly low-key life in her home state of Georgia, periodically making rock 'n' roll and trouble. "Handsome" Dick Manitoba and Andy Shernoff of the Dictators both got into the liquor business: the former opening the landmark bar Manitoba's, at 99 Avenue B in the East Village, in 1999; the latter working as a wine expert and sommelier. Dick and Jayne eventually kissed and made up.

Following a spoken-word cameo on Lou Reed's 1978 album *Street Hassle*, Bruce Springsteen became Elvis Presley: the archetypal American rock hero. Except that he has never allowed himself to fall off. The image of the bloated King that he and Miami Steve Van Zandt saw at the Philly Spectrum in '77 evidently stayed with him. The Hold Steady, Arcade Fire, Titus Andronicus, and other twenty-first-century bands have clearly studied Springsteen's records like he and Jon Landau studied *The Sun Sessions*.

The CBGB band once voted least likely to succeed, Blondie, blew up bigger than anyone, making it into the early '80s before things fell apart. They refracted the music around them. Of their four number 1 pop hits, one was deeply informed by disco ("Heart of Glass" in 1979), another by hip-hop ("Rapture" in 1981—the first "rap song" to top the charts).

Talking Heads lasted until 1991. More than any of their CBGB peers, they tuned in to the city's multiple creative frequencies, channeling ideas from funk, hip-hop, salsa, African music, disco, and minimalism into their polyglot 1980 masterpiece *Remain in Light*, expanding their lineup with additional singers and players until it was almost bursting at the seams. And of all the Bowery rockers, David Byrne remained the most active in the New York scene, living for years on Twelfth Street, where he ran his Luaka Bop label, then elsewhere around town, with a walk-up workspace loft in Chinatown. He contributed to an opera, of sorts, with Philip Glass and Robert Wilson (1984's *the CIVIL warS: a tree is best measured when it is down*). He made a salsa record, of sorts, with Willie Colón, Johnny Pacheco, and Celia Cruz (1989's *Rei Momo*). He made a disco record, of sorts, with the DJ/producer Fatboy Slim and various pop singers (2010's *Here Lies Love*, a song cycle about the unlikely folk hero Imelda Marcos). An éminence grise in the 2000s, he's indefatigable, working in numerous media, collaborating with veterans and newcomers alike. Hair gone white in a semi-pompadour, he bikes around the city and remains an obsessive live music fan, easy to spot at shows. "I go out a lot," he told me in 2007. "But sometimes I go out to these shows and I go, 'Where are my peers?' You know? Where are the musicians from my generation, or the generation after mine? Don't they go out to hear music? Do they just stay home? Are they doing drugs? What's going on?"

The Academy of Music on East Fourteenth Street—where Iggy fell apart, Gene Simmons set his hair on fire, and (after it was reborn as the Palladium) Bruce Springsteen triumphed—became a disco in the '80s, repurposed by Studio 54's Steve Rubell and Ian Schrager after their prison stint for tax evasion. It was demolished in 1999, and NYU built a residence hall on its footprint. They named it the Palladium dorm.

The storefront beneath the Performance Studio on East Twentieth Street, where the Ramones played their first show, became Trixie + Peanut, a shop selling designer pet clothes.

Disco dominated pop for a little while longer in the wake of *Saturday Night Fever*. The Rolling Stones and David Bowie dabbled in it; even Kiss had a disco hit (1979's "I Was Made for Lovin' You"). The antidisco backlash was consecrated on July 12, 1979, in Chicago's Comiskey Park when, in between games of a White Sox–Detroit Tigers double-header, a local radio station staged "Disco Demolition Night," a ritual burning of dance music records that turned into a rampage of out-of-control rock fans. It made television newscasts nationwide. The effect in the mainstream was nearly immediate: within months, disco as a genre fell from the Top Ten, and "Disco Sucks" T-shirts were being sold in malls. Racism, homophobia, and sexism informed the backlash, no doubt, but so did a lot of terrible music churned out by hacks and promoted by aesthetically bankrupt broadcasters. In 1978, my graduating class at Jamaica High School in Queens numbered around a thousand students, a pretty equal mix of black, white, and Hispanic kids. Our senior prom, booked at the Copacabana disco in Manhattan, was canceled due to lack of interest.

So disco downscaled and returned to its home in the clubs. There's an appealing irony to the fact that its creative rebirth came in the '80s not in New York but in the two cities represented that day in Comiskey Park. House music grew in Chicago, with inspiration from the New York transplant Frankie Knuckles, just as New York's loft jazz scene was inspired by the AACM musicians. And techno was born in Detroit, as Afrika Bambaataa's "Planet Rock" and its Kraftwerk-inflected electro-funk kin seeded an even more futuristic style that, together with house and MDMA, redefined club and pop music around the world.

Among the history-minded, the Loft's David Mancuso and the Gallery's Nicky Siano are revered, and as of this writing, you can still catch them behind turntables in New York from time to time, working their magic. Lenny Bellezza, the guy who fine-tuned Mancuso's mind-blowing sound system, still works at Lyric Hi-Fi up on Broadway near Eighty-third Street. He runs the place now, and he'd be happy to help you put a system together just like the Loft's.

Arthur Russell died of AIDS in 1992. He never had a mainstream hit, but he released some visionary dance tracks, and left behind a thousand tapes of unreleased music. In the 2000s, his work was rediscovered, illuminated by reissues, a biography, and a documentary film. Some of his former colleagues got together a group to perform his music; they're called Arthur's Landing.

Around the time Jerry Masucci sold Fania Records in 1980, semi-retiring as a very wealthy man, salsa was being replaced by *meringue* and power-ballad *salsa romantica*, and the South Bronx–Spanish Harlem barrio ceded its title as a global center of Spanish-language music. Héctor Lavoe struggled with his addictions, attempted suicide in 1988, and died of AIDS-related complications in 1993. The rest of the Fania team kept playing music, part-time if not full-time, and only rarely in Madison Square Garden. Many of them were bitter over deals that gave them no royalties on classic LPs that continue to be reissued.

Ray Barretto won a Grammy in 1990 for *Ritmo en el Corazón*, a team-up with Celia Cruz. He also continued to play jazz. He died of heart failure in 2006.

Rubén Blades left Fania in the early '80s to sign a major label deal with Elektra, and recorded with all sorts of musicians over the years, including Lou Reed and Steve Van Zandt. He starred in *Crossover Dreams*, a semiautobiographical film about a salsa singer, in 1985. He did a lot more acting over the years. He collaborated with Paul Simon on a Broadway musical, *Capeman*, which never quite got off the ground. In 2004, he was appointed Panama's minister of tourism. After serving a five-year term, he returned to making movies and music.

Willie Colón, a community hero, also got into politics, running for a congressional seat in '94 (he lost) and working later with Mayor Michael Bloomberg as a liaison to the Latino community. It's probably fair to say that Colón's mobster posturings on many of his '70s LP covers were among the prototypes of '80s gangsta rap iconography. To paraphrase the *New York Times* critic Jon Pareles, New York City politics, like New York salsa, has always thrived on coalition building.

In 2007, the Héctor Lavoe bio-pic *El Cantante* was released. Its leads were the royal couple of Latin pop: Jennifer Lopez, a Bronx Latina from Castle Hill who grew up with salsa, and her husband, Marc Anthony, a Puerto Rican house music singer turned *salsero* from Spanish Harlem. As fate and small communities would have it, Anthony's dad had been Lavoe's attendant during his final days at Terence Cardinal Cooke Hospital. The film was a boilerplate melodrama, although Lopez and Anthony both did their best, and the music wasn't bad at all.

Lavoe's nephew, "Little" Louie Vega, became one of house music's greatest DJs and producers.

Eddie Palmieri remains as mercurial as ever, playing for both concert audiences and dancers. Last time I saw him, in 2009, he'd reconvened an iteration of his '60s La Perfecta Band in the posh new Jazz at Lincoln Center theater up at Columbus Circle. They were blazing and, with little amplification, loud as hell. Yet trouble still seems to follow the artist. In 2010, his wife, Iraida, was shot by their eighty-one-year-old downstairs neighbor in the elevator of their Forest Hills apartment, apparently spurred by a long-standing noise complaint.

In August 2010, Larry Harlow led a performance of *La Raza Latina* with a fifty-piece band in Lincoln Center's Damrosch Park. Rubén Blades sang; the violinists included Alfredo de la Fé, the New York Cuban whose soloing on Eddie Palmieri's *The Sun of Latin Music* and Willie Colón's *El Baquiné de Angelitos Negros* soundtrack are among the great performances in New York music, right up there with Tom Verlaine's guitar explorations and Grandmaster Flash's beat-juggling. Soloing in the soft summer night alongside Harlow's Brooklyn College pal Lewis Kahn— New York salsa's other great violinist—he called down the orishas.

After being shuttered for eight years, between 1999 and 2007, Record Mart reopened on the mezzanine level of the Times Square subway station, about fifty feet from the location where, over forty years, it became the best-known Latin music shop in the city. The recorded legacy of salsa has been grossly mismanaged over the years, as the catalogs of

Fania and its competitors (like Harvey Averne's Coco, which went
Chapter 11 in the late '70s) were passed from company to company. But
Record Mart was farily well stocked with old titles the last time I
stopped in, and Héctor Lavoe's version of "El Cantante" was blasting
through the sound system.

The loft-jazz scene wound down as the cost of living downtown went
up—the usual story of music bringing a neighborhood back to life and
attracting people who make the place too expensive for musicians to live
there. At the end of the day, none of the loft-jazz pioneers were getting
rich in the lofts; many depended on arts foundation grants just to get by.
In time the musicians moved on. Some, like Anthony Braxton, took aca-
demic posts. Others found other hustles and revenue streams.

The so-called neoclassical movement of the '80s and '90s also hurt
the loft scene. It was led by the New Orleans trumpeter Wynton Marsa-
lis, son of Ellis Marsalis—an educator and musician who worked with
Ornette Coleman in the '50s, among others—and Marsalis's New York
City mentor, Stanley Crouch, who made a philosophic shift recalling
Irving Kristol's flip from young Trotskyist to neoconservative paterfa-
milias. Together, the pair preached a back-to-basics formalism, rooted in
New Orleans tradition, swing verities, hard-bop cutting contests, and
Fifty-second Street suit-and-tie fashion sense. It was welcomed among
grant-supported arts presenters at a time when edgy work of all sorts
was being defunded (or, in the case of Patti Smith's pal Robert Mapplethorpe, put on trial).

This was good news in some ways. Jazz became enshrined as a
classical music—the one truly American classical music—and it helped
recapture some of the cultural ground jazz lost in the wake of the '60s
rock 'n' roll revolution. A summer concert series in 1987 evolved over
time into Jazz at Lincoln Center, an institution anchored by three handsome spaces designed specifically for live performances, tucked into the
Time Warner Center at Columbus Circle, which had been built between
2000 and 2003 on the footprint of the demolished New York Coliseum.
In *Considering Genius: Writings on Jazz*, Crouch describes appealing to
the conscience, and vanity, of Mayor Rudy Giuliani during a one-on-one
meeting to help get JALC green-lighted. And so it was. Wynton Marsalis
became artistic director, Crouch artistic consultant. Alongside Bruce

Springsteen and Jon Landau, Marsalis and Crouch proved one of the most consequential artist-critic alliances in the history of the music business.

The downside of all this was that for years, the achievements and advances of the free jazz, loft jazz, and fusion scenes were pretty much written out of the canon. In a particularly outrageous bit of historical revisionism, Ken Burns's otherwise impressive 2001 PBS documentary *Jazz*, produced with Marsalis as senior creative consultant and Crouch as advisory board member (with both as featured talking heads), pretty much writes off the 1970s entirely, erasing a significant portion of jazz history for perhaps the largest single audience the music would ever have. In the series' final episode, Miles's electric music is dismissed as merely "playing tennis without a net." The Art Ensemble of Chicago is summed up as a group that "once found itself playing to just three people in its own hometown, and it attracted its largest following among white college students—*in France*." Gary Giddins offers perspectives on Cecil Taylor that, in the film's context, can't help but sound like apologies, while the saxophonist Branford Marsalis, Wynton's older brother, gets cast as hatchet man. He calls the demands Taylor allegedly makes of his audience "self-indulgent bullshit" and, following a section on the passing of Ellington in '74, talks about the aftermath, shrugging: "Jazz just kinda died. It just kinda went away for a while."

The spirit of the loft scene never disappeared. When the Knitting Factory opened on East Houston Street in 1987—the same year Jazz at Lincoln Center was born—it built on the lofts' genre-stretching aesthetic; the polyglot nightclub later moved to Leonard Street in TriBeCa and, in 2009, to Metropolitan Avenue in Williamsburg, setting up outposts in Los Angeles, Spokane, Reno, and Boise along the way. Saxophonist David Ware, who played with Cecil Taylor in the '70s, led one of the best jazz quartets of the '90s, re-introducing freestyle fire to the mainstream (Branford Marsalis signed him to Columbia Records—go figure—in 1997). Saxophonist John Zorn has championed the most extreme expressions of improvised music in New York City via his own work, his record label (Tzadik), and as a key player in various post-loft-era venues: Knitting Factory, Tonic, Roulette, the Stone.

The most interesting young players developed multiple personalities. The trumpeter Roy Hargrove led a fusion band and a Cuban-style jazz ensemble alongside more traditional groups. Terence Blanchard, another trumpeter, branched out into film music. In '96 the Detroit expat James

Carter released *Conversin' with the Elders*, playing his multiple saxes alternately alongside the Art Ensemble's Lester Bowie and the Count Basie Band's Harry "Sweets" Edison. In 2000, Carter released two albums on the same day: a lyrical tribute to Django Reinhardt (*Chasin' the Gypsy*) and an abstract jazz-funk record with twin electric guitars (*Layin' in the Cut*).

By the 2000s, the loft aesthetic had been absorbed into the body of jazz history—one more source of style, approach, vernacular. Jason Moran, a Houston-born New York transplant who studied with Muhal Richard Abrams, recorded *Black Stars* with Sam Rivers, and his *Modernisitic* included a cover of Afrika Bambaataa's hip-hop techno ur-text "Planet Rock." The pianist Matthew Shipp, a veteran of David Ware's quartet and a prolific experimenter, made some remarkable fusions of jazz improv and electronic music. In 2009, pianist Vijay Iyer topped the *Voice* jazz critics poll with *Historicity*, a trio album that included "Somewhere" from *West Side Story*, Julius Hemphill's "Dogon A.D.," and "Galang" by the Anglo–Sri Lankan rapper M.I.A.—a onetime Brooklyn resident whose catalog also includes a hot single based on a sample of Suicide's "Ghost Rider."

The other critical favorite of 2009 was *This Brings Us To, Volume I*, by Henry Threadgill, the AACM veteran and former member of Air, who was still based in the East Village, walking distance from the old Studio Rivbea. Some years back, Sam Rivers gave up his old loft space and, like so many maturing New Yorkers, moved to Florida. At last check, he was leading a big band in Orlando, mixing vernaculars as always. David Murray, meanwhile, set up shop in Paris, and has made a staggering array of recordings, from Senegalese and Haitian fusion collaborations to a Grateful Dead covers album. He still gets back to New York on occasion, where he plays wide. "Whenever Murray comes to any of our jam sessions," said Ahmir "?uestlove" Thompson, drummer and leader of the hip-hop band the Roots, "it's a short jam session. He'll solo so hard, there'll be twelve other cats, waiting to get on, saying, 'I ain't following *that*.'"

In January 2011, Murray led a big band up at Birdland, the famous club that opened on Broadway just off Fifty-second Street in 1949 and was revived on Forty-fourth Street just off Eighth Avenue. The night I saw them, the band did a frayed, openhearted reading of the Ellington-Strayhorn standard "Chelsea Bridge." Murray's solo was sublime: part

Ben Webster caress, part free-jazz expressionism, all Murray. It's interesting how, over the years—as Giddins has pointed out—the jazz avant-garde has proven itself more inclusive, and no less durable, than the jazz mainstream.[3]

An object lesson would be the Vision Festival, begun in 1996 by dancer Patricia Nicholson Parker and her husband, bassist William Parker, another longtime member of David Ware's quartet. The city's post-loft-era avant-garde has convened yearly for the event, which usually takes place in various corners of Lower Manhattan. The festival's purpose is to advance avant-jazz, which its mission statement defines as "not a freedom from melody or composition or rhythm" but the freedom for musicians "to choose any tradition or vocabulary as part of their palette when either composing or improvising"—a pretty succinct summary of the loft aesthetic. The 2010 edition featured Muhal Richard Abrams and other scene veterans; a tribute to the late Rashied Ali; and showcases by a new generation of players.

Jazz-pop fusion, meanwhile, continues to thrive. Rap producers have had a long love affair with '70s soul-jazz—Roy Ayers's recordings, the CTI/Kudu catalog—giving the music a new lease on life. Grover Washington's "Mr. Magic" has been sampled and remade on numerous recordings. The electric piano and sitar ambience of "Lonely Fire," from Miles Davis's roundly ignored '74 release *Big Fun*, was flipped by the producer Lord Finesse to underscore "Suicidal Thoughts" by the Notorious B.I.G.—one of the greatest, most bone-chilling raps ever recorded. Jazz and hip-hop's shared roots have produced surprising shoots. When the trumpeter Olu Dara played the Studio Rivbea festival in '76, his son, Nasir, was two years old. The kid would often pick up his dad's horn; by the time he was four, he could even play a bit. He eventually made his name as a rapper, known simply as Nas.

The city remains the global center of jazz, a hive of players and fans. My first date with my longtime partner—we met on an aged E train that broke down under the East River—was spent in part standing outside the original Knitting Factory on a soft summer night listening to John Zorn and Tim Berne play Ornette Coleman tunes, which wafted out through the club's open window over Houston Street. We were both wowed. I knew then and there that things would probably work out between us.

•

When Steve Reich's *Music for 18 Musicians* was finally released on ECM in '78, Reich stepped into a new realm. His ensemble toured the country, doing interviews on progressive-rock radio stations and playing in nightclubs. In New York, like Smith and Springsteen, he sold out the Bottom Line.[4]

Reich is still at home uptown and downtown. Shortly after a series of seventieth-birthday concerts at Carnegie Hall, the new-music group Signal performed *Music for 18 Musicians* at Le Poisson Rouge, a venue on the site of the old Village Gate, on Bleecker Street. Players set up their instruments on the floor, as the stage was too small; the audience stood around or sat on the ground among them, drinking beer. The members of Signal—who play modern composed music and avant-garde jazz in other settings, too—grew up with Reich's music as part of the canon.

Philip Glass finally got *Einstein on the Beach* issued as a four-LP box set in '79. Unfortunately, he saw little money from it, and the label that released it, Tomato, soon went belly-up. But by then the composer was on to the next project. After seeing *Einstein* in Holland, Hans de Roo of the Netherlands Opera had asked Glass if he was interested in making "a *real* opera." Indeed he was.[5]

A superstar of sorts since the '80s, Glass still produces music—film scores, chamber music, "real operas," et cetera—at a prodigious rate. He also mentors young musicians. When I interviewed him in 2008 at Dunvagen, his recording studio and publishing offices on Broadway ("We're just a stone's throw from my old place on Elizabeth Street," he said, pointing out the window), we were interrupted by Nico Muhly, a young composer and part-time Dunvagen employee who had been the subject of a glowing ten-page *New Yorker* profile that week. Muhly is another hybridizer: he's worked with the New York newcomers Björk and Antony Hegarty, among other genre-dodging pop musicians, and performed his own work—like Glass before him—at the Kitchen, now located over on West Nineteenth Street, near where the old SoHo art scene has reconstituted itself.

A full-scale revival of *Einstein* was planned for the 2009–10 New York City opera season with Wilson and Glass at the helm, returning the production to Lincoln Center for the first time since 1976. (It would probably be "the last revival of it in our lifetimes," Glass noted wistfully.) The production never got off the ground: in the new economy, it was simply too expensive. An international touring production was eventu-

ally planned, with U.S. dates at the Brooklyn Academy of Music. I saw
the 1984 revival there, and its epic, time-suspending sweep changed
the way I listened—afterward, there was no such thing as "background
music." All was foreground.

Rhys Chatham finally perfected his droning E-string composition
and called it *Guitar Trio.* He debuted it in 1978 with Nina Canal and
Glenn Branca. After playing awhile with Chatham, Branca went off to
develop his own music using multiple electric guitars with unusual tun-
ings. Thus began one of the most spectacular rivalries in modern music,
in which the two men gradually escalated their artillery. In the summer
of 2001, Branca premiered *Symphony No. 13 (Hallucination City)* for
one hundred electric guitars on the plaza of the World Trade Center. In
2009, Chatham conducted *A Crimson Grail*, his composition for two
hundred electric guitars, outside Lincoln Center in Damrosch Park.

The New York minimalist composers have had a marked influence on
rock bands, beginning with the Velvet Underground. In '79, Lee Ranaldo
had "some sort of ecstatic experience" listening to Chatham and Branca
perform *Guitar Trio* at Max's Kansas City. He and Thurston Moore would
eventually play with both Chatham and Branca, and form their own
group, Sonic Youth. In 2007, Sufjan Stevens premiered a Philip Glass–
indebted suite as part of a multimedia production at the Brooklyn Academy of Music; its unlikely subject was the reviled Brooklyn-Queens
Expressway. Anthony Braxton's son Tyondai, who played guitar in the
premiere of Branca's *Symphony No. 13*, builds Reich-like melodic webs
using digital loops on his own recordings. The list could go on. The most
impressive bit of synergy between rock and minimalism I've encountered
recently is a YouTube video of a young man in a Metallica T-shirt named
Cory Arcangel, who has arranged Bruce Springsteen's entire *Born to Run*
LP for solo glockenspiel. If Reich needs a new mallet-instrument player,
Arcangel could be his man.

La Monte Young and Marian Zazeela, minimalism's sannyasi elders,
are still married, and still live in the loft at 275 Church Street that they
moved to in 1963. For years they have presented *The Dream House*,
their "sound and light environment" exploring the psychoacoustic aesthetics of drones. It's open most Thursdays, Fridays, and Saturdays from
2:00 p.m. to midnight. Suggested donation: five dollars.

Meredith Monk still lives in the sixth-floor TriBeCa walk-up loft
space she moved to in 1972, where she still makes unclassifiable art.

She was nominated for a Grammy in 2008 for her recording *imperma-nence*. In 2010 she premiered an orchestral piece, *Weave*; the same year, she issued a remarkable collection of early recordings on John Zorn's Tzadik label, *Beginnings*, and was the subject of a documentary film, *Inner Voice*. Monk's ensemble still attracts adventurous vocalists: the last time I saw her, it featured the outstanding Theo Bleckmann, a German-born jazz singer and composer who, like so many before him, took his music to New York City.

Laurie Anderson still works in the Canal Street loft she rented in 1975, the window behind the mixing console of her home studio still overlooking the ruins of Hudson River piers. Anderson had one of the strangest hits in pop history with her single "O Superman," released on the tiny downtown sound-art label One Ten, and it launched her un-likely career as a major-label recording artist. Where she once loaded a jukebox with her own recordings as an art installation, she suddenly had a song in jukeboxes around the world: "O Superman" reached number 2 on the British pop charts in '81. And like Monk and Glass before her, she, too, completed a lengthy "opera" of sorts, titled *United States*, which premiered in full in '83 at the Brooklyn Academy of Music. In 2003, Anderson became NASA's first, and to date only, artist-in-residence.

Monk's work, and Anderson's, too, has been critically undervalued, it seems to me, in part because it collapses disciplines, dissolving the boundaries between music, theater, film, dance (in Monk's case), visual art (in Anderson's case), and storytelling. Yet it's precisely their interdis-ciplinary approaches that made them perhaps the most prescient musi-cians on the New York scene at the time, anticipating an era when recorded music is no longer a singular commodity but a component in a computer-assisted matrix of sound and image.

Laurie Anderson met Lou Reed for the very first time in Munich in 1992. They became best friends, then sweethearts; they finally mar-ried in 2008. If David Byrne is the Prince Charles of New York's art music scene, Reed and Anderson are its king and queen, bestowing on events—like a Muhly concert at the Kitchen—a benediction of history.

Hip-hop, meanwhile, grew up to rule the world. Rappers began making records, something that was inconceivable during the early days of the park jams. The Sugarhill Gang, a bunch of guys pulled together in New Jersey by the enterprising Sylvia Robinson of Sugar Hill Records, had a worldwide smash in 1979 with the ur-text "Rapper's Delight." Grandmaster Flash and the Furious Five recorded their first single, "Superrappin'," the same year. So did Kurt Walker, a Harlem kid known as Kool DJ Kurt and later as Kurtis Blow. His "Christmas Rappin'" became a hit that winter. For his next single, he went into Greene Street Recording Studios—formerly Big Apple Recording, where Philip Glass recorded *Einstein on the Beach*—and cut "The Breaks."

Over the decades hip-hop has had various creative centers: South Central L.A., Atlanta, New Orleans, Paris, Dakar. But its spiritual home remains its birthplace, New York City and its outskirts, home of the superheroes Herc and Grandmaster Flash, Run-DMC and Rakim, KRS-One and Public Enemy, Biggie and Puffy, Nas and Jay-Z.

On March 12, 2007, amid the tuxedos and gowns, I watched from a far corner of the Waldorf's Grand Ballroom as Jay-Z inducted Grandmaster Flash and the Furious Five into the Rock 'n' Roll Hall of Fame. Patti Smith was inducted the same night, and for all the dubious pomp, Flash, Melle Mel, Smith, Lenny Kaye, and the rest of their crews— R.I.P. Cowboy and Richard Sohl—appeared deeply moved. As a fan and journalist, I was, too: twenty years earlier, I worked the ceremony as a setup/breakdown tech, and spent the entire ceremony stuck out of earshot, watching my strung-out supervisor smoke crack rocks in an equipment storage room.

After accepting his award, Flash went straight to the airport to catch a plane, headed to a gig in Singapore.

It was amazing to watch hip-hop evolve over the years. I saw Afrika Bambaataa blow up the Roxy roller disco on West Eighteenth, back when he used to hold court there in the '80s, break dancers pulling impossible moves. I saw KRS-One bring out thousands to Central Park's Rumsey Playground for a free show in the spirit of Bambaataa's park jams, promoting peace after years of rap-concert violence had made it nearly impossible to produce a hip-hop show in the city. I saw Long Island's Public Enemy and Staten Island's Wu Tang Clan. On a documentary film shoot in the South Bronx, I watched Theodore Livingston—Grandwizard Theodore—dissect "Apache" with a pair of vinyl pressings in an epic act of turntablism. And thirty-seven years after Kool Herc rocked 1520 Sedgwick Avenue, I saw him rock Crotona Park, a jam sponsored by the City

Parks Department. Instead of having to jack into a lamppost, he was plugged into four 5,500-watt Wen Power Pro generators. Graying B-boys and B-girls were out with their kids. Herc played "The Mexican" and the smiles stretched wide; he played "Apache", and everyone got down. Old-schoolers dropped to the ground to show their moves, and no one was sure they'd get back up again. Meanwhile, the rent-controlled apartment building at 1520 Sedgwick had been put up for sale to real estate developers. Herc hadn't lived there for more than twenty years, but he and Coke La Rock made media appearances, speaking out for the tenants' rights, hoping to get the building landmark status, based on its role in global music history.

Grandmaster Caz and his sidekick JDL can sometimes be found leading hip-hop history tours of the Bronx and Harlem (www.hush hiphoptours.com). The one I took in 2009 cost me around seventy bucks. A dozen of us—two Belgians, two Japanese couples, a few Aussies, and a middle-aged Dutch woman—got picked up in Midtown in a plush mini-bus and driven around the city. Outside the school yard of Jackie Robinson Middle School, at 106th Street and Park Avenue in Harlem, Caz opened the base of a streetlamp and pulled out the wiring, showing everyone how to fire up a street jam. Then we headed north to 1520 Sedgwick Avenue, where he pointed out the steel-gated community room windows, and the side door near the Dumpsters that kids propped open at that first party back in '73—to let in air, or to slip out and smoke weed, while Herc's funk floated out over the Major Deegan Expressway and up toward River Park Towers, seeding the neighborhood.

Caz also talked a little about the song "Rapper's Delight" that day, hip-hop's formal recorded debut, "written" in part, as the story goes, using pieces of his personal rhyme book, which he'd given to his manager Hank Jackson, later known as "Big Bank" Hank, in a moment of esprit de corps. No performer, Hank had nevertheless been drafted for a studio project when one of the folks from Sugar Hill Records heard him rhyming along to a Caz tape at the New Jersey pizza joint where he held down a day job.

The song became an international hit; Caz never received cash or credit. More or less resigned after exploring his options, Caz did what any true MC would do: he wrote some rhymes about it, which he finally recorded on a poignant and hilarious LP titled *Mid Life Crisis*. His business card reads: GRANDMASTER CAZ: PIONEER & CULTURAL AMBASSADOR.

•

On September 11, 2001, Jay-Z released *The Blueprint*, arguably his greatest record. I'd gone out early that morning to purchase it at a Best Buy in upstate New York, and wound up in the store for hours, talking to the staff, watching the planes fly into the World Trade Center towers over and over again on dozens of wide-screen TVs.

That night in Chicago, Laurie Anderson performed "O Superman," whose meaning had changed overnight. "Here come the planes," she intoned, the pivotal line in an ominous phone message; "They're American planes."

Performing that night in Germany at the Stuttgart Liederhalle, Björk sang the wordless "Gotham Lullaby" from Meredith Monk's 1973 *Education of the Girlchild*—vowels leaping, weeping, praying, beyond language, beyond cultural designation, sound ascending into darkness.[6]

Some days later, my friend Jon and I walked past the wreckage of the towers. The air smelled of burned metal—the smell of soda cans thrown into a campfire. Then we headed over to the Knitting Factory on Leonard Street to catch a set by the trumpeter Roy Campbell, Jr., a veteran of Jemeel Moondoc's Muntu Ensemble. Campbell played a solo version of "The Star-Spangled Banner," breaking the iconic melody apart like Hendrix did up at Woodstock thirty-some years earlier—Hendrix, who inspired Miles and Patti Smith, who built Electric Lady Studios, who jammed with Sam Rivers, and who, if a story Richard Lloyd tells is to be believed, once shed tears on the young rock guitarist's hands.[7]

It was a night for tears.

On January 20, 2009, with Barack Obama newly sworn in as president, Animal Collective performed at the Manhattan Center on Thirty-fourth Street, up in the seventh-floor Grand Ballroom, a handsome space above the larger, ground-level Hammerstein Ballroom. The Manhattan Center was built in 1906, primarily as an opera house, by the theater impresario Oscar Hammerstein I, the grandfather of the lyricist Oscar Hammerstein II. The New York Dolls played it in their heyday; more recently, it hosted shows by Jay-Z and the Wu-Tang Clan.

Animal Collective's *Merriweather Post Pavilion* had been released that day, riding a full-page feature in *The New York Times* and a glowing advance review from the online indie-rock bible *Pitchfork* (it would top the year's Pazz & Jop poll). The group is devotedly experimental, making pop songs swimming in loops, reverb, and outsized electronic beats, altering "conventional" instruments—guitar, drums—to where they are nearly unrecognizable. They also produce gloriously strange vocal harmonies, processing their voices to sound like a very agitated, cybernetic version of the Beach Boys. Buddies from Baltimore who came to New York in 2001, the members represent, like their '70s predecessors, a vanguard of sorts, reinventing music for a trying-to-be-brave new world. In its fierce joyousness and pie-eyed trippiness, it's not hard to see their music as a reaction to the endlessly video-looped nightmare of September 11.

Many in the largely teenaged and twenty-something crowd wore Obama T-shirts and buttons. A clutch of music critics talked shop: Jon Caramanica of *The New York Times*; Kelefa Sanneh of *The New Yorker*; Hua Hsu, a freelancer who wrote the *Times* feature. The preshow DJs were also New York music journalists: the Russian émigré Piotr Orlov, and the Texas émigré Andy Beta. They played a 1975 live version of the Grateful Dead's "U.S. Blues," with its mandate to "wave that fla-a-ag." Then Lee Dorsey's 1970 version of Allen Toussaint's "Yes We Can Can," the pre-disco funk hit that launched the Pointer Sisters' career when they released their version in 1973. Then Mr. Fingers's "Can You Feel It?," the one-nation-under-a-groove anthem of house music, born in Obama's adopted home of Chicago. Eventually the president's voice entered the mix, stirring oratory meshing with the surging uplift of the grooves. "America: we have come so far, we have seen so much. And there is so much more to do."

Then the music faded, the lights dropped out, and three schleppy dudes stepped up to tables covered with keyboards, mixing consoles, and assorted electronic gadgetry. There were drums and cymbals, too, and a lone electric guitar sitting on a stand. A low-frequency synthesizer chord rumbled out of the speakers, and eventually a song bloomed, as if via stop-motion photography, whose dramatic high point came when the singer Noah Lennox, a.k.a. Panda Bear, wishfully wondered, "If I could just leave my body for a night," before a burst of strange chords— timbres flashing somewhere between the sound of calliopes and steel drums—crashed in. Later the band played "Summertime Clothes," a song about a heat wave and the fizzy deliciousness of love that inverts the Ramones' bratty sentiment on "I Don't Wanna Walk Around with You" with a chorus declaring "I *want* to walk around with you," swooning affirmation replacing sneering rejection. The energy level escalated; clouds of high-grade weed smoke billowed through the room, and the crowd's bouncing turned to unhinged dancing. A girl, apparently very stoned, clutched the balcony rail like she was on the prow of a boat in gale-force winds.

The set ended with "Brother Sport," a sort of techno-samba that showed how seamlessly Animal Collective fold styles together in their music. That polyglot impulse was an emblem of the most interesting New York rock bands at the end of the 2000s: Vampire Weekend, Dirty Projectors, Gang Gang Dance, Akron/Family. Animal Collective's Noah Lennox worked for a while at Other Music, the Fourth Street record store known as a source of handpicked, often obscure recordings, heavy on electronic and international styles. It was a key influence on the city's music culture in the 2000s, not unlike what Village Oldies/Bleecker Bob's—where Lenny met Patti—was to the '70s. Lennox was on his way to work there on the morning of 9/11.

After an encore, as the revelers filed out toward the frigid night and the year ahead, the DJs slipped on a gentle acoustic number: a cover of Suicide's "Dream Baby Dream" by, of all people, Bruce Springsteen. Springsteen played the song as a coda to nearly every show on his solo 2005 *Devils and Dust* tour. This particular version, a hypnotizing mantra-cum-lullaby-cum-benediction, was released on an import-only compilation right around Alan Vega's seventieth birthday.

Springsteen had always liked Suicide: he was especially impressed by the story-song "Frankie Teardrop." When he was working on *The River* in '79, he and Vega crossed paths up at 914 Studios in Blauvelt, where Springsteen had recorded so much of his early work. Vega and Marty Rev were finishing their second LP, which included "Dream Baby Dream." Bruce and Vega talked about rock 'n' roll, taking nips off Vega's flask. "You know, if Elvis came back from the dead," Springsteen said later, "I think he would sound like Alan Vega."[8]

CBGB closed on October 16, 2006, with a final set by the Patti Smith Group. It was an international media clusterfuck, and I decided to stay home rather than try to wedge myself in. The last time I'd been to the club was a few months earlier. I paid $4.50 for a Pabst and watched some hardcore/emo band—I didn't catch their name—holler songs to a crowd of maybe twenty friends and strangers. The dirt-crusted neon beer lights—Stroh's, Budweiser, Miller, Red Stripe—glowed bright, the six black speaker cabinets hanging above the stage blasted bright noise. The men's bathroom remained as appalling as ever, the three low urinals and, up on a platform, the single toilet—its seat, like everything else, covered in graffiti ("Bobby Head is HOT!"). There was no stall: you needed to shit, you had to shit in front of everybody.

I listened to the satellite radio broadcast of Smith's show and recorded it, for old times' sake, on two Maxell C90 cassettes. It was pretty good: she opened with "Piss Factory," then worked through some apropos covers: the Velvets' "Pale Blue Eyes," Television's "Marquee Moon" (with Richard Lloyd), a version of Blondie's cover of the Paragons' "The Tide Is High," a Ramones medley, and the Who's "My Generation," which has been part of her repetoire for so long, she's really a co-owner of it.

The night after CBGB closed, I interviewed the guys in TV on the Radio, one of the city's best rock bands, for a cover story in *Spin* magazine. I asked them if they felt part of the mythic continuum of New York musicians. The singer-guitarist Kyp Malone humbly allowed that maybe, along with their friends, they did, kinda. He mentioned a gallery exhibit of early Gerard Malanga photos, including the famous shot of Patti Smith on a subway platform. He was struck by both its iconic power and by Smith's anonymity. "She was just some kid," he said admiringly.

A few years later I spoke with Dave Longstreth, leader of Dirty Projectors, about what had developed in Brooklyn in the 2000s: the promiscuous art and music scene that spread from Williamsburg to Greenpoint, Bushwick, Bed-Stuy, Ditmas Park, and beyond, staked out by acts like the Yeah Yeah Yeahs, LCD Soundsystem, TV on the Radio, and dozens of others, informing a culture as vital in its way as downtown Manhattan in the '70s, with clubs, galleries, and semilegal performance spaces set up in residential lofts. He conceded it was something special. "We don't sit around getting hammered and passing the acoustic guitar around," he said of his neighbors. "But it is a community of people working side by side. And it's a really cool time to be making pop music. It is like making classical music in the teens and twenties, or making jazz in the sixties—where the basic devices and components have been soaking into the culture for half a century, so the most fertile ground for expressing things is abstraction and innovation. People are really primed. I feel really lucky to be involved in it."

Pieces of CBGB remain scattered around the city, literally. For a while, the dirty white awning and the phone booth were on display at the Rock 'n' Roll Hall of Fame Museum Annex at 76 Mercer Street, a few blocks down from the site of the Mercer Arts Center; in an amusing nod to Duchamp, one of the urinals was there, too, mounted on the wall outside the well-scrubbed restrooms in a Plexiglas vitrine. An outpost of the long-running museum in Cleveland, the Annex lasted just over a year, shutting down in 2010, a victim of the latest recession.

John Varvatos, a clothing designer with a punk aesthetic, transformed CBGB's original location, 315 Bowery, into a boutique in 2007. He preserved something of the club's vibe, keeping the black paint job and bolting Plexiglas panels over sections of the sticker-and-graffiti-encrusted walls. He even clears out the racks for an occasional concert; not long ago, in a remarkable moment of historical full-circling, David Johansen and Sylvain Sylvain, lone survivors of the New York Dolls after the 2004 death of Arthur Kane (Thunders and Nolan died within months of each other in the early '90s), staged a release party there for a new Dolls record. When they launched into "Trash" from the first Dolls LP, you could feel the ghosts swarm.

The former Ali's Alley, at 77 Greene, also became a high-end clothing boutique, operated by the mass-market superstar Nicole Miller, who was at RISD around the time Chris and Tina and David went there. It's fitting: before it was a jazz club, the ground-floor space belonged to a guy who baled and sold rags, a *schmatta* OG. Ali remained in the second-floor loft until his death in 2009, a section of his floor-to-ceiling shelves stacked with boxes of open-reel tapes, hours' worth of recordings of shows and sessions at Ali's Alley from back in the day. When I last spoke with him, in fall 2008, I suggested he try to put the music out. He thought someday he might. Then he opened up his Mac and clicked on a YouTube video of James Blood Ulmer, Don Cherry, and himself playing downstairs in the club in the late '70s.

"Pretty good, huh?" he asked.

New York City tends to erase its history, endlessly reinventing itself: that is its way. But the music remains. At Cielo on Little West Twelfth, François Kevorkian has held down a Monday-night residency, called Deep Space, for years. Afrika Bambaataa celebrated the thirty-sixth anniversary of the Zulu Nation with a jam at the still-unfinished Museum of Hip Hop, on the second floor of the Magic Johnson Theater on 124th Street. Grandmaster Caz, Disco Wiz, and Grand Wizard Theodore host park parties up at Crotona in the Bronx and St. Nicholas in Harlem. Except for the Japanese break-dancers, the botanically advanced weed, the Republican mayor, the iPods, the pocket-sized Flip video cameras, the openly gay kids, and the relative lack of menace, it seems not unlike the old days.

After the death of Fred "Sonic" Smith in 1994, Patti Smith left Detroit, where she'd been living since 1979, and returned to New York City. During the 2000s, as in the 1970s, she would usually play a series of year-end shows. Many were held at the Bowery Ballroom, a few blocks down from the site of CBGB. In 2012, it's still the best small rock venue in Manhattan; has been for a while.

On December 30, 2009, Smith's sixty-third birthday, she comes onstage in a faded Knicks T-shirt, skinny jeans, and the familiar black sports jacket. She notes with amusement, and some agreement, that a *New York Times* critic said unkind things about the previous night's show. She mentions that PBS is airing a documentary about her— *Dream of Life*—at this very moment, and how proud her late parents would have been to see it. A memoir of her relationship with Robert Mapplethorpe, *Just Kids*, would be published in a few weeks.

The band ramps up into the opening of "Gloria," and out come Jesus and Johnny and the sweet young thing leaning on the parking meter. In the middle of the song "Land," Smith begins freestyling: "All the memories that we've built up thru the years," she incants, her band working the groove, "Johnny walks over them, stone by stone . . ."

And everyone there, young and old, walks with him.

NOTES

BIBLIOGRAPHY

DISCOGRAPHY

FILMOGRAPHY

ACKNOWLEDGMENTS
AND THANKS

INDEX

NOTES

1973: WILD SIDE WALKING

1. Lyrics from "So You Want to Be (a Rock 'n' Roll Star)," *Wave* (Arista, 1979). Original written by Roger McGuinn and Chris Hillman, and recorded by the Byrds, although this line is Patti's invention. She rocked some pretty hot Rickenbacker feedback on a performance of it in Koln, Germany, that year: www.youtube.com/watch?v=Cppyn-u3Djw.
2. www.archive.org/details/gd73-03-15.sbd.cotsman.14035.sbeok.shnf (accessed 3/11). Middling sound quality but some emotional moments nevertheless.
3. John Rockwell, "'Lady of Late' Adds Color with Vocals by Meredith Monk." *New York Times*, January 13, 1973.
4. Ibid.
5. John Hammond (with Irving Townsend), *John Hammond on Record* (Penguin, 1977), p. 393.
6. I spoke with Springsteen at the Paramount Theater in Asbury Park in April 2006 for a *New York Times* piece about his folk-revival project *We Shall Overcome: The Pete Seeger Sessions*. His reflections were touching. It was watching those guys on the beach, singing folk tunes and Top Forty hits, that first inspired him to pick up the guitar, hoping for little more than to be able to, one day, sidle into the circle with them and play along. As reprinted online: www.nytimes.com/2006/04/16/arts/music/16herm.html?pagewanted=all.
7. Dave Marsh, *Born to Run: The Bruce Springsteen Story, Volume 1* (Thunder's Mouth Press, 1996).
8. Lester Bangs. Review of *Greetings from Asbury Park, New Jersey*, *Rolling Stone*, July 5, 1973. As reprinted online: www.rollingstone.com/music/albumreviews/greetings-from-asbury-park-nj-19730705.
9. http://brucebase.wikispaces.com/1972#090872. There are recordings and even video footage from the '72 solo gigs at Max's floating around the Internet: www.youtube.com/watch?v=7dy7RTicVr0&feature=player_embedded#at=29.
10. Date of recording listed incorrectly as February 17 in *Tracks* liner notes, which was likely the date of first broadcast on the syndicated radio program *The King Biscuit Flower Hour*, which had taped the show. See http://brucebase.wikispaces

.com/1973#030173 and www.wolfgangsvault.com/bruce-springsteen/concerts/maxs-kansas-city-january-31-1973.html (accessed 3/11).

11. Andreas Killen, *1973 Nervous Breakdown* (Bloomsbury, 2006), p. 1.
12. Andrew Sarris, "Out, Out, Damned Demon!" *Village Voice*, January 3, 1974, p. 51.
13. Killen, *1973 Nervous Breakdown*, p. 198.
14. Victor Bockris, *Transformer: The Lou Reed Story* (Da Capo, 1995; reprint, 1997), p. 60.
15. Keith Potter, *Four Musical Minimalists* (Cambridge University Press, 2000), pp. 60, 72.
16. "Art Rock" in *The Rolling Stone Illustrated History of Rock & Roll*, ed. Jim Miller (Rolling Stone Press, 1976), p. 325.
17. Tim Mitchell, *Sonic Transmission: Television, Tom Verlaine, Richard Hell* (Glitter Books, 2006), p. 22.
18. Greg Shaw, liner notes to *Nuggets: Original Artyfacts from the First Psychedelic Era, 1965–1968* (Rhino reissue, 1998).
19. Clinton Heylin, *From the Velvets to the Voidoids: A Pre-Punk History for a Post-Punk World* (Penguin, 1993), p. 101.
20. See Hell's website, www.richardhell.com/helllit.html#voidoid (accessed 3/11).
21. www.vasulka.org/archive/Kitchen/KBR/KBR1.pdf (accessed 3/11).
22. Nina Antonia, *The New York Dolls: Too Much Too Soon* (Omnibus Press, 1998), p. 72.
23. Photo-gallery narration by Bob Gruen, from *New York Dolls—All Dolled Up: Films by Bob Gruen and Nadya Beck* (Music Video Distributors, 2005).
24. www.workers.org/2006/us/lavender-red-73/ (accessed 3/11). A brief history of STAR, the Street Transvestite Action Revolutionaries.
25. Mitchell, *Sonic Transmission*, p. 12.
26. Antonia, *The New York Dolls*, pp. 31–32.
27. Interview with author, 2006.
28. www.thevillager.com/villager_104/genefrankel85.html (accessed 3/11).
29. David Nobakht, *Suicide: No Compromise* (SAF, 2005), p. 49.
30. Antonia, *The New York Dolls*, p. 95, and *Johnny Thunders . . . In Cold Blood* (Jungle Books, 1987), p. 33.
31. See Whitney Balliett, *Collected Works: A Journal of Jazz, 1954–2000* (St. Martin's Press, 2000), pp. 358–59.
32. Stuart Nicholson, *Jazz Rock: A History* (Schirmer, 1998), p. 112.
33. Miles Davis, *Miles: The Autobiography* (Touchstone, 1989), p. 326.
34. Nicholson, *Jazz Rock*, pp. 122–23; Ian Carr, *Miles Davis: The Definitve Biography* (Thunder's Mouth Press, 1999), pp. 315–16.
35. Interview in *Tuba Frenzy* no. 4, 1998.
36. Author interview with Rashied Ali; see also Juma Sultan's video archive at web2.clarkson.edu/projects/jumasarchive/video_pages/pharoah-sanders-vid.php.
37. Balliett, *Collected Works*, pp. 371–72.
38. www.pointofdeparture.org/PoD27/PoD27Muntu.html (accessed 3/11).
39. Peter Shapiro, *Turn the Beat Around: The Secret History of Disco* (Faber and Faber, 2005), pp. 182, 321.
40. As told to Mark Schwartz. "Players Club," *Guilt & Pleasure* no. 6, fall 2007.
41. Juan Moreno Velásquez, liner notes to *Hommy: A Latin Opera* (Fania reissue, 2006).

42. Advertisement, *Village Voice*, April 19, 1973, p. 67.

43. Jerry Dee Lewis, "Born in the Bronx," in *Born in the Bronx*, ed. Johan Kugelberg (Universe, 2007), p. 194.

44. As recalled by Kurtis Blow in "Cheeba, Cheeba Y'all: Original House Rocker Eddie Cheba" by Mark Skillz (MarkSkillz@aol.com), reprinted at Davey D's MySpace blog: www.myspace.com/mrdaveyd/blog/321666119.

45. Shapiro, *Turn the Beat Around*, p. 27. Henry Post, "The Front," *New York*, December 4, 1978.

46. Dan Charnas, *The Big Payback: The History of the Business of Hip-Hop* (New American Library, 2010), p. 13.

47. Shapiro, *Turn the Beat Around*, p. 292.

48. Tim Lawrence, *Love Saves the Day: A History of American Dance Music Culture, 1970–1979* (Duke University Press, 2003), pp. 114–15; Shapiro, *Turn the Beat Around*, p. 35.

49. en.wikipedia.org/wiki/Bomba (accessed 3/11).

50. Jeff Chang, blog post January 5, 2004, www.cantstopwontstop.com/blog/2004/01/che-che-cole-to-future-just-want-to.html. (This entry seems to have gone missing in the blog's reformatting, but will perhaps reappear at a future date.)

51. Ned Sublette, *Cuba and Its Music: From the First Drums to the Mambo* (Chicago Review Press, 2004), p. 33.

52. Eddie Palmieri at his best: www.youtube.com/watch?v=zOcj8j_KPS0&feature=related (accessed 3/11), and César Rondón, *The Book of Salsa* (University of North Carolina Press, 2008).

53. Jack Stewart, *Graffiti Kings* (Abrams, 2009), pp. 83–85; Jeff Chang blog cited above; timeline in Kugelberg, *Born in the Bronx*, pp. 56–57.

54. The Topps Company, Inc., *Wacky Packages* (Abrams, 2008).

55. Antonia, *The New York Dolls*, pp. 85, 89.

56. Ibid., p. 100; Arthur Bell, "Waldorf Nation," *Village Voice*, November 8, 1973, pp. 25, 30.

57. *New York Dolls—All Dolled Up: Films by Bob Gruen and Nadya Beck*.

58. Antonia, *The New York Dolls*, p. 103.

59. Phil Lesh, *Searching for the Sound: My Life with the Grateful Dead* (Little, Brown, 2005), pp. 37–38.

60. K. Robert Schwarz, *Minimalists* (Phaidon, 1996), p. 71.

61. Keith Potter, *Four Musical Minimalists* (Cambridge University Press, 2000), p. 200.

62. Alan Rich, "A Lot of Night Music: Surging Forward by Standing Still," *LA Weekly*, March 15, 2006.

63. This account drawn from Michael Tilson Thomas's vivid liner notes to Steve Reich's *Works*, 1997.

64. Harold C. Schonberg, "Music: A Concert Fuss," *New York Times*, January 20, 1973.

65. Tom Johnson, "A Galleryful of Spinets," *Village Voice*, May 24, 1973.

66. Ibid.

67. Potter, *Four Musical Minimalists*, p. 25.

68. Interview with La Monte Young and Marian Zazeela by Gabrielle Zuckerman, American Public Media, July 2002, musicmavericks.publicradio.org/features/interview_young.html. Great material, and nearly as long as one of Young's compositions.

69. Legs McNeil and Gillian McCain, *Please Kill Me: The Uncensored Oral History of Punk* (Grove Press, 1996), p. 4.
70. Potter, *Four Musical Minimalists*, p. 51.
71. Schwarz, *Minimalists*, p. 33.
72. Potter, *Four Musical Minimalists*, p. 61.
73. John Cale, Tony Conrad, Angus Maclise, La Monte Young, and Marian Zazeela, *Inside the Dream Syndicate, Volume I: Day of Niagara (1965)* (Table of the Elements, 2000).
74. Mark Prendergast, *The Ambient Century: From Mahler to Trance—The Evolution of Sound in the Electronic Age* (Bloomsbury, 2000), pp. 92–93, 152–53.
75. Potter, *Four Musical Minimalists*, p. 67.
76. McNeil and McCain, *Please Kill Me*, p. 4.
77. Potter, *Four Musical Minimalists*, p. 323.
78. Schwarz, *Minimalists*, pp. 108–19; also interview with author, 2008.
79. Potter, *Four Musical Minimalists*, p. 303.
80. John Rockwell, *All American Music: Composition in the Late Twentieth Century* (Knopf, 1983; Da Capo reprint, 1997), pp. 109–10.
81. Steven Lee Beeber, *The Heebie-Jeebies at CBGB's: A Secret History of Jewish Punk* (Chicago Review Press, 2006), p. 82.
82. Roman Kozak, *This Ain't No Disco: The Story of CBGB* (Faber and Faber, 1988), p. 2.
83. Clinton Heylin, *From the Velvets to the Voidoids*, pp. 68–70.
84. Footage of Wayne County in swastika and garters shot by Anton Perich: www.youtube.com/watch?v=_mSExLSGB4w&feature=related.
85. Luc Sante, *Low Life: Lures and Snares of Old New York* (Farrar, Straus and Giroux, 1991), pp. 105–106.
86. Ibid., pp. 119–20.
87. www.nycroads.com/roads/west-side/ (accessed 3/11).
88. McNeil and McCain, *Please Kill Me*, p. 160.
89. Patti Smith, *Patti Smith Complete: Lyrics, Notes and Reflections* (Anchor, 1999), p. xxiii.
90. Patti Smith, "Masked Bawl," *Creem*, April 1974. As reprinted in Ann Powers and Evelyn McDonnell, eds., *Rock She Wrote* (Delta, 1995).
91. Bernard Gendron, "The Downtown Music Scene," in Marvin J. Taylor, ed., *The Downtown Book: The New York Art Scene 1974–1984* (Princeton University Press, 2006), p. 52.

1974: INVENT YOURSELF

1. From chronology in Marvin J. Taylor, ed., *The Downtown Book: The New York Art Scene 1974–1984* (Princeton University Press, 2006), p. 176.
2. Vincent J. Cannato, *The Ungovernable City* (Basic Books, 2001), p. 564.
3. *New York Times*, January 1, 1974.
4. Legs McNeil and Gillian McCain, *Please Kill Me: The Uncensored Oral History of Punk* (Grove, 1996), p. 161.
5. Tom McCarthy, "Patti: Poet as Macho Woman," *Village Voice*, February 7, 1974, p. 47.

6. Undated, smooth-as-hell stream from the period, www.powerhouseradio.com/frankiecrocker.html.

7. Patricia Morrisroe, *Mapplethorpe: A Biography* (Random House, 1995), p. 92; Heylin, *From the Velvets to the Voidoids: A Pre-Punk History for a Post-Punk World*, p. 107.

8. Heylin, *From the Velvets to the Voidoids*, p. 108.

9. Patti Smith, *Patti Smith Complete: Lyrics, Notes and Reflections* (Anchor, 1999), p. xxi.

10. Interviews with Leee Black Childers and Wayne County, *The Sacred Triangle: Bowie, Iggy & Lou 1971–1973* (Sexy Intellectual DVD, 2010).

11. Heylin, *From the Velvets to the Voidoids*, p. 118.

12. Frank Rose, "Rising Starshine," in Riffs, *Village Voice*, January 31, 1974.

13. Heylin, *From the Velvets to the Voidoids*, pp. 44–45.

14. Liner notes to Arthur Russell, *Another Thought* (Point, 1994).

15. Liner notes to Arthur Russell, *First Thought Best Thought* (Audika Records, 2006).

16. John Rockwell, "Under New Chief, The Kitchen Has Regained Some of Its Zip," *New York Times*, September 17, 1987.

17. Tim Lawrence, *Love Saves the Day: A History of American Dance Music Culture, 1970–1979* (Duke University Press, 2003), p. 125.

18. Ibid., pp. 125–30.

19. Ibid., p. 120.

20. Ibid., p. 125.

21. Ibid., p. 108.

22. Richard Lloyd interviewed in *Punk* no. 21, fall 2007.

23. Ibid.

24. See the 2005 compilation *Spurts: The Richard Hell Story* (Rhino).

25. Lisa Robinson, "Rebel Nights," *Vanity Fair*, November 2002.

26. Heylin, *From the Velvets to the Voidoids*, p. 114.

27. Patti Smith, "Television: Escapees from Heaven," *Soho Weekly News*, June 27, 1974.

28. Victor Bockris and Roberta Bayley, *Patti Smith: An Unauthorized Biography* (Simon & Schuster, 1999), p. 103.

29. Heylin, *From the Velvets to the Voidoids*, pp. 172–73, as quoted from *Punk* no. 3, April 1976.

30. Heylin, *From the Velvets to the Voidoids*, p. 168.

31. Mickey Leigh with Legs McNeil, *I Slept with Joey Ramone* (Touchstone, 2009), pp. 95–97.

32. Heylin, *From the Velvets to the Voidoids*, p. 176.

33. Leigh, *I Slept with Joey Ramone*, p. 123.

34. Ibid., p. 115.

35. As quoted in Jayne County with Rupert Smith, *Man Enough to Be a Woman* (Serpent's Tail, 1995), pp. 106–107.

36. www.robertchristgau.com/cg.php (accessed 3/11).

37. Ben Ratliff, *Coltrane: The Story of a Sound* (Farrar, Straus and Giroux, 1997), p. 186.

38. Publisher's Page, *Latin NY*, April 1976, p. 6.
39. Max Salazar, *Mambo Kingdom* (Schirmer Trade, 2002), pp. 255–57; Vernon W. Boggs, *Salsiology* (Greenwood Press, 1992), p. 188. Larry Harlow related the story of his nickname in the liner notes of *Salsa* (Fania, 1974).
40. Robert Caro, *The Power Broker* (Vintage, 1974), p. 893.
41. Robert Worth, "Guess Who Saved the South Bronx," *Washington Monthly*, April 1999, www.washingtonmonthly.com/features/1999/9904.worth.bronx.html (accessed 1/09).
42. Interview with author, 2006. See also Jim Fricke and Charlie Ahearn, *Yes Yes Y'all: The Experience Music Project Oral History of Hip-Hop's First Decade* (Da Capo, 2002), p. 29, and Jeff Chang, *Can't Stop Won't Stop* (Picador, 2006), pp. 81–82.
43. http://brucebase.wikispaces.com/1973#030173, entry for March 13, 1973.
44. Grandmaster Flash with David Ritz, *The Adventures of Grandmaster Flash* (Broadway, 2008), pp. 32–34.
45. Ibid.
46. Chang, *Can't Stop Won't Stop*, p. 79.
47. *Village Voice*, June 13, 1974, p. 55.
48. Interview with author, 2008.
49. Munkacsi, interview with author, 2008.
50. An epic interview with Harvey Averne by singer and radio host Ernesto "Chico" Alvarez Peraza, "Arvito: The Harvey Averne Story," *Latin Jazz Network* website, posted June 13, 2009: www.latinjazznet.com/2009/07/27/features/harvey-averne-interview-2/ (accessed 12/10).
51. Celia Cruz with Ana Christina Reymundo, *Celia: My Life* (Rayo/HarperCollins), 2004, p. 135.
52. Liner notes to *Celia and Johnny* reissue (Fania, 2006).
53. As Smith recalls in her memoir *Just Kids*, the recorded take of "Piss Factory" was finished at precisely midnight.
54. *Village Voice*, July 11, 1974, p. 51.
55. *Village Voice*, August 8, 1974, p. 52.
56. Concert stream of the second and final night's performance from Wolfgang's Vault, www.wolfgangsvault.com/bob-dylan-and-the-band/concerts/madison-square-garden-january-31-1974-set-1.html.
57. *Village Voice*, October 31, 1974, p. 82.
58. *Village Voice*, June 6, 1974, p. 73.
59. *Hit Parader*, September 1974, pp. 17, 22–25; Nina Antonia, *Too Much Too Soon*, pp. 132–33.
60. Antonia, *Too Much Too Soon*, pp. 144–48.
61. Lester Bangs, "Smack as Catch Can: The Shape of Dope Today," *Creem*, September 1974, p. 40.
62. Laurie Anderson, *Stories from the Nerve Bible: A Retrospective 1972–1992* (HarperCollins, 1994), pp. 78, 103.
63. *Village Voice*, October 17, 1974, p. 5.
64. *Village Voice*, December 2, 1974, p. 9.
65. Lawrence, *Love Saves the Day*, pp. 144–45.
66. Ibid., pp. 72–73.
67. Ibid., p. 146.

68. *Billboard*, November 2, 1974, p. 10.
69. Lawrence, *Love Saves the Day*, p. 149.
70. Ibid., p. 205.
71. Ibid., p. 212.
72. Mel Cheren, *Keep On Dancin': My Life and the Paradise Garage* (24 Hours for Life, 2000), p. 144.
73. As quoted by John Storm Roberts in *Village Voice*, October 31, 1974, p. 85.
74. John Holmstrom, ed., *Punk: The Original* (High Times Press, 1998), p. 26.
75. Philip Glass, *Music by Philip Glass* (Harper & Row, 1987), pp. 28–29.
76. Steve Reich, *Writings on Music 1965–2000* (Oxford, 2002), p. 90.

1975: JUNGLELAND

1. Howard Smith and Brian Van Der Horst, "Street Plunker" in Scenes, *Village Voice*, January 27, 1975, p. 20.
2. www.latinamericanstudies.org/puertorico/Fraunces-Tavern-communique.jpg (accessed 3/11), blog.insidetheapple.net/2010/01/bombing-of-fraunces-tavern-january -24.html (accessed 3/11).
3. Jeff Chang, *Can't Stop Won't Stop* (Picador, 2006), p. 98.
4. Jeff Chang, Timeline in Johan Kugelberg, ed., *Born in the Bronx: A Visual Record of the Early Days of Hip Hop* (Rizzoli, 2007), pp. 56–57.
5. Dan Charnas, *The Big Payback* (New American Library, 2010), p. 15.
6. As recalled by Kurtis Blow in "Cheeba, Cheeba Y'all: Original House Rocker Eddie Cheba" by Mark Skillz (MarkSkillz@aol.com), reprinted at Davey D's My-Space blog: www.myspace.com/mrdaveyd/blog/321666119.
7. *New York Times*, January 1, 1975.
8. Andy Gill and Kevin Odegard, *A Simple Twist of Fate: Bob Dylan and the Making of Blood on the Tracks* (Da Capo, 2005), pp. 37–39.
9. David Sheppard, *On Some Faraway Beach: The Life and Times of Brian Eno* (Chicago Review Press, 2008), pp. 77–78.
10. Interview with author, 2007.
11. Roman Kozak, *This Ain't No Disco: The Story of CBGB* (Faber and Faber, 1988), pp. 28–29. See also Clinton Heylin, *From the Velvets to the Voidoids* (Penguin, 1993), p. 157.
12. Legs McNeil and Gillian McCain, *Please Kill Me*, p. 172. Harry details this encounter in the book. See also Gary Valentine, *New York Rocker* (Thunder's Mouth Press, 2006), p. 60, and CBGB advertisement, *Soho Weekly News*, March 13, 1975.
13. Heylin, *From the Velvets to the Voidoids*, p. 161.
14. Nina Antonia, *Too Much Too Soon*, p. 162.
15. Valentine, *New York Rocker*, pp. 60–61.
16. Wayne Robbins and Robert Christgau, "Al Green at 7 and 11," *Village Voice*, March 24, 1975, p. 110.
17. Jamaica Kincaid, "Sly Ashamed," *Village Voice*, January 27, 1975, pp. 113–14.
18. www.latinamericanstudies.org/faln.htm (accessed 3/11).
19. See the excellent and mysterious MP3 blog *Magic of Juju*: magicofjuju.blogspot .com/2006_09_01_archive.html (accessed 11/10).

20. Victor Bockris and Roberta Bayley, *Patti Smith: An Unauthorized Biography*, p. 107; for Kaye on Richman, see Kozak, *This Ain't No Disco*, p. 37.

21. Stuart Nicholson, *Jazz Rock: A History* (Schirmer, 1998), pp. 127–28.

22. Gary Giddins, "Ed Beach: The Persistence of a Jazz Jock," *Village Voice*, March 17, 1975, p. 116.

23. Author interview, 2008.

24. George Lewis, *A Power Stronger Than Itself: The AACM and American Experimental Music* (University of Chicago Press, 2008), p. 226.

25. Braxton spoke about chess, valium, and other topics with critic Graham Lock for *Forces In Motion: The Music and Thoughts of Anthony Braxton* (Da Capo, 1988), pp. 84–86, 136–37.

26. Gilles Peterson and Stuart Baker, eds., *Freedom Rhythm & Sound* (Soul Jazz Records Publishing, 2009), pp. 4–5, 32, 39.

27. Jim Fricke and Charlie Ahern, eds., *Yes Yes Y'all: The Experience Music Project Oral History of Hip-Hop's First Decade* (Da Capo, 2002), p. 61.

28. Ibid., p. 63.

29. When I interviewed Chris Stein, he bristled at the mention of David Bowman's *This Must Be the Place: The Adventures of Talking Heads in the 20th Century* (Harper Entertainment/HarperCollins, 2001), saying it was full of "misinformation and bullshit." David Byrne is a big fan of Sytze Steenstra's *Song and Circumstance: The Work of David Byrne from Talking Heads to the Present* (Continuum, 2010), which quotes him in a cover blurb describing the volume as "scrupulously researched and uncannily on-the-money." I referred to both these books here, along with interviews and other material.

30. Heylin, *From the Velvets to the Voidoids*, p. 213.

31. Interview, *Rolling Stone*, May 3–17, 2007. In her memoir *Just Kids*, Smith suggests she took LSD with Mapplethorpe in '74, noting, "There was a garbage strike." The big New York City garbage strike was in July '75. So it's likely that's when their trip occurred.

32. Thurston Moore, notes to Patti Smith's "Jukebox Crucifix," reprinted in Robert Matheu and Brian J. Bowe, *Creem: America's Only Rock 'n' Roll Magazine* (Collins, 2007), p. 104.

33. Bill Adler, *Tougher Than Leather: The Rise of Run-DMC* (Consafos Press, 2002), p. 22.

34. This scene was composed from a few accounts: Bockris and Bayley, *Patti Smith*, pp. 122–23; Paul Williams, "All Down the Line," *Soho Weekly News*, July 3, 1975; Danny Fields, column, *Soho Weekly News*, July 3, 1975; James Wolcott, "Dylan Calls on Patti Smith," *Village Voice*, July 7, 1975.

35. Jerry Leichtling, "Buddy Holly, Can You Spare a Dime?," *Village Voice*, July 14, 1975.

36. Peter Shapiro, *Turn the Beat Around* (Faber and Faber, 2005), p. 190.

37. Lawrence, *Love Saves the Day*, pp. 212–13.

38. Shapiro, *Turn the Beat Around*, p. 107.

39. Richard Szathmary and Lucian K. Truscott IV, "Inside the Disco Boom," *Village Voice*, July 21, 1975. My description of the July 1 scene at Le Jardin is informed by this groundbreaking piece.

40. Shapiro, *Turn the Beat Around*, p. 184.

41. Ibid., p. 194.

42. Louis Laffitte, "Eddie Palmieri: The Sun of Latin Music," *Latin Beat*, August 2002.

43. Pablo "Yoruba" Guzman, "We Are the Source," *Soho Weekly News*, September 4, 1975, p. 30.

44. Leighton Kerner, "Nilsson Sings the World Away," *Village Voice*, April 28, 1975, p. 108.

45. Alex Ross, *The Rest Is Noise: Listening to the Twentieth Century* (Farrar, Straus and Giroux, 2007), p. 507.

46. Heylin, *From the Velvets to the Voidoids*, p. 215.

47. Dave Marsh, *Born to Run*, p. 123.

48. Ken Tucker, "Bruce Springsteen's Sublime Excessiveness," *Soho Weekly News*, August 21, 1975, p. 29; Paul Nelson, "Is Bruce Springsteen Worth the Hype?" *Village Voice*, August 25, 1975, p. 96.

49. Danny Fields, column, *Soho Weekly News*, February 27, 1975.

50. Patricia Morrisroe, *Mapplethorpe*, p. 159.

51. Phil Tracy, "What Will Happen When the City Defaults?" *Village Voice*, August 4, 1975.

52. Howard Blum, "Gasoline Gomez: Legendary Arsonist of the Bronx," *Village Voice*, June 23, 1975, p. 10.

53. Katherine Pritchard, "Village Crime Wave," *Soho Weekly News*, October 30, 1975; Howard Blum, "Groupie with a Gun Creates Interest at Local Bank," *Village Voice*, October 30, 1975; and a bizarre clip of the avuncular Scott Muni talking to the robber: www.scottmuni.com/audio/cat_olsen.mp3.

54. Howard Blum, "A Heroin War Is Coming to Harlem," *Village Voice*, November 3, 1975.

55. Stanley Crouch, "Keith Jarrett: Practice Does Not Make Up for the Lack of a Story," *Village Voice*, November 25, 1975.

56. This scene was constructed from the photos and history in Jack Stewart's *Graffiti Kings: New York City Mass Transit Art of the 1970s* (Melcher Media/Abrams, 2009), pp. 53, 161–63.

57. Richard Goldstein, "George Maciunas: The Phantom Co-oper," *Village Voice*, March 21, 1977.

58. Arnie Kantrowitz, "A Gay Struggles with the New Acceptance," *Village Voice*, November 11, 1975, p. 36.

59. Bockris and Bayley, *Patti Smith*, p. 134.

60. John Rockwell, "Patti Smith Battles to a Singing Victory," *New York Times*, December 28, 1975, p. 31.

61. Danny Fields, column, *Soho Weekly News*, November 27, 1975.

62. www.youtube.com/user/IvanKralVault#p/u/4/c1y3ETs8PuA. Ivan Kral also posted this CBGB party clip, with some musical background, on his Facebook site; send him a friend request and maybe he'll let you see it.

1976: THESE ARE THE DAYS, MY FRIENDS

1. John Holstrom, ed., *Punk: The Original*, p. 3.

2. Cynthia Heimel and Stephen Saban, "Invasion of the Body Twitchers," *Soho Weekly News*, December 4, 1975.

NOTES TO PAGES 162-178

3. Vince Aletti, "I Won't Dance, Don't Ask Me," *Village Voice*, April 26, 1976.
4. Corrine Robins, "Soho Discos: Board Votes to Stop the Music," *Soho Weekly News*, April 29, 1976.
5. Andrew Mason, "RIP Harry Whitaker," www.waxpoetics.com/2010/11/rip-harry-whitaker/.
6. Legs McNeill and Gillian McCain, *Please Kill Me*, pp. 178–79.
7. Eric Gonzalez, "Andy Gonzalez: The Cultural Warrior, Part II," *Latin Beat Magazine*, June/July 2006.
8. Roberto Ernesto Gyemant, "Cali Cartel," *Wax Poetics* no. 19, October/November, p. 54.
9. Pablo "Yoruba" Guzman, "Gunfight at the Latin Corral—Part 1," *Soho Weekly News*, November 20, 1975; "Gunfight at the Latin Corral—Part 2," *Soho Weekly News*, December 4, 1975.
10. Pablo "Yoruba" Guzman, "Salsa's Radio Battle (Part 1)," *Soho Weekly News*, March 4, 1976; "Salsa's Radio Battle (Part 2)," *Soho Weekly News*, April 15, 1976.
11. Epigram to Julie Coryell and Laura Friedman, *Jazz-Rock Fusion* (Delacorte, 1978), p. ii.
12. See Frederic Dannen's memorable account of the label's hijinks in *Hit Men* (Crown, 1990), pp. 161–81.
13. Howard Mandel, liner notes to *Wildflowers: The New York Loft Jazz Sessions* (Knit Classics reissue, 1999).
14. Gary Giddins, "The Highs and Lows of a Great Jazz Club," *Village Voice*, February 10, 1976. See also Andy Schwartz, "The Tin Palace," in *Perfect Sound Forever*, www.furious.com/perfect/tinpalace.html (accessed 3/11).
15. Peter Keepnews, "To Africa and Beyond," *Soho Weekly News*, May 20, 1976, p. 34.
16. See the 1978 Swedish TV documentary *Don Cherry: Det Aer inte min music* (It Is Not My Music), directed by Urban Lasson (www.youtube.com/watch?v=6S9eGFOcBEY, accessed 5/10).
17. Gary Giddins, "Don Cherry: Sa Ri Ga Ma Pa Dha Ni Sa," *Village Voice*, June 9, 1975, p. 112; Peter Ochiogrosso, "Getting in Touch with Planet Earth," *Soho Weekly News*, June 5, 1975.
18. Gary Giddins, "Rabbi Monk Reasserts His Mastery," *Village Voice*, April 12, 1976, p. 99.
19. Gary Valentine, "Blondies Behind Bars," *New York Rocker*, March 1976, p. 4. Valentine comes clean about smoking a joint that night in his autobiography, also titled *New York Rocker* (Thunder's Mouth Press, 2006), pp. 117–20.
20. David Byrne, "David Byrne's Laundry Hints," *New York Rocker*, March 1976, p. 6. See also Heylin, *From the Velvets to the Voidoids*, pp. 242–43.
21. Philip Glass, *Music by Philip Glass* (Harper & Row, 1987), p. 37.
22. Ibid., p. 35.
23. Tim Lawrence, *Hold On to Your Dreams: Arthur Russell and the Downtown Music Scene 1973–1992* (Duke University Press, 2009), p. 107.
24. Rhys Chatham, Notes on *Guitar Trio (1977)*. From booklet included with CD box set *An Angel Moves Too Fast to See: Selected Works 1971–1989* (Table of the Elements, 2002).
25. Interview with the composer, 2009.
26. Rhys Chatham, Notes on *Guitar Trio (1977)*, op. cit.

27. Robert Palmer, "Extraordinary Sound Is Produced by Reich," *New York Times*, April 26, 1976, p. 53.

28. Bockris and Bayley, *Patti Smith*, pp. 148–49.

29. Larry Harris, *And Party Every Day: The Inside Story of Casablanca Records* (Backbeat, 2009), p. 148.

30. See Miles, "Patti Smith: At Last, the Lower Manhattan Show," *New Musical Express*, May 22, 1976, accessed at www.rocksbackpages.com/article.html?ArticleID= 712&SearchText=Patti+Smith (3/11).

31. As quoted in Bockris and Bayley, *Patti Smith*, p. 154; Mary Harron, "Johnny Rotten—To the Core," *Punk* no. 8, March 1977.

32. Gene Simmons, quote in booklet for *Kissology: The Ultimate Kiss Collection, Vol. 1 1974–1977* (VH1 Classic).

33. Bockris and Bayley, *Patti Smith*, p. 150.

34. Danny Fields, column, *Soho Weekly News*, March 11, 1976. See also McNeil and McCain, *Please Kill Me*, pp. 272–77; John Holstrom and Mark Rosenthal, "The Dictators Story," *Punk*, 1977, reprinted at www.thedictators.com/punkmag.html (accessed 3/11).

35. Lester Bangs, "Who Are the Real Dictators?" Unpublished piece, 1976. Originally posted at Punkmagazine.com, reposted at www.jimdero.com/Bangs/Bangs%20Punk .htm (accessed 3/11).

36. Frank Lauria, "The Grass Is Gone," *Soho Weekly News*, July 8, 1976, p. 6.

37. Valentine, *New York Rocker*, p. 130.

38. Stewart, *Graffiti Kings*, p. 178.

39. Leigh and McNeil, *I Slept with Joey Ramone*, p. 151.

40. Jon Savage, *England's Dreaming* (St. Martin's Press, 1992), pp. 178, 194.

41. Leigh and McNeil, *I Slept with Joey Ramone*, pp. 151–52.

42. John Robb, *Punk Rock: An Oral History* (Ebury Press, 2006), pp. 198, 201.

43. Geoffrey Stokes, "Let Them Eat Smack," *Village Voice*, June 14, 1976.

44. Bowman, *This Must Be the Place*, p. 85.

45. James Wolcott, "John Cale Refuses to Die," *Village Voice*, August 2, 1976, p. 71.

46. Yvonne Sewall-Ruskin, *High on Rebellion: Inside the Underground at Max's Kansas City* (Thunder's Mouth Press, 1998), p. 274.

47. Philip Glass, *Music by Philip Glass*, p. 58.

48. Ibid., p. 48.

49. Robb Baker, "Waves of Power," *Soho Weekly News*, August 12, 1976, p. 13.

50. Pete Hamill, "New York Has Its Best Summer," *Village Voice*, August 23, 1976, p. 11.

51. Howard Smith and Brian Van der Horst, "Garden of Ego," *Village Voice*, October 4, 1976, p. 26.

52. Clark Whelton, "What Price Peace in the Park?" *Village Voice*, September 27, 1976, p. 16; Frederic C. Weiss, "Washington Sq. Riot Is Not Over," *Soho Weekly News*, September 23, 1976, p. 6.

53. Lawrence, *Love Saves the Day*, pp. 242–43.

54. www.nii.net/~obie1/deadcd/wall_of_sound.htm (accessed 3/11).

55. Lawrence, *Love Saves the Day*, p. 237.

56. Ibid., p. 242.

57. Old-school addresses compiled at www.b-boys.com/classic/hiphoptapes.html (accessed 3/11).

58. Grandmaster Flash with David Ritz, *The Adventures of Grandmaster Flash* (Broadway, 2008), pp. 120–26. There's no known recording of the September '76 jam—indeed, there are no recordings of hip-hop parties from the '73–'76 era in circulation, as far as I can tell—but there is an extraordinary one of Grandmaster Flash and the Furious Four (Mr. Ness, Melle Mel, Kid Creole, and Cowboy) performing at the Audubon Ballroom dated December 23, 1978, that's not hard to find: www.youtube.com/watch?v=bWBucLnKRZU.

59. Bowman, *This Must Be the Place*, p. 88; see also Source Notes, p. 369.

60. Lawrence, *Hold On to Your Dreams*, pp. 89–90, 102–103.

61. Ibid., pp. 126–27.

62. César Rondón, translated by Francis R. Aparicio, with Jackie White, *The Book of Salsa* (University of North Carolina Press, 2008), pp. 100–101. A tremendous addition to the scant amount of English language scholarship on '70s salsa.

63. Joe Conzo, *Mambo Diablo: My Journey with Tito Puente* (AuthorHouse, 2010), pp. 338–39. Conzo was Puente's best friend and right-hand man; this is as intimate a profile of the great bandleader as we will probably ever get.

64. Ivan Sanchez and Luis "Disco Wiz" Cedeño, *It's Just Begun* (Powerhouse, 2009), p. 45.

65. Jim Fricke and Charlie Ahearn, eds., *Yes Yes Y'all*, pp. 44–52.

66. Lester Bangs, "Peter Frampton Is Nice, Nice, Nice," *Village Voice*, October 25, 1976, p. 71.

67. Mitchell, *Sonic Transmission: Television, Tom Verlaine, Richard Hell*, pp. 68–69.

68. Heylin, *From the Velvets to the Voidoids*, pp. 258–59.

69. Nobakht, *Suicide: No Compromise*, p. 84.

70. Gary Giddins, "Ali and Jenkins Blow Swiftly," *Village Voice*, September 6, 1976.

71. Dan Oppenheimer, "The Outcasts of WRVR," *Soho Weekly News*, December 9, 1976, p. 37.

72. www.schmitt-hall-studios.com/ron/JohnCale_Set.List.htm (accessed 3/11).

73. Ross Wetzsteon, "There's No Business Like the Avant-Garde Business," *Village Voice*, December 6, 1976, pp. 23–28. Glass, pp. 53–55. My description is drawn largely from Wetzsteon's vividly reported piece; the bit about the *Einstein* audience is from Glass's memoir *Music By Philip Glass*, p. 53. He was right, but only to an extent. The Met hardly became a bastion of the avant-garde.

74. Interview with the artist, 2010. See also Paula Court, *New York Noise* (Soul Jazz, 2007), p. 200.

75. Alexander Cockburn, "Press Clips," *Village Voice*, December 13, 1976, p. 41.

76. Jonathan Mahler, *Ladies and Gentlemen, the Bronx Is Burning* (Farrar, Straus and Giroux, 2005), pp. 33, 72–76.

77. Ibid., p. 46.

78. Nina Antonia, *Johnny Thunders . . . In Cold Blood*, p. 75.

79. McNeil and McCain, *Please Kill Me*, p. 262.

80. Vivian Gornick, "Born Again at the Plaza Club," *Village Voice*, November 22, 1976. Also Mahler, *Ladies and Gentlemen, the Bronx Is Burning*, p. 67.

81. Joe Brancatelli, "Computer Logic Says Your Home Is Next," *Village Voice*, November 15, 1976, p. 65; Robert Smith, "The Fight to Ban Video Recorders," *Village Voice*, December 20, 1976, p. 85.

1977: LA RESURRECCIÓN

1. The Clash, "1977," from *The Clash* (CBS UK, 1977).
2. Dillinger, "Cokane in My Brain," from *CB200* (Island, 1976).
3. Robert Christgau, "Save This Rock&Roll Hero," *Village Voice*, January 17, 1977, pp. 14–16.
4. Interview with Stanley Snadowsky and Allan Pepper, supplement to *Soho Weekly News*, February 10, 1977.
5. Bockris and Bayley, *Patti Smith*, pp. 166–67. See also Julie Burchill and Tony Parsons, *The Boy Looked at Johnny* (Faber and Faber, 1987).
6. As quoted in Bockris and Bayley, *Patti Smith*, p. 175. The description of Smith's accident is drawn mainly from this book and Patricia Morrisroe's excellent *Mapplethorpe: A Biography*, pp. 174–76.
7. As quoted in Bockris and Bayley, *Patti Smith*, p. 178.
8. Morrisroe, *Mapplethorpe*, pp. 177–80.
9. Nobakht, *Suicide: No Compromise*, p. 81.
10. Ibid., 91.
11. Bert Blanco, "Musica Jibara . . . and Salsa," *Latin N.Y.*, March 1977, pp. 18–20.
12. Louis Laffitte, "Eddie Palmieri: the Sun of Latin Music Part 2," *Latin Beat Magazine*, August 2002.
13. Sanchez and Cedeño, *It's Just Begun*, p. 46.
14. Mark Skillz, "One Night at the Executive Playhouse," *Hip Hop 101A* blog, hiphop101a.blogspot.com/2007/05/one-night-at-executive-playhouse.html (accessed 3/11). Originally published in *Wax Poetics*.
15. Vince Aletti, *The Disco Files 1973–78* (Djhistory.com, 1998), pp. 260–63; Harris, *And Party Every Day*, pp. 181–83.
16. Howard Smith and Brian Van der Horst, "Scenes," *Village Voice*, March 14, 1977.
17. Arthur Bell, "Looking for Mr. Gaybar," *Village Voice*, January 24, 1977, pp. 19–20.
18. Mahler, *Ladies and Gentlemen, the Bronx Is Burning*, p. 123.
19. Dennis Hamill, "A Brooklyn Neighborhood Battles City Hall," pp. 30–31.
20. Alexander Cockburn and Jack Newfield, "Why We Hate the Subways."
21. Mitchell, *Sonic Transmission*, p. 87.
22. Leigh and McNeil, *I Slept with Joey Ramone*, pp. 173–74.
23. Albertine told this story onstage at the Knitting Factory in Brooklyn in 2009 during a rambling, riveting solo set, opening up for her punk-veteran compadres the Raincoats.
24. Lawrence, *Hold On to Your Dreams*, p. 103.
25. Ibid., p. 105.
26. Cruz, *Celia: My Life*, p. 124.
27. Aletti, *The Disco Files 1973–1978*, pp. 282–89.
28. Ibid., p. 286.
29. Lawrence, *Hold On to Your Dreams*, p. 273; Anthony Haden-Guest, *The Last Party* (It, 2009), pp. 45–46.
30. Ibid., 272.
31. David Sheppard, *On Some Faraway Beach: The Life and Times of Brian Eno* (Chicago Review Press, 2009), p. 249.
32. Lawrence, *Hold On to Your Dreams*, pp. 285–86.

33. Stanley Crouch, "Jazz Lofts: A Walk Through the Wild Sounds," *New York Times*, April 17, 1977.
34. Benjamin Looker, *Point from Which Creation Begins: The Black Artists' Group of St. Louis* (Missouri Historical Society Press, 2004), pp. 232–33.
35. As reprinted in Whitney Balliett, *Collected Works* (St. Martin's Press, 2000), pp. 497–503. See also Lewis, *Born in the Bronx*, p. 344.
36. Hubert Saal and Abigail Kuflik, "Jazz Comes Back!," *Newsweek*, August 8, 1977.
37. Judith Coburn, "Far Up! Terrifying! God Bless!," *Village Voice*, June 6, 1977.
38. Glass, *Music by Philip Glass*, pp. 55–56, 88.
39. K. Robert Schwarz, *Minimalists* (Phaidon, 1996), pp. 84–86.
40. Jim DeRogatis, *Let It Blurt* (Broadway Books, 2000), pp. 145–46, 152.
41. Antonia, *Johnny Thunders . . . In Cold Blood*, p. 81.
42. Scott Muni aircheck, WNEW-FM, 7/14/77, www.scottmuni.com/audio/.
43. Allen Tannenbaum and Roberta Bayley, oral history bits from "Where Were You When the Lights Went Out? The Blackout of 1977," *Powerhouse Magazine* no. 2, June 2007, pp. 90–91.
44. Robert Palmer, "Pop Music: Modern Meets Rock," *New York Times*, May 6, 1977.
45. Lawrence, *Hold On to Your Dreams*, p. 107.
46. Ibid., p. 109.
47. David McGee, "Bruce Springsteen Reclaims the Future," *Rolling Stone*, August 11, 1977.
48. http://brucebase.wikispaces.com/1977#070277.
49. Charles M. Young, "Rock Is Sick and Living in London," *Rolling Stone*, October 20, 1977.
50. Lester Bangs, "How Long Will We Care?" *Village Voice*, August 29, 1977.
51. Craig Castleman, "The Origins of Graffiti," in Murray Forman and Mark Anthony Neal, eds., *That's The Joint!: The Hip-Hop Studies Reader* (Routledge, 2011), pp. 39–41. In his bio, *It's Just Begun*, Wiz recalls the battle as taking place in the summer at the Webster Police Athletic League gym. The VH1 documentary *NY77* depicts it as happening outdoors. Queen's "We Will Rock You," the flip of a double-A-side single with "We Are the Champions," wasn't released until October 7. Specifics aside, it's a great story.
52. Much of this description is drawn from the excellent VH1 documentary *NY77*, www.youtube.com/watch?v=iuFWzU6xwA0 (accessed 1/10).
53. Lewis, *Born in the Bronx*, pp. 194–95.
54. Mahler, *Ladies and Gentlemen, the Bronx Is Burning*, pp. 260–64.
55. Lawrence, *Hold On to Your Dreams*, pp. 290–92.
56. Mahler, *Ladies and Gentlemen, the Bronx Is Burning*, pp. 299–301.
57. Ibid., p. 301.
58. Dave Marsh, *Born to Run: The Bruce Springsteen Story Volume 1* (Thunder's Mouth Press, 1996), pp. 173–76; Bockris and Bayley, *Patti Smith*, pp. 183–84.
59. McNeil and McCain, *Please Kill Me*, pp. 288–90.
60. Savage, *England's Dreaming*, p. 430.
61. Sheppard, *On Some Faraway Beach*, pp. 268–70.
62. Lawrence, *Hold On to Your Dreams*, pp. 137–38.
63. As mentioned in Howard Smith and Leslie Harlib's "Scenes" column, *Village Voice*, January 23, 1978.

64. Greil Marcus, "Ramones Loosen Up," *Village Voice*, December 12, 1977.
65. Allan Wolper, "Blowing Up the South Bronx," *Soho Weekly News*, January 5, 1978.
66. I drew this scene from Lee's lengthy interview in Craig Castleman's *Getting Up: Subway Graffiti in New York* (MIT Press, 1999) and Jack Stewart's descriptions and photos in *Graffiti Kings*. Both are seminal texts on the graffiti era's early years.
67. Interview with Lee in Castleman, *Getting Up*, pp. 3–17.
68. Interview with Gilbert "El Pulpo" Colón, 2008, www.descarga.com/cgi-bin/db/archives/Interview57.
69. Shapiro, *Turn the Beat Around*, pp. 103–104.
70. Greg Milner, *Perfecting Sound Forever: An Aural History of Recorded Music* (Faber and Faber, 2009), pp. 198, 201–202.
71. Some random notes on the Anderson Theater from an ex–New Yorker blogging in 2005 as "Signed D.C." from Toronto, streetsyoucrossed.blogspot.com/2005/07/still-hangin-out-on-second-avenue.html.
72. Bob Weiner, column, *Soho Weekly News*, January 5, 1978.
73. Daryl Easlea, *Everybody Dance: Chic and the Politics of Disco* (Helter Skelter, 2004), pp. 114–15.

EPILOGUE

1. kauhajokinyt.fi/~jplaitio/levykans/markykirje020104.html#japan (accessed 3/11). The Internet is crazy.
2. As Springsteen told Elvis Costello on the show *Spectacle*, January 2010.
3. Gary Giddins and Scott DeVeaux, *Jazz* (W. W. Norton, 2009), p. 471.
4. Keith Potter, *Four Musical Minimalists* (Cambridge University Press, 2000), pp. 246, 249.
5. Glass, *Music by Philip Glass*, pp. 55–56, 88.
6. www.youtube.com/watch?v=ken0A39FY1A.
7. See *The Sam Rivers Sessionography* by Rick Lopez, www.bb10k.com/RIVERS.disc.html#76.00.00-2 (accessed 3/11); author conversation with Richard Lloyd before his gig at Otto's Shrunken Head on East Fourteenth Street, January 2008.
8. *Mojo*, October 2005, via www.springsteenlyrics.com/lyrics/d/dreambabydream.php.

BIBLIOGRAPHY

Adler, Bill. *Tougher Than Leather: The Rise of Run DMC*. Los Angeles: Consafos Press, 2002.

Alava, Silvio H. *Spanish Harlem's Musical Legacy, 1930–1938*. Chicago: Arcadia Publishing, 2007.

Aletti, Vince. *The Disco Files, 1973–1978*. London: Djhistory.com, 1998.

Alkyer, Frank, ed. *The Miles Davis Reader: Interviews and Features from DownBeat Magazine*. New York: Hal Leonard Books, 2007.

Anderson, Iain. *This Is Our Music: Free Jazz, the Sixties, and American Culture*. Philadelphia: University of Pennsylvania Press, 2007.

Anderson, Laurie. *Stories from the Nerve Bible: A Retrospective, 1972–1992*. New York: HarperCollins, 1994.

Antonia, Nina. *Johnny Thunders . . . in Cold Blood*. London: Cherry Red Books, 2000.

———. *Too Much Too Soon: The Makeup & Breakup of the New York Dolls*. London: Omnibus Press, 1998.

Balliett, Whitney. *Collected Works: A Journal of Jazz, 1954–2000*. New York: St. Martin's Press, 2000.

Bangs, Lester. *Psychotic Reactions and Carburetor Dung*. Edited by Greil Marcus. New York: Alfred A. Knopf, 1987.

———. *Mainlines, Blood Feasts, and Bad Taste: A Lester Bangs Reader*. Edited by John Morthland. New York: Anchor Books, 2003.

Beeber, Steven Lee. *The Heebie-Jeebies at CBGB's: A Secret History of Jewish Punk*. Chicago: Chicago Review Press, 2006.

Bessman, Jim, with the Ramones. *Ramones: An American Band*. New York: St. Martin's Press, 1993.

Bockris, Victor. *Keith Richards: The Biography*. New York: Da Capo Press, 2003.

———. *Transformer: The Lou Reed Story*. New York: Da Capo Press, 1997.

Bockris, Victor, and Roberta Bayley. *Patti Smith: An Unauthorized Biography*. New York: Simon & Schuster, 1999.

Bockris, Victor, and John Cale. *What's Welsh for Zen: The Autobiography of John Cale*. New York: Bloomsbury Publishing, 1999.

Boggs, Vernon W. *Salsiology*. Westport, CT: Greenwood Press, 1992.

Bowman, David. *This Must Be the Place: The Adventures of Talking Heads in the 20th Century*. New York: HarperEntertainment, 2001.

Broughton, Frank, and Bill Brewster. *Last Night a DJ Saved My Life*. New York: Grove Press, 2000.

Buckland, Gail. *Who Shot Rock & Roll: A Photographic History, 1955–Present*. New York: Alfred A. Knopf, 2009.

Caro, Robert A. *The Power Broker: Robert Moses and the Fall of New York*. New York: Vintage Books, 1975.

Castleman, Craig. *Getting Up*. Cambridge, MA: MIT Press, 1982.

Cepeda, Raquel, ed. *And It Won't Stop*. New York: Faber and Faber, 2004.

Chang, Jeff. *Can't Stop Won't Stop*. New York: St. Martin's Press, 2005.

———, ed. *Total Chaos: The Art and Aesthetics of Hip-Hop*. New York: Basic Civitas Books, 2006.

Charnas, Dan. *The Big Payback*. New York: New American Library, 2010.

Cheron, Mel, with Gabriel Rotello. *My Life and the Paradise Garage/Keep On Dancin'*. New York: 24 Hours for Life, 2000.

Conzo, Joe, with David A. Pérez. *Mambo Diablo: My Journey with Tito Puente*. Bloomington, IN: AuthorHouse, 2010.

County, Jayne, with Rupert Smith. *Man Enough to Be a Woman*. New York: Serpent's Tail, 1995.

Crouch, Stanley. *Considering Genius: Writings on Jazz*. New York: Basic Civitas Books, 2006.

Cruz, Celia, with Ana Cristina Reymundo. *Celia*. New York: Rayo, 2004.

Currid, Elizabeth. *The Warhol Economy: How Fashion, Art, and Music Drive New York City*. Princeton, NJ: Princeton University Press, 2007.

Dávila, Arlene. *Barrio Dreams: Puerto Ricans, Latinos, and the Neoliberal City*. Los Angeles: University of California Press, 2004.

Davis, Francis. *Jazz and Its Discontents: A Francis Davis Reader*. Cambridge, MA: Da Capo Press, 2004.

Davis, Miles, with Quincy Troupe. *Miles, The Autobiography*. New York: Touchstone, 1989.

DeGroot, Gerard. *The Seventies Unplugged*. London: Macmillan, 2010.

DeRogatis, Jim. *Let It Blurt: The Life & Times of Lester Bangs, America's Greatest Rock Critic*. New York: Broadway Books, 2000.

———. *The Velvet Underground: An Illustrated History of a Walk on the Wild Side*. Minneapolis: Voyageur Press, 2009.

Easlea, Daryl. *Everybody Dance*. London: Helter Skelter Publishing, 2004.

Eliot, Mark, with Mike Appel. *Down Thunder Road: The Making of Bruce Springsteen*. New York: Simon & Schuster, 1992.

Fernandez, Raul A. *From Afro-Cuban Rhythm to Latin Jazz*. Los Angeles: University of California Press, 2006.

Fink, Robert. *Repeating Ourselves: American Minimal Music as Cultural Practice*. Los Angeles: University of California Press, 2005.

Fletcher, Tony. *All Hopped Up and Ready to Go: Music from the Streets of New York, 1927–77*. New York: W. W. Norton, 2009.

Freeman, Phil. *New York Is Now: The New Wave of Free Jazz*. Brooklyn: The Telegraph Company, 2001.

Fricke, James, and Charlie Ahearn, eds. *Yes Yes Y'all: The Experience Music Project Oral History of Hip-Hop's First Decade*. Cambridge, MA: Da Capo Press, 2002.

Fuentes, Leonardo Padura. *Faces of Salsa*. Washington, DC: Smithsonian Institution, 2003.

García, David. *Arsenio Rodríguez and the Transnational Flows of Latin Popular Music*. Philadelphia: Temple University Press, 2006.

Gendron, Bernard. *Between Montmartre and the Mudd Club: Popular Music and the Avant-Garde*. Chicago: University of Chicago Press, 2002.

George-Warren, Holly. *Punk 365*. New York: Harry N. Abrams, 2007.

Gerard, Charley, with Marty Sheller. *Salsa: The Rhythm of Latin Music*. Tempe, AZ: White Cliffs Media Company, 1989.

Giddins, Gary. *Weather Bird: Jazz at the Dawn of Its Second Century*. New York: Oxford University Press, 2004.

Giddins, Gary, and Scott DeVeaux. *Jazz*. New York: W. W. Norton, 2009.

Gilbert, Pat. *Passion Is a Fashion: The Real Story of the Clash*. Cambridge, MA: Da Capo Press, 2005.

Glass, Philip. *Music by Philip Glass*. New York: Harper & Row, 1987.

Goldberg, RoseLee. *Laurie Anderson*. New York: Harry N. Abrams, 2000.

Gooch, Curt. *Kiss Alive Forever: The Complete Touring History*. New York: Billboard Books, 2002.

Grandmaster Flash with David Ritz. *The Adventures of Grandmaster Flash: My Life, My Beats*. New York: Broadway Books, 2008.

Gruen, Bob. *New York Dolls: The Photographs of Bob Gruen*. New York: Abrams Image, 2008.

Haden-Guest, Anthony. *The Last Party*. New York: It Books, 2009.

Harris, Larry. *And Party Every Day*. New York: Backbeat Books, 2009.

Hebdige, Dick. *Subculture: The Meaning of Style*. London: Routledge, 1979.

Heylin, Clinton. *Bob Dylan: Behind the Shades Revisited*. New York: HarperCollins, 2003.

———. *From the Velvets to the Voidoids: The Birth of American Punk Rock*. Chicago: A Capella Books, 2005.

Holman, Bob, and Miguel Algarín, eds. *Aloud*. New York: Henry Holt, 1994.

Isoardi, Steven L. *The Dark Tree: Jazz and the Community Arts in Los Angeles*. Berkeley and Los Angeles: University of California Press, 2006.

Jowitt, Deborah, ed. *Meredith Monk*. Baltimore: The Johns Hopkins University Press, 1997.

Kahn, Douglas. *Noise, Water, Meat: A History of Sound in the Arts*. Cambridge, MA: MIT Press, 2001.

Kane, Arthur. *I, Doll: Life and Death with the New York Dolls*. Chicago: Chicago Review Press, 2009.

Kasher, Steven, ed. *Max's Kansas City: Art, Glamour, Rock and Roll*. New York: Abrams Image, 2010.

Kent, Nick. *Apathy for the Devil: A 70s Memoir*. Cambridge, MA: Da Capo Press, 2010.

Killen, Andreas. *1973 Nervous Breakdown: Watergate, Warhol, and the Birth of Post-Sixties America*. New York: Bloomsbury USA, 2006.

Kozak, Roman. *This Ain't No Disco: The Story of CBGB*. Winchester, MA: Faber and Faber, 1988.

Kruth, John. *Bright Moments: The Life and Legacy of Rahsaan Roland Kirk*. New York: Welcome Rain Publishers, 2000.

Kugelberg, Johan, ed. *Born in the Bronx*. New York: Rizzoli International Publications, 2007.

———, ed. *The Velvet Underground: New York Art*. New York: Rizzoli International Publications, 2009.

Kuntz, Tom, and Phil Kuntz. *The Sinatra Files: The Secret FBI Dossier*. New York: Three Rivers Press, 2000.

Lawrence, Tim. *Hold On to Your Dreams*. Durham, NC: Duke University Press, 2009.

———. *Love Saves the Day*. Durham, NC: Duke University Press, 2003.

Leigh, Mickey, with Legs McNeil. *I Slept with Joey Ramone*. New York: Touchstone, 2009.

Lesh, Phil. *Searching for the Sound: My Life with the Grateful Dead*. New York: Little, Brown, 2005.

Lewis, George E. *A Power Stronger Than Itself: The AACM and American Experimental Music*. Chicago: University of Chicago Press, 2008.

Licht, Alan. *Sound Art: Beyond Music, Between Categories*. New York: Rizzoli International Publications, 2007.

Lindberg, Ulf. *Rock Criticism from the Beginning: Amusers, Bruisers, and Cool-Headed Cruisers*. New York: Peter Lang Publishing, 2005.

Litweiler, John. *Ornette Coleman: A Harmolodic Life*. New York: William Morrow, 1992.

Lock, Graham. *Forces in Motion: The Music and Thoughts of Anthony Braxton*. Cambridge, MA: Da Capo Press, 1988.

Long, Kat. *The Forbidden Apple: A Century of Sex & Sin in New York City*. Brooklyn, NY: Ig Publishing, 2009.

Looker, Benjamin. *"Point from which Creation Begins": The Black Artists' Group of St. Louis*. St. Louis: The Missouri Historical Society Press, 2004.

Lydon, John, with Keith and Kent Zimmerman. *Rotten: No Irish, No Blacks, No Dogs*. New York: Picador, 1994.

Mahler, Jonathan. *Ladies and Gentlemen, the Bronx Is Burning: 1977, Baseball, and the Battle for the Soul of the City*. New York: Farrar, Straus and Giroux, 2005.

Mandel, Howard. *Future Jazz*. New York: Oxford University Press, 1999.

———. *Miles, Ornette, Cecil: Jazz Beyond Jazz*. New York: Routledge, 2008.

Marsh, Dave. *Born to Run: The Bruce Springsteen Story, Volume I*. New York: Thunder's Mouth Press, 1996.

Matheu, Robert, and Brian J. Bowe. *Creem: America's Only Rock 'n' Roll Magazine*. New York: Collins, 2007.

McCoy, Alfred W. *The Politics of Heroin: CIA Complicity in the Global Drug Trade*. Chicago: Lawrence Hill Books, 2003.

McDonnell, Evelyn and Ann Powers, eds. *Rock She Wrote: Women Write About Rock, Pop, and Rap*. New York: Delta, 1995.

McNeil, Legs, and Gillian McCain. *Please Kill Me: The Uncensored Oral History of Punk*. New York: Grove Press, 1996.

Melendez, Mickey. *We Took the Streets*. New York: St. Martin's Press, 2003.

Miles, Barry. *William Burroughs: El Hombre Invisible*. New York: Hyperion, 1992.

Milkowski, Bill. *Rockers, Jazzbos & Visionaries*. New York: Billboard Books, 1998.

Milner, Greg. *Perfecting Sound Forever: An Aural History of Recorded Music*. New York: Faber and Faber, 2009.

Mitchell, Tim. *Sonic Transmission: Television, Tom Verlaine, Richard Hell*. London: Glitterbooks, 2006.

———. *There's Something About Jonathan: Jonathan Richman and the Modern Lovers*. London: Peter Owen Publishers, 2000.

Morales, Ed. *The Latin Beat*. Cambridge, MA: Da Capo Press, 2003.

———. *Living in Spanglish*. New York: St. Martin's Press, 2002.

Morgan, Ted. *Literary Outlaw: The Life and Times of William S. Burroughs*. New York: Henry Holt, 1988.

Morrisroe, Patricia. *Mapplethorpe: A Biography*. New York: Da Capo Press, 1997.

Nicholson, Stuart. *Jazz-Rock: A History*. New York: Schirmer Books, 1998.

Nobakht, David. *Suicide: No Compromise*. London: SAF Publishing, 2005.

Nyman, Michael. *Experimental Music: Cage and Beyond*. Cambridge, UK: Cambridge University Press, 1999.

Odegard, Kevin, and Andy Gill. *A Simple Twist of Fate: Bob Dylan and the Making of Blood on the Tracks*. Cambridge, MA: Da Capo Press, 2005.

Palmer, Robert. *Blues & Chaos: The Music Writing of Robert Palmer*. Edited by Anthony Decurtis. New York: Scribner, 2009.

Peck, Abe, ed. *Dancing Madness*. Garden City, NY: Rolling Stone Press, 1976.

Peterson, Gilles, and Stuart Baker, eds. *Freedom Rhythm & Sound: Revolutionary Jazz Original Cover Art, 1965–83*. London: SJR Publishing, 2009.

Porter, Dick, and Kris Needs. *Trash!: The Complete New York Dolls*. London: Plexus Publishing, 2006.

Potter, Keith. *Four Musical Minimalists*. Cambridge, UK: Cambridge University Press, 2000.

Prial, Dunstan. *The Producer: John Hammond and the Soul of American Music*. New York: Farrar, Straus and Giroux, 2006.

Radano, Ronald M. *New Musical Figurations: Anthony Braxton's Cultural Critique*. Chicago: University of Chicago Press, 1993.

Ratliff, Ben. *Coltrane: The Story of a Sound*. New York: Farrar, Straus and Giroux, 2007.

Riley, Tim. *Fever: How Rock 'n' Roll Transformed Gender in America*. New York: St. Martin's Press, 2004.

Robb, John. *Punk Rock: An Oral History*. London: Ebury Press, 2006.

Roberts, John Storm. *Black Music of Two Worlds*. Tivoli, NY: Original Music, 1972.

———. *The Latin Tinge*. Tivoli, NY: Original Music, 1985.

Rockwell, John. *All American Music: Composition in the Late Twentieth Century*. New York: Da Capo Press, 1997.

Rombes, Nicholas. *A Cultural Dictionary of Punk, 1974–1982*. New York: Continuum, 2009.

Rondón, César. translated by Francis R. Aparicio with Jackie White, *The Book of Salsa*. Chapel Hill: University of North Carolina Press, 2008.

Ross, Alex. *The Rest Is Noise: Listening to the Twentieth Century*. New York: Farrar, Straus and Giroux, 2007.

Salazar, Max. *Mambo Kingdom*. New York: Schirmer Trade Books, 2002.

Sanchez, Ivan, and Luis Cedeño. *It's Just Begun.* New York, NY: powerHouse Publishing, 2009.

Sante, Luc. *Kill All Your Darlings: Pieces, 1990–2005.* Portland, OR: YETI/Verse Chorus Press, 2007.

———. *Low Life: Lures and Snares of Old New York.* New York: Farrar, Straus and Giroux, 2003.

Santelli, Robert. *Greetings from E Street: The Story of Bruce Springsteen and the E Street Band.* San Francisco: Chronicle Books, 2006.

Savage, Jon. *England's Dreaming: Anarchy, Sex Pistols, Punk Rock, and Beyond.* New York: St. Martin's Press, 1992.

Schloss, Joseph G. *Foundation.* New York: Oxford University Press, 2009.

Schwarz, K. Robert. *Minimalists.* London: Phaidon Press, 1996.

Sewall-Ruskin, Yvonne. *High on Rebellion: Inside the Underground at Max's.* New York: Thunder's Mouth Press, 1998.

Shapiro, Marc. *Passion and Pain.* New York: St. Martin's Griffin, 2007.

Shapiro, Peter. *Turn the Beat Around.* New York: Faber and Faber, 2005.

Shaw, Suzy, and Mick Farren, eds. *Bomp!* Pasadena, CA: Ammo Books, 2007.

Shepard, Sam. *The Rolling Thunder Logbook.* Cambridge, MA: Da Capo Press, 2004.

Sheppard, David. *On Some Faraway Beach: The Life and Times of Brian Eno.* Chicago: Chicago Review Press, 2009.

Silverman, Kenneth. *Begin Again: A Biography of John Cage.* New York: Alfred A. Knopf, 2010.

Smith, Patti. *Just Kids.* New York: HarperCollins, 2010.

———. *Patti Smith Complete: Lyrics, Notes and Reflections.* New York: Anchor Books, 1999.

Steenstra, Styze. *Song and Circumstance: The Work of David Byrne from Talking Heads to the Present.* New York: Continuum, 2010.

Steward, Sue. *¡Musica!* San Francisco: Chronicle Books, 1999.

Stewart, Jack. *Graffiti Kings.* New York: Abrams, 2009.

Stosuy, Brandon, ed. *Up Is Up, but So Is Down: New York's Downtown Literary Scene.* New York: New York University Press, 2006.

Sublette, Ned. *Cuba and Its Music.* Chicago: Chicago Review Press, 2004.

Sweet, Robert E. *Music Universe, Music Mind: Revisiting the Creative Music Studio, Woodstock, NY.* Ann Arbor, MI: Arborville Publishing, 1996.

Szwed, John F. *Space Is the Place: The Lives and Times of Sun Ra.* New York: Pantheon Books, 1997.

Taylor, Marvin J., ed. *The Downtown Book: The New York Art Scene, 1974–1984.* Princeton, NJ: Princeton University Press, 2006.

Thompson, Dave. *Dancing Barefoot: The Patti Smith Story.* Chicago, IL: Chicago Review Press, 2011.

Tompkins, Dave. *How to Wreck a Nice Beach.* Brooklyn, NY: Melville House Publishing, 2010.

Troupe, Quincy. *Miles and Me.* Berkeley and Los Angeles: University of California Press, 2000.

Valentine, Gary. *New York Rocker: My Life in the Blank Generation with Blondie, Iggy Pop, and Others, 1974–1981.* New York: Thunder's Mouth Press, 2006.

Villoerente, David, and Todd Jams. *Mascots & Mugs.* New York: Testify Books, 2007.

Washburne, Christopher. *Sounding Salsa*. Philadelphia: Temple University Press, 2008.

Wax Poetics Anthology: Volume 1. Brooklyn, NY: Wax Poetics, 2007.

Wax Poetics Anthology: Volume 2. Brooklyn, NY: Wax Poetics, 2007.

Wein, George, with Nate Chinen. *Myself Among Others: A Life in Music*. Cambridge, MA: Da Capo Press, 2003.

Weisbard, Eric, ed. *Listen Again*. Durham, NC: Duke University Press, 2007.

Willis, Ellen. *Beginning to See the Light: Pieces of a Decade*. New York: Alfred A. Knopf, 1981.

———. *Out of the Vinyl Deeps: Ellen Willis on Rock Music*. Edited by Nona Willis Aronowitz. Minneapolis: University of Minnesota Press, 2011.

Wilmer, Valerie. *As Serious as Your Life: John Coltrane and Beyond*. London: Serpent's Tail, 1992.

Yedgar, Ariella, and Mark Sladen, eds. *Panic Attack: Art in the Punk Years*. London: Merrell Publishers, 2007.

Yglesias, Pablo. *¡Cocinando!* New York: Princeton Architectural Press, 2005.

Young, Rob, ed. *Undercurrents: The Hidden Wiring of Modern Music*. London: Continuum, 2007.

DISCOGRAPHY

Air, *Air Raid* (Whynot/Candid)

———, *Air Song* (Whynot/Candid)

Ali Plays the Blues featuring Royal Blue, *N.Y. Ain't So Bad* (Survival/Knitting Factory)

Anthony Braxton, *The Complete Arista Recordings of Anthony Braxton* (Arista/Mosaic)

———, *For Alto* (Delmark)

———, *In the Tradition Vol. 1* (Steeplechase)

———, *In the Tradition Vol. 2* (Steeplechase)

Arthur Russell, *Another Thought* (Point Music)

———, *Calling Out of Context* (Audika)

———, *First Thought Best Thought* (Audika)

———, *Love Is Overtaking Me* (Audika)

———, *The World of Arthur Russell* (Soul Jazz)

———, *World of Echo* (Audika)

Bee Gees, *The Ultimate Bee Gees* (Reprise)

Bernard Herrmann, *Taxi Driver Soundtrack* (Arista)

Bill Conti, *Rocky Soundtrack* (Capitol)

Blondie, *Blondie* (Private Stock/Chrysalis)

———, *Greatest Hits: Sound & Vision* (Capitol)

———, *Plastic Letters* (Chrysalis)

Blue Öyster Cult, *Agents of Fortune* (Columbia)

Bob Blank, *The Blank Generation: Blank Tapes NYC 1975–1985* (Strut)

Celia Cruz, *¡Azucar!* (Fania)

Celia Cruz and Johnny Pacheco, *Celia & Johnny* (Fania)

Celia Cruz and Willie Colón, *Only They Could Have Made This Album* (Vaya)

Cerrone, *Love in C Minor* (Malligator)

David Holland Quartet, *Conference of the Birds* (ECM)

David Murray, *Flowers for Albert: The Complete Concert* (India Navigation)

———, *Interboogieology* (Black Saint)

———, *Live at the Lower Manhattan Ocean Club: Volumes 1&2* (India Navigation)

———, *Low Class Conspiracy* (Adelphi)

Deodato, *Deodato 2* (Sony)
———, *Prelude* (CTI Records)
Don Cherry, *Brown Rice* (A&M/Universal)
Don Cherry, Dewey Redman, Charlie Haden, Eddie Blackwell, *Old and New Dreams* (Black Saint)
Double Exposure, *My Love Is Free: The Best of Double Exposure* (Koch)
Dr. Buzzard's Original Savannah Band (RCA)
Eddie Kendricks, *Keep On Truckin': The Motown Solo Albums, Vol. 1* (Motown)
Eddie Palmieri, *Lucumi, Macumba, Voodoo* (Epic/Sony Japan)
———, *Vámonos Pa'l Monte* (Fania)
Eddie Palmieri and Cal Tjader, *Bamboleate* (Fania)
Eddie Palmieri and Friends, *The Sun of Latin Music* (Coco Records)
Eddie Palmieri and Lalo Rodriguez, *Unfinished Masterpiece* (Coco/Musical Produc-tions/La Nota)
Eddie Palmieri with Israel Quintana, *Sentido* (Coco/Musical Productions/La Nota)
Fania All Stars, *Campeones* (Fania)
———, *Delicate And Jumpy* (Fania)
———, *Latin-Soul-Rock* (Fania)
———, *Live at Yankee Stadium Vol. 1* (Fania)
———, *Live at Yankee Stadium Vol. 2* (Fania)
———, *San Juan 73* (Fania)
———, *Tribute to Tito Rodriguez* (Fania)
Ghetto Brothers, *Power-Fuerza* (Mary Lou)
Glenn Branca, *Lesson No. 1* (99/Acute)
Grandmaster Caz, *Midlife Crisis* (self-released)
Grandmaster Flash, *Essential Mix: Classic Edition* (WSM)
Grover Washington, Jr., *Mister Magic* (Kudu/Motown)
Grupo Folklorico y Experimental Nuevayorquino, *Concepts in Unity* (Bethlehem/ Sony/Salsoul)
Harlem River Drive (Roulette/Stateside/EMI)
Harry Whitaker, *Black Renaissance* (Luv N' Haight)
Héctor Lavoe, *Comedia* (Fania)
———, *De Ti Depende* (Fania)
———, *La Voz* (Fania)
Herbie Hancock, *Head Hunters* (Columbia)
Iggy and the Stooges, *Double Danger: Academy of Music/Latin Casino—Live 1973* (Bomp)
———, *Raw Power* (Columbia)
Incredible Bongo Band, *Bongo Rock* (Mr. Bongo Records)
Isaac Hayes, *Black Moses* (Stax)
Jemeel Moondoc, *Muntu Recordings* (NoBusiness)
Jobriath, *Creatures of the Street* (Collector's Choice)
———, *Jobriath* (Collector's Choice)
Joe Bataan, *Joe Bataan Anthology* (Salsoul/Koch)
———, *Under the Streetlamps: Anthology, 1967–1972* (Fania)
Joe Cuba, *Cocinando la Salsa* (Fania)
———, *El Alcalde del Barrio* (Fania)

Joe Lee Wilson, *Shout for Trane* (Whynot/Candid)

John Cale, *The Academy in Peril* (Reprise)

———, *Fear* (Island)

———, *Helen of Troy* (Island)

———, *Paris 1919* (Reprise)

———, *Seducing Down the Door: A Collection, 1970–1990* (Rhino)

———, *Slow Dazzle* (Island)

———, *Vintage Violence* (Reprise)

John Cale, Tony Conrad, Angus Maclise, La Monte Young, Marian Zazeela, *Inside the Dream Syndicate, Volume I: Day of Niagara (1965)* (Table of the Elements)

Johnny Pacheco, *El Maestro* (Fania)

Johnny Pate, *Shaft in Africa* (Geffen)

Johnny Thunders, *After the Dolls, 1977–1987 (Track and Jungle Records Studio Sessions)* (Cleopatra)

Johnny Thunders and the Heartbreakers, *Down to Kill* (Jungle)

Julius Hemphill, *Dogon A.D.* (Arista Freedom)

Keith Jarrett, *The Köln Concert* (ECM)

———, *Fort Yawuh* (GRP)

Kid Creole, *Going Places: The August Darnell Years, 1974–1983* (Strut)

Lester Bowie, *The 5th Power* (Black Saint)

Lou Reed, *Berlin* (RCA)

———, *Coney Island Baby* (Legacy)

———, *Metal Machine Music* (RCA/Buddha)

———, *NYC Man: The Collection* (BMG Heritage)

———, *Rock and Roll Heart* (Arista)

———, *Rock N Roll Animal* (RCA)

———, *Sally Can't Dance* (RCA)

———, *Transformer* (RCA)

Lou Reed (with Don Cherry), *Claim to Fame: Roxy Theater, Los Angeles, 12/1/76* (bootleg)

Matthew Shipp, *4D* (Thirsty Ear)

———, *Nu Bop* (Thirsty Ear)

———, *Pastoral Composure* (Thirsty Ear)

Meredith Monk, *Beginnings* (Tzadik)

———, *Dolmen Music* (ECM)

———, *Ink* (Lovely Music)

———, *Our Lady of Late* (Wergo)

———, *Songs from the Hill/Tablet* (Wergo)

MFSB, *MFSG* (Philadelphia International)

———, *Love Is The Message* (Philadelphia International)

Miamis, *The Miamis* (self-released)

Miles Davis, *Agharta* (Columbia)

———, *Bitches Brew 40th Anniversary* (Columbia)

———, *The Complete Bitches Brew Sessions* (Columbia)

———, *The Complete Jack Johnson Sessions* (Columbia)

———, *The Complete On the Corner Sessions* (Columbia)

———, *Miles Davis on Columbia* (Columbia)

———, *Pangaea* (Columbia)
Modern Lovers, *The Modern Lovers* (Beserkley/Rhino)
———, *The Original Modern Lovers* (Bomp)
———, *Precise Modern Lovers Order: Live In Berkeley and Boston* (Rounder)
Muhal Richard Abrams, *1-OQA+19* (Black Saint)
New York Dolls, *Great Big Kiss* (Sanctuary)
———, *Lipstick Killers: The Mercer Street Sessions, 1972* (ROIR)
———, *New York Dolls* (Mercury)
———, *Too Much Too Soon* (Hip-O Select)
Orchestra Harlow, *El Judio Maravilloso* (Fania)
———, *Hommy: A Latin Opera* (Fania)
———, *La Raza Latina: A Salsa Suite* (Fania)
———, *Salsa* (Fania)
Patti Smith, *Horses* (Arista)
———, *Twelve* (Columbia)
Patti Smith and friends, *CBGB 10/15/06* (Sirius radio broadcast bootleg)
Patti Smith Group, *Easter* (Arista)
———, *Radio Ethiopia* (Arista)
Philip Glass, *Analog* (Orange Mountain)
———, *Einstein on the Beach* (CBS)
———, *Music in Twelve Parts* (Nonesuch)
———, *Music with Changing Parts* (Nonesuch/Elektra)
———, *Two Pages; Contrary Motion; Music in Fifths; Music in Similar Motion* (Nonesuch/Elektra)
Ramones, *All the Stuff (And More): Volume One* (Sire)
———, *Anthology: Hey Ho Let's Go!* (Rhino)
———, *Leave Home* (Sire)
———, *Ramones* (Sire)
———, *Rocket to Russia* (Sire)
Rashied Ali and Frank Lowe, *Duo Exchange* (Survival/Knitting Factory)
Rashied Ali and Leroy Jenkins Duo, *Swift Are the Winds of Life* (Survival/Knitting Factory)
Rashied Ali Quartet, *New Directions in Modern Music* (Survival/Knitting Factory)
Rashied Ali Quartet and Quintet, *Moon Flight* (Survival/Knitting Factory)
Ray Barretto, *Acid* (Fania)
———, *Barretto* (Fania)
———, *Baretto Live: Tomorrow* (KOCH)
———, *Indestructible* (Fania)
———, *The Other Road* (Fania)
———, *Que Viva la Musica* (Fania)
Reggie Lucas, *Survival Themes* (Inner City)
Return to Forever, *The Anthology* (Concord)
Revolutionary Ensemble, *The Psyche* (Mutable Music)
Rhys Chatham, *An Angel Moves Too Fast to See* (Table of the Elements)
———, *Die Donnergötter (The Thundergods)* (Table of the Elements)
———, *Two Gongs* (Table of the Elements)
Richard Hell, *Spurts: The Richard Hell Story* (Rhino)

Richard Hell and the Voidoids, *Blank Generation* (Sire)

Rivingtons, *Papa Oom Mow Mow* (Shout)

Rubén Blades, *De Panama a New York* (Fania)

————, *Poeta del Pueblo* (Fania)

Sam Rivers, *Crystals* (ABC/Impulse)

————, *Sizzle* (ABC/Impulse)

————, *Streams* (ABC/Impulse)

Steve Reich, *Music for 18 Musicians* (ECM)

————, *Works, 1965–1995* (Nonesuch)

Suicide, *Live, 1977–1978* (Blast First Petite)

————, *Suicide* (Mute Records)

Talking Heads, *More Songs About Buildings and Food* (Sire)

————, *Popular Favorites, 1976–1992: Sand in the Vaseline* (Sire)

————, *Remain in Light* (Sire)

————, *'75 Demos, CBS Studios* (bootleg)

————, *Talking Heads* Box Set (Rhino)

————, *Talking Heads: 77* (Sire)

————, *The Name of This Band Is Talking Heads* (Sire)

Television, *Adventure* (Elektra/Rhino)

————, *The Blow-Up* (ROIR)

————, *Eno Demos '75* (bootleg)

————, *Marquee Moon* (Elektra/Rhino)

————, *1975 Cleveland* (bootleg)

Terry Riley, *In C* (Columbia)

Tipica 73, *Tipica 73 Orchestra* (Fania)

Tite Curet Alonso, *Alma De Poeta* (Fania)

Tom Moulton (Various Artists), *A Tom Moulton Mix* (Soul Jazz)

Uncle Monk, *Uncle Monk* (Airday)

Various Artists, *Creative Music Studio: Archive Selections: Volume 1* (Creative Music Studio)

————, *Creative Music Studio: Woodstock Jazz Festival 1* (Knitting Factory)

————, *Creative Music Studio: Woodstock Jazz Festival 2* (Knitting Factory)

————, *CTI: The Master Collection* (Epic/Legacy)

————, *The Disco Box* (Rhino)

————, *The Disco Years, Vol. 1: Turn the Beat Around, 1974–1978* (Rhino)

————, *Fania DJ Series: Gilles Peterson* (Fania)

————, *Fania Records 1964–1980: The Original Sound of Latin New York* (Strut)

————, *Fire in My Bones: Raw Rare + Otherworldly African American Gospel (1944–2007)* (Tompkins Square)

————, *Get Down Tonight: The Disco Explosion* (Shout Factory)

————, *Grandmaster Flash Essential Mix: Classic Edition* (FFRR/Essential)

————, *The House That Al Built: The Alegre Records Story, 1957–1977* (Fania)

————, *Journey into Paradise . . . The Larry Levan Story* (Rhino)

————, *Kenny Gamble, Leon Huff & the Story of Brotherly Love (1966–1976)* (Epic)

————, *Kurtis Blow Presents the History of Rap Vol. 1* (Rhino)

————, *Live at CBGB's* (Atlantic)

————, *Max's Kansas City 1976* (ROIR)

————, *New York Latin Hustle: The Sound of New York* (Soul Jazz)

————, *New York Rocks: Original Punk Classics of the 70's* (Koch)

————, *Nicky Siano's The Gallery: The Original New York Disco, 1973–1977* (Soul Jazz)

————, *No New York* (Island)

————, *Nu Yorica! Culture Clash in New York City: Experiments in Latin Music, 1970–1977* (Soul Jazz)

————, *Nuggets: Original Artyfacts from the First Psychedelic Era, 1965–1968* (Rhino)

————, *Salsa: A Musical History* (Fania)

————, *Tommy Boy Presents: Hip Hop Roots* (Tommy Boy)

————, *Wildflowers: The New York Loft Jazz Sessions* (Knitting Factory)

Wayne County, *At the Trucks* (Munster)

Weather Report, *Forecast: Tomorrow* (Columbia)

Willie Colón, *Cosa Nuestra* (Fania)

————, *Crime Pays* (Fania)

————, *El Baquiné de Angelitos Negros* (Fania)

————, *El Malo* (Fania)

————, *La Gran Fuga* (Fania)

Willie Colón and Mon Rivera, *There Goes the Neighborhood* (Fania)

Willie Colón and Rubén Blades, *Siembra* (Fania)

Willie Colón featuring Héctor Lavoe and Yomo Toro, *Asalto Davideño—Deluxe Edition* (Fania)

Willie Colón presents Rubén Blades, *Metiendo Mano!* (Fania)

Willie Colón with Héctor Lavoe, *The Good, the Bad, the Ugly* (Fania)

World Saxophone Quartet, *Point of No Return* (Moers)

————, *Steppin with the World Saxophone Quartet* (Black Saint)

FILMOGRAPHY

Alphabet City (1984)
The Blank Generation / Dancing Barefoot (1976)
Death Wish (1974)
Deep Throat (1972)
End of the Century: The Story of the Ramones (2003)
The Exorcist (1973)
From Mambo to Hip Hop: A South Bronx Tale (2006)
Kissology: Vol. 1, 1974–1977 (2006)
Latin Music USA (2009)
MC5: A True Testimonial (2002)
MC5: Kick Out the James (1999)
Midnight Blue Vol. 2—Porn Stars of the 70's (2006)
Miles Electric: A Different Kind of Blue (2004)
Nashville (1975)
New York Doll (2005)
New York Dolls: All Dolled Up: Films by Bob Gruen and Nadya Beck (2005)
New York, New York (1977)
The Omega Man (1971)
"Our Latin Thing": The Fania All-Stars and New York's Latin People (1972)
Phil Ochs: There But for Fortune (2010)
Ramones Raw (2004)
The Rocky Horror Picture Show (1975)
The Sacred Triangle: Bowie, Iggy, & Lou, 1971–1973 (2010)
Salsa (1974)
Salsa: Latin Pop Music in the Cities (1979)
Saturday Night Fever (1977)
Search and Destroy: Iggy & the Stooges' Raw Power (2010)
Short Eyes (1987)
Solaris (1972)
Soul Power (2008)

Soylent Green (1973)
Style Wars (1984)
Taxi Driver (1976)
Westworld (1973)
Wild Combination: A Portrait of Arthur Russell (2008)

ACKNOWLEDGMENTS AND THANKS

This book is the product of six-plus years of research/reporting, and thirty-plus years of following music in New York City.

I had a lot of help. Thanks to Sunya Bhutta, Kate Brady, Jeff Canino, Abby Everdell, Michael Parayannilam, Phoebe Reilly, and Dana Sagona for assorted research and transcription assists. And thanks to my editors and producers over the years who have given me space to ruminate on the music: Nathan Brackett, Nick Catucci, Jason Fine, Ben French, Christian Hoard, Joe Levy, and Melissa Maerz at *Rolling Stone*; Tom Kuntz, Sia Michel, Fletcher Roberts, and Scott Veale at *The New York Times*; Brendan Banaszak, Bob Boilen, Robin Hilton, and Frannie Kelley at NPR; Charles Aaron, Doug Brod, Jon Dolan, Michael Hirschorn, Dave Itzkoff, Steve Kandell, Craig Marks, Tracey Pepper, Lee Smith, and Eric Weisbard at *Spin*; Bob Christgau, Chuck Eddy, Rob Harvilla, Brian Parks, and Allison Benedikt at *The Village Voice*; Jim Nelson and Mark Healy at *GQ*; Helen Antrobus, Julie Caniglia, Rob Nelson, Steve Perry, Terri Sutton, Michael Tortorello, and Jim Walsh at *City Pages*; Mark Schoofs at the *Windy City Times*; Richie Unterberger at *Option*.

A big chunk of the book was completed during a summer residency at Yaddo, an inspiring, humbling, altogether amazing place, and it got off the ground at the beautiful, chill, equally inspiring Virginia Center for the Creative Arts; *merci* for the support, y'all. The State University of New York at New Paltz also provided research support; Seattle's Experience Music Project enabled me to share an early draft as part of its always-awesome annual Pop Conference. Marvin Taylor at NYU Fales

Library, Michael Basinski at the SUNY Buffalo Library Poetry Collection, and Rus Springer at the SUNY New Paltz Sojourner Truth Library, along with their respective staffs, helped me access data, as did the fine people in Room 100 (the microfilm parlor) of the New York Public Library at Forty-second Street and their colleagues at the Library for the Performing Arts at the Lincoln Center. Props to all who preserve New York City's cultural history—especially the stuff that may never be digitized.

Online history, meanwhile, transformed the writing of this book over five years. Lost film and video clips appeared like time-warp portals on YouTube: Celia Cruz and the Fania All-Stars rehearsing "Guantanamera" in an empty stadium in Kinshasa, Zaire, in '74; a six-month-old Talking Heads playing "Psycho Killer" as a trio at CBGB in '75. We are near a mind-boggling moment when something approaching the entire history of recorded sound will be available with a few clicks. I am very grateful to the shadowy online community of music archivists, most of whom don't make a dime off their efforts and, in spite of what legal briefs may say, generally maintain high standards of (admittedly self-made) ethics; as Dylan sang, "to live outside the law, you must be honest." Special thanks to Ish for out-of-print jazz and funk gems, Croz for the Television demos and the NYC *Blood on the Tracks* sessions, Wolfgang's Vault for other bootlegs. YouTube song posts saved me hours of crate-digging, as did Spotify, the Swedish stream-on-demand music service that kindly granted me access to their archives while they were still jumping U.S. licensing hurdles.

Shout-outs to Facebook and Twitter, which proved to be small journalistic miracles for story leads and source access, in spite of their time-sucking seductiveness. Special punk-rock huzzahs to Phyllis Stein, whose astonishing Facebook photo archive of the CBGB and Max's scenes—and the online conversation threads it has spurred—was a help and an inspiration.

The bibliography is contained elsewhere in this volume, but some books were beacons: Tim Lawrence's disco history *Love Saves the Day*; Jeff Chang's hip-hop history *Can't Stop Won't Stop*; Clinton Heylin's U.S. punk history, *From the Velvets to the Voidoids*; Legs McNeil and Gillian McCain's U.S. punk gossip-fest-cum-history, *Please Kill Me*; George Lewis's history of the Association for the Advancement of Creative Musicians, *A Power Stronger Than Itself*; Alex Ross's history of twentieth-century music, *The Rest Is Noise*; Vince Aletti's collected *Record World* columns in *The Disco Files, 1973–1978*; Jonathan Mahler's paean to 1977 New York City, *The Bronx Is Burning*. The '70s music coverage in *The Village Voice* and the *Soho Weekly News*, which I revisited on crumbling newsprint and faded microfilm, was invaluable.

Further credit where credit is due: The ever-growing archive of salsa-related interviews at Descarga.com. The mother of all Springsteen databases: Brucebase.wikispaces.org. The crate-digging bible Wax Poetics. Tom Johnson's *The Voice of New Music*, an anthology of the writer-composer's *Village Voice* columns downloadable for free at www.editions 75.com. And the great, long-running online music magazine *Perfect Sound Forever*, still produced by my Madison Square Park pal and former roomie Jason Gross in his spare time—which I always accepted as the reason he rarely cleaned the apartment.

Thanks to the many who granted (sometimes multiple) interviews specifically for this project, or for articles that informed it, including Muhal Richard Abrams, Viv Albertine, Rashied Ali, Laurie Anderson, Marc Antony, Afrika Bambaataa, Karl Berger, Björk, Rubén Blades, Ernie Brooks, David Byrne, Rhys Chatham, Robert Christgau, Gilberto "Pulpo" Colon, Willie Colón, Adegoke Steve Colson, Michael Cuscuna, Carola Dibbell, Dennis Elsas, Chris Frantz, Gary Giddins, Philip Glass, Grandmaster Caz, Bob Gruen, Larry Harlow, Debbie Harry, Richard Hell, John Holmstrom, Leon Ichaso, JDL, David Johansen, Lenny Kaye, Kool DJ Herc, Jon Landau, Richard Lloyd, Dave Longstreth, Felipe Luciano, Handsome Dick Manitoba, Ilene Marder, Meredith Monk, Eddie Montalvo, Kurt Munkacsi, David Murray, Johnny Pacheco, Tommy Ramone, Steve Reich, Izzy Sanabria, Luc Sante, Andy Shernoff, Patti Smith, Bruce Springsteen, Chris Stein, Sufjan Stevens, Ned Sublette, Sylvain Sylvain, TV on the Radio, Alan Vega, and Tom Wynbrandt.

Gracias to the fine folks who connected me with music and musicians, including Nils Bernstein, Ruza Blue, Jenny Boddy, Bill Bragin, Joe Cohen, Melissa Cusick, Paul Dryden, Felice Ecker, Mary Fuss, Sonya Kolowrat, Jana La Sorte, Marilyn Laverty, Aleix Martinez, Judy Miller, Tina Pelikan, Tim Putnam, Michael Rucker, Carla Sacks, Claudia Sanchez, Mark Satloff, Benny Tarantini, Zooey Tidal, Ulla in Madrid, Lupita Valdes, Clint Weiler, Krista Williams, Christie Z-Pabon, and Blake Zidell.

Thanks for random data, leads, laughs, cocktails, encouragement:

Jon Caramanica, Daphne Carr, Jeff Chang, Joe Conzo, Jr., Joe Conzo, Sr., Geeta Dayal, Jim DeRogatis, Jon Dolan, Brent Hayes Edwards, Tony Fletcher, Dan Forrer, Ezra Gale, Andy Gensler, Holly George-Warren, Ward Harkavy, Hua Hsu, Peter Keepnews, Chuck Klosterman, Ernesto Lechner, Sara Marcus, Michaelangelo Matos, Greg Milner, the Mishpucha massive, Jon Pareles, Ann Powers, Joy Press, Ben Ratliff, Simon Reynolds, Tricia Romano, Mike Rubin, Jules Schumacher, Rob Sheffield, Laura Sinagra, Alvin Singleton, Brandon Stosuy, Sarah Vowell, Mark Zip. To my sound dealers, past and present: Keith Ambrose of the Brats (aka Dominique) at the Music Box on Union Turnpike, the defunct Korvettes in Douglaston, the legendary Binky Phillips at Sounds on St. Mark's Place, the Vinyl Mania dudes on Carmine Street, J&R Music World, the awesome Other Music on Fourth Street, Rhino and Jack's Rhythms in New Paltz. Special thanks to Bleecker Bob's for always making me feel uncool, but in an inspiring way.

The extended fam: Matt, Scott, Adam, Russell, and the Queens music freaks. Kirk McElhearn, who recalled Cunningham Park memories from the French Alps via Facebook. The *Jukin'* editorial cabal: Jon Stahl, Howard Wolfe, and Dan Morse, who donated a well-preserved copy of the *Daily News* "Ford to City: Drop Dead" edition and helped in countless other ways. The WHRW-FM continuum. Ron Drumm, music guru. Barb, for crash space after countless late-night "research" sessions. Tim, Meredith, John, Reagan, Bill, Candice for drinks and child-care swaps. Jeff S. and the Tuesday night group. Rivka Tadjer. David Stern. Sara Delphine. Adam Weiss, the best photographer I've ever worked with. My sister, Liz, hip to Patti Smith and the Ramones before anyone else in Jamaica High School.

To my editor, Paul Elie, and my agent, Paul Bresnick, who share my passion for the music and the city: this book wouldn't exist without y'all. Muchas gracias. To Karen Maine, Susan Mitchell, Zach Brown, and the rest of the FSG crew, thanks for making it happen. To John McGhee, thanks for the musical copyediting. To Mark Alan Stamaty, whose cartoons in the *Voice* in the '70s and '80s embodied the era's beautiful craziness, thanks for the fantastic cover art. Large-font gratitude to anyone I've forgotten here.

No single volume, let alone a readable one, could cover the entire breadth and depth of New York's creative output during this era. As history should never be spoken of in the singular, here's hoping my fellow writers will step in where deserving stories are undertold or untold here.

R.I.P. Rashied Ali, Tite Curet Alonso, Ray Barretto, Ed Beach, Lester Bowie, Mel Cheren, Clarence Clemons, Cowboy, Joe Cuba, Joel Dorn, Danny Federici, Arthur "Killer" Kane, Hilly Kristal, Héctor Lavoe, Robert Mapplethorpe, Jerry Masucci, Malcolm McLaren, Ralph Mercado, Scott Muni, Billy Murcia, Jerry Nolan, Dee Dee Ramone, Joey Ramone, Johnny Ramone, John Storm Roberts, Richard Sohl, Holly Solomon, Gerard Smith, Johnny Thunders, Ellen Willis, etc.

Dedicated to my dad, a jazz fan and record collector who gave me my love of music, and my mom, a bookworm who gave me my love of writing. And to Queens, New York City's fattest borough and the most culturally diverse county in the United States, for giving me an appetite for just about everything. To Anne and Gia, more thanks than words can contain.

For the record, Talking Heads' debut single is titled "Love —> Building on Fire." But it's often rendered, and remains known colloquially, as "Love Goes to Building on Fire." Because this book is in part about the way creative work is a shared chain-reaction of inspirations, I took the liberty of borrowing and tweaking it. I hope the band is cool with that. To them, and to all the artists whose work enriches the world, I raise my glass.

INDEX

INDEX